MW00814280

THE SICK CHILD IN
EARLY MODERN ENGLAND,
1580–1720

The Sick Child in Early Modern England, 1580–1720

HANNAH NEWTON

OXFORD

UNIVERSITY PRESS

OXFORD
UNIVERSITY PRESS

Great Clarendon Street, Oxford, OX2 6DP,
United Kingdom

Oxford University Press is a department of the University of Oxford.
It furthers the University's objective of excellence in research, scholarship,
and education by publishing worldwide. Oxford is a registered trade mark of
Oxford University Press in the UK and in certain other countries

© Hannah Newton 2012

The moral rights of the author have been asserted

First Edition published in 2012

Impression: 1

British Library Cataloguing in Publication Data

Data available

Library of Congress Cataloguing in Publication Data
Library of Congress Control Number: 2012930331

ISBN 978–0–19–965049–1

Printed in Great Britain
on acid-free paper by
MPG Books Group, Bodmin and King's Lynn

For Mum

Acknowledgements

This book began as a PhD thesis, which I researched and wrote at the University of Exeter in 2006–2009/10. My greatest debt is to my wonderful supervisors, Professor Alex Walsham and Dr Sarah Toulalan, for their unstinting support, expertise, and patience throughout my doctoral studies and beyond. Truly, I cannot imagine two better supervisors. I would also like to thank the Wellcome Trust for generously funding my MA and doctorate, without which this book could never have been written. Special thanks are due to my PhD examiners, Dr Margaret Pelling and Dr Jonathan Barry, for their meticulous reading of the thesis, and their invaluable suggestions about how my work could be further developed. I am most grateful to the Readers commissioned by Oxford University Press for their constructive feedback about the manuscript, and to Stephanie Ireland and Emma Barber for guiding me through the publication process so smoothly. Most of my research was carried out in the British Library and Wellcome Library, so I would like to thank the staff at both institutions for their help. My thanks go also to Dr Caroline Bowden, who conducted a fruitful search of the Cecil correspondence database on my behalf, and to Dr Alun Withey, for sharing with me a collection of letters from the Campbell family. Other historians to whom I owe thanks are Anthony Fletcher, Henry French, Ralph Houlbrooke, Mark Jackson, Lauren Kassell, Steve King, Bill MacLehose, Jonathan Reinarz, Philip Rieder, and Andrew Williams, who all took the time to talk to me about my subject. I would also like to thank Sir Edmund Verney for allowing me to reproduce two letters from his family archive, and the archivist, Sue Baxter, for her great assistance in locating and copying these items. Some of the material used in this book has been published as articles in the journals *Medical History* and *Social History of Medicine;* I am grateful to the referees who provided useful feedback about these pieces, which has helped strengthen the book significantly. Finally, a huge thank you to Mum, Dad, my sisters, Kathryn and Lydie, and to all my friends and relatives, for their love and encouragement, and for putting up with my endless stream of early modern anecdotes!

Contents

List of Figures

List of Abbreviations

BL	British Library, London
KJV	King James Version of the Bible
OBP	Old Bailey Proceedings (www.oldbaileyonline.org)
ODNB	Oxford Dictionary of National Biography (www.oxforddnb.com)
OED Online	Oxford English Dictionary Online (www.oed.com)
WL	Wellcome Library, London

All the quotations from contemporary manuscript and printed works retain original punctuation, capitalization, italics, and spelling. The use of i, j, u, and v, however, have been modernized, and the archaic letter 'thorn' has been transcribed as 'th'. Standard abbreviations and contractions have been silently expanded, and long titles have been curtailed. In the bibliography and footnotes, the place of publication is London, unless otherwise stated.

Introduction

One morning in 1678, 'as he lay in Bed very ill', five-year-old Joseph Scholding from Suffolk said to his mother, 'Mother . . . I am thinking how my Soul shall get to Heaven when I die; my Legs cannot carry it, [because] the Worms shall eat them'. His mother 'took up his Fingers, which were half dead', and explained, 'God will send his Angels, and they shall carry it to Heaven'.[1] At bedtime in October 1625, three-year-old Elizabeth Wallington, 'then being merry', told her father, 'Father I goe abroode tomorrow and bye you a plomee pie'. Her father recorded in his diary, 'these were the last words that I did heere my sweete child speeke', for a few hours later 'the very panges of death seassed upon her', and 'she continued in great agonies, which was very grievous unto us the beholders', and died at four o'clock in the morning.[2] Fifty years later, in Battersea, twelve-year-old Caleb Vernon, sick of consumption, announced, '*Now I think I shall die*'. He bequeathed 'all his toyes' to his sisters Nancy and Betty, and told his mother '*I love your company dearly*'. Seeing his father 'gush into tears', he pleaded, '*Father do not weep, but pray for me*[:] *I long to be with God*'. Caleb began to grow breathless, 'as if choaked with plegm', and his father, who was 'in great care for him', ran downstairs to fetch some medicines 'for his relief'. Returning quickly, he saw his son 'thrusting, first, his finger, and then his whole hand in to his mouth' to clear his throat. Hearing his father coming, Caleb gasped, '*O Father, what shall I do!*', and then 'immediately lay back', uttered '*God, God*', and died.[3]

Early modern children never seem more alive than when they are dying. Usually mute in the primary sources, during illness their voices call out with disarming poignancy. Parents and relatives recorded the words, thoughts, and actions of their sick offspring in detail, acutely aware that these might soon be cherished as last memories. The resulting evidence provides rare and intimate insights into the lives and deaths of early modern children, and sparks numerous questions relating to the treatment, perception, and experience of illness in childhood. What happened to children when they fell ill? Who cared for them, and how were they treated? Were children's medicines the same as those given to adults? How were children's bodies depicted, and what were the perceived causes of their

---

[1] William Bidbanck, *A present for children. Being a brief, but faithful account of many remarkable and excellent things utter'd by three young children* (1685), 75–6.

[2] Guildhall Library, London, MS 204, [his pagination] 408–9 (Nehemiah Wallington, 'A Record of the Mercies of God: or A Thankfull Remembrance').

[3] John Vernon, *The compleat scholler; or, a relation of the life, and latter-end especially, of Caleb Vernon* (1666), 66, 73–5.

diseases? How did the young experience illness, pain, and death? What emotions
did suffering provoke? Finally, how did parents respond to the diseases and deaths
of their offspring? By addressing these questions, this book seeks to illuminate an
aspect of the past which was widely experienced, and yet has received little scholarly
attention. A quarter to a third of children died before the age of fifteen, and for
every one thousand babies born alive, between 123 and 154 did not live beyond
their first birthdays.[4]

SUMMARY OF ARGUMENTS

This book is about sick children in England between approximately 1580 and 1720.
It investigates medical perceptions of children, asking how doctors, medical authors,
and laypeople understood and treated the bodies, minds, and diseases of the young.
The central argument is that children were distinguished fundamentally from adults
in their physiology and medical treatment. They abounded in moist and warm
humours, which rendered their bodies more tender and weak than those of their
elders, vulnerable to a different set of maladies, and in need of medicines of a gentler
and less aggressive nature. Ideas about disease causation, diagnosis, and prognosis
were also specific to children. The term I have coined to refer explicitly to the notion
that children were distinct in medical opinion, is 'children's physic'. It would have
been tempting to use the word 'paediatrics' instead, but since this term was not
widely adopted until the nineteenth century, its use here would be anachronistic.[5]
Besides, to use the modern term would be to imply that there exists a universal
concept of children's medicine, which is identical in all time periods. In fact, an
essential premise to this book is that medical ideas about children are cultural
constructions, which vary across time. I seek to understand early modern views of
children on their own terms, revealing the internal logic to their beliefs, and the
historical specificity of children's physic. Children's physic was rooted in the ancient
traditions of Hippocratic and Galenic medicine: it was the child's unique humoral
make-up that underpinned all medical ideas about children, and distinguished the
young from other ages of human beings. This humoral view of children persisted into
the eighteenth century, despite the rise of new chemical theories of medicine.

The notion that children were unique in medical opinion contributes to the
historiographical debates about concepts of 'childhood' in the past. Philippe Ariès
initiated these debates with the publication of his book, *L'Enfant et la Vie Familiale
sous l'Ancien Régime* in 1960.[6] Ariès proposed that in medieval times, societies did

---

[4] Edward Anthony Wrigley and Roger Schofield, *The Population History of England, 1541–1871:
A Reconstruction* (Cambridge: 1981), 249; Edward Anthony Wrigley and Roger Schofield, 'Infant and
Child Mortality in the Late Tudor and Early Stuart Period', in Charles Webster (ed.), *Health, Medicine
and Mortality in the Sixteenth Century* (Cambridge: 1979), 61–95.
[5] Jacalyn Duffy, 'No Baby, No Nation: History of Pediatrics', in her book *The History of Medicine:
A Scandalously Short Introduction* (2000), 301–36, at 301.
[6] Philippe Ariès, *Centuries of Childhood: a Social History of Family Life*, trans. Robert Baldick (1962,
first publ. 1960).

not appreciate the distinctiveness of children, as demonstrated by the practice of dressing infants in small-scale adult clothing.[7] Since the 1980s, many historians have found evidence to refute this thesis, arguing that 'There is no doubt that childhood was both recognised and indulged' in medieval and early modern times.[8] In the context of medical history, however, Ariès' legacy lives on, with scholars continuing to assert that until as late as the nineteenth century, doctors neither recognized 'the physiological differences in infants, young children, adolescents, and adults', nor 'acknowledged the need for . . . treatment designed specifically for children's unique physiology'.[9] *The Sick Child* challenges these views, thereby bringing the history of medicine in line with the current consensus in the history of childhood, and closing the gap between these hitherto separate fields.

By examining medical understandings of children, this book highlights the importance of age more generally in early modern medicine. The patient's constitution, disease vulnerability, and treatment, were intimately tied to age. Historians have often overlooked age as a category, instead concentrating on gender as the organizing principle of early modern medicine.[10] For example, Thomas Laqueur's book, *Making Sex* (1990), assesses the extent to which past medical theories distinguished between males and females. He asserts that over the course of the early modern period, doctors were increasingly inclined to view men and women's bodies as two discrete types or 'models'.[11] My book demonstrates that medicine at this time actually adopted a multifaceted approach to the body, in which humans were differentiated according to several factors, including age and sex.[12] It further argues that gender, which was evidently so crucial in medical perceptions of adults, was far less significant in understandings of children. This finding has important

[7] Ibid. 128.

[8] Linda Pollock, *Forgotten Children: Parent-Child Relations from 1500 to 1900* (Cambridge: 1983), 102. Other revisionists include Ralph Houlbrooke, *The English Family 1450–1700* (1984); Alan Macfarlane, *The Family Life of Ralph Josselin, a Seventeenth-Century Clergyman: an Essay in Historical Anthropology* (1970). For historians of medieval childhood, see Nicholas Orme, *Medieval Children* (2001); Shulamith Shahar, *Childhood in the Middle Ages* (1990); Barbara A. Hanawalt, *Growing Up in Medieval London: the Experience of Childhood in History* (Oxford: 1993); Albrecht Classen (ed.), *Childhood in the Middle Ages and the Renaissance* (Berlin: 2005).

[9] A. R. Colon, *Nurturing Children: a History of Pediatrics* (London and Westport, Conn.: 1999), p. xiv. See Ch. 2, footnotes 1–6 for further examples.

[10] For example, Gianna Pomata, 'Menstruating Men: Similarity and Difference of the Sexes in Early Modern Medicine', in V. Finucci and K. Brownlee, *Generation and Degeneration: Tropes of Reproduction in Literature and History from Antiquity through Early Modern Europe* (London: 2001), 109–52; Barbara Duden, *The Woman Beneath the Skin: A Doctor's Patients in Eighteenth-Century Germany*, trans. Thomas Dunlap (Cambridge, Mass.: 1991); Karen Harvey, 'The Substance of Sexual Difference: Change and Persistence in Representations of the Body in Eighteenth-Century England', *Gender and History*, 14 (2002), 202–23; Michael Stolberg, 'A Woman Down to Her Bones: The Anatomy of Sexual Difference in the Seventeenth and Early Seventeenth Centuries', *Isis*, 94 (2003), 274–99; Kaara Peterson, *Popular Medicine, Hysterical Disease, and Social Controversy in Shakespeare's England* (Farnham: 2010). An exception to this focus on gender over age is provided by Daniel Schäfer, *Old Age and Disease in Early Modern Medicine* (2011).

[11] Thomas Laqueur, *Making Sex: Body and Gender from the Greeks to Freud* (London and Cambridge, Mass.: 1990).

[12] This view is also expressed by Wendy Churchill in, 'The Medical Practice of the Sexed Body: Women, Men, and Disease, 1600–1740', *Social History of Medicine*, 18 (2005), 3–22, at 21.

implications for the historiography of childhood and gender, which currently assumes that every aspect of children's lives was influenced by their sex, especially after the age of seven.[13]

As well as exploring medical perceptions of children, this book is concerned with the family's experience. It uncovers the practical repercussions of child illness and death, demonstrating that parents and other relatives were heavily involved in the care of their sick children, and that this involvement was often physically, socially, and financially burdensome. Parents stayed up at night nursing their ill children, bestowing earnest prayers, administering remedies, and trying desperately to prepare their offspring spiritually for death. There appears to have been no clear gender division in the roles of parents as carers: fathers as well as mothers looked after their sick offspring, even though historians have often assumed that women monopolized childcare and domestic medicine.[14] Above all, the energy and attentiveness with which parents and other close relatives tended their ailing children reveals the depth of love between these relations, thereby adding weight to the historiography which opposes Lawrence Stone's pessimistic interpretation of family relationships.[15]

Far more exhausting than the practical demands occasioned by the child's illness was the emotional impact: witnessing one's child suffer pain, grow weak and pale, and eventually die, provoked the most painful passions imaginable in parents. While scholars have occasionally examined parents' emotional responses to children's deaths, few have considered their reactions to illness itself.[16] It is asserted that the dolour of mothers and fathers was equally intense: both genders experienced feelings of extreme anguish, despite the fact that females were considered to be more emotional than males.[17] Such emotional parity constitutes strong evidence

---

[13]   Sara Mendelson and Patricia Crawford, *Women in Early Modern England, 1550–1720* (Oxford: 2003, first publ. 1998), 77–8; Colin Heywood, *A History of Childhood: Children and Childhood in the West from Medieval to Modern Times* (Cambridge: 2001), 103; Elizabeth Foyster, 'Boys will be Boys? Manhood and Aggression, 1660–1800', in Tim Hitchcock and Michele Cohen (eds.), *English Masculinities, 1660–1800* (1999), 151–66; Linda Pollock, '"Teach Her to Live Under Obedience": the Making of Women in the Upper Ranks of Early Modern England', *Continuity and Change*, 4 (1989), 231–58; Anthony Fletcher, *Growing up in England: The Experience of Childhood 1600–1914* (London and New Haven, CT: 2008).

[14]   The historiography which emphasizes woman's roles includes: Linda Pollock, *With Faith and Physic: the Life of a Tudor Gentlewoman, Lady Grace Mildmay, 1552–1620* (1993); Sara Pennell, 'Perfecting Practice? Women, Manuscript Recipes, and Knowledge in Early Modern England', in Victoria Burke and Jonathan Gibson (eds.), *Early Modern Women's Manuscript Writing* (Aldershot and Burlington, VT: 2004), 237–58; Susan Broomhall, *Women's Medical Work in Early Modern France* (Manchester: 2004), 156–85, at 159; Patricia Crawford, *Parents of Poor Children in England, 1580–1800* (Oxford: 2010), 121–2, 128–9, Rebecca Tannenbaum, *The Healer's Calling: Women and Medicine in Early New England* (London and Ithaca, NY: 2002).

[15]   Lawrence Stone, *The Family, Sex and Marriage in England 1500–1800* (London and New York: 1990, first publ. 1977). Similar interpretations were given by Lloyd De Mause (ed.), *The History of Childhood: The Untold Story of Child Abuse* (New York: 1974); J. H. Plumb, 'The New World of Children in Eighteenth-Century England', *Past and Present*, 67 (1975), 64–95; Edward Shorter, *The Making of the Modern Family* (1976). Many scholars have challenged this thesis, including Pollock, *Forgotten Children* and Houlbrooke, *The English Family*.

[16]   See Ch. 5 for historiographical details.

[17]   Historiography which suggests that maternal grief was greater than paternal grief is cited in Ch. 4, footnote 5.

that parents of both sex dearly loved their children, daughters as well as sons. There is little sign that fathers 'found it easier to protect themselves from unbearable sorrow' at the deaths of their offspring 'by remaining emotionally aloof from their children'.[18] These arguments discredit the enduring notion that high rates of infant mortality served to desensitize parents to the sickness or death of a child in the early modern period.[19]

Besides taking the perspectives of doctors and families, this book attempts to reconstruct the experiences of sick children themselves: it explores the emotional, spiritual, physical, and social dimensions of illness, pain, and death. What was it like being a patient at this time? How did children respond emotionally to pain and the prospect of death? I argue that children's experiences were characterized by profound ambivalence: on the one hand, illness was often painful and frightening, and a source of spiritual grief and guilt. But on the other hand, it could be a time of sympathy, love, and power, and occasionally, spiritual and emotional elation. This ambivalence stemmed from the religious beliefs in salvation, the providential origin of sickness, and the value of suffering, together with the more practical and social consequences of patienthood, such as attention and affection from parents. The idea that illness could in some ways be experienced positively acts as an antidote to the common historiographical assumption that, owing to the backwardness of medicine in the early modern period, patienthood at this time was a wholly miserable experience.[20] This interpretation also nuances our understanding of the psychological culture of Protestantism, by demonstrating that Calvinist doctrines could be comforting, as well as corrosive, to the morale.[21]

By seeing sickness through the eyes of the child, this book departs radically from the usual approach to the history of childhood. Generally, scholars have studied children from the standpoints of adults, institutions, or didactic authors, rather than the children themselves. Margaret Pelling has imputed this approach partly to the primary sources, which were almost always composed by adults.[22] The tide may be turning, however: in *Growing Up in England* (2008), Anthony Fletcher devotes several chapters to the experiences of young diarists, aged twelve to twenty, from the period 1750–1914. His intention was to allow 'teenagers . . . to speak for themselves' about their lives.[23] Encouraged by this study, *The Sick Child* investigates the experiences of an even younger age group, those under fifteen, in an earlier

---

[18] Michael MacDonald, *Mystical Bedlam: Madness, Anxiety and Healing in Seventeenth-Century England* (Cambridge: 1981), 84.

[19] The desensitizing effect of high rates of child mortality was suggested by Ariès, in *Centuries of Childhood*.

[20] For examples of this pessimistic interpretation, see Ch. 5, footnotes 3–4.

[21] Negative pictures of the psychological effects of Protestantism have been given by John Stachniewski, *The Persecutory Imagination: English Puritanism and the Literature of Religious Despair* (Oxford: 1991); Max Weber, *The Protestant Ethic and the Spirit of Capitalism*, trans. Talcott Parsons (Guildford: 1976, first published 1930), 95–139; S. E. Sprott, *The English Debate on Suicide: from Donne to Hume* (La Salle, Ill.: 1961), ch. 2; David E. Stannard, *The Puritan Way of Death: a Study in Religion, Culture, and Social Change* (Oxford: 1977).

[22] Margaret Pelling, 'Child Health as a Social Value in Early Modern England', *Social History of Medicine*, 1 (1988), 135–64, at 137.

[23] Fletcher, *Growing Up in England*.

chronology. Ultimately, I hope to show that it *is* possible to glimpse the thoughts and feelings of early modern children, even though the evidence is oblique.

A theme that threads through many of the chapters is the link between religion and medicine in the early modern period. Sickness was largely a spiritual experience: young patients and their families engaged in passionate prayer, read the Bible, and contemplated the afterlife. Such activities were motivated by the belief that God had ordained sickness as a punishment for sin: it was up to the sick and their loved ones to elicit the Lord's forgiveness through religious devotion and contrition, so that He would recover the patient. Religious acts were also part of the process of preparation for death, necessary for demonstrating inward faith and likely salvation after death. These spiritual aspects of sickness and medicine, which endured throughout the period, have attracted only a limited amount of attention in the historiography.[24]

Through investigating the emotional experiences of sick children and their parents, this book explores concepts of emotions in the early modern period. The 'passions', as they were known, were depicted as tangible fluids that welled up within the body and mind, bringing physical effects.[25] The reciprocal relationship between the mind and body is also examined, and in particular, the perceived impact of physical pain on the emotions. Although the bodily effects of the passions have been investigated thoroughly by historians, less work has been conducted on the influence of the body on the emotions.[26] It is argued here, that just as the

---

[24] Exceptions include Andrew Wear, 'Puritan Perceptions of Illness in Seventeenth-Century England', in Roy Porter (ed.), *Patients and Practitioners: Lay Perceptions of Medicine in Pre-Industrial Society* (Cambridge: 1985), 55–99; Jonathan Barry, 'Piety and the Patient: Medicine and Religion in Eighteenth Century Bristol', in Porter (ed.), *Patients and Practitioners,* 145–75; Andrew Wear, 'Religious Beliefs and Medicine in Early Modern England', in Hilary Marland and Margaret Pelling (eds), *The Task of Healing: Medicine, Religion and Gender in England the Netherlands, 1450–1800* (Rotterdam: 1996), 145–69; David Harley, 'The Theology of Affliction and the Experience of Sickness in the Godly Family, 1650–1714: The Henrys and the Newcomes', in Ole Peter Grell and Andrew Cunningham (eds), *Religio Medici: Medicine and Religion in Seventeenth-Century England* (Aldershot: 1996), 273–92; John Hinnells and Roy Porter (eds), *Religion, Health, and Suffering* (London and New York: 1999); Jan Frans van Dijkhuizen, 'Partakers of Pain: Religious Meanings of Pain in Early Modern England', in Jan Frans van Dijkhuizen and Karl A. E. Enenkel (eds), *The Sense of Suffering: Constructions of Physical Pain in Early Modern Culture,* Yearbook for Early Modern Studies, vol. 12 (Leiden and Boston: 2008), 189–220; Jenny Mayhew, 'Godly Beds of Pain: Pain in English Protestant Manuals (*c.* 2550–1650)', in van Dijkuizen and Enenkel (eds), *The Sense of Suffering,* 299–322; Alexandra Walsham, 'In Sickness and in Health: Medicine and Inter-Confessional Relations in Post-Reformation England', in C. Dixon, Freist Dagmar, and Mark Greengrass (eds), *Living with Religious Diversity in Early Modern Europe* (Aldershot: 2009), 161–82.
[25] Gail Kern Paster, *Humoring the Body: Emotions and the Shakespearean Stage* (Chicago: 2004), 17; Ulinka Rublack, 'Fluxes: The Early Modern Body and the Emotions', *History Workshop Journal,* 53 (2002), 1–16.
[26] For the perceived impact of the mind on the body, see: MacDonald, *Mystical Bedlam,* 72–3; Andrew Wear, 'Fear, Anxiety and the Plague in Early Modern England: Religious and Medical Responses', in John Hinnells and Roy Porter (eds), *Religion, Health and Suffering* (1999), 339–63; Fay Bound Alberti (ed.), *Medicine, Emotion and Disease, 1700–1950* (Basingstoke and New York: 2006), p. xvii, 2–15; Penelope Gouk and Helen Hills (eds), *Representing Emotions: New Connections in the Histories of Art, Music and Medicine* (Aldershot and Burlington, VT: 2005), 21; Jan Frans van Dijkhuizen and Karl A. E. Enenkel (eds), *The Sense of Suffering: Constructions of Physical Pain in Early Modern Culture,* Yearbook for Early Modern Studies, vol. 12 (Leiden and Boston: 2008).

emotions could have bodily consequences, physical pain was thought to have an emotional impact.

This book seeks to rebalance our knowledge of parent–child relationships in the early modern period, by exploring children's feelings for their parents as well as parents' feelings for their children. While numerous scholars have investigated parents' relationships with their children, few have considered the other side of this relationship.[27] The following chapters show that parental affection was fiercely reciprocated: children expressed sincere appreciation for their parents' tender care during illness, a concern about their happiness and spiritual health, and a strong desire to be reunited in heaven.

The time frame of this study—approximately 1580 to 1720—has been depicted as one of dramatic upheaval. Developments were occurring in industry and agriculture, towns were growing; the period saw an extension of government's powers, and religious and civil strife. In a medical context, several 'revolutions' were underway: there was an upturn in the demand for the services of doctors during serious illness,[28] new theories of medicine were springing up in opposition to the ancient traditions of Galenism,[29] and the volume of drugs being imported into England was expanding.[30] Changes may have also been occurring in religious practices and beliefs: some historians have suggested that by the close of the seventeenth century, spiritual physic was being supplanted by medicine, the providential interpretation of illness was beginning to fade,[31] and the existence of hell was being called into question.[32] Likewise, the period has been associated with transformations in the nature of family relationships: scholars writing in the 1970s argued that over the course of the early modern period, parents' feelings for their children evolved from indifference to love.[33] Although this view is no longer widely accepted, historians continue to emphasize the changing ideological status of the family in the eighteenth century, and in particular, the increasing tendency of fathers to express affection for their offspring.[34]

---

[27] See footnote 15 above.

[28] Ian Mortimer, 'The Triumph of the Doctors: Medical Assistance to the Dying, *c.*1570–1720', *Transactions of the Royal Historical Society*, 15 (2005), 97–116; Ian Mortimer, 'The Rural Medical Marketplace in Southern England, *c.*1570–1720', in Mark S. R. Jenner and Patrick Wallis (eds), *Medicine and the Market in England and its Colonies, c.1450–c.1850* (Basingstoke and New York: 2007), 69–87; Ian Mortimer, *The Dying and The Doctors: The Medical Revolution in Seventeenth-Century England* (Woodbridge and Rochester, NY: 2009).

[29] One of the most important challenges to Galenism was chemical medicine; see Ch. 1 for details. For discussions of some of the other changes in medicine, see Roger French and Andrew Wear (eds), *The Medical Revolution of the Seventeenth Century* (Cambridge: 1989).

[30] Patrick Wallis, 'Exotic Drugs and English Medicine: England's Drug Trade, *c.*1550–*c.*1800', *Social History of Medicine* (advanced access, 2011), doi: 10.1093/shm/hkr055, 1–27.

[31] See footnote 28 above; Keith Thomas, *Religion and the Decline of Magic* (1991, first publ. 1971), 126–7 (for demise of providentialism) and ch. 22 (for decline of prayer); Wear, 'Puritan Perceptions of Illness', 75–7.

[32] The most famous exponent of this view was given by Daniel Pickering Walker, *The Decline of Hell: Seventeenth-Century Discussions of Eternal Torment* (1964); Ralph Houlbrooke offers a more tentative interpretation in, *Death, Religion and the Family in England, 1480–1750* (Oxford: 1998), 50–6.

[33] See footnote 15 above.

[34] For example, Joanne Bailey, 'Reassessing Parenting in Eighteenth-Century England' in H. Berry and E. Foyster (eds.), *The Family in Early Modern England* (Cambridge: 2007), 209–32; idem.,

Choosing this time period therefore promises to provide opportunities for the reassessment of some of these changes. It is argued that, despite the wider contextual developments, the fundamental ways in which children's illnesses were perceived, treated, and experienced, remained relatively unchanged. The keystone to children's physic, the notion that children were humid and tender, lasted throughout the whole period, and was embraced by practitioners of diverse theoretical perspectives. Children continued to be treated by an assortment of lay and learned healers, regardless of any changes that have been detected by scholars in the employment of physicians. The experience of sickness was also characterized by continuity: the pain of illness, and the prospect of death, provoked similar responses in children and their parents across the period. This was probably because the religious doctrines that held most significance during sickness—providence and salvation—remained prominent throughout the years, especially among pious families.[35] Finally, it seems that family relationships were typically affectionate across the period, in spite of any ideological shifts: expressions of love and concern by both fathers and mothers are ubiquitous. Through this argument, I support Andrew Cambers' assertion that 'continuities might be both as interesting and as important as changes' in history.[36]

DEFINITIONS AND PARAMETERS

In this book, 'child' is defined as beginning at birth and ending at the onset of puberty at the age of about fourteen or fifteen. Such a definition is consistent with those given by contemporary medical authors and physicians. The midwifery expert 'W. S.', for example, took 'childhood' to mean 'Children, from their Birth, to 14 Years of Age'.[37] The term 'infant' was also used in this period; it usually referred to babies and young children up to the age of six or seven. Childhood was regarded as both a distinct phase of life, and a graduated phenomenon: it was a time during which the individual's constitution, body, and mind, underwent significant change.

Various types of medical practitioner are mentioned in this book. Generally, the terms 'doctor', 'physician', and 'learned practitioner' are used synonymously, to denote those individuals who had studied medicine at university, some of whom possessed licenses to practise medicine. This category also includes those who had

---

'"Think Wot a Mother Must Feel": Parenting in English Pauper Letters, *c.*1760–1834', *Family & Community History*, 13 (2010), 5–19.

[35] For historiography which emphasizes the continuities in Protestant beliefs and practices over the course of the early modern period and early eighteenth century, see Andrew Cambers, *Godly Reading: Print, Manuscript and Puritanism in England, 1580–1720* (Cambridge: 2011); W. M. Jacob, *Lay People and Religion in the Early Eighteenth Century* (Cambridge: 1996); Jane Shaw, *Miracles in Enlightenment England* (2006); Barry, 'Piety and the Patient'. Some of these scholars refer explicitly to the endurance of providential interpretations of illness and the recourse to prayer at times of illness.

[36] Ibid. (Cambers) 247.

[37] W. S., *A family jewel, or the womans councellor* (1704), title page.

read other subjects at university, but had taught themselves medicine through use of academic medical texts. Next, 'surgeons' were men who had undertaken training as apprentices in surgery, and whose principal tasks were operations.[38] Finally, the terms 'lay' or 'laity' comprise the vast numbers of men and women who existed outside the universities, from elite to poor, who may have been well versed in medical theory, but lacked a humanist education. Many of these people practised medicine regularly, providing remedies to their neighbours.[39] It must be admitted that the above vocabulary is not ideal: it sets up an artificial dichotomy between doctors (and surgeons) and the rest of society, and implies a stark contrast between the two in medical knowledge and practice.[40] 'Lay' suggests a crude understanding of disease and treatment, whereas 'learned' intimates sophistication and expertise. The vocabulary fails to capture the complexity of the 'medical marketplace'. For example, it does not accommodate those individuals who styled themselves as 'physicians' even though they had not undertaken any university studies.[41] Nevertheless, it is necessary to use these terms in order to interrogate them, and highlight their deficiencies. A key argument in this book is that medical cultures were shared in the early modern period, and that children's physic was embraced by physicians and laypeople alike.

Many of the children who feature in this study came from puritan backgrounds. 'Puritans' are defined here as the 'hotter sort of providentialists'—they believed ardently in the doctrine of providence, were particularly hostile to the Catholic Church, and experienced an especially intense relationship with God.[42] Central to this definition is the idea that these individuals were on a spectrum of Protestant religiosity: their views differed from those of other Protestants in intensity rather than substance. Words that are used interchangeably with 'puritan', are 'godly' and 'pious': these share the meaning outlined above, because conspicuous piety was at the core of puritanism.[43]

Since a principal concern of this book is the emotional relationship between parents and their offspring, the discussions tend to centre around those children who lived with, or were in regular contact with, their biological parents. Nevertheless, to give a more representative picture of early modern residential patterns, examples are also given of children who resided beyond their nuclear families, such as apprentices, school-boarders, and wet-nursed infants, as well as those who cohabited with members of their extended families. As historians have shown,

---

[38] For a summary of these definitions, see Lauren Kassell, *Medicine & Magic in Elizabethan London: Simon Forman* (Oxford: 2009; first publ. 2005), 5–6.

[39] Margaret Pelling and Charles Webster spearheaded the research on the activities of lay healers: 'Medical Practitioners', in Charles Webster (ed.), *Health, Medicine and Mortality in the Sixteenth Century* (Cambridge: 1979), 165–235.

[40] For a critique of the elite/lay dichotomy (in reference to popular culture), see Peter Burke, *Popular Culture in Early Modern Europe* (Farnham: 2009, first publ. 1978); for a medical context, see Doreen Nagy, *Popular Medicine in Seventeenth-Century England* (Ohio: 1988).

[41] For a discussion of the 'medical marketplace', see Ch. 3.

[42] Alexandra Walsham, *Providence in Early Modern England* (Oxford: 2003, first publ. 1999), 2; Patrick Collinson, *The Elizabethan Puritan Movement* (1967), 26–7.

[43] Andrew Cambers justifies the interchangeable use of these words, in: 'Reading, the Godly, and Self-Writing in England, c. 1580–1720', *Journal of British Studies*, 46 (2007), 796–825, at 801.

many children at this time lived with 'surrogate' parents, owing to the high rates of parental death, and the institutions of apprenticeship and domestic service.[44]

This book focuses predominantly on children's experiences of serious diseases, many of which ended in death. It was usually these conditions that provoked the most comment from contemporaries. Precedence has been given to non-surgical cases because surgery seems to have been comparatively uncommon in child patients, owing to concerns about safety.[45] Finally, the discussions concentrate on what today would be considered 'physical illness', as opposed to 'mental illness'. Although this division may seem anachronistic, doctors from the period did actually distinguish between these conditions when discussing children, stating 'Phrenzy and Madness . . . are not . . . among Childrens Diseases'.[46]

HISTORIOGRAPHY

The subject of children's sickness eludes easy categorization: it straddles several historiographical fields, including the histories of childhood, medicine, bodies, emotion, religion, death, pain, and gender. By engaging with all these areas, and highlighting their interconnections, *The Sick Child* seeks to draw these fields closer together. In particular, it attempts to consolidate the links between the history of childhood and the history of medicine, sub-disciplines, which have rarely enjoyed much interaction. Points of intersection include domestic medicine and the experience of the emotions.[47] Domestic medicine is relevant to historians of childhood, since it involved vital negotiations between parents about the treatment of offspring. Likewise, the history of emotions features in both historiographies: medical historians are interested in the impact of the emotions on the body, while childhood scholars are often concerned with the quality of emotional relationships between relatives.[48] It was, in fact, the pioneer of childhood history, Lawrence Stone, who spearheaded the study of the emotions. Thus, by investigating the emotional experiences of sick children, and the role of the family in the provision of medicine, this book hopes to bridge the gap between medical and childhood history more generally.

The historiography of childhood has rapidly expanded in recent years, and now encompasses topics as diverse as children's books, theatre, clothing, and sexual identities. Its theoretical underpinnings have also shifted considerably: childhood is no longer regarded as a 'timeless category', but is seen as a cultural construct, which

---

[44] Crawford, *Parents of Poor Children*, 10–11; Naomi Tadmor, 'The Concept of the Household-Family in Eighteenth-Century England', *Past & Present*, 151 (1996), 111–40.

[45] See Ch. 2 for the dangers of surgical procedures.

[46] J. S., *Paidon nosemata; or childrens diseases both outward and inward* (1664), 87. This was because these diseases were caused by dry humours, and children's bodies were naturally moist—see Ch. 1.

[47] Linda Pollock provides a link between these fields: for domestic medicine, see *With Faith and Physic*; on childhood, see *Forgotten Children;* and on the emotions, see 'Anger and the Negotiation of Relationships in Early Modern England', *The Historical Journal*, 47 (2004), 567–90.

[48] See footnote 15 above.

differs according to particular 'historical, social, cultural or economic contexts'.[49] Despite these notable developments, the themes of children's illness and medicine have rarely entered the historiography. These subjects have also been largely absent from the history of medicine, including the studies of patients which emerged in the 1980s in response to Roy Porter's criticism of the 'too doctor-focused' stances taken by conventional medical historians.[50] The issue of gender rather than age has tended to dominate this historiography: scholars have explored women's experiences of pregnancy and childbirth, but less has been written about medical encounters involving children, or other ages.[51]

Why has the sick child been overlooked in the historiography? One reason may be that historians have assumed that doctors rarely treated children in the early modern period. 'Summoning practitioners for children's illnesses, and indeed physicking them in general, were bones of contention', wrote Roy and Dorothy Porter in 1988.[52] 'Many doctors felt unable to deal with childhood illness . . . children possessed a disquieting tendency to succumb to whatever disease afflicted them', echoed Linda Pollock.[53] Coupled with the notion that doctors did not treat children, is the idea that 'there was no notion that children might be treated any differently from the adults . . . when they were unwell'.[54] This book challenges these views.

The history of child illness has not been neglected entirely however. From the early twentieth century, a number of paediatricians wrote histories of their specialty, the most famous of which were penned by John Ruhrah and George Still.[55] Many of these works are teleological accounts of the rise of modern paediatrics: they aim to uncover the origins of current medical knowledge in the past, and to identify retrospectively the 'real conditions' behind diagnoses. My book intentionally avoids making comparisons between past and present paediatric practices, instead, exploring early modern children's medicine for its own sake.

[49] Anja Müller (ed.), *Fashioning Childhood in the Eighteenth Century: Age and Identity* (Aldershot and Burlington ,VT: 2006), 3.

[50] Roy Porter (ed.), *Patients and Practitioners: Lay Perceptions of Medicine in Pre-Industrial Society* (Cambridge: 2002, first publ. 1985), 1; idem., 'The Patient's View: Doing Medical History from Below', *Theory and Society*, 14 (1985), 175–98.

[51] Adrian Wilson, 'Participant or Patient? Seventeenth Century Childbirth from the Mother's Point of View', in Roy Porter (ed.), *Patients and Practitioners: Lay Perceptions of Medicine in Pre-Industrial Society* (Cambridge: 1985), 129–44; H. Roodenburg, 'The Maternal Imagination: the Fears of Pregnant Women in Seventeenth-Century Holland', *Journal of Social History*, 21 (1988), 701–16; Linda Pollock, 'Embarking on a Rough Passage: The Experience of Pregnancy in Early Modern Society', in Valerie Fildes (ed.), *Women as Mothers in Pre-Industrial England* 1990), 39–67; Duden, *The Woman Beneath the Skin*; Sharon Howard, 'Imagining the Pain and Peril of Seventeenth-Century Childbirth: Travail and Deliverance in the Making of an Early Modern World', *Social History of Medicine*, 16 (2003), 367–82.

[52] Roy Porter and Dorothy Porter, *In Sickness and in Health: The British Experience, 1650–1850* (1988), 82.

[53] Linda Pollock, *A Lasting Relationship: Parents and Children Over Three Centuries* (1987), 93.

[54] Fletcher, *Growing Up in England*, 59.

[55] John Ruhrah, *Pediatrics of the Past* (New York: 1925); George Still, *The History of Paediatrics: the Progress of the Study of Diseases of Children up to the End of the 18th Century* (Oxford: 1931).

Children's illnesses have also been mentioned in the historiography of parent–child relations. Scholars have taken evidence of parents' care of ill children, and grief upon their deaths, to argue that parents loved their offspring. Linda Pollock's *Forgotten Children* (1983) falls into this category.[56] She argues that 'most parents were clearly anxious and upset by the ill-health of a child', and therefore 'the 16th and 17th century texts do not support' the argument that early modern parents did not love their children.[57] The emphasis in these studies is on parent–child relationships, and consequently, sickness has not been considered from the child's viewpoint.

Occasionally, the sick child has been examined 'outside the circumscribed context of the family'. Margaret Pelling, in her seminal article, 'Child Health as a Social Value in Early Modern England' (1988), remarked, 'the child has been treated as a passive element within the family, a hostage to conflicting interpretations of relationships between children and parents'.[58] She sought to 'glimpse the child as an individual in his or her own right' by exploring the care provided by local authorities to the sick children of the urban poor.[59] Several scholars have followed Pelling's example, examining the medical services available to poor children.[60]

Historians have sometimes used a case-study approach to investigate sickness in childhood. James Riley analysed the diary of the Essex clergyman Ralph Josselin to provide a window into children's health in the seventeenth century: he compared the mortality and morbidity rates of Josselin's children to those of children living in modern developing countries.[61] Likewise, the scholar Isabelle Robin-Romero has examined a number of diaries from eighteenth-century France to create a 'carnet de santé' for children.[62] Neither of these studies takes the perspective of the child.[63]

[56] Pollock, *Forgotten Children*, 124–40. For a similar approach, see Angela Margaret Thomas, 'Parent-Child Relationships and Childhood Experiences: the Emotional and Physical Aspects of Care for Children in Early Modern Britain, 1640–1800' (unpubl. PhD thesis, University of Reading, 2000)', 167–88.

[57] Pollock, *Forgotten Children*, 127.

[58] Pelling, 'Child Health as a Social Value'. This article is also printed in Pelling's book, *The Common Lot: Sickness, Medical Occupations, and the Urban Poor in Early Modern England* (Harlow: 1998), 105–33.

[59] Ibid. ('Child Health'), 136.

[60] Alysa Levene, *Childcare, Health, and Mortality at the London Foundling Hospital, 1741–1800: 'Left to the Mercy of the World'* (Manchester: 2007); Broomhall, *Women's Medical Work*, 156–85; Crawford, *Parents of Poor Children*, 127–9; Iris Ritzmann, in 'Children as Patients in German-Speaking Regions in the Eighteenth Century', in Müller (ed.), *Fashioning Childhood*, 25–32.

[61] James Riley, 'The Sickness Experience of the Josselins' Children', *Journal of Family History*, 14 (1989), 347–63, at 349. This diary has also been used by Lucinda McCray Beier in, 'In Sickness and in Health: A Seventeenth Century Family's Experience', in Roy Porter (ed.), *Patients and Practitioners: Lay Perceptions of Medicine in Pre-Industrial Society* (Cambridge: 2002, first publ. 1985), 101–28.

[62] Isabelle Robin-Romero, 'L'Enfant Malade dans les Écrits Privés du XVIIIe', *Histoire Économie et Société*, 22 (2003), 469–86.

[63] One exception is a chapter by Arianne Baggerman and Rudolf Dekker, which uses the diary of a Dutch boy from the 1790s to investigate eighteenth-century attitudes to illness: *Child of the Enlightenment: Revolutionary Europe Reflected in a Boyhood Diary*, trans. Diane Webb (Leiden: 2009), 444–70.

Occasionally, historians have explored physicians' views of ill children. Andrew Williams examined the theories of John Locke and Thomas Willis, both of whom displayed a special interest in children's conditions.[64] He argued that the study of children's diseases pre-dated the establishment of children's hospitals in the nineteenth century. Likewise, Adriana Benzaquén has traced the rise of medical interest in children from the 1740s, as exemplified by the proliferation of paediatric treatises. She attributes this trend to certain 'political, economic, moral and pedagogical concerns'.[65] Finally, Iris Ritzmann and Urs Boschung have analysed the practice of the eighteenth-century German doctor, Albert Haller, asserting that by 1800 something akin to a concept of paediatrics existed.[66] An implicit concern in many of these works is the development of children's medicine as an area of special medical interest. In short, little has been published about ill children, and what has been written usually focuses on the poor, the perceptions of adults, and a later time period.

SOURCES

A diverse array of sources has been deployed in this study because it is concerned with a diverse range of perspectives—medical, emotional, and spiritual, of doctors, parents, and children. The sources are seen as cultural constructs, rather than as factual repositories: they contain the expression of experience, not the actual experiences themselves. It has therefore been necessary to analyse the sources critically, with an appreciation of the cultural processes that might have been at work during their production.

To uncover medical perceptions and treatments of children, vernacular medical texts have been analysed.[67] Many types of medical text were published in the early modern period, from practical books of popular remedies, to treatises of a more academic style. Most useful for providing insights into ideas about children are midwifery manuals and treatises about children's diseases. Midwifery manuals

[64] Andrew Williams, 'Eighteenth-Century Child Health Care in a Northampton Infirmary: A Provincial English Hospital', *Family and Community History*, 10 (2007), 153–16; idem., '"To Observe . . . and Thence to Make Himself Rules": John Locke's Principles and Practice of Child Health Care', *Journal of Medical Ethics; Medical Humanities*, 33 (2007), 22–34.
[65] Adriana S. Benzaquén, 'The Doctor and the Child: Medical Preservation and Management of Children in the Eighteenth Century', in Anja Müller (ed.), *Fashioning Childhood in the Eighteenth Century: Age and Identity* (Aldershot and Burlington, VT: 2006), 13–24.
[66] Iris Ritzmann and Urs Boschung, ' "Dedi Clysterem Purgantem": Haller et la Médecine de L'Enfance (1731–1736)', *Canadian Bulletin of Medical History*, 22 (2005), 175–82. Ritzmann has also published a book in German about children's health: *Sorgenkinder: Kranke und Behinderte Mädchen und Jungen im 18. Jahrhundert* (Cologne, Germany: 2008).
[67] For information about medical texts, see Paul Slack, 'Mirrors of Health and Treasures of Poor Men: The Uses of the Vernacular Medical Literature of Tudor England', in Charles Webster (ed.), *Health, Medicine and Mortality in the Sixteenth Century* (Cambridge: 1979), 237–73; Mary Fissell, 'Readers, Texts and Contexts: Vernacular Medical Works in Early Modern England', in Roy Porter (ed.), *The Popularisation of Medicine 1650–1850* (London: 1992), 72–96; and Elizabeth Lane Furdell, *Publishing and Medicine in Early Modern England* (Woodbridge: 2002).

contain sections on the *'various maladies of new born babes'* in addition to the information about childbirth and women's health.[68] Vernacular treatises about children's diseases were published in England from the mid-sixteenth century onwards. One of the most detailed is, *Paidon nosemata; or childrens diseases,* by the author 'J. S.': it is over 170 pages in length, and discusses thirty-seven diseases 'incident to children'.[69] The function of these texts was to provide *'useful Directions'* to parents, medical practitioners, and midwives about *'the Health of Children ... with Causes, Signs, and Remedies of Diseases'.*[70] The authors were physicians and surgeons from England and Europe; medical knowledge at this time was transcontinental owing to the trade of books between countries, and the tendency of English doctors to study medicine abroad. Many possessed licences to practise medicine, having read medicine at university. Francis Glisson (*c.* 1599–1677), the author of *A treatise of the rickets* (1651), obtained his MD at Cambridge in 1634, and then went on to become Regius Professor.[71] The content of the medical texts was not new in the early modern period: authors routinely acknowledged earlier writers, most notably the ancient 'fathers of medicine', Hippocrates (*c.* 460–370 BC) and Galen (AD 129–199/217), together with numerous medieval writers. For instance, Thomas Phaer's *The booke of children* (1544) describes a cure for the 'stifnes of ... limmes' in children, which was 'manye tymes approved' by the Islamic medieval practitioners Avicenna (980–1037) and Rhazes (*c.* 865–935/32).[72] Likewise, the physician J. S. began his book with *'A Catalogue of the* Authors *used in this Work'*, which comprises 36 ancient and medieval writers.[73] This practice of parroting earlier authors may explain why ideas about children's medicine altered so little across the course of the early modern period.

It is difficult to estimate the extent to which the medical texts represent the opinions of most learned doctors in early modern England. The vast majority of practising physicians did not publish medical texts, and even fewer wrote treatises specifically about children. Consequently, it could be argued that the physiological uniqueness of children that is conveyed in the midwifery texts and treatises on children's diseases may be misleading, since by definition the authors believed that the young were worthy of special attention. Nevertheless, the fact that many of these treatises went through multiple editions suggests that there was a large demand for medical information of this kind, and that the texts therefore held some resonance with their buyers. The aforementioned treatise by Phaer was one of the most widely read and frequently reprinted medical texts of the Tudor era.[74] Furthermore, it is possible to ascertain whether the authors of these treatises were

---

[68] James MacMath, *The expert midwife ... [and the] various maladies of new born babes* (Edinburgh: 16).
[69] J. S., *Paidon nosemata.*
[70] W. S., *A family jewel,* preface.
[71] ODNB; article by Guido Giglioni.
[72] Thomas Phaer, ' "The Booke of Children: The Regiment of Life by Edward Allde" (1596, first publ. 1544), in John Ruhrah (ed.), *Pediatrics of the Past* (New York: 1925), 157–95, at 167–8.
[73] J. S., *Paidon nosemata,* 'to the Reader'.
[74] ODNB; article by Philip Schwyzer.

unusual in their views by making comparisons with other, more general medical texts, which deal with all ages of humans, since these were written from a less explicitly child-focused perspective.

Other documents that shed light on medical perceptions of children are doctors' casebooks and observations, notes kept by medical practitioners about the treatment of particular patients.[75] The advantage of these sources is their potential for revealing what was actually happening in practice, as opposed to the theory conveyed in the medical textbooks above. Casebooks vary in their content, from brief lists of remedies, to extensive accounts of patients' symptoms and treatments. Doctors sometimes incorporated extracts from their casebooks into their published medical treatises, using the patients' histories to illustrate their theories or treatments. The observations of the Dutch physician Ysbrand van Diemerbroeck (1609–74), for example, were printed in Latin in his anatomical treatise *Anatome corporis humani,* and then after his death, translated into English.[76] Other casebooks were published separately—such as John Hall's *Select observations on English bodies* (1679). It is likely that these published documents were censored, with authors selecting especially successful cases to enhance their professional reputations. The surgeon James Yonge, for instance, published an account of his remarkable cure of a child's head injury: he wished to disprove the common view that such a task was '*impossible to be performed*', thereby demonstrating his superior skills.[77] However, some casebooks were published posthumously, without the knowledge of their authors. The notes of the Oxfordshire physician Thomas Willis, for example, were first put into print in 1981.[78] According to the editor, Kenneth Dewhurst, this document depicts 'more accurately than printed sources the pattern of bygone medical practice . . . we find him studying medicine at the patients' bedside' without any attempt to conceal his failures.[79] Some casebooks were never published at all, such as those belonging to the surgeon Joseph Binns (1633–63), which remain in manuscript form.[80] The reliability of the unpublished material must not be overestimated, however, for even in private documents, writers may have been engaging in a 'self-fashioning' exercise, recording their medical cases in such a way as would serve to bolster their sense of self-worth.[81]

---

[75] Studies of doctors' casebooks include MacDonald, *Mystical Bedlam*; Ronald Charles Sawyer, 'Patients, Healers, and Disease in the Southeast Midlands, 1597–1634' (unpubl. PhD thesis, University of Wisconsin, 1986); Joan Lane, *John Hall and his Patients: The Medical Practice of Shakespeare's Son-in-Law* (Stratford-upon-Avon: 1996); Duden, *The Woman Beneath the Skin*; Lauren Kassell, 'How to Read Simon Forman's Casebooks: Medicine, Astrology and Gender in Elizabethan London', *Social History of Medicine,* 12 (1999), 3–18, and her book *Medicine & Magic*; Olivia Weisser, 'Boils, Pushes and Wheals: Reading Bumps on the Body in Early Modern England', *Social History of Medicine,* 22 (2009), 321–39.

[76] The version used in my book is Ysbrand van Diemerbroeck, *The anatomy of human bodies . . . to which is added a particular treatise of the small pox* (1689).

[77] James Yonge, *Wounds of the brain proved curable . . . the remarkable history of a child four years* (1682).

[78] Thomas Willis, *Willis's Oxford Casebook (1650–52),* ed. Kenneth Dewhurst (Oxford: 1981).

[79] Ibid. pp. vii–viii.

[80] BL, Sloane MS 153 (Casebook of Joseph Binns, 1633–63).

[81] The idea of 'self-fashioning' was developed by Stephen Greenblatt in his book, *Renaissance Self-Fashioning: From More to Shakespeare* (Chicago: 1980).

To find out how laypeople treated sick children, and to make comparisons between 'lay' and 'learned' medicines, manuscript domestic recipe books have been deployed.[82] Written mainly by housewives of gentry and middling status, these books contain instructions for the making of medicines and culinary items for use in the home.[83] Some were composed in one sitting, while others were written over longer periods in many different hands.[84] Ninety-one per cent of the recipe books consulted in this research describe remedies that were specifically intended for children, hence their value in this study. Although some scholars have expressed doubt as to whether the books were actually used, the fact that they were often annotated with comments about efficacy or usage, does strongly suggest the contrary.[85] The Evelyn recipe book, for example, states 'I gave my sonne' a treatment for 'the chin cough' when he was '1 yeare old'.[86] A special advantage of recipe books is that they represent a surprisingly large spectrum of society: authors credited a range of individuals for particular recipes, including doctors, apothecaries, noblemen, servants, yeomen, and even occasionally, beggars. Some recipes had complicated histories. Anne Brumwich's medicine for the stone was originally owned by 'old Dr Ridgley'; he then gave it to a 'particular friend of his', who passed it to 'Mrs Higley', who then sent it to Lady Cavendish, who at last recommended the recipe to Anne Brumwich.[87]

The above sources illuminate medical and lay perceptions and treatments of children. To investigate the emotional and spiritual experiences of illness, from the perspectives of children and their families, four groups of sources have been analysed: firstly, diaries and autobiographies. Emerging from the 1580s in England, these documents were usually kept as spiritual exercises: authors tracked God's interventions in their lives, recorded their sins, and attempted to discern marks of 'election'—signs of their salvation.[88] Since sickness was thought to be divinely

---

[82] For studies which use recipe books, see Sara Pennell, 'Perfecting Practice? Women, Manuscript Recipes, and Knowledge in Early Modern England', in Victoria Burke Jonathan and Gibson (eds.), *Early Modern Women's Manuscript Writing* (Aldershot and Burlington, VT: 2004), 237–58; Elaine Leong and Sara Pennell, 'Recipe Collections and the Currency of Medical Knowledge in the Early Modern "Medical Marketplace"', in Mark Jenner and Patrick Wallis (eds), *Medicine and the Market in England and its Colonies, c.1450–1850* (Basingstoke and New York: 2007), 133–52; Elaine Leong, 'Making Medicines in the Early Modern Household', *Bulletin for the History of Medicine*, 82 (2008), 145–68.

[83] Jennifer L. Stine, 'Opening Closets: The Discovery of Household Medicine in Early Modern England' (unpubl. thesis, Stanford University, 1996), 2.

[84] An example of a book written over a long period is Thomas Davies's 'Medical Recipes arranged in alphabetical order of common complaints' (BL, Egerton MS 2,214). By contrast, Mary Doggett's 'Her Booke of Receits' (BL, Additional MS 27466), seems to have been written in one sitting, since it uses the same hand.

[85] Leong and Pennell, 'Recipe Collections', 138.

[86] BL Additional MS 78337, fol. 20v (Evelyn papers, medical and culinary recipes, 1651–1700s).

[87] WL, MS 160, fol. 70v (Anne Brumwich and others, 'Booke of Receipts or medicines', c.1625–1700).

[88] For discussions of early modern autobiographies, see Ronald Bedford, Lloyd Davis, and Philippa Kelly (eds), *Early Modern Autobiography: Theories, Genres, Practices* (Ann Arbor, Mich.: 2006); Meredith Anne Skura, *Tudor Autobiography: Listening for Inwardness* (2008); Adam Smyth, *Autobiography in Early Modern England* (Cambridge: 2010). On diaries, see Cambers, 'Reading, the Godly, and Self-Writing'; Tom Webster, 'Writing to Redundancy: Approaches to Spiritual Journals

ordained, it appears very frequently.[89] Ralph Josselin's diary, for instance, contains 136 entries relating to his children's illnesses.[90] The second type of source is personal correspondence, letters sent between relatives and friends about domestic matters. These documents refer to children's illnesses regularly, because people were keen to keep one another informed about their health.[91] A year's correspondence between members of the Verney family from Buckinghamshire contains over five thousand words about children's diseases and deaths.[92] Thirdly, biographies of pious children have been analysed: these are published accounts of puritan children's lives and deaths, written by parents, friends, or clergymen, to eulogize the deceased child.[93] For example, *The admirable and glorious appearance of the eternal God* (1684), by Thomas Camm, describes the life of his eight-year-old daughter Sarah, who had died two years previously. Some of the biographies were collected together and published as anthologies: *A token for children* (1671–73), by the nonconformist minister James Janeway, recounts the life histories of thirteen children.[94] The special value of these sources for my research is their tendency to provide lengthy narratives of children's final illnesses. The fourth group of sources are printed possession cases, accounts of children's illnesses that were attributed to the Devil or to witches. Diabolical sickness was a form of illness, only differing from other diseases in its directly supernatural causation, and its strange assortment of symptoms.[95] These documents are useful because they describe in detail the physical sufferings of children, as well as their treatments, which in the case of possession, was prayer.

One of the most significant problems of the above sources is their over-representation of the intensely religious in society. In this period, medicine and religion were intimately connected: God brought illness for the punishment of sin,

---

and Early Modern Spirituality', *The Historical Journal,* 39 (1996), 33–56'; Margo Todd, 'Puritan Self-Fashioning: The Diary of Samuel Ward', *The Journal of British Studies,* 31 (1992), 236–64.

[89] For the purpose of diaries, see Effie Botonaki, 'Seventeenth-Century Englishwomen's Spiritual Diaries: Self-Examination, Covenanting, and Account Keeping', *Sixteenth-Century Journal,* 30 (1999), 3–21, and the literature listed in footnote 88 above. For the medical content of diaries, see Wear, 'Puritan Perceptions of Illness'.

[90] Riley, 'The Sickness Experience of the Josselins' Children', 347.

[91] For a critique of the use of letters in medical history, see Willemijn Ruberg, 'The Letter as Medicine: Studying Health and Illness in Dutch Daily Correspondence, 1770–1850', *Social History of Medicine,* 23 (2010), 492–508.

[92] Frances Parthenope Verney and Margaret M. Verney (eds), *The Verney Memoirs, 1600–1659,* vol. 1 (1925, first publ. 1892) and BL, MS 636/7–10 (Verney papers on microfilm, 1646–50).

[93] These sources have received little attention, with the exceptions of Ralph Houlbrooke, 'Death in Childhood: the Practice of the Good Death in James Janeway's "A Token for Children"', in Anthony Fletcher and Stephen Hussey (eds), *Childhood in Question: Children, Parents and the State* (Manchester: 1999), 37–56; and Lucinda Becker, who has used the pious biographies of women (and several girls) to explore the gendered experience of death: *Death and the Early Modern Englishwoman* (Aldershot and Burlington, VT: 2003).

[94] James Janeway, *A token for children being an exact account of the conversion, holy and exemplary lives and joyful deaths of several young children* (1671); James Janeway, *A token for children. The second part* (1673).

[95] James Sharpe, 'Disruption in the Well-Ordered Household: Age, Authority and Possessed Young People', in Paul Griffiths, Adam Fox, and Steve Hindle (eds), *The Experience of Authority in Early Modern England* (Basingstoke: 1996), 187–212, at 195.

and disease could be cured through prayer and repentance.[96] The experience of sickness would therefore have been influenced by the religiosity of the patient and family.[97] These pious individuals may, for example, have been more likely to interpret sickness providentially, or to resort to spiritual physic at times of illness, than other, perhaps less religious people. In the case of the diarists and autobiographers, the majority were puritans or Quakers, and many of the male writers were clerics.[98] This was because, as was mentioned above, the motives for writing these documents were religious. The biographies of pious children share this religious slant: most of the child subjects were from puritan backgrounds, and these documents fulfilled religious functions. Authors sought to commemorate the child's godly life, and convince the family that he or she had gone to heaven.[99] They also wished to glorify God for using the child as a mouthpiece for his Holy Spirit. William Bidbanck, the author of several biographies, stated that he intended 'that all [readers] may magnify his [God's] Work which they behold, giving God the Glory'.[100] Ultimately, the biographies were didactic: it was hoped that the child's exemplary life would encourage other Christians to live and die in a similarly pious manner. This intention is revealed in some of the titles of the documents—the biography of fourteen-year-old Sarah Howely is entitled, *An account of the admirable conversion of one Sarah Howley ... very good for the use of children, to read and imitate.*[101] In order to achieve these functions, it is likely that authors sometimes exaggerated certain aspects of children's piety. This is suggested implicitly by the tendency of the authors to anticipate or remark upon their readers' sceptical reactions. James Janeway stated, '*I am persuaded by some*' that the intense religiosity displayed by a two-year-old child '*was scarce credible*'.[102]

Possession cases are equally biased towards the religious elites; historians have analysed the backgrounds of the children, and found that most came from puritan families.[103] Like the biographers above, the authors may have embellished certain elements of their accounts, such as the effectiveness of prayer as a means of recovery. This was because possession literature acted as religious propaganda: a successful dispossession enhanced the reputation of the demoniac's religious group by proving that God had answered its prayers.[104]

Religious representation might not be as problematic as it first appears however. While the children in the sources were unusually pious, they were not abnormal:

[96] Wear, 'Puritan Perceptions'.
[97] Wear, 'Religious Belief and Medicine'.
[98] About two-thirds of the authors were male, and many of these were clergymen or ministers.
[99] Becker, *Death and the Early Modern Englishwoman*, 20, 105.
[100] Bidbanck, *A present for children*, 31.
[101] *An account of the admirable conversion of one Sarah Howley, a child of eight or nine years old* (Edinburgh: 1704).
[102] Janeway, *A token for children (part 2)*, preface.
[103] Keith Thomas, *Religion and the Decline of Magic* (1991, first publ. 1971), 572–4.
[104] Philip Almond, *Demonic Possession and Exorcism in Early Modern England: Contemporary Texts and their Cultural Contexts* (Cambridge: 2004), p. x. See also Daniel Walker, *Unclean Spirits: Possession and Exorcism in France and England in the Late 16th and Early 17th Centuries* (Philadelphia: 1981), 4; Michael MacDonald (ed.), *Witchcraft and Hysteria in Elizabethan London* (1991), pp. xix–xx.

religion was pervasive in early modern society, and therefore it is likely that these children were at the extreme end on a scale of conventional piety.[105] Patricia Crawford has shown that children of all social levels, down to the very poorest, encountered Christianity in many contexts. Church attendance was compulsory until 1689, providential ballads were routinely chanted in public places, and illustrations depicting Biblical scenes were pasted to walls.[106] Religion was 'in the social air which everyone alike breathed'.[107] As such, the experiences of puritan children may not have differed vastly from those of others.

While the piety displayed by the children in these sources may seem scarcely credible to modern eyes, when one considers early modern attitudes to childhood, it begins to appear more plausible.[108] Children enjoyed a 'special religious status' at this time: they were thought to be especially beloved by God, and capable of 'startling divine insight'.[109] This was because they had committed fewer sins than adults—childhood was the most innocent part of man's life, despite the inheritance of original sin.[110] These ideas were rooted in the Biblical passage, Matthew 18, verses 3–5:

> And Jesus called a little child unto him, and set him in the midst of them, and said, Verily I say unto you, Except you be converted, and become as little children, you shall not enter into the kingdom of heaven. Whosoever therefore shall humble himself as this little child, the same is greatest in the kingdom of heaven. And whoso shall receive one such little child in my name receiveth me.

The spiritual potential of childhood was also indicated by God's decision to send His son into the world as a little child.[111] Given this cultural backdrop, and the intense religious conditioning of children from an early age, it is quite conceivable that some children would have been able to attain a sophisticated knowledge of Christian precepts, which may then have shaped their experiences of illness.[112] Put another way, since adults' expectations strongly influence children's behaviour, it is likely that children who were brought up in environments that nurtured precocious spirituality, may have sometimes been able to meet, and even surpass,

---

[105] Houlbrooke, 'Death in Childhood', 47–51; Walsham, *Providence*.

[106] Crawford, *Parents of Poor Children*, 130–2. For discussions of the religious content of ballads, see Tessa Watt, *Cheap Print and Popular Piety 1550–1640* (Cambridge and New York: 1991).

[107] Peter Laslett, *The World We Have Lost* (1965), 60.

[108] Gillian Avery, 'Intimations of Mortality: the Puritan and Evangelical Message to Children', in Gillian Avery and Kimberley Reynolds (eds), *Representations of Childhood Death* (Basingstoke: 2000), 87–110, at 104; Houlbrooke, 'Death in Childhood', 51.

[109] Alexandra Walsham, ' "Out of the Mouths of Babes and Sucklings": Prophecy, Puritanism, and Childhood in Elizabethan Suffolk', in Diana Wood (ed.), *The Church and Childhood*, Studies in Church History, vol. 31 (Oxford: 1994), 285–300, at 286, 295.

[110] See Ch. 1 for a discussion of children's moral status.

[111] William MacLehose, *A Tender Age: Cultural Anxieties over the Child in the Twelfth and Thirteenth Centuries* (New York: 2006) [Columbia University Press in conjunction with the American Historical Association's Gutenberg-e series], ch. 2, para.54.

[112] Alison Shell, ' "Furor Juvenilis": Post-Reformation English Catholicism and Exemplary Youthful Behaviour', in Ethan H. Shagan (ed.), *Catholics and the 'Protestant Nation': Religious Politics and Identity in Early Modern England* (Manchester: 2005), 185–206, at 189.

these expectations.[113] Thus, we should resist the urge to dismiss these children as improbable caricatures, because such a view may partly be a reflection of the disparity between early modern and modern assumptions about childhood.[114] Rather than judging the sources according to their levels of authenticity, perhaps they should be treated as cultural representations. Whether invented, exaggerated, or real, the piety of the children in the sources is a manifestation of a cultural idea about ideal childhood and sickness conduct. Since this idea was part of the social and religious framework within which everyone lived, it probably coloured the experiences of illness for many people beyond the individual puritan families featured in the sources.

Besides the issues of religious representation, the sources may suffer from censorship and omission. In the case of diaries, autobiographies, and letters, authors may have left out information which they found too upsetting to relate, such as the details of their child's suffering. This is implied by the tendency of parents to say little about children's pains, other than that they were 'in pain' or 'sore'. Censorship and omission may have also resulted from the authors' anticipation of 'reader reception': writers expected their personal documents to be read by other people, and therefore may have tailored their writings to make themselves appear in the best light. This was even the case with diaries and autobiographies, documents which have traditionally been regarded as private places for the confession of 'regrets, hopes and dreams without fear of ridicule'.[115] As Andrew Cambers has shown, diaries were 'written and designed to be read', 'shared, and circulated among godly communities': authors routinely addressed their readers directly, and many were prefaced with dedicatory epistles.[116] Henry Newcome dedicated his journal '[for] the use of my children after me, that they might remember the God of their father, so . . . that they might have their hope in God, and not forget the works of God, but keep his commandments'.[117] Diaries might also be handed round in church, or borrowed by friends, to demonstrate the author's exemplary life.[118] Some were even published, and distributed to wider audiences, including the memoirs of Gervase Disney, which were put into print in 1692.[119] In these instances, it is likely that the authors sought to portray themselves positively by omitting anything that might have provoked censure, and emphasizing their virtues. Samuel Jeake, an astrologer from Sussex, admitted that there were certain things he had not mentioned in his autobiography, on the grounds that they were 'inconvenient for me to

---

[113] Helena M. Wall, '"My Constant Attension on My Sick Child": The Fragility of Family Life in the World of Elizabeth Drinker', in James Alan Marten (ed.), *Children in Colonial America* (2007), 155–67, at 157.

[114] Shell, 'Furor Juvenilis', 188–9.

[115] Cambers, 'Reading, the Godly, and Self-Writing', 801.

[116] Ibid. 804, 824.

[117] Henry Newcome, *The Autobiography of Henry Newcome*, ed. Richard Parkinson, Chetham Society, vol. 26 (Manchester: 1852), 1, 2.

[118] Cambers, 'Reading, the Godly, and Self-Writing', 822–3.

[119] Gervase Disney, *Some remarkable passages in the holy life and death of Gervase Disney* (1692).

relate, and liable to certaine exposure'.[120] Even those documents that were not published until the nineteenth or twentieth centuries are not free from these problems, because editors may have left out what they considered to be of 'little interest . . . tedious, repetitive or embarrassing'.[121]

Of course, not all diaries and autobiographies were intended for public viewing; perhaps these documents were less likely to have been censored.[122] Anthony Walker assured the readers of his wife's autobiography that she 'could not have the least *prospect* that her writings 'should ever see *publick light;* and . . . therefore [she] did not dress them up, to appear with the best *advantage*'.[123] Some authors explicitly stated their desire to provide comprehensive accounts of their lives, with no omissions. The minister Isaac Archer prayed that God would help him to 'conceale nothing that may make for thy glory, though it be for my owne shame!'[124] This honesty is perhaps unsurprising, since the very purpose of spiritual diaries was to confess personal sin. In fact, one could argue that authors were more likely to have concealed their successes than their failings, on the grounds that this genre of writing encouraged self-critical reflection. In other words, a different sort of censorship was at work, with the emphasis being placed on sin. By presenting themselves in this lowly manner, puritan writers may have been fashioning themselves identities as conscientious Christians, because self-deprecation was a religious duty.[125] Thus, what might now be seen as unhealthy introspection may have been experienced in the early modern period as a positive practice, necessary for reaffirming one's Christian identity.

Letters were also subject to censorship and editing. Susan Wyman believes that correspondents were acutely aware of their readers' reactions, and framed their narratives to make them socially acceptable.[126] A rare insight into the editorial process is provided by a draft letter, written by the Buckinghamshire gentleman Ralph Verney in 1647, to his uncle, Dr William Denton, about the illness of his eight-year-old daughter Pegg (see **Figure 1**). The letter is heavily corrected, with several crossings out and additions. For example, Verney had initially stated that Pegg 'goes to stoole 14. 16. or 18 times in 24 howers'; he then crossed out '14', and

[120] Samuel Jeake, *An Astrological Diary of the Seventeenth Century: Samuel Jeake of Rye 1652–1699*, eds Michael Hunter and Annabel Gregory (Oxford: 1988), 25.

[121] Joan Lane, '"The Doctor Scolds Me": The Diaries and Correspondence of Patients in Eighteenth-Century England', in Roy Porter (ed.), *Patients and Practitioners: Lay Perceptions of Medicine in Pre-Industrial Society* (Cambridge: 2002, first publ. 1985), 205–48, at 214.

[122] Sara Heller Mendelson, 'Stuart Women's Diaries and Occasional Memoirs', in Mary Prior (ed.), *Women in English Society 1500–1800* (London and New York, 1985), 181–212, at 183.

[123] Elizabeth Walker, *The vertuous wife: or, the holy life of Mrs Elizabeth Walker*, ed. Anthony Walker (1694), preface.

[124] Isaac Archer, *Two East Anglian Diaries 1641–1729*. ed. Matthew J. Storey, Suffolk Record Society, vol. 36 (Woodbridge, 1994), 43.

[125] For discussions of the construction of religious identities, see Todd, 'Puritan Self-Fashioning', and Webster, 'Writing to Redundancy'.

[126] Susan Wyman, 'Paper Visits: the Post-Restoration Letter as Seen Through the Verney Family Archive', in Rebecca Earle (ed.), *Epistolary Selves: Letters and Letter-Writers, 1600–1945* (Aldershot: 1999), 15–36, at 20; Gary Schneider, *The Culture of Epistolarity: Vernacular Letters and Letter Writing in Early Modern England, 1500–1700* (Newark: 1984), 43; James Daybell, *Women Letter-Writers in Tudor England* (Oxford: 2006), 77.

added 'or 20 . . . and sometimes oftner'. He also inserted information about a 'new and deeper sore' that had appeared in her mouth. Together, the alterations emphasize the severity of Pegg's illness, and provide the reader with a more detailed picture of her condition. The probable reason for this editing was that Verney was seeking medical assistance from his correspondent, and as such, wished to supply as full a history as possible, so that the advice could be tailored appropriately. He may have also been trying to ensure that Denton took the case seriously, through stressing the gravity of the symptoms. This letter is a useful reminder that even correspondence between close relatives was subject to revision. It also reveals the richness of letters as evidence of parents' feelings for their children. The final

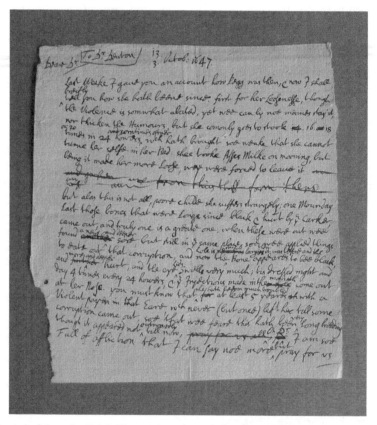

Fig. 1. A draft letter by Ralph Verney about his sick daughter Pegg, 13/3 October 1647; by kind permission of Sir Edmund Verney, and with the assistance of the archivist, Mrs Sue Baxter. The reason for the two dates is that Ralph was writing from France, while his correspondent, Dr William Denton, was in England. At this time, the calendars of the two countries were separated by ten days (England was using the Julian calendar, but France had adopted the Gregorian calendar).

statement poignantly encapsulates the parent's experience of child sickness: 'Oh Dr I am soe Full of affliction that I can say noe more but pray for us'.[127]

The biographies of pious children may have also been carefully filtered, with authors omitting anything that might have undermined the image of the saintly child, which they were trying to create. However, occasionally these sources do mention when children failed to achieve the required state of godliness, or behaved inappropriately. Four-year-old Mary Stubbs 'had her Infirmities and Fits of Passion, for which she would be grieved, and very sorry; but it was no wonder, considering her violent Pain, and long Affliction', wrote her biographer.[128] Possession cases are especially useful for revealing the more subversive behaviours of children: instead of concealing bad conduct, these documents describe in detail the ungodly acts of children. This was because rebellion against religious devotion was a sign of the Devil's presence, which needed to be emphasized if the possession was to be judged genuine. Commonly, these young patients refused to pray or partake in any religious duties.[129]

Omissions may have occurred due to lapse of memory. This is especially likely in the autobiographies, which were often recorded long after the events. Isaac Archer admitted that, 'Some things I write from tradition, others from weake recollections, and the rest from attentive observation and watch', thus implying that his memories were not always reliable.[130] Perhaps letters are less problematic in this respect, since they were usually written at the very moment, or shortly after, the child's sickness.[131] In a letter sent in 1713, Lady Elizabeth Hervey told her husband John that five hours previously their seven-year-old son James had had 'a very odd fit, for he was only convulsd of his left side, and that very strong, in his eye, mouth, hand and leg'. The next day, she sent an update, bewailing that 'between seven & eight a clock this morning I was alarmd again with another fit', which was so violent that 'I am afraid there is but very little hopes of him'.[132] The composed tone of the autobiographies is replaced by a sense of urgency and panic. Perhaps more than any of the other sources, letters transport us into the sick chamber.

A further problem is that the sources are often patterned and stereotyped, influenced by literary convention. Diaries and autobiographies frequently adhere to a set format, in which authors systematically catalogued their sins and God's providences, using stock phraseology. Authors probably learned how to write these documents from diary-writing models, such as John Beadle's *The journal or diary of a thankful Christian* (1656), or from the diaries of their godly friends.[133] Correspondents may have also been influenced by literary conventions. Letter-writing manuals,

---

[127] BL, M.636/8, this manuscript is unfoliated (Verney papers on microfilm, 1646–50).
[128] Bidbanck, *A present for children*, 68.
[129] Almond, *Demonic Possession*, 5–6.
[130] Archer, *Two East Anglican Diaries*, 44.
[131] See Robin-Romero, 'L'Enfant Malade dans les Écrits Privés', for discussions of the value of letters.
[132] John Hervey, *Letter-Books of John Hervey, First Earl of Bristol*, ed. S. H. A. Hervey, 3 vols (Wells, 1894), vol. 1, 370–1.
[133] Cambers, 'Reading, the Godly, and Self-Writing', 814.

such as William Fulwood's *The enemie of idlenesse* (1568), lay out appropriate templates for letters. Even family letters, which appear so spontaneous and informal, do not escape these conventions, since the very formula for these letters included 'a plain, unaffected style, and the expression of affect and intimacy'.[134] The influence of epistolary etiquette is especially conspicuous in the letters that were sent to grieving parents: similar phrases of condolence were used. Likewise, possession cases follow a distinctive blueprint.[135] The symptoms of possession were so well known that authors may have been prone to 'imagining how the possessed ought to have behaved rather than describing how they did behave'.[136] Nevertheless, James Sharpe believes that, within the parameters of contemporary perceptions, these texts are 'factual accounts rather than fictionalized moral tales'.[137] The biographies of pious children also follow a predictable pattern: they usually begin with a description of the child's religious upbringing; next, they recount the child's response to the onset of illness, which involved a sudden sense of sin, and a fear of hell. Eventually, after receiving intense spiritual counsel, the child becomes convinced of God's forgiveness, and dies a 'good death', confident about heaven. The formulaic nature of these sources do not reduce their value, however, since the particular sequence of events would not have become entrenched unless it had been regarded as believable.

The most intractable problem presented by all the above sources for the purpose of accessing the child's experience of illness, is the fact that they were written by adults. As Peter Stearns has recently stated, the 'granddaddy issue' faced by historians of childhood is the 'virtually unprecedented' problem of 'getting information from children themselves, as opposed to adult perspectives'.[138] Especially difficult, is uncovering the experiences of infants, who could not yet speak, or were less articulate than older children. Even when children did leave records, their writings were often edited by adults. This was the case for eleven-year-old James Bassett in the mid-sixteenth century: he wrote to his mother telling her that he had a sore eye, but that otherwise he was perfectly happy at school. A few days later, he wrote again, stating that his previous letter had been dictated 'sore against my will' by his schoolmaster. The boy was miserable, and complained that in the event of his being 'ill-handled', he would not have been permitted to say so, as was the case with many of his schoolfellows, who had been 'ill a month' and yet were forced to write home saying they were 'merry and in good health'.[139]

Nonetheless, although the sources were penned by adults, they do make it possible to glimpse the feelings of sick children: authors often recorded children's own words and actions in considerable detail.[140] John Evelyn described in his diary

[134] Schneider, *The Culture of Epistolarity*, 113.
[135] Walker, *Unclean Spirits*, 4.
[136] Sharpe, 'Disruption in the Well-Ordered Household', 192.
[137] Ibid. 192.
[138] Peter Stearns, 'Challenges in the History of Childhood', *Journal of the History of Childhood and Youth*, 1 (2009), 35–42 at 35.
[139] Muriel St Clare Byrne (ed.), *The Lisle Letters*, 6 vols (Chicago: 1981), vol. 4, 496–7.
[140] For the use of autobiographies/diaries for revealing childhood experiences, see Rudolf Dekker, *Childhood, Memory and Autobiography in Holland from the Golden Age to Romanticism* (Birmingham: 1999).

the illness of his five-year-old son Richard in 1658, and included an account of the boy's behaviour, responses to pain, and feelings about death.[141] Since children usually 'rely on and respond to and incorporate their own parents' perceptions and actions' into their own experiences, the fact that it was adults who wrote the accounts may not be quite so problematic as first appears.[142]

Autobiographies provide especially valuable insights into children's experiences, because they usually begin with accounts of childhood, including early illnesses. Samuel Jeake recounted at least twelve bouts of sickness that had occurred to him before the age of fifteen.[143] Of course, the memories conveyed in these documents are sometimes incomplete or vague—as time passed, authors frequently forgot the details of their ailments. According to Ilana Krausman Ben-Amos, memories of childhood emotions are especially likely to have been 'moulded by the experience and understanding acquired in the time that had elapsed'.[144] Autobiographers, through hearing their parents reminisce about childhood maladies, may have gradually come to adopt these as their own. Nonetheless, some recollections appear to be so lucid that they can be viewed more positively. The dictionary writer Samuel Johnson, for instance, remembered his trip to London to be treated for the 'King's Evil':

> I always retained some memory of this journey, though I was then but thirty months old. I remembered a little dark room behind the kitchen, where the jack-weight fell through a hole in the floor, into which I once slipped my leg. I . . . played with a string and a bell, which my cousin Isaac Johnson gave me; and that there was a cat with a white collar, and a dog, called Chops, that leaped over a stick.[145]

Johnson seems to have been captivated by the new environment in which he found himself. Cases of serious illness may have been particularly memorable because they were events considered at the time to be important, and were associated with extreme physical and emotional feelings.

The biographies of pious children may surpass all the other sources in their potential to convey the child's experience of illness. This is because sickness is the main focus of these texts—it was a rite of passage in the child's spiritual development, and the moment at which he or she realized the importance of salvation. Particularly useful is the tendency of these sources to report verbatim the child's words. The biography of Martha Hatfield is 171 pages in length, and contains hundreds of her own words, which the author claims to be authentic; her speeches are dated, presumably to add legitimacy.[146] Likewise, Sarah Camm's biography includes all her 'Memorable and Weighty sayings', which her father wrote down as he sat by her bedside, so that 'God may have the glory of his own Work'.[147] Of

---

[141] John Evelyn, *John Evelyn's Diary: A Selection*, ed. Philip Francis (1963), 385–8.
[142] Wall, ' "My Constant Attension" ', 157.
[143] Jeake, *An Astrological Diary*, 85, 86, 88, 89–90, 91, 92, 98–100.
[144] Ilana Krausman Ben-Amos, *Adolescence and Youth in Early Modern England* (1994), 50.
[145] Samuel Johnson, *An Account of the Life of Dr. Samuel Johnson, from his Birth to his Eleventh Year, Written By Himself* (1805), 17–18.
[146] Fisher, *The wise virgin.*
[147] Camm, *The admirable and glorious appearance,* 3.

course, these statements are no guarantees of accuracy—it seems unlikely that parents and friends could have remembered every utterance, however profound. Like all sources, the biographies were subject to processes of authorial and editorial filtering. Nonetheless, they remain highly valuable sources, owing to the sheer volume of information they provide about children's illnesses.

The final, and by no means least significant, limitation of the primary sources, is their under-representation of the lower socio-economic groups. Few sources survive which provide detailed, qualitative evidence of the illnesses and medicines of the poorer sectors. In the case of the diarists, autobiographers, and letter-writers, the majority were landowners from the middling and upper classes, engaged in legal, clerical, or parliamentary careers. Finance probably affected many aspects of the experience of sickness, such as the quality of medical care that could be afforded, and the physical environment in which an ill child lay. Poorer children may have also been more vulnerable to disease, owing to their lower levels of nutrition, and damp, overcrowded housing.[148]

Although the majority of the sources are products of the wealthy sectors, some authors did come from more humble backgrounds. The puritan diarist Nehemiah Wallington (1598–1658), for example, worked as a woodturner in London.[149] Besides, even the most elite families could find themselves struggling financially on occasions: Alice Thornton, daughter of the Lord Deputy of Ireland, recorded in her autobiography the economic crisis suffered by her family after the outbreak of unrest in Ireland in 1641.[150] The biographies of pious children help to broaden the socio-economic representation of the research, since these children were born into a variety of social groups, ranging from the higher clergy to the very poor.[151] Likewise, doctors' casebooks frequently mention child patients of lower social status. In the 1730s, Dr William Brownrigg treated the 'poor baby' of Henry Hutchinson, a plasterer.[152] The editor of John Hall's casebook claims that this doctor saw patients from every social level.[153]

Nevertheless, there is still an undeniable skew towards the wealthier echelons, which must be corrected as far as possible. To this end, several additional types of evidence have been selected for analysis: firstly, records from the Proceedings of the Old Bailey, which refer incidentally to children in the period after 1674. Scholars have shown that although these documents convey 'the words of scribes, not the voices of the past', they do offer valuable glimpses into the lives of people

---

[148] Crawford, *Parents of Poor Children*, 127.
[149] Nehemiah Wallington, *The Notebooks of Nehemiah Wallington, 1618–1654, A Selection*, ed. David Booy (Aldershot: 2007).
[150] The editor of Alice Thornton's autobiography wrote that although Thornton was of 'good birth and fortune' she spent at least fifty years struggling with poverty: *The Autobiography of Mrs Alice Thornton*, ed. Charles Jackson, Surtees Society, vol. 62 (1875), p. xii.
[151] Houlbrooke, 'Death in Childhood', 39.
[152] William Brownrigg *The Medical Casebook of William Brownrigg, MD, FRS (1712–1800) of the Town of Whitehaven in Cumberland*, eds Jean E. Ward and Joan Yell, Medical History Supplement, vol. 13 (1993), 25.
[153] Lane, *John Hall and His Patients*, p. xiii.

below the level of middling status.[154] Newspaper advertisements for children's remedies are also potentially fruitful sources, since they often include testimony from parents of humble means about the medicine's efficacy. Regardless of whether these parents were real or fictional, their testimonies must have been sufficiently believable to contemporaries, otherwise they would not have succeeded in persuading readers into purchasing the medicines. Other sources that mention the treatment of poor children, are published accounts of hospitals and workhouses, institutions which provided health care to their pauper inmates, including children. For instance, *An account of the general nursery, or colledg of infants* (1686), describes a 'large House' in Middlesex, established by the Justices of the Peace to bring up orphans. These sources offer few insights into the personal experiences of children, but they do at least provide some basic information about medical provision. Popular ballads, the 'lowest common denominator of print', are similarly useful for shedding light on this subject, because they regularly mention children.[155] These texts were commonly 'Hawked and chanted' in public places, and 'borrowed, exchanged, shared, and passed on', and therefore it is probable that they would have been within earshot of all levels of society, including the destitute poor.[156] Although this does not mean that these documents constitute a 'mirror of the tapestry of habits, attitudes, and beliefs' of the poor, it is likely that they held some resonance with their consumers, otherwise they would not have been so notoriously popular.[157] Finally, it will be possible to draw upon the work conducted by historians who have used poor law records in their investigations of the medical care provided to poor children.[158] Throughout the book, examples from the above sources will be used wherever appropriate.

STRUCTURE

This book is divided into three parts, each of which comprises two chapters. The first part examines medical perceptions and treatments of children: Chapter One focuses on medical ideas about children's bodies, minds, and diseases, and Chapter Two investigates their medical treatment.[159] The second section takes the family's perspective: Chapter Three explores the family's involvement in, and experience

---

[154] Crawford, *Parents of Poor Children, 27.*

[155] Mary Fissell, *Vernacular Bodies: The Politics of Reproduction in Early Modern England* (Oxford: 2006, first publ. 2004), 2. For the production and readership of ballads, see Margaret Spufford, *Small Books and Pleasant Histories: Popular Fiction and its Readership in Seventeenth-Century England* (1981). For the use of ballads by historians of childhood, see Crawford, *Parents of Poor Children.*

[156] Walsham, *Providence,* 33–4.

[157] Ibid. 36–7. Tessa Watt makes a similar statement: *Cheap Print,* 52.

[158] See footnotes 58–60 above.

[159] Material from Chs 1 and 2 has been published as the following article: 'Children's Physic: Medical Perceptions and Treatment of Sick Children in Early Modern England, c. 1580–1720', *Social History of Medicine,* 23 (2010), 456–74. I am grateful to this journal for allowing me to use the material here.

of, caring for sick children. Chapter Four then asks how parents responded emotionally to their children's illnesses, pains, and deaths. The third part of the book is devoted to the child's viewpoint: Chapter Five investigates children's experiences of the practical consequences of sickness—care or 'patienthood'. Finally, Chapter Six explores children's emotional, physical, and spiritual experiences of pain, suffering, and death.[160]

---

[160] Chapter 6 is based on the following article: '"Very Sore Nights and Days": The Child's Experience of Illness in Early Modern England, *c.* 1580–1720', *Medical History*, 55 (2011), 153–82. My thanks go to this journal for granting permission for the use of this material.

PART I

MEDICAL PERCEPTIONS

1

Humid Humours:
Children's Bodies and Diseases

While at play one day in March 1640, a boy of eight years old 'fell down of a sudden, quite senseless, writh'd his Eyes, and clutch'd his two Thumbs hard in his Fists'. The next day, the fit returned more vehemently, attended with 'manifest convulsions of the body', which were so violent that the 'Boy's Brain was affected'. His parents recalled that a few weeks previously, their son had 'first become sad', and then 'complain'd of a grievous Head-ach'. The fits continued for a year, coming 'twice, thrice, and four times a Week'. The boy's doctor, Ysbrand van Diemerbroeck, diagnosed the condition as 'Epilepsie', a disease common in children owing to their peculiarly 'moist brain[s]'. Contributing to the disease was the boy's 'greedy devouring of bad or raw fruit', which bred great quantities of 'crude and phlegmatic humours' in his brain. Despite the gravity of the illness, the doctor assured the boy's parents that 'the Strength and Age of the Patientt gave great hopes of Cure[,] For being but a Child, the very change of Youth out of one Age into another many times effects the Cure'.

The above medical case was recorded in the mid-seventeenth century by Dr van Diemerbroeck, a physician from Utrecht; some forty years later, it was published in England in his *[P]articular treatise of the small pox ... and observations*.[1] The case provides insights into medical perceptions of children's bodies and diseases, the subjects of this chapter. Children had moist brains, which predisposed them to certain distempers. Epilepsy was a children's disease, affecting the young more than other ages. The cause of the boy's condition—the gluttonous eating of fruit—was specific to the age of childhood. Prognosis was dependent partly on the patient's age: when the patient passed from one age into another, such as from childhood to youth, recovery was likely.

This chapter examines medical perceptions of children's constitutions, bodies, minds, and diseases, from the viewpoints of doctors and laypeople. It argues that children were distinguished fundamentally from adults, and that a concept of 'children's physic' existed.[2] Children's bodies and brains were filled with moist and warm humours, which made them weaker than grown persons, and vulnerable

---

[1] Ysbrand van Diemerbroeck, *The anatomy of human bodies ... to which is added a particular treatise of the small pox ... and observations* (1689), 190–1.
[2] See the Introduction for a definition of 'children's physic'.

to a different set of diseases. These humoral qualities influenced the functioning of children's body parts, as well as the inclinations of their minds and emotions. Children were thus defined by their humid humours: all contemporary medical ideas about children were rooted in this belief. This argument refutes the view common among historians that until the nineteenth century, doctors did not recognize 'the physiological differences in infants, young children, adolescents, and adults'.[3] It also taps into the historiographical debates about concepts of 'childhood' in past societies, and contributes to the revisionist work that challenges Philippe Ariès' famous thesis.[4] Nevertheless, while children were distinguished from adults, this chapter acknowledges that contemporaries did recognize certain physiological commonalities between all the ages.

Early modern physicians frequently criticized the 'vulgar practices' of the laity. The physician James Primrose (1598–1659), declared that 'physic and surgery cannot be known but by a skilful Physician', and that the laity 'ought not so rashly and adventurously to intermeddle with them'.[5] Such statements have created the impression that there must have been a vast gulf separating the medicine of elite doctors from that of the non-learned masses.[6] By examining the views of laypeople alongside those of learned medical authors, this chapter will add to the body of historiography which has sought to demonstrate the shared nature of early modern medical cultures, thereby dispelling the myth created by contemporary doctors about the supremacy of their own knowledge.[7]

The seventeenth century was a time of great debate between Galenic and chemical physicians. Broadly speaking, 'Galenic' doctors were those who endorsed the humoral theory espoused by the ancient Greeks Hippocrates and Galen; they believed that disease resulted from the corruption, blockage, or imbalance of the body's fluids, the 'humours'. Chemical physicians, by contrast, usually supported the theories of the Swiss medical reformer Paracelsus (1493–1541) and the Flemish physician Jan Baptista van Helmont (1579–1644). These practitioners believed that disease was caused by the malfunctioning of certain chemical processes, rather than by the humours.[8] In the 1640s, hostility between these two groups mounted in England: numerous Galenic doctors complained of the 'new upturned brood' of 'chymists' who were a threat to the 'old and settled and approved practice of physick', and chemists attacked the Galenic physicians for their tendency to 'kill

---

[3] R. Colon, A. R., *Nurturing Children: a History of Pediatrics* (London and Westport, Conn.:1999), p. xiv.

[4] See the Introduction for a summary of this historiography.

[5] James Primrose, *Popular errours, or the errours of the people in physick,* trans. Robert Wittie (1651), 19–20.

[6] See also John Cotta, *A short discoverie of severall sorts of ignorant and unconsiderate practisers of physicke* (1619).

[7] For example, Doreen Nagy, *Popular Medicine in Seventeenth-Century England* (Ohio: 1988); Michael Stolberg, 'Medical Popularization and the Patient in the Eighteenth Century', in Willem De Blécourt and Cornelie Usborne (eds), *Cultural Approaches to the History of Medicine: Mediating Medicine in Early Modern and Modern Europe* (Basingstoke: 2004), 89–107; Laurence Brockliss and Colin Jones, *The Medical World of Early Modern France* (Oxford: 1997), 279.

[8] See Elizabeth Lane Furdell, *Publishing and Medicine in Early Modern England* (Woodbridge: 2002), for a summary of these theories.

enough' patients through their 'heathen' practices.[9] Such disputes have informed historiographical understandings of Galenic and chemical theories, by suggesting that the two types of medicine must have been irreconcilable. Many historians of the 1960s and 1970s supported this view in their teleological histories of medicine, asserting that chemical philosophy represented a move towards the modern, enlightened, and empirical medicine that now reigns.[10] The following discussion seeks to redress this interpretation in the context of children's bodies and diseases, demonstrating that while there were subtle differences between the theories of chemical and Galenic writers, the basic ideas espoused by the groups were similar. Medical perceptions of children thus underwent little change over the course of the early modern period, in spite of the rise of chemical medicine. These arguments support the recent historiography that emphasizes the endurance of Galenism over time, and the easy assimilation of chemical ideas into humoral medicine.[11]

Since there were so many coexisting, competing strands to chemical medicine in this period, it has been necessary to be selective, focusing principally on one 'brand' of chemical physic when making comparisons between chemical and Galenic medicine.[12] The chosen type of medicine is that advocated by the renowned Dutch physician and chemist, Franciscus Sylvius (1614–72) and his supporters. Sylvius wrote extensively about children, publishing a treatise entitled *Dr. Franciscus de le Boe Sylvius of childrens diseases,* which was translated into English after his death in 1682.[13] Many other practitioners embraced his ideas, and therefore the comparisons are likely to be 'representative' of a reasonably large body of chemical doctors. Sylvius was born in Germany, but worked as a physician and chemist in Holland; he studied under van Helmont.

The first part of this chapter examines medical perceptions of children's constitutions, bodies, and minds, and shows that all of these were in some way unique to children. The second section focuses on children's diseases, and analyses contemporary ideas about disease causation and prognosis in this age group.

---

[9] These extracts were cited by Michael Hunter, *Science and Society in Restoration England* (Cambridge: 1981),138; and Harold J. Cook, *The Decline of the Old Medical Regime in Stuart London* (1986), 122. Charles Webster has investigated the divisions between chemists and Galenists, in, *The Great Instauration: Science, Medicine and Reform 1626–1660* (Oxford: 2002; first publ. 1975).
[10] For example, Henry M. Leicester, *The Historical Background of Chemistry* (New York:1956), and Lester S. King, *The Road to Medical Enlightenment 1650–1695* (1970).
[11] For example, Allen Debus, *The Chemical Philosophy: Paracelsian Science and Medicine in the Sixteenth and Seventeenth Centuries,* vol. 1 (New York: 1977), 60; Andrew Wear, 'Medical Practice in the Late Seventeenth- and Early Eighteenth-Century England: Continuity and Union', and *Knowledge and Practice in English Medicine, 1550–1680* (Cambridge: 2000), 294–320; Louise Hill-Curth, *English Almanacs, Astrology and Popular Medicine: 1550–1700* (Manchester: 2007), 2.
[12] For a summary of the diverse theories of chemists, see Antonio Clericuzio, 'From van Helmont to Boyle. A Study of the Transmission of Helmontian Chemical and Medical Theories in Seventeenth-Century England', *British Journal for the History of Science,* 26 (1993), 303–34.
[13] Franciscus Sylvius, *Dr. Franciscus de le Boe Sylvius of childrens diseases* (1682).

CHILDREN'S CONSTITUTIONS, BODIES, AND MINDS

Children's constitutions and bodies were characterized, above all, in terms of their distinctive humours. Hippocratic and Galenic medical traditions taught that all living beings were ultimately reducible to four qualities: heat, coldness, moisture, and dryness. Four corresponding liquids ('humours') embodied these qualities in varying proportions: blood (which was warm and moist), choler (warm and dry), phlegm (cold and moist), and melancholy (cold and dry). The precise balance of the humours in each human being was determined largely by age, for it was understood that as people grew older, their humoral make-up gradually altered. As declared by the medical author J. S. in 1664, 'The Life of Man consists in Heat and Moisture, the Heat consumes by degrees the Moisture, whereby necessarily follow several Changes of the Temperament, which are called Ages'.[14] Life was a 'continuall combat' between the 'ever-jarring elements' of heat and moisture, wherein 'heate without any the least intermission or pause, worketh upon our moisture'.[15] The ages through which humans passed were: 'infancy' or 'childhood' (from birth to about fourteen), 'youth' (from fifteen to approximately twenty-five or thirty), 'ripe age' or adulthood (roughly thirty years to fifty or fifty-five), and finally old or 'decrepit age' (fifty-five or sixty until death).[16] At birth, the temperature was warm; it then rose until the end of youth, after which point it began to decline. By contrast, moisture was greatest at birth, and then progressively fell until death. Death occurred when all the body's moisture had been depleted. **Figure 2** depicts these changing constitutions.

Thus, for each age, the humoral balance was distinct:

> [O]ur infancy [is] ful of moisture, as the fluid substance of our flesh manifestly declareth: our youth bringeth a farther degree of solidity: our riper age ever temperate: thence still inclineth our body unto cold and drinesse, till at length death ceaseth . . . our bodies, being the last end . . . of our life.[17]

In childhood, bodies contained great quantities of the humour blood, and therefore tended to be warm and moist. As confirmed by the midwifery expert W. S. in 1704, 'children . . . are full of Blood . . . and abound with heat'.[18] These characteristics had an effect on the child's bodily strength and texture, making it soft and weak, or 'tender'.[19] Youths were then associated with the humour choler: they were hotter, drier, and stronger than children. Adults, the most 'temperate' age, were cooler, drier, and stronger than the preceding ages, and were linked to the humour phlegm.[20] Finally, the elderly were characterized by their high levels of melancholy, and the

---

[14] J. S., *Paidon nosemata; or childrens diseases both outward and inward* (1664), 2. Some scholars believe J. S. may have been John Starsmere, while others have suggested Jane Sharpe.

[15] Henry Cuffe, *The differences of the ages of mans life* (1607), 113.

[16] For a discussion of the ages of man, see Alexandra Shepard, *Meanings of Manhood in Early Modern England* (Oxford: 2003), 54–8.

[17] Cuffe, *The differences of the ages*, 114.

[18] W. S., *A family jewel, or the womans councellor* (1704), 72.

[19] J. S., *Paidon nosemata*, 2–3, 26–8.

[20] Cuffe, *The differences of the ages*, 114–15.

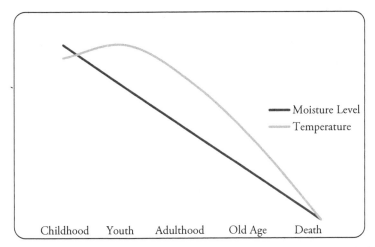

Fig. 2. A graph to depict the humoral constitutions of the different ages, compiled by author.

corresponding qualities of coolness, dryness, and brittleness.[21] Some of the characteristics of children were shared with other ages or groups of humans: weakness, for instance, was associated with the elderly, moisture, with women, and warmth with youths and males. However, no other category exhibited all these characteristics, and therefore it seems safe to conclude that children were perceived to be humorally unique. This notion, which underpinned all medical ideas about children, was accepted by doctors throughout the early modern period.[22]

To illustrate these various humoral constitutions, contemporaries drew parallels with the seasons of the year, each of which experienced a similar degree of heat and moisture. Childhood was likened to the Spring, 'wherein all things [exhibit a] pleasant verdour and greenish flourish, and by a plenfifull supply of moisture, continually increase in growth'. Youth was then equated with 'Summer, for that groweth strength of the body and minde', while '*man-age*' was associated with '*Autumn* or *Harvest*', when 'after manifold turmoiles and dangers of our fore-spent life, the good giftes and indowments of our minde . . . receive a kind of seasonable and timely ripenesse'. Finally '*old age*' resembled 'the colde and troublesome *Winter season*, very fitly thereby expressing the cumbersome coldnesse of the latter end of our life'.[23] Other analogies were used when depicting the bodily strength and texture of the different ages. The military surgeon Felix Wurtz (1518–1575)

---

[21] Andrew Wear, *Knowledge and Practice in English Medicine 1550–1680* (Cambridge: 2000), 38; Pat Thane (ed.), *The Long History of Old Age* (2005), 127.
[22] For example, compare Thomas Phaer, '"The Booke of Children: The Regiment of Life by Edward Allde" (1596, first publ. 1544)', in John Ruhrah (ed.), *Pediatrics of the Past* (New York:1925), 157–95, at 157, 160, 166, with François Mauriceau, *The diseases of women with child . . . With fit remedies for the several indispositions of new-born babes* (1710), 345.
[23] Cited in Cuffe, *The differences of the ages*, 115–16.

observed, 'The bodies of such little Children, may be compared to a young and tender root or twigg of a Tree...[they] are like soft Wax, or young Trees'.[24] This comparison with soft wax evoked both the softness, and the humidity, of children's bodies. By contrast, the bodies of adults were likened to mature trees which were solid and strong, while the elderly were thought to resemble ancient trees that were dry and brittle.

Why were children moist and warm? William Bullein offered one explanation in 1595, stating, 'children's...temperaments or complections, be hot and moist, very like unto the seed whereof they bee procreated'.[25] Thus, the qualities of the sperm and egg determined the characteristics of children's bodies. This notion probably derived from the ancient theories of Galen. A 1652 edition of Galen's *Art of physick* states, 'Is not I say [the] seed of Man hot and moist, which is the *Causa Formans* of the Child? Is not the Mothers Blood whereof the Child is formed, naturally hot and moist also? Is not the Cell of the Womb in which the Child is formed, hot and moist?'[26] Some practitioners believed that the influence of the planets—space—contributed to children's unique humoral make-up. As explained by Henry Cuffe, 'our Infancie age is allotted to the Moones milde and moist dominion, cherishing us with her sweet influence which she hath especially upon moist bodies', whereas youth was controlled by 'Venus', adulthood, by 'the Sunnes lively operation', old age, by 'Jupiter', and finally, 'Decrepit age' by Saturn, which 'sucketh the poisonous infirmities of crasie sicknesse and wayward petishnesse'.[27] Thus, there was a sympathetic link between each age and a particular celestial body. Children's bodies were influenced by the moon, and gradually assumed its qualities of humidity and weakness.

Chemical physicians agreed with Galenists about the basic characteristics of children's constitutions, especially in relation to their weakness. Sylvius declared, 'children are tender, and may die upon a small occasion',[28] while Everard Maynwaring (1628–1699), noted that '*Infants* and *Children*' have 'tender soft bodies'.[29] Occasionally, chemists also acknowledged children's moisture and warmth. Robert Johnson stated that 'Children...abound with moisture, and are full of excrements'.[30] This apparent similarity between the views of the chemical and Galenic authors seems to undermine the notion that the two groups embraced very different theories. Chemical practitioners had allegedly rejected the humours as 'frivolous... fictions', and replaced them with the three or four immaterial elements or 'principles', the *tria prima*, sulphur, mercury, and salt.[31] The reason for this similarity may

[24] Felix Wurtz, '"An Experimental Treatise of Surgerie in Four parts...Whereunto is Added...the Childrens Book", trans. Lenertzon Fox (1656)', in John Ruhrah, *Pediatrics of the Past* (New York: 1925), 198–220, at 205, 366.

[25] William Bullein, *The government of health* (1595, first publ. 1558), 10; see also, Helkiah Crooke, *Mikrokosmographia a description of the body of man* (1615), 56.

[26] Claudius Galen, *Galens art of physick* (1652), 43.

[27] Cuffe, *The differences of the ages*, 121.

[28] Sylvius, *Of childrens diseases*, 37.

[29] Everard Maynwaring, *The method and means of enjoying health* (1683), 40.

[30] Robert Johnson, *Praxis medicinae reformata: or, the practice of physick* (1700), 58.

[31] The quotation is from Joan Baptista van Helmont, *Van Helmont's works, containing his most excellent philosophy, physick, chirurgery, anatomy* (1664), 1.

be that chemical physicians needed to make their treatises accessible to the predominantly Galenic lay audience. This was the case for Maynwaring, who admitted that the humours 'being so familiar, and well known to such for whom chiefly this work is intended, I shall retain these names' rather than to 'impose new words... not so well understood' upon the reader.[32] The humours may also have been so deeply entrenched within early modern medical culture, that chemical practitioners found it impossible to escape from the basic ideas about the changing constitutions of different ages.

Nevertheless, when the chemical texts are examined more closely, they sometimes do convey slightly different views of children. While agreeing on the basic qualities of children's constitutions, certain authors disagreed about the content of the humidity and weakness, attributing it not to a humour, but to a chemical, and more specifically, an acidic or sour substance. Johann Dolaus (1651–1707) stated that 'Children abound' in 'a viscous Acid'.[33] His contemporary, the chemical empiric William Salmon (1644–1713), concurred, noting that an '*acid Matter or Spirit extravagantly prevails in little ones*'.[34] The notion that children were particularly acidic was so persuasive that many of the allegedly Galenic physicians incorporated it into their depictions of children. The royal physician Walter Harris (1647–1732), who had at times been extremely critical of chemical physic, stated, 'children... do all abound with Humidity, which is easily changed into a Praeternatural Acid'.[35] Thus, Galenic and chemical writers were sometimes prepared to compromise, conceding on the subject of children's basic humoral characteristics, while also acknowledging their peculiarly acidic temperaments. This compromise was possible because the theories of Galenists and chemists were compatible, at least at a simplistic reading: both implied that humans were composed of certain substances (humours or chemicals), so it made sense to ascribe to these substances such qualities as moisture or tenderness. In theory, this thinking was erroneous, because the chemical *tria prima*, unlike the humours, were immaterial entities. However, in practice chemical physicians often 'disguised many of the properties' of the Galenic humours and 'reintroduced them under the terminology of mercury, sulfur, and salt'.[36]

Laypeople probably also regarded children to be humorally unique. Popular books of rhymes, such as John Raymond's *Folly in print* (1667), described the age of infancy as 'most tender' and 'moist'.[37] William Basse's, *A miscelany of merriment* (1619), includes a short poem about the seasons and their resemblance to the different ages:

---

[32] Maynwaring, *The method and means*, 155.
[33] Johann Dolaus, *Systema medicinale. A compleat system of physick* (1686), 359.
[34] William Salmon, *Medicina practica, or, practical physick* (1692), 76–7.
[35] Walter Harris, *An exact enquiry into, and cure of the acute diseases of infants*, trans. William Cockburn (1693), 73.
[36] Lester S. King, *The Philosophy of Medicine: the Early Eighteenth Century* (1978), 66.
[37] John Raymond, *Folly in print, or a book of rymes* (1667), 35–6.

1. His Infancy to the Spring, hote and moist.
2. His Youth to the summer, hote and drie.
3. His Manhood to the Autumne, cold and moist.
4. ...old age to Winter, colde and drye.[38]

Most people of middling status or above would have been able to afford these texts, and even the illiterate poor may have had access to them, since they were commonly read aloud in market squares and 'borrowed, exchanged, shared, and passed on'.[39] As such, it can be speculated that the content of these books, including the idea that children were humorally distinct, was probably within the reach of most socio-economic levels. Medical historians might agree, since they have shown that the laity 'possessed fairly sophisticated and detailed medical knowledge... the cognitive distance between medical expert knowledge and lay knowledge was much smaller than today'.[40]

The laity may have also been familiar with the notion that children were especially weak. The Yorkshire gentlewoman Alice Thornton (1626–1707) described the 'accidents and casultys incident to that feble and weake estate of infants and childe-hoods'.[41] This association between weakness and childhood was also expressed by the antiquary Simonds D'Ewes (1602–50), who wrote in his autobiography of the 'great weakness' of his 'young body' during his 'tender infancy'.[42] However, it is difficult to determine the extent to which terms such as 'weak' and 'tender' were meant in their technical medical senses, or in fact, denoted slightly different meanings, such as 'youthful' or 'immature'.[43]

Within the age of childhood, the constitutions of individual children varied. There were three categories of variation: firstly, age. Medical authors believed that infants were weaker and wetter than older children because 'humidity is lessened by Age'.[44] As infants grew older, their temperatures rose, and this had a drying and strengthening effect. Francis Glisson provided a detailed account of this process, when explaining why rickets, a disease caused by moist and cold humours, was more common in infants than older children. He wrote,

> [T]he yonger Children are of a colder temperament than the Older. For the heat of the temperament is augmented from the time of birth to mans estate, at which time it standeth at a stay... but afterwards delineth by degrees into extream old age... The yonger Children are more moist than the older, for to wax old, if it be taken in a sound sense, is to wax dry.[45]

---

[38] William Basse, *A helpe to discourse. Or, a miscelany of merriment* (1619), 236.

[39] Alexandra Walsham, *Providence in Early Modern England* (Oxford: 2003, first publ. 1999), 34.

[40] Stolberg, 'Medical Popularization and the Patient', 90.

[41] Alice Thornton, *The Autobiography of Mrs Alice Thornton,* ed. Charles Jackson, Surtees Society, vol. 62 (1875), 4.

[42] Simonds D'Ewes, *The Autobiography and Correspondence of Sir Simonds D'Ewes, Bart.,* ed. J. O. Halliwell, 2 vols (1845) vol. 1, 30–1.

[43] These meanings are given by the OED Online.

[44] J. S., *Paidon nosemata,* 91–2.

[45] Francis Glisson, George Bate, and Assuerus Regemorter, *A treatise of the rickets being a diseas common to children,* trans. Philip Armin (1651), 188–90.

Although the bodies of older children differed from those of infants, medical authors did not believe that older children were identical to adults: they were still firmly distinguished in their humoral make-up, being weaker than older people. The distinctions within childhood were of degree rather than substance.

A second way that children's humoral constitutions differed was in relation to their individual strength and weight or size. In 1721, the physician Charles Maitland wrote to Sir Hans Sloane on the subject of two young brothers, Joseph and William Heath: 'What a Mighty difference there is to be obser'd, Between these two boyes!' he exclaimed, for one was of a 'clean Habit', slim and strong constitution, while the other child had a weak, 'fat . . . [and] foul constitution'.[46] Although all children had a general tendency to humidity and weakness, individuals were thought to vary on this scale. The distinctions were mentioned most regularly in the context of ascertaining why certain children were more inclined to particular diseases than others. Felix Wurtz, for example, asserted that 'Some Children are weaker in their backs and sinews than others', and consequently, were more likely to develop lameness than children of more robust constitutions.[47] The reason for these differences, according to François Mauriceau, was nature: 'Very often,' he stated, the children who contracted venereal disease, had been 'weak at their Birth . . . by Nature'.[48] However, nurture was also important in fostering these constitutional characteristics. John Locke claimed that 'children's constitutions are either weakened or spoiled by [the] cockering and tenderness' of parents, but that if they were brought up in a 'plain rustick way', and encouraged to go out in 'both wind and sun', they would become 'strong . . . and hardy'.[49]

The third constitutional variable was gender. J. S. highlighted one difference between girls and boys when discussing the tendency of males to contract smallpox more frequently than females: 'Boys are more di[s]po'd to it then Girles, by the disparity of heat in them, boys being hotter'.[50] Since smallpox was caused by hot humours, boys were predisposed to the disease. Thus, boys' humours, like those of adult males, were warmer than those of females. The reason for this difference in temperature was that 'Males are generated out of a hotter seede, Females of colder . . . Adde hereunto the nature and condition of the place [or womb], for Males for the most part are generated in the right side [whereas] Females in the left . . . the right side is hotter than the left'.[51] Girls and boys also differed in their strength, as is demonstrated in the casebook of John Locke in 1678: he noted that the disease 'lameness' was more common in 'girles that are tenderer, than boys who are stronger and sooner out of their swaddling clouts'.[52] Although it is likely that

---

[46] BL, Sloane, MS 4034, fol. 20r–20v.

[47] Wurtz, 'An Experimental Treatise', 219.

[48] Mauriceau, *The diseases of women*, 320. He suggested that this might be exacerbated by a premature birth.

[49] John Locke, *The Correspondence of John Locke*, ed. E. S. De Beer, 8 vols, (Oxford: 1976–89), vol. 2, 624–9, 686–9; vol. 3, 56; vol. 4, 719–23.

[50] J. S, *Paidon nosemata*, 59.

[51] Crooke, *Mikrokosmographia*, 308.

[52] John Locke, *John Locke (1632–1704): Physician and Philosopher: A Medical Biography, with an Edition of the Medical Notes in his Journals*, ed. Kenneth Dewhurst (1963), 130.

most medical writers agreed about these physiological differences, gender does not seem to have been as significant as the other variables discussed above, since it was mentioned far less frequently. This is intriguing because in adulthood, gender differentiation was crucial in medical narratives. Wendy Churchill believes the reason for this situation was that children's bodies were 'unsexed' until the onset of puberty.[53] Gender historians, while showing much interest in the gendering of children's upbringings, have neglected this issue in the context of children's physiology and medicine.[54]

It was not just children's general constitution that was thought to be humorally distinct. Every single body part shared these characteristics: the bones and carti-lages, for example, were 'most humid . . . perfectly soft and flexible', whereas in old men, they are 'dry and wither'd'.[55] The stomach was 'tender' because the muscle 'fibres' were 'softer'.[56] Medical authors were especially preoccupied with the subject of children's bones. The surgeon Paul Barbette noted in 1687 that 'The *number* of Bones is greater in Children than in adult People; for by years, many of them grow together, as that they cannot be separated any more'.[57] But by the age of 'seven yeares', the bones, such as those in the lower jaw began to be 'conjoined . . . and growe fewer'.[58] Children's bones also differed in texture: whereas those of adults were 'very dry' and 'hard, thick, and firm', the bones of children were 'tender, loose, soft, and thin', like 'soft Wax', 'curdled or gathered butter, and coagulated or sammed cheese'.[59] This distinct consistency stemmed from the 'plenty of Heat & Moysture' within the bones.[60] Thus, medical depictions of children's internal physiologies matched the more general humoral constitution discussed above, resembling soft wax.

Another physiological characteristic of children was their extreme sensitivity to pain.[61] Felix Wurtz, in an attempt to persuade children's nurses to handle their charges gently, asked them to consider 'how tender and soft' their own skin felt after a 'swelling or wound': he then declared that this sensation was how a newborn infant's skin felt permanently.[62] He added that the pain suffered by a child was 'twice worse' than that in an adult, owing to the sensitivity of the 'new grown flesh'.[63] One consequence of this sensitivity was the child's tendency to 'crye upon

---

[53] Wendy Churchill, 'The Medical Practice of the Sexed Body: Women, Men, and Disease, 1600–1740', *Social History of Medicine*, 18 (2005), 3–22, at 19–20.

[54] For example, Sara Mendelson and Patricia Crawford, *Women in Early Modern England, 1550–1720* (Oxford: 2003, first publ. 1998), 77–123; Ralph Houlbrooke, *The English Family 1450–1700* (1984), 150–1; Anthony Fletcher, *Growing up in England: The Experience of Childhood 1600–1914* (London and New Haven, CT: 2008).

[55] Harris, *An exact enquiry*, 3–4.

[56] Crooke, *Mikrokosmographia*, 163.

[57] Paul Barbette, *Thesaurus chirurgiae: the chirurgical and anatomical works of Paul Barbette* (1687, first publ. 1676), 209.

[58] Crooke, *Mikrokosmographia*, 982.

[59] Ibid. 982; John Brown, *A compleat discourse of wounds* (1678), 121, 137.

[60] Ibid. (Brown) 137.

[61] See Ch. 6 for a discussion of how children experienced physical pain.

[62] Wurtz, 'An Experimental Treatise', 201–4.

[63] Ibid. 205.

any litle harme they suffer and the least pain that befalls them'.[64] In turn, the 'materiall cause of Teares' in children, according to Jacques Ferrand, was 'the same with that of Spittle; which is, the Abundance of serosity remaining in the Braine . . . by reason [of which] . . . young children, are more inclined to weeping then [sic] any other'.[65] Once again, children's moist humours accounted for their physical traits.

Children were also differentiated in terms of their mental, emotional, and moral capacities. Cuffe declared, '*in their infancie*' children had '*no actuall evident use of their reason*':[66] they were like 'young Lyons and Beares'.[67] In early modern philosophy, the human soul was divided into three hierarchical sections: the 'rational soul' or 'seat of reason', the superior part, which possessed powers of reason and understanding; the animal soul, which controlled perception and the emotions; and at the bottom of the triangle, the 'vegetal soul', which oversaw the body's basic functions.[68] Thus in children, the lower souls (animal and vegetal) were more active than the highest, rational soul, hence their weak powers of reason. This situation arose once again due to the child's moist humours: the rational soul was 'drowned and drunk with moisture and humours'.[69] The reason moisture was associated with drunkenness may have been that alcohol was the most common form of drink in this period—liquid thus conjured images of irrationality. This image of the soul, a supposedly immaterial entity, becoming saturated with liquid, demonstrates the inseparability of mind and body in early modern thought, and confirms Gail Kern Paster's assertion that both mental and bodily processes were imagined in physical terms.[70]

Children's weak powers of reason had detrimental effects on their memories: 'in yong Children', there is 'forgetfulness and doltish foolishnes', whereas in adults, 'the memory [is] stedfast, firme & retentive', wrote Levinus Lemnius in 1559.[71] As children grew older, however, the moisture in their brains began to lessen, and their memories and rational powers therefore improved. Infants had 'no discretion or knowledge', but older children 'growe . . . to have more understanding and judgement', stated Jacques Guillemeau in his 1635 midwifery treatise.[72] Owing to their enhanced memories, older children were thought particularly 'inclineable to learne'.[73] In fact, of all the ages, William Gouge believed that children learn 'with much ease and small charge', since 'the parts of those who are growne in yeares are

[64] Locke, *The Correspondence*, vol. 3, 219–55.

[65] Jacques Ferrand, *Erotomania or a treatise discoursing . . . love, or erotique melancholy* (1640), 129.

[66] Cuffe, *The differences of the ages*, 127.

[67] John Pechey, *A general treatise of the diseases of infants and children* (1697), 12–13; J. S., *Paidon nosemata*, 87.

[68] F. M. Coeffeteau, *A table of humane passions* (1621), images 1–21; Thomas Dixon, *From Passions to Emotions: The Creation of a Secular Psychological Category* (Cambridge and New York: 2003), 22.

[69] J. S., *Paidon nosemata*, 87.

[70] Kail Kern Paster, *Humoring the Body: Emotions and the Shakespearean Stage* (Chicago: 2004), 12.

[71] Levinus Lemnius, *The touchstone of complexions*, trans. Thomas Newton (1576), 69.

[72] Jacques Guillemeau, *Child-birth, or the happy delivery of women . . . To which is added, a treatise of the diseases of infants* (1635, first publ. 1612), 37.

[73] Basse, *A helpe to discourse*, 236.

not so fresh and fit to learne, as in child-hood they were'.[74] It was the soft, moist texture of children's brains that enabled them to retain memories: the information became stamped and ingrained on the wax-like substance of the brain. The age by which children had attained this increased use of reason was estimated by J. S. to be about seven, the age at which children started school, or in the lower social groups, apprenticeships.[75] Historians have recognized that this age was a 'significant life stage', the point at which children were thought to be 'capable of reason', and boys were put into breeches for the first time.[76]

Medical authors sometimes implied that children's emotions were more powerful than those of adults. In 1615 Helkiah Crooke stated that children often experienced anger more strongly than older people because they had 'weake mind[s] which cannot moderate it selfe'.[77] Thus, it was the weakness of the rational soul that allowed children's passions to become inordinate. To illustrate the 'strength [of] Passion' in children, the surgeon John Brown gave a case history of a fifteen-year-old boy who had suffered a fracture to his skull: initially, the wound had healed well, but after the 'Child being vexed, and moved to Anger', he suddenly 'fell into a Fever' and died.[78] Laypeople as well as doctors recognized children's potential to feel strong emotions. Alice Thornton recorded that her seven-year-old daughter Alice, upon hearing 'guns, or drums, or noyses, and shouting' during the Civil Wars, was 'soe extremely scaired' that she was 'allmost out of her poore witt'.[79]

Children also differed from other ages in their moral dispositions. Unlike adults, the young were morally impressionable: '[C]hildren . . . are most pliable . . . as is evident by the ordinary course of nature in all things Clay, wax, and such other things while they are soft recive any impression: twigs while they are tender are bowed any way', declared William Gouge in 1622.[80] Children were born with blank minds and moral dispositions, having the potential and predisposition to sin; but through careful nurture by parents, their minds could be inculcated with morals. 'Many are the evils which children by nature are prone unto, even as ranke ground is subject to bring forth many weeds', but 'good nurture' by parents would breed 'genuity, amiablenesse, curtesie, and kindnesse' of mind, and enable children to repudiate sin.[81] On the other hand, inadequate nurture and 'cockering' would cultivate 'crooked, perverse, stubborne, churlish, surly, doggish' disposi- tions.[82] The moral dispositions of adults, by contrast, were thought to be 'head- strong: much like a strong bigge arme of a tree, which if a man goe about to straiten, he cannot easily make it bow'.[83] Thus, the disparity between the impressionability of adults and children's minds stemmed from their distinctive humoral constitu- tions: the moistness of the young was associated with flexibility, whereas adults'

---

[74] William Gouge, *Of domesticall duties eight treatises* (1622), 534.
[75] J. S., *Paidon nosemata*, 87.
[76] Patricia Crawford, *Parents of Poor Children in England, 1580–1800* (Oxford: 2010), 213.
[77] Crooke, *Mikrokosmographia*, 276.
[78] Brown, *A compleat discourse of wounds*, 148.
[79] Thornton, *The Autobiography*, 128–9.
[80] Gouge, *Of domesticall duties*, 544.
[81] Ibid, 532, 544.   [82] Ibid. 532, 537.   [83] Ibid. 547.

hard humours had connotations of permanence. The laity seem to have held a similar view, as is evidenced in popular ballads from the time. *A warning to all lewd livers* (1684–86) reminds parents that children are like 'Twigs', which when 'green you may ... ply', but with age become 'dry ... so stiff and stubborn ... You cannot bend them'.[84] Many of the above descriptions conjure an image of a 'blank slate': infants' minds were unblemished places for the imprinting of morals. Although the philosopher John Locke is usually credited for this understanding of childhood, the fact that comparable ideas were in circulation in the early 1600s suggests that it was not such a novel view.[85]

Although children were 'in danger' of some of the same sins as 'grown Persons', each age was also disposed to a number of specific sins.[86] The clergyman Isaac Watts identified eight particular sins associated with children: 'niceness' (a tendency to be fussy), *'peevishness'* (irritableness), *'Impatience'*, *'Selfishness'* and *'uncleanliness'*, *'Heedlessness'* (rashness), *'Fickleness'* (always wanting 'something new ... new Books, new Lessons, and new Employments'), and finally, 'A talkative or tattling Humour'.[87] Other sins that were commonly mentioned, especially in autobiographical accounts of childhood, were disobedience and greed. Authors implied that children's general tendency to immorality stemmed from their weak powers of reason.

While older children were capable of the above sins, there was a general acceptance that infancy was 'the most innocent Part of our Lives', in which time 'we are without all appearance of Evil, and we neither do, nor think amiss ... we are incapable of sinister Designs, and do in all our Actions express a perfect Innocence'.[88] Owing to their moral purity, young children were thought to be peculiarly vulnerable to 'divine impressions'.[89] Only as children grew older did the 'Seeds of Sin' present in all humans from birth begin to 'ripen', hence the numerous 'follies and sins' committed by older children outlined above.[90] But there was a degree of ambivalence surrounding the issue of infants' moral status, for some churchmen believed that even newborn babies would crave 'adultery, fornication, impure desires, lewdness, idol worship, belief in magic ... anger' and so forth, due to original sin. Infants were 'innocent vipers', characterized paradoxically by their innocence and wickedness.[91]

As well as being distinguished from adults in their bodies and minds, children were set apart by their behaviour. Firstly, regarding sleep, W. S. wrote in 1704, that 'Children for some time after they come into the World sleep not moderately, as having had a long Repose in the Womb, and therefore [are] naturally in [their]

[84] *A warning to all lewd livers* (1684–86).
[85] For a critique of historians' interpretations of Locke, see Anthony Krupp, *Reason's Children: Childhood in Early Modern Philosophy* (Lewisburg, PA: 2009).
[86] Isaac Watts, *Preservative from the sins and follies of childhood and youth* (1734), 9.
[87] Ibid. 41–9.
[88] Bunyan, *Meditations on the several ages*, 14.
[89] Alexandra Walsham, '"Out of the Mouths of Babes and Sucklings": Prophecy, Puritanism, and Childhood in Elizabethan Suffolk', in Diana Wood (ed.), *The Church and Childhood*, Studies in Church History, vol. 31 (Oxford: 1994), 285–300.
[90] John Bunyan, *Meditations on the several ages of man's life* (1700), 21.
[91] Cited by Colin Heywood, *A History of Childhood: Children and Childhood in the West from Medieval to Modern Times* (Cambridge: 2001), 34.

Infancy desirous of Rest'.[92] Children remembered sleeping in the womb—they were 'mindfull of the perpetual sleep'—and so wished to continue to do so after birth.[93] Children's humours also contributed to this behaviour: J. S. explained, 'children . . . never sleep moderately . . . because his body is very moist, not only by the abounding with humours, but by the solid parts being moist and soft'.[94] By contrast, 'in old men . . . having solid dry parts of their heads . . . makes them most watchfull'.[95] Thus, sleep and moisture were linked in early modern opinion; this was probably because moisture resembled alcohol, which was known for its soporific effects.

Another distinctive behavioural characteristic of children related to their diet. It was widely believed that 'All children are naturally very greedy, and gluttonous and therefore many times, and especially when they grow somewhat big, and are wained [weaned], they doe fill themselves with much milke or with store of divers other victuals'.[96] This idea of children's greediness derived from Hippocrates' aphorisms, which stated that, 'Old men can most easily endure fasting, next to them such who are arrived at their full Age; Young men worst of all; but among all, Boys chiefly, and among them such as are active and prone to action'.[97] Physicians usually explained this trait by referring to children's growing bodies, which needed constant nourishment.[98]

Children loved playing. The religious author John Bunyan wrote in 1700 that, 'before we are well got out of our Mother's Lap, we betake our selves to Play . . . in this Age [we] contend . . . eagerly for Rattles and Hobby-Horses'.[99] Play fulfilled a useful function in medical opinion: it enabled the release of the child's sometimes wild passions. Daniel Sennert advised parents to 'Let them play to temper the affection'.[100] Play also served as a form of physical exertion, and as such, was linked to the non-natural of exercise. Glisson suggested that children suffering from rickets should 'exercise' by means of 'playing [with] some little Ball or Cat before them that they may be often kicking [their feet]'.[101] The perspiration caused by play evacuated the excess humours, thereby maintaining or restoring the humoral balance.[102] Play may have been regarded as a child-specific form of the non-natural exercise since young children were probably excluded from the more adult methods, such as shooting and horse-riding.

Laypeople also associated play with children. The Royalist army officer, Hugh Cholmley (1600–57), reminisced that as a child, he had been 'naturally given to all

---

[92] W. S., *A family jewel*, 50.
[93] J. S., *Paidon nosemata*, 105.
[94] Ibid.
[95] Ibid.
[96] Guillemeau, *Child-birth*, 68.
[97] Hippocrates, *The eight sections of Hippocrates aphorismes* (1665), 35.
[98] Daniel Sennert, *Practical physick the fourth book in 3 parts: section 2: of diseases and symptoms in children* (1664), 231.
[99] Bunyan, *Meditations on the several ages*, 17.
[100] Sennert, *Practical physick*, 231.
[101] Glisson, *A treatise of the rickets*, 362.
[102] Mulcaster, *The training up of children*, 45.

sports and recreations and inclinable to play'.[103] Attitudes to play were mixed: it was sometimes regarded fondly by parents. The London woodturner Nehemiah Wallington wrote with pleasure in 1625 that his 'sweete Sonne John . . . was very merry that night and full of play'.[104] It is unclear whether this positive comment stemmed from an appreciation of the medical benefits, or was elicited simply from observing the child's enjoyment. However, when play was excessive, or threatened to disrupt education, it provoked censure. The puritan Richard Baxter admitted that during his own childhood, he had been 'excessively addicted to play', which he lamented 'troubled' his conscience for 'a great while' later in life.[105]

In sum, it appears that medical authors and laypeople believed that children were distinctive in their constitutions, bodies, minds, and behaviour. Underpinning all these characteristics was their distinctive humoral humidity and tenderness.

CHILDREN'S DISEASES

Many of the maladies suffered by children were different from those contracted by other ages. As J. S. asserted, the 'Diseases of Children are so called, not only such which trouble and affect only Children . . . but also such Diseases[,] which most frequently happen to Children'.[106] In the treatises devoted entirely to the subject of children's medicine, authors usually listed between thirty and forty-five diseases, which included conditions as diverse as smallpox, 'pissing the bed' (incontinence), and nightmares. Among the most commonly cited children's diseases in all the medical texts were worms, rickets, convulsions, gripes, fever, 'breeding of teeth' (teething), and thrush. There was little change over time in the types of maladies mentioned,[107] although the terminology occasionally did alter. The disease epilepsy, for example, tended to be known as 'falling sickness' in the first half of the seventeenth century.

The laity also believed that children were vulnerable to a specific set of diseases. **Figure 3** shows the nine most commonly cited diseases of children in the domestic recipe books; it includes the numbers and percentages of the authors who cited each disease at least once in their manuscripts.

These figures indicate that the laity and the medical authors associated the same diseases with children. Like the medical texts, there was little evidence of change over time in the types of diseases appearing in the recipe books.[108]

---

[103] Hugh Cholmley, *The Memoirs and Memorials of Sir Hugh Cholmley of Whitby 1600–1657*, ed. Jack Binns, Yorkshire Archaeological Society, vol. 153 (Woodbridge: 2000), 82–3.

[104] Guildhall Library, London, MS 204 (Nehemiah Wallington, 'A Record of the Mercies of God: or A Thankfull Remembrance').

[105] Richard Baxter, *The Autobiography of Richard Baxter Abridged from the folio 1696*, ed. J. M. Lloyd Thomas (1931), 5–6.

[106] J. S. *Paidon nosemata*, 5.

[107] For example, compare Phaer, 'The Booke of Children', 157–95, with Pechey, *A general treatise*.

[108] This similarity can be observed by comparing Mrs Corylon's recipe book with those in Thomas Davies': WL, MS 213 and BL, Egerton MS 2,214 .

Diseases	Number of recipe books referring to each disease (from a total of 37 books)	Percentage of all recipe book authors
Worms	21	57
Convulsions/ falling sickness/ epilepsy	19	51
Rickets	17	46
Gripes/ collick/ fretts	11	30
Smallpox/ measles	10	27
Ague/ fever	10	27
Sore gums/ teething	9	24
Chin cough	9	24
Thrush	8	22

Fig. 3. A table to show the most commonly cited children's diseases in recipe books, compiled by author.

The precise range of diseases to which children were susceptible was thought to vary according to their age. Hippocrates' *Aphorisms* state that newborn babies suffer from 'creeping Ulcers...Vomitings, Coughs, Watchings...Inflamations about the Navil, and moistnesse of the Ears'. At the age of about seven months, infants contracted 'prickings of the Gums, Feavers, Convulsions'. When 'they are somewhat older', the common diseases were 'Inflamations of the Tousills...beatings upon the inward part of the Vertebra...difficulty breathing, the Stone, Round-wormes... swellings about the Neck...small pustules or pimples'.[109] This apportioning of diseases was repeated identically in many of the medical treatises. Laypeople also made the connection between the child's age and illness. Foremost among the ailments associated with infants were 'the breeding of teeth', gripes, and thrush, which appear numerous times in parents' personal letters and diaries. Lady Chicheley, for example, recorded that her baby daughter was 'very weak and a little hotter... than ordinary...occasioned by a tooth which lyes swelled and ready to cutt'.[110]

Children's strength and weight also impacted on their disease vulnerability. In 1693 Walter Harris stated that, 'Corpulent and fat Infants [are] troubled with Defluxions, and having an open Mould, are most subject to the Rickets, Chin-Cough, Kings-Evil, and almost incurable Thrushe', whereas 'Lean and Scraggy

[109] Hippocrates, *The eight sections of Hippocrates*, Section 3, aphorisms 24–9, [p] 56–7.
[110] Evelyn Caroline Legh Newton, *Lyme Letters, 1660–1760* (1925), 98.

Children are, the most tender and very subject to the worst Fevers'.[111] Weak children
were more susceptible to rickets, syphilis, and coughs, whereas strong children were
more 'liable' to fevers, smallpox, and vomiting.[112] By contrast, the child's gender had
a comparatively small impact on the range of diseases contracted by children. Boys
were 'much troubled at this day with the rupture', declared Guillemeau.[113] The
diseases associated with the male genitalia were obviously confined to males.[114] Even
fewer diseases were associated particularly with girls—they might suffer from the
'closed up womb' or other conditions related to their reproductive organs.[115] This
comparative lack of 'gendered' diseases in both sexes is at odds with medical
understanding of the diseases of adult women, which were almost always linked to
gender.[116]

As has been implied above, older people were thought to suffer from different
diseases. In youth, the 'Diseases usuall' were 'spittings of Blood, Consumptions,
[and] acute Feavers', while adults contracted 'Asthmaes, Plurisies, inflamations of
the Lungs, Lethargies, Phrensies... [and] Flux of the Hemorrhoide[s]'.[117] The
maladies 'incident to Old Age' included 'Catarrhes... pains in the joynts... Ver-
itgoes, Apoplexies... [and] difficulty of hearing'.[118] The fact that each age group
was ascribed its own set of diseases is a useful reminder that childhood was not
entirely unique in medical opinion: children were not the only ones who suffered
from a distinct range of ailments. Nor were all diseases categorized according to age:
some were universal. As Thomas Phaer stated in 1596, 'there be innumerable...
diseases, whereunto the bodye of man is subjecte, and as well maye chaunce in the
yonge as in the olde'.[119] These shared conditions included 'the Diseases of the Sight
and Hearing', which were 'the same... in men' as in children.[120] Even so, these
shared diseases did not affect all ages in a like manner. For example, in adults, the
disease 'lice' was contracted only by those who 'live nastily and wear foul Cloaths',
whereas in the young, this condition were less discriminating, even troubling
'Gentlemen[']s Children'.[121] The distinctiveness of children is thus conveyed
consistently in the medical discussions.

It is essential to examine the perceived causes of children's diseases, in order to
assess whether they were specific to the age of childhood. The fundamental cause of
illness, God for the punishment of sin, was applicable to all ages, since every human

---

[111] Harris, *An Exact Enquiry*, 38.

[112] Wurtz, 'An Experimental Treatise', 219; Mauriceau, *The diseases of women,* 320.

[113] Guillemeau, *Child-birth,* 71.

[114] Ibid. 82–3; Mauriceau, *The Diseases of Women,* 324.

[115] Guillemeau, *Child-birth,* 91, 79.

[116] Mendelson and Crawford, *Women in Early Modern England,* 23–9; Patricia Crawford, *Blood,
Bodies and Families in Early Modern England* (Harlow: 2004), 24–6; Kaara Peterson, *Popular Medicine,
Hysterical Disease, and Social Controversy in Shakespeare's England* (Farnham: 2010); Lauren Kassell,
Medicine & Magic in Elizabethan London (Oxford: 2009, first publ. 2005), 162.

[117] Hippocrates, *The eight sections of Hippocrates,* Section 3, aphorisms 24–9, [p] 57–8.

[118] Ibid. 58.

[119] Phaer, 'The Booke of Children', 159–60.

[120] J. S., *Paidon nosemata,* 110.

[121] Ibid. 61.

being, down to the smallest infant, was tarnished with original sin.[122] Likewise, the overarching natural cause of disease, humoral imbalance, corruption, or blockage, which the Lord used to bring disease into fruition, was universal, applying to all humans and even to animals.[123] This combination of divine and natural causation was accepted by Galenic doctors and laypeople alike.

Chemical physicians, while agreeing that God was the ultimate cause of illness, seem to have embraced a rather different theory regarding the natural cause of disease.[124] Sylvius and his supporters, influenced by the famous chemist van Helmont, believed that all creatures were composed of three or four 'principles' or chemicals, including salt, mercury, and sulphur.[125] The body was depicted as a site of chemical processes, the most important of which was 'fermentation', a process which took place in the stomach, and involved the separation of the impure 'excrement' from the pure 'chyle'.[126] This fermenting process was promoted by the presence of special chemicals or 'ferments' within the body.[127] Fermentation (and the production of chyle) was the source of nourishment for the entire body, and was therefore responsible for the maintenance of health. Sickness occurred when fermentation was disrupted: this disruption was caused by the malignant alteration of the bodily ferments from their normal state. Sylvius stated, '*when any*' of the ferments '*are out of temper; it also makes the body so*'.[128] In the case of children's diseases, the offending ferments were often thought to be particularly sour or acidic. For example, the common ailment 'thrush' was caused by 'sharp and sowre Humours *or Vapours* brought upward from the small Gut and Stomach', and the sharpness of the 'Spittle'.[129] The ferments responsible for adults' diseases, by contrast, were characterized by a greater variety of qualities, not just acidity and sharpness. The 'hypochondriac disease' in adults, for instance, was attributed to 'various' qualities of the ferments, including 'thinner or thicker; too Viscous, or Fluid; Bitter, or Acid, or Salt, or harsh, or Sweet, or Insipid; Yellow, or Green, or Ceruleous, or Black, or White, or Watry'.[130] Thus, unlike Galenic physicians, chemical authors seem to have regarded the fundamental natural cause of children's diseases as specific to this age group: their diseases were caused by 'a Praeternatural Acid', a chemical which was particularly abundant in children.[131]

---

[122] Ralph Houlbrooke, 'Death in Childhood: the Practice of the Good Death in James Janeway's "A Token for Children"', in Anthony Fletcher and Stephen Hussey (eds), *Childhood in Question: Children, Parents and the State* (Manchester: 1999), 37–56.

[123] For disease causation in animals, see Louise Hill Curth, 'The Care of the Brute Beast: Animals and the Seventeenth-Century Medical Market-Place', *Social History of Medicine*, 15 (2002), 375–92 and her book, *The Care of Brute Beasts: A Social and Cultural Study of Veterinary Medicine in Early Modern England* (Leiden and Boston: 2011), 32–49.

[124] George Acton, *A letter in answer to certain quaeries and objections ... against ... chymical physick* (1670), 4.

[125] Debus, *The Chemical Philosophy*, 107; King, *The Philosophy of Medicine*, 74–5.

[126] Sylvius, *Of childrens diseases*, apparatus.

[127] See Franciscus Sylvius, *New Idea of the Practice of Physic* (1675), 51–2.

[128] Sylvius, *Of childrens diseases*, apparatus.

[129] Ibid. 61. See also James MacMath, *The expert midwife ... [and the] various maladies of new born babes* (Edinburgh: 1694), 329.

[130] Sylvius, *New idea*, 63.

[131] Harris, *An exact enquiry*, 72.

The chemical notion that children's diseases were caused by an acidic chemical was often assimilated into the theories of Galenic physicians. Walter Harris, for instance, believed that 'the genuine Parent' of all diseases in children 'is an Acid Distemper'.[132] This author admitted that he had taken the idea from Sylvius, stating that, '*Sylvius de le Boe* has written the best Treatise of any that ever I did read on the Diseases of Infants, for he did valiantly maintain an Acid to be their true and general Cause'.[133] Galenists and chemists juxtaposed humoral and chemical language, apparently seeing the two theories as compatible. W. S. stated that the 'little risings in the heads' of children were 'for the most part . . . produced by a Salt Phlegm, mixed with choler, or of a nitrous salt Humour in the Blood'.[134] Even devout chemists like Sylvius continued to use humoral language.[135] The reason for this sharing of Galenic and chemical terminology may be that the actual theories of causation were similar: disease in both cases was caused by a malignant substance. This was recognized by Dolaus, who explained, 'All Childrens Diseases proceed from an Acid, and a Viscid. The Galenists blame a Gross and Acid Phlegm. The Paracelists an Acid Salt or Tartar'.[136]

Having considered the overarching supernatural and natural causes of disease, we now turn to the secondary or subsidiary causes—the factors that contributed to the humoral or chemical corruption. Crucially, many of these *were* unique to children. Physicians invoked these child-specific causes to explain 'how it comes to pass, that they which are grown to mans estate are not infested with these evils, as wel as children'.[137] One of the most important causes was the weakness of the child's body:

> Young Trees are scarce rais'd out of the Earth . . . but often many of them soon after die; because their Bodies, by reason of the tenderness of their Sub[s]tance, easily receive alteration, and cannot without great difficulty resist the smallest opposition, until they become a little bigger, and have taken deeper Root: So likewise we see daily above half of the youg Children die . . . as well because of the tenderness of their Bodies, as by reason of the feebleness of their Age.[138]

Thus the high rate of child morbidity and mortality was attributed to bodily weakness: the child's body was unable to resist or suppress the processes of humoral or chemical alteration. To give an example of a disease caused in this way, 'the cough' was thought to 'happen . . . unto them, because their lungs are weake and tender, which for every little thing that troubleth them, they endeavour to discharge and rid themselves of it, with some striving agitation'.[139] Diseases associated with the weakness of a muscle, such as incontinence, were also imputed to this cause.[140]

---

[132] Ibid. 79.   [133] Ibid. 40.   [134] W. S., *A family jewel*, 35–6.
[135] For example, Sylvius stated that gripes in the belly were caused by '*Sowre* and *Sharp* **Humours**' and '*Tough* **Phlegm**' (my bold): *Of childrens diseases*, 31–3.
[136] Dolaus, *Systema medicinale*, 317.
[137] Glisson, *A treatise of the rickets*, 186.
[138] Mauriceau, *The diseases of women*, 317.
[139] Guillemeau, *Child-birth*, 47.
[140] Ibid. 79.

Children's distinctive humoral constitution—their moisture and warmth—was another major cause of disease. J. S. asserted that 'Every Age is obnoxious to all kinds of Diseases, but one Age is more disposed to some diseases, then another is; for every Age hath a peculiar temper, and so a similitude with some Diseases'.[141] Since diseases were caused by humours, the humoral make-up of the patient predisposed him or her to the diseases which shared its humoral cause. Thus, in children, their 'hot and moist temper' inclined them to diseases that were caused by humours of these qualities. One such disease was lice: Nicholas Culpeper explained in 1662 that *'Lice are creatures that breed... chiefly in children... that are hot and moist have many excrements that are fit to breed Lice'*.[142] In medical practice as well as prescription, doctors mentioned this cause: Ysbrand van Diemerbroeck attributed the 'Epileptic Convulsions' in his patient of seven months old to the fact that 'the Brains of Children are very moist, and thence arise many watry and flegmatic Vapors'.[143] Doctors of chemical persuasions also mentioned this cause of disease, thus once again reflecting their shared understanding of children's general constitutions. Robert Johnson, for instance, stated that 'Catarrhs happening to Children' are caused by 'plenty of humours, because they abound in moisture, and are full of excrements'.[144]

Another cause of disease in children was the infection of the 'generative seed' during gestation. As explained by Crooke in 1615, 'diseases are... communicated from the Father or Mother to the childe... by [the] seede. These seeds contain in them potentially the Idea, Formes and Properties of all the partes' of the child's body.[145] It was believed that the seeds of the parents sometimes contained pernicious properties, which, after birth, would transmute into harmful humours, and produce disease. An example of such a disease was French Pox: James MacMath wrote in 1694, 'This is a dangerous and loathsome Disease generated of vicious and corrupt Humours sometimes from the Seed of the Parents'.[146] Conditions caused in this way were commonly termed 'inherited diseases', and they included lameness, epilepsy, and baldness.[147] Although the diseases could be inherited from either parent, it was usually the mother's seed that was held responsible. This may have been owing to the entrenched conviction that women's bodies were inferior to men's.[148]

Disease could also be transmitted through the 'impure blood' of the mother, which seeped into the foetus's body during pregnancy, and caused many ailments throughout childhood.[149] 'Children are disposed to very many Diseases' because of

[141] J. S., *Paidon nosemata*, 2–3.
[142] Nicholas Culpeper, *Culpeper's directory for midwives: or, a guide for women... the diseases and symptoms in children* (1662), 239.
[143] Van Diemerbroeck, *The anatomy of human bodies*, 134.
[144] Johnson, *Praxis medicinae reformata*, 58, 25–6.
[145] Crooke, *Mikrokosmographia*, 292, 285.
[146] MacMath, *The expert midwife*, 382; Mauriceau, *The Diseases of Women*, 362.
[147] Crooke, *Mikrokosmographia*, 279.
[148] William MacLehose, *A Tender Age: Cultural Anxieties over the Child in the Twelfth and Thirteenth Centuries* (New York: 2006) [Columbia University Press in conjunction with the American Historical Association's Gutenberg-e series], ch. 1.
[149] Patricia Crawford, 'Attitudes to Menstruation in Seventeenth-Century England', *Past and Present*, 91 (May 1981), 47–73, at 52.

the 'Impurity of the nourishment in the Womb', declared J. S.[150] There were two ways by which the mother's blood became corrupt: one was through lack of menstrual purging during pregnancy. Menstruation, according to most medical writers, resulted from the inefficiency of women's bodies: they were unable to purify their own blood, and therefore had to shed the excess or impure matter in the form of monthly periods.[151] During pregnancy, this blood, 'which was wont to be evacuated every month, and those vitious humours that are wont to be carried off with it, being detained nine whole months in the Womb, it may easily happen that the Child be injured there by'.[152] The second way by which the menstrual blood could become corrupt was through the poor regimen or the sickness of the mother herself. If the mother's six 'non-naturals' were immoderate, her bodily humours would become unbalanced or corrupt, and these would then impair the health of the foetus. Diet was the most regularly mentioned non-natural: according to John Pechey, certain foods caused 'vitious humours [to be] communicated to the Fetus... which... disorder Children in the Womb, and sometimes after they are Born, occasion various Diseases and Symptoms'.[153] The most harmful foods, according to chemical physicians, were '*Sallets,* Citrons, Oranges, unripe and sowre fruits, and other Meats which for their loathsomness are pickled with much sowre and sharp liquors'.[154] All these foods were acidic, hence their association with acidic chemical ferments. Galenic physicians pointed to similar foods, and particularly, spicy, hot, salty meats, which were capable of engendering a choleric or melancholic state in the mother's blood.[155]

Other subsidiary causes were those relating to children's natural physiological developments, such as the falling off of the 'navel string' (umbilical cord) shortly after birth. W. S. stated in 1704 that, 'The cutting of the Navel String to give freedom' occasions 'Inflamations and Pains... which must trouble and enfeeble the Child'.[156] Medical writers identified three diseases caused in this way: the swelling of the navel, which 'may happen when the Navel is not well bound, and when it is cut too long',[157] the 'inflammation of the navel', which occurred when 'the Ligature is not rightly made',[158] and the 'gaping of the navel', which was a condition whereby the 'navel... would not come together' because of 'the unskilful cutting' of the navel string by the midwife.[159] These diseases were caused by the pain generated at the cutting of the cord: the smart drew the body's blood to the site of the navel, 'and so heats and causes this Inflamation, [and] the Symptoms... of Swellings,

---

[150] J. S., *Paidon nosemata,* 2–3.
[151] Crawford, 'Attitudes to Menstruation', 49–51; Mendelson and Crawford, *Women in Early Modern England,* 21–3.
[152] Pechey, *A general treatise,* 14.
[153] Ibid. 14. This is echoed by W. S., *A family jewel,* 34, and J. S., *Paidon nosemata,* 2–3
[154] Sylvius, *Of childrens diseases,* 87.
[155] J. S., *Paidon nosemata,* 83–4; W. S., *A family jewel,* 25.
[156] Ibid. (W. S.), 34. See also J.S., *Paidon nosemata,* 4.
[157] Robert Pemell, *De morbis puerorum, or a treatise of the diseases of children* (1653), 47.
[158] Pechey, *A general treatise,* 135.
[159] John Symcotts, *A Seventeenth Century Doctor and his Patients: John Symcotts, 1592?-1662,* eds F. N. L. Poynter and W. J. Bishop, Bedfordshire Historical Record Society, vol. 31 (Streatley: 1951), 80.

Hardness, Redness, Heat, Pulsation, and a Feavour'.[160] Thus, pain was thought to be a cause, as well as a symptom, of illness: it heated the humours, and forced their movement around the body, instigating humoral imbalances or obstructions. In practice as well as in medical theory, doctors were aware of the effects of the cutting of the navel string. The Bedfordshire physician, John Symcotts, for example, recorded in 1650 that he went to see 'Mr. Corbet's child' living in Huntingdon, who, 'by the unskilful cutting of her navel string, her navel gaped and would not come together, seemed an omphacele, and so continued for three years at least'.[161]

Another natural development that caused disease in children was teething, at the age of about seven months.[162] This may seem contradictory, for earlier it was suggested that teething was actually a disease in itself. However, in this period, it was quite legitimate to label a particular condition as a disease, a cause, and a symptom. The illnesses resulting from teething included the 'swelling of the gummes & jawes...fevers, crampes, palsies, fluxes, Reumes, and other infirmities'.[163] Chemical physicians listed a similar array of diseases.[164] Teething caused diseases by bringing pain: children's gums were 'exquisitely tender', and the teeth were 'sharp' and 'hard', and therefore great pain resulted when the teeth 'bruised and crushed' the gums as they pierced the flesh.[165] In turn, this pain unsettled the humoral balance of the body by heating and augmenting the hot humours choler and blood. As Mauriceau explained, 'looseness' (diarrhoea), 'happen[s] to them by reason of the great Pain they have at the cutting of their Teeth; for all the Humours are so overheated'.[166] Laypeople were also aware that teething caused disease in infants. In the late seventeenth century, the Cornish gentlewoman, Mrs Frances Godolphin, recorded that her 'poor boy was very froward & sick yesterday & last night', which she attributed to his growing teeth.[167]

Children's diseases could also be caused by their environment—the 'non-naturals'. Three non-naturals were mentioned most regularly: firstly, diet. Physicians believed that a key cause of disease in 'sucking infants' (breastfed babies) was the change in nourishment from the 'pure' blood in the womb, to the 'corrupt' breast milk of the wet nurse or mother. This was revealed by W. S. in 1704: 'in the Womb [children] are nourished with the pure Blood...but after the Child is born, Milk...is necessary...The Milk they suck from the Breast may be vitiated or bad', in which case, 'many fevourish Distempers' result.[168] There is a degree of contradiction in this causation theory, for it is based on the supposition that the blood of the womb was 'pure' in contrast to the breast milk: as was stated earlier, the mother's menstrual blood could also be seen as corrupt. Such a contradiction

[160] W. S., *A family jewel*, 37.
[161] Symcotts, *A Seventeenth Century Doctor*, 80.
[162] W. S., *A family jewel*, 34–5.
[163] Phaer, 'The Booke of Children', 174.
[164] Sylvius, *Of childrens diseases*, 95.
[165] J. S., *Paidon nosemata*, 132–3.
[166] Mauriceau, *The diseases of women*, 345.
[167] BL, Additional MS 28052, fol. 14r (Domestic correspondence of the family of Godolphin, 1663–1782, no date given).
[168] W. S., *A family jewel*, 34–5.

reflects the ambivalent attitudes surrounding the mother's blood—it was simultaneously 'murderous' and 'nourishing', according to Barbara Duden.[169] The diseases generated by the milk included 'wringing of the Belly, Flux, Watching,
Leaness, Thrush, and Falling sickness', 'want of Appetite', and 'Pustules'.[170] The
cause of the milk's corruption was usually the poor diet of the wet nurse or mother,
thus confirming the earlier observation that ideas of female physical inferiority
underpinned understandings of infant health.[171]

Laypeople also regarded the impure breast milk as a cause of disease in children.
In 1656, Alice Thornton wrote, 'It pleased God to take from me my deare
childe Betty...which I conceived was caused by ill milke of two nurses'.[172]
Several decades later, Abigail Harley told her husband that their child, 'is broken
out on the body' with 'the itch', which she believed was caused by the milk of 'Ann
Wo[o]dhouse', who 'suckled' the child.[173] Occasionally mothers blamed themselves rather than their wet nurses. In 1709, the mother of Samuel Johnson (the
dictionary writer) decided that the 'scrofulous sores' on her infant's body came not
from 'the bad humours of the nurse', but instead, from her own family.[174] The
question how this theory of disease causation—which laid the blame with
mothers—might have affected parents emotionally, will be discussed in Chapter 4.

Another cause that was related to diet was the child's 'naturally very greedy and
gluttonous' instinct and 'tender belly'.[175] As Crooke explained, the 'retentive and
expulsive' faculties of children's stomachs were 'weaker, because they have tender
bellies', and therefore, their 'continuall eating and greedy appetites' caused an
accumulation of undigested food in the stomach, which would begin to become
'vicious'.[176] Consequently, many diseases associated with evacuation and putrefac-
tion were occasioned, such as vomiting and diarrhoea. Mauriceau stated, 'One need
not wonder at the Vomiting of little Children.... they often draw more Milk than
their...Stomachs can easily...digest, with which...they are oblig'd to cast it
up'.[177] Galenic and chemical physicians seem to have agreed, although the former
spoke of the decomposing 'humours' in the food, while the latter referred to the
acidic ferments or vapours. Sylvius, for example, wrote that children, as 'great
eaters', had a tendency to devour *too much meat, especially Flesh, and green Fruit:*
which not fermenting enough...turn into...*sharp vapours* which then produced
worms.[178] In practice as well as in prescription, this cause was mentioned. Dr van

---

[169] Barbara Duden, *The Woman Beneath the Skin: A Doctor's Patients in Eighteenth-Century Germany*, trans. Thomas Dunlap (Cambridge, Mass.: 1991), 167–9. See also MacLehose, *A Tender Age*, ch. 1, para. 80.
[170] Sennert, *Practical physick*, 228; Dolaus, *Systema medicinale*, 314–15.
[171] Harris, *An exact enquiry*, 17–19; MacLehose, *A Tender Age*, ch.1
[172] Thornton, *The Autobiography*, 94.
[173] BL, Additional MS 70115, this manuscript is unfoliated (Harley papers).
[174] Samuel Johnson, *An Account of the Life of Dr Samuel Johnson, from his Birth to his Eleventh Year, Written By Himself* (1805), 12.
[175] Crooke, *Mikrokosmographia*, 163–4.
[176] Ibid. 163–4.
[177] Mauriceau, *The diseases of women*, 347.
[178] Sylvius, *Of childrens diseases*, 129.

Diemerbroeck attributed the epilepsy of his eight-year-old patient to his 'Bad Diet' and 'greedy devouring of bad or raw Fruit', which 'heap[ed] up Crude and Flegmatic Humors' in the stomach, and sent vapours of 'peculiar pravity and acrimony', to the brain.[179] The image evoked here, of vapours rising through the body, confirms Gail Kern Paster's assertions that the early modern body was a 'semipermeable, irrigated container', in which the humours moved about unconstrained and free.[180] Overeating as a cause of disease applied to 'Older children...as well as the younger',[181] but some writers believed that children 'grown somewhat big, and are weaned' were especially subject to this cause, perhaps because they were more active in their play, and therefore required greater nourishment.[182] The foods desired most insatiably by children were fruits and sweet things.[183]

Laypeople also acknowledged diet as a cause of disease in children, although they did not usually provide detailed physiological explanations. Martha Hodges, in her recipe book dated 1675, wrote that 'The voracious Feeding of young Persons, often produces putrid Fevors, & ill conditioned small Pocks, Measles, Ulcers, foul eruptions of the skin, bleeding at the Nose'.[184] Likewise, the Buckinghamshire gentleman Ralph Verney attributed the sickness of his eight-year-old daughter Pegg to 'nothing but that when I was abroad on Thursday she stole [took] some raisons of the sun and ate too many of them'.[185] Children themselves sometimes blamed their diseases on this cause. In 1624, Nathaniel Bacon told his wife Jane that their young son Nick 'sends you word of...a disaster he escaped at my beinge w[i]th him; he ate so much milke porrage at supper that he cryed out, (O Lord!) I think I have almost broake myne guutt' from eating too much; the father 'was fayne to walke him a turne or...[two] about the chamber to digest it' until he felt better.[186]

The second non-natural that was mentioned regularly as a cause of children's diseases was the perturbation of the mind. As was established earlier, medical authors often believed that children's passions were especially powerful, owing to the weakness of their rational souls. Consequently, it was thought that children were particularly likely to suffer from diseases caused by this non-natural. John Pechey stated in 1697, 'violent Passions of the mind make great impressions upon the Body' of children 'and so occasion the falling Sickness and other Diseases'.[187] Of all the passions, 'sudden Fright', sorrow, and anger were mentioned most frequently in reference to disease causation in children.[188] The passions caused

---

[179] Van Diemerbroeck, *The anatomy of human bodies*, 191.
[180] Gail Kern Paster, *The Body Embarrassed: Drama and the Disciplines of Shame in Early Modern England* (Ithaca, NY: 1993), 8.
[181] Pemell, *De morbis puerorum*, 22.
[182] Guillemeau, *Child-birth*, 68.
[183] Maynwaringe, *The method and means*, 94.
[184] WL, MS 2844 fol. 100r (Martha Hodges and others, Collection of cookery receipts, including a few medical receipts, *c.* 1675–1725).
[185] BL, M.636/8, this manuscript is unfoliated (Verney papers on microfilm, 1646–50).
[186] [Cornwallis], *The Private Correspondence of Jane Lady Cornwallis, 1613–1644*, ed. Lord Braybrooke (1842), 99.
[187] Pechey, *A general treatise*, 12–13.
[188] Ibid. 31.

disease by harming various organs of the body, and especially the heart: 'this Passion of Sorrow fixes the Blood in the Heart, and hinders it from circulating through the several Parts, being depriv'd of this Humour, that is necessary to the very Being, grow lean, and fall away, beyond a Possibility of being restor'd', wrote one anonymous author.[189] Thus, the passions drew the blood and other humours to the heart, thereby depriving the rest of the body of its vital nourishment.[190]

The laity also believed that children's passions could cause disease. In 1710, Anne Clavering bewailed that 'Jacky', her young half-brother 'has been ill of a rash' which she believed was occasioned 'by fretting' over beatings he was given at school for 'faults he dos not comitt', and also because the school mistress 'won't lett him lye in his own sheets or use his silver porringer'.[191] Although this vignette does not reveal the precise ways by which the emotions were thought to bring disease, it does suggest that the laity linked children's passions with their illnesses.

The third non-natural that was commonly mentioned in the context of children's diseases was the air. Galenic medical theory taught that the temperature and consistency of the air resembled the bodily humours; when a person was exposed to the air, their internal state would therefore be influenced. Robert Burton explained how this occurred: 'Aire is a cause of great moment [importance], it producing Disease, being that it is still taken into our bodies by respiration, and our more inner parts'.[192] Thus, the power of air as a cause derived from its ability to penetrate the innermost regions of the body through the mechanism of breathing. Chemical physicians also referred to this non-natural, believing that 'Northern and Sharp' winds in particular produced 'sharp' chemical ferments, which then initiated diseases such as rickets.[193] The air could affect all ages, but children were particularly susceptible owing to the permeability of their skin. As Felix Wurtz stated, 'If Childrens shoulders are left open' to cold air 'it is great hurt to them, by reason of the pores, which are more open than aged peoples, because their skin is very tender'.[194] In the case of newborns, their vulnerability was even greater, because they were 'not used to the Air, For Infants live in the womb in the greatest Lukewarmnes and Tranquility, but as soon as they feel the cold Air outwardly and breath it in; they are hurt'.[195] The diseases occasioned by this non-natural included the running of the nose, cough, and difficult breathing.[196] Physicians sometimes seemed to be angry when discussing this cause of disease, imputing it to the negligence of mothers and nurses. Thomas Willis, for instance, wrote in his casebook that the infant daughter of 'F. Bodily' contracted the measles because she had been 'carelessly exposed to cold air' by her nurse.[197]

[189] *The nurse's guide* (1729), 55.
[190] See Ch. 4 for a discussion of the nature of the passions, and their bodily impact.
[191] James Clavering, *The Correspondence of Sir James Clavering*, ed. Harry Thomas Dickinson, Surtees Society, vol. 178 (Gateshead: 1967), 73–4.
[192] Robert Burton, *The anatomy of melancholy* (1621), 109.
[193] Sylvius, *Of childrens diseases*, 137.
[194] Wurtz, 'An Experimental Treatise', 216.
[195] J. S., *Paidon nosemata*, 4.
[196] Pechey, *A general treatise*, 93.
[197] Thomas Willis, *Willis's Oxford Casebook (1650–52)*, ed. Kenneth Dewhurst (Oxford: 1981), 140.

Laypeople as well as medical authors blamed the air for their children's diseases. In 1638, Brilliana Harley complained that her son Robert 'left of[f] some of his cloth[e]s, and tooke a great coold, and yesterday was exceedingly ill'.[198] Over half a century later, Anne Clavering informed her husband James that her twelve-year-old sister Betty 'went out' on Sunday 'for air, as farr as Kensington, without a hood, which gave her cold. She had a sore throat, a cough, a violent diffluction of rheum and some uneasiness in her breathing'.[199] Thus, the laity and physicians were in agreement about the role of cold air in causing illness. However, it is difficult to tell whether it was common sense that explained the association between coldness and illness, or an actual medical understanding of the effects of air on the humours. Andrew Wear implies that it was the latter, stating that 'patients had . . . been educated into the ways of rational medicine' including 'the non-naturals'.[200]

In short, while the providential and humoral causes of disease were not specific to children, the factors that contributed to the humoral corruption were often uniquely related to this age group. Children's extreme humidity, combined with their natural developments and environmental habits, predisposed them to a range of diseases to which other ages were less susceptible. This understanding of children's diseases is indicative of the existence of a concept of children's physic.

A discussion of disease prognosis provides further evidence of the children's physic concept, since it was within the context of estimating the gravity of an illness and its likely outcome, that physicians invoked the peculiarity of children's constitutions. This was because prognosis depended largely upon the degree of resemblance between the nature of the disease and the nature of the patient; the greater the dichotomy between the two, the worse the prognosis. Thus, in children, diseases that hindered their natural habits and constitutions, such as their great need for sleep, were particularly dangerous. J. S. asserted that, 'The want of sleep in Children is very hurtful, being contrary to their nature, who by the greatest and most large sleep . . . and being used to sleep much, it causes sharp humours, alters the temper of the brain, makes *Feavers* and Crudities, and weakens Children'.[201] Of all the diseases that had this effect, 'watching' was the most severe, for it was literally defined as the inability to sleep. W. S. bemoaned, 'Watching . . . is very hurtful, especially to Children, as contrary to their Nature'.[202] So ingrained was the association between lack of sleep and sickliness, that children's sleeping habits were used as an indication of their general health.[203] Laypeople also expressed concern over diseases that disturbed the child's sleep. Nehemiah Wallington recorded in 1630 that his infant Samuel suffered fits of convulsions that were 'so stronge' that he 'did start very much in his sleepe and groone very much'; upon

[198] Brilliana Harley, *Letters of the Lady Brilliana Harley*, ed. Thomas Taylor Lewis (1853), 12.
[199] Clavering, *The Correspondence of Sir James Clavering*, 31.
[200] Wear, 'Medical Practice: Continuity and Union', 311.
[201] J. S., *Paidon nosemata*, 108.
[202] W. S., *A family jewel*, 52–3.
[203] Pechey, *A general treatise*, 72.

observing these symptoms, Nehemiah felt 'small hope of his life'.[204] Clearly, this father regarded the child's inability to sleep as a foreboding sign.

Another group of diseases that was regarded as particularly hostile to children's natures were those associated with the 'stoppage' of the natural evacuations of the body. Children's bodies contained an excess of humours, owing to their naturally moist constitutions: to remain healthy, these liquids needed to be discharged through the mechanisms of urination, perspiration, and defecation. Consequently, it was believed that 'all distempers in Children' that impeded 'the natural evacuative faculties are dangerous'.[205] These diseases included costiveness (constipation), bladder stones, and stranguary (the inability to urinate). Regarding costiveness, the Kentish physician Robert Pemell declared, 'ill vapours arise . . . and cause gripings of the belly, pain of the head, and many other distempers'.[206] Jacques Guillemeau was so convinced of the dangerousness of stranguary that he insisted that if children 'bepisse themselves', they should not be 'chidden or beaten' in case this makes them 'hold their water by force' and develop difficulties in 'voiding it'.[207] Barbara Duden has noted that women's diseases were also regarded as particularly hazardous when they involved the retention of the body's humours, because female bodies were also thought to abound in moist humours.[208] This similarity is a useful reminder that women and children shared this humoral characteristic.

By contrast, diseases that were sympathetic to children's natures were reckoned to be far less serious. This notion probably stemmed from Hippocrates' *Aphorisms*, wherein it was stated that 'They . . . are in less danger, whose Maladies are more familiar and convenient to their Nature and Temperament, or their Age, Custom of Living, or the Season, than they whose Disease hath no respect to any of these things'.[209] For children, maladies of this kind were those that involved evacuation, such as vomiting, diarrhoea, and milky scab. The young were naturally moist, and would therefore benefit from the purging induced by these illnesses. Of vomiting, Pemell wrote, 'Vomiting in children is most times little dangerous' because 'if the vitious humours . . . be cast out by vomit, it is the better then if they were retained in the stomach'.[210] Likewise, diarrhoea was 'an Indisposition convenient to a Child's Nature and moist Habit' because their excess moisture required purgation.[211] Some doctors regarded these ailments so favourably that they were reluctant to attempt a cure: Mauriceau considered that doctors 'need not wonder at the Vomiting of little Children', because ''tis an Accident more ordinary and common in them. . . . nor need one be very careful to stop it'.[212] In medical practice as well as

---

[204] Guildhall Library, London, MS 204, [his pagination] 433 (Nehemiah Wallington, 'A Record of the Mercies of God: or A Thankfull Remembrance').

[205] J. S., *Paidon nosemata*, 145.

[206] Pemell, *De morbis puerorum*, 39.

[207] Guillemeau, *Child-birth*, 76.

[208] Duden, *The Woman Beneath the Skin*, 132.

[209] Cited in Mauriceau, *The diseases of women*, 345.

[210] Pemell, *De morbis puerorum*, 27. Likewise Culpeper declared, 'it is for the most part without danger in children and they that vomit from their birth are the lustiest': *Culpeper's directory*, 253.

[211] Mauriceau, *The diseases of women*, 345.

[212] Ibid. 347.

prescription, evacuative diseases were sometimes regarded optimistically. In 1714, the surgeon Daniel Turner wrote that his own child, a boy of seven, 'had not a Speck' of the disease the itch 'upon his Body', which meant that 'Nature ... not being able to Purge the Body of vitious Humours', the child's blood became 'polluted', and he died. From this lesson, he warned, 'Let Mothers have a Care how they set about the Cure' of the itch.[213] 'Itch' was a skin complaint characterized by a continuous oozing of pus, and as such, it was seen as useful for purging bad humours.

Laypeople as well as medical authors viewed evacuative diseases in this positive way. In 1667, Elizabeth Walker, the daughter of a tobacconist from London, noted in her autobiography that her young daughter, Margaret, 'Vomited tough Flegm' which she hoped would 'contribute much to her future health ... for the abundance of corrupt Matter which came away must needs have been very prejudicial to her, if it had been retained'.[214] Some years later James Tyrrell made a similar statement in his personal correspondence, stating that he believed that his son Jemmy's 'violent Cough' had served to discharge 'the greatest part of the ... malignity' from his body.[215] People lower down the social scale also understood the benefit of these diseases, as is implied in the writings of elite doctors. Daniel Sennert commented that, 'The Vulgar' think that scabs are 'healthful, when they run, because Nature sends them forth'.[216] Thus once again, the notion that there was a deep divide between lay and learned medicine is challenged.

Besides comparing the child's nature with that of the ailment, prognosis depended upon the longevity of the disease. If it was short-lived, the illness was generally deemed trivial, but once it became prolonged, it would inevitably lead to other, more dangerous diseases, and could potentially be mortal. The disease St Anthony's Fire (shingles), for example, was 'without danger' if treated immediately, but if it 'be neglected', a 'worse disease' might follow, such as 'Frenzie'.[217] Likewise, the gripes of the belly (stomach ache) 'if they continue long' will 'weaken the spirits, and many times bring Convulsions and the Falling sicknesse'.[218] Mauriceau provided an explanation: 'the Child, compos'd of a tender and soft Substance ... be too much enfeebled by it, because of the great dissipation of Spirits, which the continual Evacuation of Humours flowing thro the Belly effects'.[219] Thus, it was the extreme weakness of young patients that occasioned their vulnerability during prolonged disease—they were unable to withstand the effects of persistent illness.

Laypeople also attached greater danger to long-lasting disease in children. In 1647 Ralph Verney expressed 'fear' for a child under his care, the son of Robert Busby: the boy had been suffering from a 'troublesome ague' which had 'been his constant companion for 9 or 10 weekes together'.[220] Over sixty years later, the

---

[213] Daniel Turner, *De morbis cutaneis, a treatise of diseases incident to the skin* (1714), 44–5.
[214] Elizabeth Walker, *The vertuous wife: or, the holy life of Mrs Elizabeth Walker*, ed. Anthony Walker (1694), 94–5.
[215] Locke, *The Correspondence*, vol. 2, 569–71.
[216] Sennert, *Practical physick*, 235.   [217] Pemell, *De morbis puerorum*, 57.
[218] Ibid. 32.   [219] Mauriceau, *The diseases of women*, 345.
[220] BL, M.363/8, this manuscript is unfoliated.

Yorkshire gentleman John Yorke, wrote to his brother-in-law about 'the lingering indisposition' of his son James, who was ill of an 'impostumation of the lungs'. He admitted that it had given him 'great uneasiness' because it had lasted for over two months.[221] Although these sources do not provide explanations for their prognoses, it is clear that there was a perceived connection between the duration and the gravity of illnesses.

Medical writers debated whether diseases were more or less dangerous in children than in adults.[222] Several groups of diseases were considered less hazardous, and easier to cure in children: firstly, wounds, hernias, broken bones, and dislocations. Mauriceau noted that '*Hernias . . .* are sooner cur'd than in ancient Persons, because the Parts dilated are easier reunited . . . by reason of their Tenderness'.[223] Likewise, in reference to broken bones, Helkiah Crooke stated,

> [I]n Children and moyst natures, all the spermaticall parts, even the bones may reunite by a homogenie meane; in those that are growne some parts may, but not all; veines often, arteries more rarely; bones never. In old men there is no hope of coalition in a nerve, membrane, arterie, veine or skin.[224]

The reason for the favourable prognosis was that 'while the Child is yet yong and tender, they may be reduced to their Natural habit' of health, whereas 'once the Child is grown up and the parts are hardened, 'tis impossible to reduce them, and indeed all errors in the Body are easier to be amended while the Body grows then afterwards'.[225] Thus, children's natural humoral constitution explained their disease prognosis: moisture and softness were qualities associated with healing.

A second collection of diseases that received this positive prognosis were those associated with sweating, such as fevers, agues, smallpox, and measles. Mauriceau explained that children 'are not in so great danger as older Persons' when suffering from smallpox 'in as much as this Disease is more agreeable to their Age and Nature, and that they also have a thinner and softer Skin, thro which this Matter is easier expel'd, than thro theirs that is harder, and whose Pores are less open'.[226] Children's soft, permeable skin allowed the noxious matter to escape more easily in the form of sweat. This view was not confined to medical theory: the practising physician, John Symcotts told the parent of his young patient that 'the danger' of smallpox 'is much greater' in adults 'than in children' because 'the body' of older people is 'less transpirable' and of greater 'solidity', and consequently, 'a greater accession and a more violent fever' is produced, which 'suffocates the vital spirits'.[227] Laypeople may have also been aware of this notion: the Kentish courtier and poet, Robert Sidney, told his wife that he was 'afraid of' the prospect of his

---

[221] Clavering, *The Correspondence of Sir James Clavering*, 162.
[222] Adriana Benzaquén, 'The Doctor and the Child: Medical Preservation and Management of Children in the Eighteenth Century', in Anja Müller (ed.), *Fashioning Childhood in the Eighteenth Century: Age and Identity* (Aldershot and Burlington, VT: 2006), 13–24, at 17.
[223] Mauriceau, *The diseases of women*, 348.
[224] Crooke, *Mikrokosmographia*, 55.
[225] Galen, *Galens art of physick* (1652), 103–4.
[226] Mauriceau, *The diseases of women*, 357.
[227] Symcotts, *A Seventeenth Century Doctor*, 18–19.

adolescent children coming to stay with him because the town was infected with the smallpox, which is 'exceeding dangerous here' for 'bigger . . . children'.[228]

The disease 'falling sickness' (epilepsy) was also thought to be less grave in children than in adults: 'They who are troubled with the Falling Sicknesse before they attain the age of Fourteen, may be freed from it; but they who are taken with it at the Age of five and twenty, are usually accompanied therewith to their death'.[229] This was because in children 'the great humidity[,] which is the cause of this Diseases is lessened by Age', whereas in adults 'the . . . moisture [is already] lessened, & cannot overcome the cause of the Disease'.[230] In other words, during childhood, the humoral moisture was in decline, and therefore the cause of the disease would gradually be eradicated; but in adults, a large proportion of their moisture had already been consumed, and as a result, the chance of recovery was slimmer. Practising doctors made similar statements: Dr van Diemerbroeck observed that the epilepsy of his eight-year-old patient was curable because 'the very change of Youth out of one Age into another many times effects the Cure'.[231] Since the passage from childhood to youth was marked by a substantial change in humoral make-up, diseases that had been caused by the child's particular humoral constitution would be cured by the change.

While many diseases were thought to be less dangerous in children, some were considered to be more deadly. 'A compleat *Cure*' of the French Pox 'is rarely wrought in *Infants,* for that because of their *Non-Age* and *Imbecility,* they cannot take, nor endure the proper *Remedies* without peril of Life', declared MacMath.[232] Of the same disease, Mauriceau explained, '[the] Symptoms of it do much easier make Impressions' upon children's bodies 'because of the Delicacy and Tenderness of them, than upon such who are more advanc'd in years'.[233] Thus it was a combination of two factors that explained children's vulnerability: their inability to endure violent remedies, and their general bodily weakness. In casebooks as well as in the treatises, this view is expressed. After describing the case of a 'very poor . . . little boy' suffering from hydrocephalus (water on the brain) Dr van Diemerbroeck lamented, 'This Disease is dangerous in tender Age that will not bear strong Remedies'.[234]

Laypeople also articulated this pessimistic prognosis in relation to certain diseases in children. When Simonds D'Ewes's daughter Anne became ill of an ague in 1632, he lamented, 'being not yet two years old . . . we much feared we should have lost her'.[235] He implied that the child's young age made her more vulnerable during illness. Popular sayings and proverbs which laypeople recorded in their personal

---

[228] Robert Sidney, *Domestic Politics and Family Absence: The Correspondence (1588–1621) of Robert Sidney, First Earl of Leicester, and Barbara Gamage Sidney,* eds Margaret P. Hannay, Noel J. Kinnamon, and Michael G. Brennan (Aldershot: 2005), 100.

[229] Hippocrates, *The eight sections of Hippocrates,* section 5, aphorism 7, [p.] 18.

[230] J. S, *Paidon nosemata,* 91–2.

[231] Van Diemerbroeck, *The anatomy of human bodies,* 191.

[232] MacMath, *The expert midwife,* 382.

[233] Mauriceau, *The diseases of women,* 362–3.

[234] Van Diemerbroek, *The anatomy of human bodies,* 208.

[235] D'Ewes, *The Autobiography and Correspondence,* vol. 2, 67.

documents also provide an insight into their views on this subject. After the birth of his son, the vicar Thomas Brockbank told his father-in-law, 'a childs health is very uncertain'.[236] Likewise, Adam Martindale, a non-conformist minister from Lancashire, recorded that 'Children are uncertaine comforts'.[237] Thus, it seems there was a general recognition that children were especially vulnerable to sickness; this was proved on an almost daily basis by the high rates of child mortality.

In sum, the discussions of prognosis indicate that once again children were thought to differ from other ages: their diseases were more or less dangerous, depending on the nature of the disease, its resemblance to the child's constitution. Conditions which involved evacuation or required the fusion of flesh were less serious in children, owing to their moist natures.

CONCLUSION

Children were 'like soft wax' in medical opinion: they were tender, moist, and warm. These characteristics, which arose from the child's high levels of the humour blood, distinguished children fundamentally from other ages of human beings, and underpinned all medical ideas about the bodies, minds, and diseases of the young. The causes of children's ailments, along with the texture and strength of their muscles, bones, and brains, were explicitly linked to their humoral make-up. Children were thus defined not by their small stature, but by their humid humours. The humoral distinctiveness of child patients is evidence of the existence of a concept of children's physic among doctors, medical authors, and the laity. This finding also challenges Ariès' assertion that the idea of childhood was only beginning to emerge in the seventeenth century, since humoral medicine dated back to ancient times. Finally, the humoral uniqueness of children highlights the importance of age more generally as a category of differentiation in early modern medicine. Historians have rarely acknowledged the significance of this category, tending to dwell on gender as the organizing principle of medicine at this time.

Children's distinctiveness should not be overstated, however. There were many physiological commonalities between all ages of human beings: most importantly, children's bodies and diseases were viewed through the usual lens of Galenism or chemical theory.[238] Children's bodies contained humours just as adults' did, only varying in their proportions. Likewise, their diseases were caused by humoral imbalances or malignant chemical ferments, like those of other ages. The methods of prognosis—such as comparing the nature of the disease with the nature of the patient—were also the same for all ages of human beings.

---

[236] Thomas Brockbank, *The Diary and Letter Book of the Rev. Thomas Brockbank 1671–1709*, ed. Richard Trappes-Lomax, Chetham Society New Series, vol. 89 (Manchester: 1930), 276.

[237] Adam Martindale, *The Life of Adam Martindale*, ed. Richard Parkinson, Chetham Society, vol. 4 (Manchester: 1845), 120.

[238] Karen Harvey has offered a similar argument for the degree to which men and women's bodies were perceived to be different—she has suggested that there was 'sameness and difference' in: 'The Substance of Sexual Difference', 213.

This chapter has argued that children were not identical, but differed according to their age, individual strength and weight, and to a lesser extent, their gender. These factors played a part in determining the precise range of diseases to which each child was most vulnerable, as well as affecting the causes of disease. Of all these variables, gender featured least frequently: doctors and laypeople rarely distinguished between girls and boys when describing children's constitutions, bodies, and diseases. This was because the defining characteristics of children in medical opinion were their moisture and weakness, qualities shared by both sexes. The relative insignificance of gender is important because it constitutes another way in which children differed from adults—medical perceptions of adults were inextricably bound to issues of gender. This finding also has implications for the historiography of childhood and gender, because historians have usually assumed that from the age of seven, every aspect of children's lives was differentiated according to their sex.

Medical ideas about children's bodies and constitutions underwent little change over the course of the early modern period, despite the growing tensions between certain proponents of Galenic and chemical medicine. Doctors of diverse theoretical inclinations, including those who supported Sylvius, continued to emphasize the humidity and weakness of children's bodies, and listed the same ailments as the 'diseases of children'. They also agreed on the child-specific causes of disease, such as the impure milk and blood of the mother. The main reason for these shared views was that chemical and Galenic theories were in some ways similar: diseases were caused by a malignant substance—a humour or a ferment—and therefore the same kinds of causes, including the non-naturals, could be used to explain how these substances became corrupt.

A theme that has emerged in this chapter has been the tendency of doctors to blame mothers and wet nurses for children's diseases: women's corrupt menstrual blood and breast milk, together with their negligent cutting of the infant's umbilical cord could harm the tender body of the child. Rarely were fathers held responsible in this way. However, as will become apparent in a later chapter, while the natural causes of disease might be blamed on the mother, the supernatural cases were often blamed on fathers as well as mothers, since all parents were responsible for provoking God's providential punishments.

Finally, there does not seem to have been a great gulf separating lay and learned medical cultures. While the primary sources representing lay beliefs generally offer less detail about medical theory than those of doctors, the occasional glimpses that are provided by these documents indicate a similar understanding of disease causation in children. Perhaps the only significant difference to emerge has been the lack of evidence pertaining to lay understandings of chemical medicine. It may be that laypeople were so familiar with the entrenched theories of Galenic medicine, that they remained sceptical about alternative ideas.

2

'Cur'd in a Different Manner': Children's Physic

In the corpus of Western medical writing...certain documents did offer advice and treatment regarding diseases and medical conditions of childhood. None, however, acknowledged the need for...treatment designed specifically for children's unique physiology.[1]

There was no notion that children might be treated any differently from the adults...when they were unwell.[2]

Many doctors felt unable to deal with childhood illness...children possessed a disquieting tendency to succumb to whatever disease afflicted them.[3]

Many physicians shunned infants, feeling unprepared to cope with their high morbidity and mortality and incompetent to diagnose or cure them.[4]

[S]ummoning practitioners for children's illnesses, and indeed physicking them in general, were bones of contention.[5]

Il n'y a pas de différence de nature entre les remèdes donnés aux adultes et ceux administrés aux enfants...[6]

As illustrated by the quotations above, historians have often assumed that early modern doctors neither treated children, nor recognized the need to adapt their medicines to suit their distinctive temperaments.[7] Children were miniature patients, treated using the same remedies as adults. This chapter refutes these

---

[1] A. R. Colon, *Nurturing Children: a History of Pediatrics* (London and Westport, Conn.: 1999), p. xiv.

[2] Anthony Fletcher, *Growing up in England: The Experience of Childhood 1600–1914* (London and New Haven, CT: 2008), 59.

[3] Linda Pollock, *A Lasting Relationship: Parents and Children Over Three Centuries* (1987), 93.

[4] Samuel X. Rabill, 'Pediatrics', in Allen G. Debus (ed.), *Medicine in Seventeenth Century England* (1974), 237–82, at 237.

[5] Roy Porter and Dorothy Porter, *In Sickness and in Health: The British Experience, 1650–1850* (1988), 82.

[6] Philip Rieder, 'Vivre et Combattre la Maladie. Représentations et Pratiques dans les Régions de Genève, Lausanne et Neuchâtel au XVIIIe Siècle' (unpubl. PhD thesis, Geneva University, 2003), 234.

[7] A few historians have acknowledged some of the adaptations, including Nicholas Orme, *Medieval Children* (London and New Haven, CT: 2001), 108; William MacLehose, *A Tender Age: Cultural Anxieties over the Child in the Twelfth and Thirteenth Centuries* (New York: 2006) [Columbia University Press in conjunction with the American Historical Association's Gutenberg-e series], ch. 1, para. 65; Iris Ritzmann, 'Children as Patients in German-Speaking Regions in the Eighteenth

assumptions, demonstrating that physicians, medical authors, and laypeople regularly administered medical treatments to children, and were careful to tailor these treatments to suit their special constitutions. This argument supports the notion that 'children's physic' existed in early modern England.

Since it was necessary to diagnose disease before prescribing a treatment, the first part of this chapter focuses on the subject of diagnosis. The second section examines the different types of treatments that learned and lay practitioners considered appropriate and inappropriate for children. The final part then identifies the various ways in which children's remedies were adapted.

DIAGNOSIS

The diagnosis of diseases in children was notoriously difficult.[8] 'I know in how unfrequented, and unknown a Path I am to walk, since Children, and especially sick Infants offer nothing for a clear Diagnostick', complained the royal physician Walter Harris in 1693.[9] The following paragraphs examine the difficulties faced by practitioners when diagnosing children's diseases, and the techniques adopted to overcome these challenges. Such a discussion adds to the evidence that a concept of children's physic existed, since it demonstrates that medical authors and laypeople appreciated the uniqueness of children.

Diagnosis was difficult for three reasons. Firstly, young children lacked powers of communication, and therefore could not say 'where, nor what their pain is, nor any thing else'.[10] As Daniel Sennert explained, 'pain and inflammation are hard to be known' in children because 'they cannot relate it'.[11] In the early modern period, the patient's own account of illness was essential in the diagnosis process.[12] Consequently, when the patient was unable to give a clear history, as was often the case in children, diagnosis was impeded. The laity also recognized this difficulty: in the 1680s, John Verney complained that his two ill infants, Molly and Ralph, 'will not tell where their paines are'.[13] To overcome this problem, medical practitioners suggested taking children's histories from 'the Nurses and Women that are their constant Attendants'. These women, according to Harris,

Century', in Anja Müller (ed.), *Fashioning Childhood in the Eighteenth Century: Age and Identity* (Aldershot and Burlington, VT: 2006), 25–32, at 32.

[8] Lynda Ellen Stephenson Payne, *With Words and Knives: Learning Medical Dispassion in Early Modern England* (Aldershot: 2007), 96.

[9] Walter Harris, *An exact enquiry into, and cure of the acute diseases of infants*, trans. William Cockburn (1693), 2.

[10] Theophile Bonet, *A guide to the practical physician* (1684), 324.

[11] Daniel Sennert, *Practical physick the fourth book in 3 parts: section 2: of diseases and symptoms in children* (1664), 246–7.

[12] Peter Elmer (ed.), *The Healing Arts: Health, Disease and Society in Europe 1500–1800* (Manchester: 2004), 9–10.

[13] Frances Verney (ed.), *The Verney Memoirs, 1600–1659*, vol. 2 (1925, first publ. 1892), 376.

[K]now, if they have been troubled with Loathings and Vomitings, and how long; whether the Food or Milk that was cast up, was curdled; whether untimeous Weeping, Watching, and Disquiet... whether their Belly hath kept a due course, and if their Excrements be white, green, or filled with Bile.[14]

In practice, as well as in prescription, doctors recognized the value of speaking to children's nurses. In his casebook, the surgeon Daniel Turner complained that when he asked his six-year-old patient 'of... what he ailed', the child 'reply'd briskly enough, he could not tell, nor could he help it'. Turner therefore asked the 'Nurse of the Child' instead.[15] As well as seeking information from the child's nurse, medical writers paid attention to the child's cries. 'Little children will not cry, unless they ail somewhat', declared Felix Wurtz. 'They are not able to make their complaints any way but by crying. Hence.... good notice must be taken what these crying children aileth, wherein they are grieved or pained', he suggested.[16] Throughout the period, medical writers replicated this advice.[17] The laity also paid special attention to the cries of children. In 1654, Alice Thornton's baby daughter Nally gave 'great schriks' and 'grew blacke in her face', so that she believed the infant was suffering from convulsions.[18]

As children grew older, however, they became more articulate, and consequently, diagnosis based on their own words became increasingly possible. In the mid-seventeenth century, the Oxfordshire doctor Thomas Willis was called to see a ten-year-old boy, John Dew, who was suffering from 'terrible pains in his loins'. Upon 'carefully [enquiring] about the nature of his ailment', the boy told Willis that 'the malady began first in the upper part of his loins... then descends... it stays there with the pain persisting almost without a break... the pain seems to have taken itself from the region of the kidney, moving internally'.[19] From this description, Willis was able to pronounce confidently that the child was suffering from 'nephritis'. Laypeople also relied on the accounts of older children when diagnosing their distempers. In 1709, Elizabeth Hervey informed her husband that their six-year-old son Charles had contracted the smallpox: the diagnosis was based partly upon the boy's own complaint of pain 'in his head, after that in his hipp'.[20]

A second diagnostic difficulty involved taking children's pulses. At this time, practitioners ascribed certain qualities to the patient's pulse, such as 'hectic', 'gazelling', 'anting', and 'worming'. Since each type of pulse was associated with a

[14] Harris, *An exact enquiry*, 8.

[15] Daniel Turner, *A remarkable case in surgery... in a child about six years old* (1709), 19, 32.

[16] Felix Wurtz, '"An Experimental Treatise of Surgerie in Four parts... Whereunto is Added... the Childrens Book", trans. Lenertzon Fox (1656)', in John Ruhrah (ed.), *Pediatrics of the Past* (New York: 1925), 198–220, at 201.

[17] Thomas Collins, *Choice and rare experiments in physick and chirurgery* (1658), 136; J. S., *Paidon nosemata; or childrens diseases both outward and inward* (1664), 7, 23, 27; John Pechey, *A general treatise of the diseases of infants and children* (1697), 105.

[18] Alice Thornton, *The Autobiography of Mrs Alice Thornton*, ed. Charles Jackson, Surtees Society, vol. 62 (1875), 91–2.

[19] Thomas Willis, *Willis's Oxford Casebook (1650–52)*, ed. Kenneth Dewhurst (Oxford: 1981), 64–5.

[20] John Hervey, *Letter-Books of John Hervey, First Earl of Bristol*, ed. S. H. A. Hervey, 3 vols (Wells: 1894), vol. 1, 249.

particular group of diseases, it was possible to identify the ailment from studying
the patient's pulse. In children, however, this method could be misleading, because
'the Pulses of Children are naturally, or upon every little Alteration do become so
swift and frequent, that they always seem somewhat Feverish'.[21] Adding to this
difficulty was the fact that young children 'are for the most part, so...froward
[irritable] that not keeping their Wrest one moment in the same posture, do not
suffer their Pulse to be touched'.[22] Nevertheless, there were occasions when in
practice, doctors took children's pulses despite these problems. In October 1721
the physician Charles Maitland recorded that his two-year-old patient from
Hertford, Mary Batton, had a 'fuller and Quicker pulse'. This technique helped
Maitland to deduce that her disease was a mild form of smallpox.[23] Perhaps this
tension between theory and practice stemmed from the fact that there were few
alternative methods available for diagnosis.

Once again, diagnostic techniques were more reliable in older children. As
children aged, their pulses became less erratic, and their powers of reason developed, and therefore medical practitioners could come to rely more on pulse-taking
as a diagnostic test. Dr Brownrigg noted in his casebook that his seven-year-old
patient, a boy of 'good constitution', had 'a Pulse hard, full and strong with the
artery rather stiff and slowly dilating and contracting'. He decided that the boy
was suffering from 'a fever of the inflammatory kind'.[24] Iris Ritzmann, in her
study of the medical practice of the eighteenth-century German doctor Albert
Haller, has found that taking the pulse was actually used more frequently in
children than in adults: a third of the children were examined in this way, compared
with only a fifth of adults.[25] Although this does not seem to have been the case in
early modern England, Ritzmann's finding is useful for suggesting that in practice it
may have been more common to resort to traditional techniques.

Thirdly, children's urine had a naturally unhealthy appearance, and therefore,
the traditional diagnostic procedure of 'uroscopy', the examination of the urine,
was impeded. As explained by Andrew Wear, urine was considered a useful
indicator of health because it was thought to contain a mixture of all the bodily
humours.[26] Special attention was paid to the colour, precipitation, taste, and smell
of the urine. In children, however, the urine 'is most thick', even when 'in perfect
Health', and consequently, 'any too curious Person, unacquainted with this, could
pronounce them labouring under some grievous Distemper, though at that minute,
they do enjoy most prosperous Health', explained Harris.[27] Furthermore, the urine
of infants 'is always mixed with their Excrements in their Cloaths, so that it doth

[21] Harris, *An exact enquiry*, 9.   [22] Ibid. 9.
[23] BL, Sloane MS 4034, fol. 19r (Correspondence of Sir Hans Sloane 1720–30).
[24] William Brownrigg, *The Medical Casebook of William Brownrigg, MD, FRS (1712–1800) of the Town of Whitehaven in Cumberland*, eds Jean E. Ward and Joan Yell, Medical History Supplement, vol. 13 (1993), 35.
[25] Iris Ritzmann and Urs Boschung, '"Dedi Clysterem Purgantem": Haller et la Médecine de L'Enfance (1731–1736)', *Canadian Bulletin of Medical History*, 22 (2005), 175–82, at 179.
[26] Andrew Wear, *Knowledge and Practice in English Medicine, 1550–1680* (Cambridge: 2000), 120–1.
[27] Harris, *An exact enquiry*, 10.

rather serve for the scalding and excoriating of their Thighs'.[28] Once again, as children grew older, their urine gradually attained a more healthy consistency, and could be used with greater reliability in diagnosis. This can be inferred from the casebooks of doctors, which refer frequently to the urine of older children. The Stratford physician John Hall remarked that his twelve-year-old patient, the son of 'Mr Underhil of Loxley' had 'Urine . . . red, as in a burning Feaver, wet without thirst or desire to drink', which suggested that the disease was scurvy.[29]

In short, diagnosis was difficult in young children owing to their distinctive temperaments. Nevertheless, as will become apparent below, these challenges did not deter practitioners from attempting to treat children's diseases.

TYPES OF TREATMENTS

Did doctors and laypeople believe children should be treated, and if so, with what types of treatments? Practitioners often justified the use or avoidance of particular medicines by referring to the special constitutions of the young, and as such, an examination of these treatments will provide further evidence to show that a concept of children's physic existed. The first part of these discussions will focus on the opinions of doctors and medical authors, and the second part will concentrate on the laity.

Physicians usually agreed that children should be treated, as indicated by the fact that almost every medical text examined in this research mentioned medicines for children. Throughout the early modern period, four particular kinds of remedies were identified as being especially suitable for this age group. Firstly, environmental medicine: this involved controlling the 'six non-natural things', the patient's diet, sleep, exercise, passions of the mind, evacuation and retention, and air.[30] The rationale behind this treatment was that the cause of the disease—the humoral imbalance—was brought about by the transference of humours into the body via the patient's diet and environment. By controlling the non-naturals, the cause of disease could thus be removed or prevented. To cure the 'almonds of the ears', for instance, W. S. recommended 'A wholesome Diet, avoiding any Excess of the Air, Smoak, Sun, all violent Exercises of the Body, vehement Agitations of the Mind, especially Anger, and avoid bathing'.[31] Since the child's tender body was thought to be especially vulnerable to the effects of the non-naturals, it made sense to place extra emphasis on this form of physic. The second highly esteemed treatment for children was non-evacuating alterative internal medicine, which included drinks, potions, juleps, syrups, decoctions, and waters.[32] Made of herbs, fruits, and animal products, these medicines were taken orally, and 'worked' by altering the humoral

---

[28] Ibid. 10.   [29] John Hall, *Select observations on English bodies* (1679), 61.

[30] This is explained by Gianna Pomata, *Contracting a Cure: Patients, Healers, and the Law in Early Modern Bologna* (London and Baltimore, MD: 1998), 60.

[31] W. S., *A family jewel, or the womans councellor* (1704), 56.

[32] Daniel Tauvry, *A treatise of medicines containing an account of their chymical principles* (1700), 61, 65, 100–1.

balance internally without causing any purgation: they usually heated, cooled, dried, or moistened the body, or had strengthening effects. Thirdly, doctors recommended external physic, such as baths, fomentations, plasters, ointments, and poultices. These treatments may have been the most popular of all the medicines prescribed to children, for they appear as a cure for almost every disease in the treatises devoted to children's medicine. Daniel Tauvry defined 'ointment' as 'a Medicine of the consistence of Honey, made of Oyls, Wax, Powders, Fat, [and] Gums', while a plaster was 'more solid than Ointments . . . generally spread upon Linnen'.[33] Baths contained water, alcohol, herbs, or animal carcasses.[34] Poultices and fomentations were 'warm . . . Liquor[s] applied with a spunge'.[35] All these external medicines were spread across the skin, and functioned by drawing impure or surplus humours to the surface of the body. They also heated or cooled, moistened or dried the body.[36] The fourth pair of remedies that was considered particularly fitting for children were clysters and suppositories. '*In the Cure, use not strong Remedies . . . but Suppositories and Clysters*', commanded Nicholas Culpeper in 1662.[37] Clysters (or 'glisters') were liquid 'injections into the Guts' through the anus; suppositories were 'solid Medicines thrust up into the Fundament'.[38] Both functioned as 'benign and gentle Purgers', encouraging a slight movement of the bowels: they removed some of the humours of the body, thus eliminating the main cause of disease.[39] Clysters often contained syrup of roses, oil of violets, sugar, and egg white.[40]

The four types of physic described above could be prescribed to children of all ages and strengths, from infants of 'a moneth or two moneths old', to young adolescents.[41] When treating 'sucking infants' (breastfed babies), some physicians preferred to administer these treatments to whoever was suckling the child, in the anticipation that the medicinal effects would be transferred to the baby via the breast milk. Thomas Phaer suggested giving 'redde roses, & violettes' mixed with 'a lytle honye' to 'a tender suckynge childe', but also stated that 'the nourse . . . eat a[n] elctuary' made of mint, cumin, rose, mastic, and zedoary.[42]

Despite the alleged differences between the medicine of chemical and Galenic doctors, both groups prescribed the above types of treatment. The chemist Franciscus Sylvius, for instance, suggested that to cure thrush, '*sowre* Meats, Sauces . . . *cold Air . . . fright*, or *sorrow of mind*' should be avoided.[43] The use of environmental physic was justified on the grounds that the cause of disease, the malfunction of the

---

[33] Tauvry, *A treatise of medicines*, 108–9.   [34] Ibid. 79.   [35] Ibid. 81.

[36] Pomata, *Contracting a Cure*, 132.

[37] Nicholas Culpeper, *Culpeper's directory for midwives: or, a guide for women . . . the diseases and symptoms in children* (1662), 233.

[38] Tauvry, *A treatise of medicines*, 71, 74, 110.

[39] Francis Glisson, George Bate, and Assuerus Regemorter, *A treatise of the rickets being a diseas common to children*, trans. Philip Armin (1651), 323.

[40] For example, François Mauriceau, *The diseases of women with child . . . With fit remedies for the several indispositions of new-born babes* (1710), 332.

[41] Robert Pemell, *De morbis puerorum, or a treatise of the diseases of children* (1653), 33.

[42] Thomas Phaer, ' "The Booke of Children: The Regiment of Life by Edward Allde" (1596, first publ. 1544)', in John Ruhrah (ed.), *Pediatrics of the Past* (New York: 1925), 157–95, at 175, 167.

[43] Franciscus Sylvius, *Dr Franciscus de le Boe Sylvius of childrens diseases* (1682), 71.

body's fermentation process, was initiated by the invasion of the body by malignant acidic substances, from external, environmental origins. Likewise, alterative medicine and external physic were administered because they were able to absorb the acids that had been responsible for harming the body's fermentation process. The midwifery text writer James MacMath explained that these treatments 'infringe, contemper, blunt, securely drink up and remove ... [the] predominating *Acidity*'.[44] Usually these supposedly chemical medicines contained similar ingredients to those used by Galenic doctors.[45] However, chemical physicians also suggested adding 'testaceous' (shelly) powders, stones, and animal bones, such as mother of pearl, crabs' eyes, oyster shells, and chalk. These ingredients were alkali in character, and were therefore thought capable of neutralizing the acid. Dr James Clegg, for example, wrote that he gave his own daughter 'powder of crabs claws, oyster shells and nutmeg with sugar, to absorb the Acid' when she was feverish in 1723.[46] Galenic practitioners also regularly used these ingredients, which supports the notion that chemical and humoral medicine borrowed from one other.[47] According to Wayne Wilde, the motive for using chemical treatments was commercial—Galenic physicians wished to appear up-to-date, so that they could attract more customers.[48]

In practice as well as in prescription, doctors seem to have regularly used the four types of treatment above. In the mid-seventeenth century, the Dutch doctor Ysbrand van Diemerbroeck suggested that his young patient, an infant of only one year, should have a 'drier Diet then ordinary; as Biscuit' to cure him of hydrocephalus.[49] Dr John Symcotts remarked in 1636 that he applied external physic, 'oil of camomile and saffron', to the throat of his four-year-old patient, the son of one Richard Vincent from Huntingdon.[50] Clysters were also used frequently by practising doctors. In 1693 Harris treated 'the Daughter of *James Lowry,* a Girl scarce a year old' with 'a Clyster of sugared and salted Milk'.[51]

Having identified the most favoured types of medicines for use in children, we now turn to the more controversial and probably less common treatments: evacuative and surgical remedies. These comprised vomits, purges, bloodletting, issues, and blisters, and they all 'worked' by expelling the superfluous or impure humours that had caused the disease. Vomits and purges were taken orally, and had vomiting or laxative effects. Bloodletting and issues were surgical procedures: the former

---

[44] James MacMath, *The expert midwife ... [and the] various maladies of new born babes* (Edinburgh: 1694), 330.

[45] For example, Robert Johnson's chemical treatise described a powder which contained 'the Roots of Peony ... sweet Fennel and aniseed.... white Sugar.... and ... the Oil of sweet Almonds': *Praxis medicinae reformata: or, the practice of physick* (1700), 34.

[46] James Clegg, *The Diary of James Clegg of Chapel-en-Frith 1708–1755*, ed. Vanessa S. Doe, vol. 1 (1708–36), Derbyshire Record Society, vol. 5 (Matlock: 1978), 20.

[47] Pechey, *A general treatise,* 16–17.

[48] Wayne Wild, *Medicine-by-Post: The Changing Voice of Illness in Eighteenth-Century British Consultation Letters and Literature,* Clio Medica, vol. 79 (New York: 2006), 8, 19.

[49] Ysbrand van Diemerbroeck, *The anatomy of human bodies ... to which is added a particular treatise of the small pox* (1689), 184.

[50] John Symcotts, *A Seventeenth Century Doctor and his Patients: John Symcotts, 1592?–1662,* eds F. N. L. Poynter and W. J. Bishop, Bedfordshire Historical Record Society, vol. 31 (Streatley: 1951), 57.

[51] Harris, *An exact enquiry,* 103.

meant cutting a vein to remove blood, and the latter involved making an incision in the skin to allow bodily fluids to escape in the form of pus over a period of several days, weeks, or months. Bloodletting could also be achieved by scarifying the surface of the skin and applying warmed cups ('cupping-glasses') over the affected areas to create a vacuum and draw blood. Blisters had similar effects to issues, but were caused by the application of slightly corrosive substances: the blistered skin allowed noxious fluids to drain away.

Attitudes to surgical and evacuative medicine varied according to the child's age, size, and strength: medical authors usually advised against the use of these treatments in infants, or small or weak children.[52] 'In the Cure, use not strong Remedies, nor bleeding, nor purging', commanded Daniel Sennert about the treatment of infants in his midwifery text of 1664.[53] Roughly forty years later, Robert Johnson warned that 'vomiting is not to be provoked in very weak Children'.[54] Practitioners of chemical leanings shared this view: Johann Dolaus cautioned that 'Children cannot bear Purging'.[55] If these treatments were required, practitioners thought it best to give them instead 'to the Nurse or Mother, for the purgative quality is imparted by the Milk to the Child'.[56] By contrast, when treating adults, evacuative and surgical treatments were probably among the most common medicaments.[57]

There were several reasons for this hierarchy of preference when treating young children. The first relates to safety: the non-evacuating treatments were considered 'safe and gentle', 'innocent and simple', and 'not much receding from their [children's] Natural State'.[58] In this period, the best medicines were thought to be those which matched the constitution of the patient. In the case of infants and young children, their natural constitution was 'tenderness and weakness', and therefore, it made sense to choose medicines of a similarly mild quality.[59] James Primrose attributed the gentleness of these treatments to their tendency to 'never touch any noble part, in that they goe not beyond the great guts'.[60] The 'noble parts' of the body were those regions that were most vulnerable to damage, such as the brain, heart, and stomach. Conversely, the evacuative and surgical remedies were deemed dangerous and violent, and therefore not suited to the tender temperaments of children. 'In the cure of Infants a special regard is to be had to the Methods and Medicines', declared Pechey, 'for Children by reason of the weakness of their bodies, cannot undergo severe methods or strong Medicines... but... a Suppository ought to be used, or a Glister injected'.[61] Regarding purges,

---

[52] However, certain physicians thought it was acceptable to use these remedies in infants, including Sylvius, *Of childrens diseases*, 144.

[53] Sennert, *Practical physick*, 233.

[54] Johnson, *Praxis medicinae reformata*, 300.

[55] Johann Dolaus, *Systema medicinale. A compleat system of physick* (1686), 321.

[56] Pechey, *A general treatise*, 16; J. S., *Paidon nosemata*, 25.

[57] Pomata, *Contracting a Cure*, 130–5.

[58] Harris, *An exact enquiry*, 41; Primrose, *Popular errours, or the errours of the people in physic*, trans. Robert Wittie (1651) 280, 284.

[59] Ibid. (Harris) 41.

[60] James Primrose, *Popular errours*, 280.

[61] Pechey, *A general treatise*, 15.

Thomas Sydenham warned, 'Their tender Age will not bear . . . the raising of a great tumult in the Humours by purging Medicines'.[62] Thus children's humours, like their bodies, were depicted as weak and easily overwhelmed by aggressive remedies. Of all the evacuative remedies, vomits were often considered the most dangerous:

> [V]omits [are] . . . alwaies more harsh to Nature than any Purgation by the inferior parts, because the stomacke was not made for expulsion, but for reception; for it is one of the noble parts, and of exquisite sence, and hath a very great sympathy with the Braine and the heart, in so much as when it is affected . . . their heart akes [ache] . . . a vomit doth offer much violence to the . . . whole Body, straine head, braine, muscles of the belly, the breast, and all the intrailes.[63]

Vomits were violent because they affected the superior, 'noble' parts of the human body. The description above confirms Gail Kern Paster's assertion that 'Body parts are even imbued with their own affective capacity'—the stomach and heart could 'sympathise' and 'ake'.[64]

Another reason for favouring non-evacuating remedies in infants was that they were relatively painless. Ointments, for example, were 'in no way noisome . . . to Children', according to Dr van Diemerbroeck, because they soothed the soreness of skin illnesses and refreshed the mind.[65] Likewise, baths containing '*Marjoram* and time, Hyssop, Sage, [and] Mintes' were 'good and comfortable' for children suffering from colds, stated Thomas Collins.[66] By contrast, the surgical and evacuative remedies were 'unpleasing, ful of pain and molestation to Children', declared Francis Glisson.[67] Since children were especially sensitive to pain, the administration of these treatments was often considered cruel. 'Blisters may be drawn behind the Ears and on the Wrists' to cure children of epileptic fits, 'But because of the Torture, I never used them', stated Dolaus in 1686.[68] It was not just compassion that dissuaded practitioners from using these medicines: the pain itself was thought to be dangerous—it could overpower the child's tender body. As J. S. explained in 1664, cupping glasses should be avoided because 'this Age is wont greatly to be overcome by pain and trouble, and Cupping glasses are painful'.[69]

There was also a pragmatic motivation behind the choice of medicines: children were often uncooperative when faced with evacuative or surgical treatments, and therefore practitioners were left with few options but to use the medicines that their young patients were more willing to take. One anonymous author wrote in 1670, 'Some patients, (and especially Children) cannot be gotton to take any inward Medicine at all', and therefore he advised 'applying the Plaisters' instead.[70] Doctors

[62] Thomas Sydenham, *The compleat method of curing almost all diseases* (1694), 51–2.
[63] Primrose, *Popular errours*, 276, 447–8.
[64] Gail Kern Paster, *The Body Embarrassed: Drama and the Disciplines of Shame in Early Modern England* (Ithaca, NY: 1993), 11.
[65] Van Diemerbroeck, *The anatomy of human bodies*, 33.
[66] Collins, *Choice and rare experiments*, 142.
[67] Glisson, *A treatise of the rickets*, 317.
[68] Dolaus, *Systema medicinale*, 332.
[69] J. S., *Paidon nosemata*, 46–7.
[70] *An account of the causes of some particular rebellious distempers*, 74.

regularly mentioned this situation in their casebooks. Dr van Diemerbroeck recorded that a 'Noble Youth about six Years of Age', who was troubled with an obstructed spleen, 'loath'd Physic', and therefore 'I only prescribed him a proper Diet, and ordered him only', and laid a plaster 'upon his Spleen'.[71] When practitioners did try to give the more aggressive treatments, they frequently regretted their efforts due to the trouble such procedures occasioned. Francis Glisson complained that cupping-glasses 'are very little effectual, and we leave it to be perpended, whether the profit arising from the use of them, whatsoever it be, can recompence the trouble of the application'.[72] Daniel Turner's book of clinical cases reveals just how troublesome children could be in this context. He complained that one particular infant, 'a Gentleman's Child', 'growing restless, as being held in the same Posture' during bloodletting, 'fell into a Fit of Crying and holding the Breath', which meant that he could not properly dress the wound afterwards; consequently, it took much longer than usual to stop the bleeding, and he finished his working day late and exhausted.[73]

Despite the above reasons for avoiding the use of evacuative and surgical remedies in infants, there were occasions when such treatments were administered. Richard Wiseman, in his casebook published in 1686, acknowledged that he had purged an infant of one month's age 'with Rhubarb infused in his Drink' once in '4 or 5 days' to cure him of the King's Evil.[74] The medical treatises show that physicians were sometimes prepared to contradict their own advice regarding these treatments. Of purges, Harris had previously written 'The purging of Young Children ... doth seem most difficult and full of hazard', but a few pages later, he declared that 'It hath been my constant [opinion] ... to enjoyn Purging in the Fevers of Children and the youngest Infants'.[75] Likewise, bloodletting and blisters were occasionally permitted by the same physicians who had formerly condemned their use. Pechey, who had stated formerly that 'infants ... do not well bear bleeding', later admitted that 'I have bled the smallest Infants in the Arm ... with very great success'.[76]

The main grounds for using evacuative and surgical treatment in spite of the concerns about safety, was that doctors feared that without resorting to these drastic treatments, the gravely ill child might die. As explained by François Mauriceau in 1710,

[L]ittle Sucking Children ... by reason of the feebleness of their Age ... cannot ... take ... the Violence of Remedies ... but since there are very many [infants] who would perish before they were so much as a year or two [in age] ... one is oblig'd sometimes to undertake the Cure, tho[ugh] the Child is yet sucking. This Enterprize is ... very perilous, but one is constrain'd to resolve on it, when there is no appearance or hope that the Child can otherways escape.[77]

[71] Van Diemerbroeck, *The anatomy of human bodies*, 138.
[72] Glisson, *A treatise of the rickets*, 315.
[73] Daniel Turner, *De morbis cutaneis, a treatise of diseases incident to the skin* (1714), 339–40.
[74] Richard Wiseman, *Several chirurgical treatises* (1686, first publ. 1676), 264.
[75] Harris, *An exact enquiry*, 43, 46.
[76] Pechey, *A general treatise*, 15, 45.
[77] Mauriceau, *The diseases of women*, 362–3.

Mauriceau believed that when an infant was seriously ill, it was better to take the risk of administering a potentially hazardous but effective remedy, than to do nothing, and watch the infant die. This thinking stemmed from the belief that 'desperate diseases require desperate cures'.[78] Since illness was caused by the presence of corrupt humours, it followed that the most efficient method of treatment was the removal of these substances by powerful evacuations. Doctors thus found themselves in a catch-twenty-two situation: if infants were given the purging treatment, they might die, but if they were denied it, they might also die, and therefore it was up to the practitioner to assess the risks and act accordingly.

Physicians sometimes administered the more drastic treatments in response to parental pressure. This seems to have been the case for Thomas Willis in the early 1650s: he noted that when his ten-month-old patient 'was very ill' of a 'very acute' fever, the child's mother 'begged me urgently to give the child a vomit'. Willis acquiesced, prescribing '8 grains of squillae of Theophrastus in cooked plumbs'.[79] According to Barbara Duden this was probably not an unusual situation, since 'The doctor's prescription was... often a confirmation of the patient's own assessment. The doctor became a roundabout route, an authority used not to choose a remedy but to confirm a remedy'.[80]

Thus, there was much controversy surrounding the issue of treating infants with evacuative and surgical remedies. However, as children grew older, bigger, and stronger, doctors seem to have given these treatments with less reluctance. 'If the child... be very big, the vomiting may doe him much good', wrote Jacques Guillemeau in 1635.[81] He offered similar advice about the use of purges and bloodletting: 'If the child bee elder, let him bee purged twice with a little *Sene*... neither will it be amisse (if hee be bigger and stronger) to open a veine'.[82] This advice was repeated across the period, by both Galenic and chemical physicians.[83] Authors were usually imprecise in their instructions—they rarely stated what constituted a 'bigger', 'elder', or 'stronger' child. Perhaps this was because they assumed the meanings were too obvious to need stating, or else, it may have seemed illogical to set an exact age on the grounds that children grew at different rates. As Alius Medicus stated, '[S]ome persons of ten, are as strong as others at fifteen... if the strength be... good, the Age is inconsiderable [irrelevant]... For Age is not so much to be reckoned by the number of years, as by the habit of the Body, and its strength'.[84]

---

[78] Gail Kern Paster, 'Purgation as the Allure of Mastery: Early Modern Medicine and the Technology of the Self', in Lena Cowen Orlin (ed.), *Material London, ca. 1600* (Pittsburg: 2000), 193–205, at 197.

[79] Willis, *Willis's Oxford Casebook*, 106 (January 1650).

[80] Barbara Duden, *The Woman Beneath the Skin: A Doctor's Patients in Eighteenth-Century Germany*, trans. Thomas Dunlap (Cambridge, Mass.: 1991), 94.

[81] Jacques Guillemeau, *Child-birth, or the happy delivery of women... To which is added, a treatise of the diseases of infants* (1635, first publ. 1612), 62.

[82] Ibid. 115.

[83] J. S., *Paidon nosemata*, 10, 128–9; Collins, *Choice and rare experiments*, 156. An example of a chemical author is Dolaus, *Systema medicinale*, 327.

[84] Alius Medicus, *Animadversions on the medicinal observations of... Frederick Loss* (1674), 102–3.

In practice as well as in theory, doctors were more willing to administer evacuative or surgical treatments to older children. John Hall prescribed the twelve-year-old son of 'Mr Underhil' a purge every day to give him 'three or four stools', and a vomit.[85] Likewise, Dr van Diemerbroeck advised a gentle purge containing 'Powder of Diacarthamum, and Syrup of Succory with Rhubarb' for the five-year-old son of a domestic servant.[86] Girls as well as boys were prescribed these remedies. The '[d]aughter of *Captain Rifflaer,* about six Years of Age', was given 'one scruple of *Mercurius Dulcis*' to purge her when she had the worms.[87]

The justification for treating older children with the aforementioned medicaments was that they were stronger. Children's excessive moisture, the cause of their weakness, gradually declined with age, and therefore older children were believed to be better able to bear the violent remedies. These children were also less troublesome during the administration process, because they had attained 'more understanding and judgement'.[88] Daniel Turner found this to be the case in the early 1700s: he noted approvingly that his patient, the fourteen-year-old son of a wealthy merchant, 'bore his Cutting [operation] well enough'.[89] However, the fact that older children were more likely to be treated with these remedies than infants does not mean that they were regarded as identical to adults, or were excluded from the concept of children's physic. The impression conveyed in the medical texts and casebooks is that doctors still tended to favour the gentler, non-evacuative remedies for older children, even though they also resorted to the use of stronger treatments. Also supporting this argument is the evidence that some practitioners believed that even adolescents should not be treated with evacuative remedies. Dr van Diemerbroeck cautioned that 'in Children, before the seventeenth or eighteenth year, I do not approve of Bloodletting... Because it is very dangerous to wast[e] the strength of Children, which is apt enough to decay of it self'.[90]

Did ideas about the treatment of infants and children change over time? Advice about the types of medicines suitable for these ages remained the same across the period—non-evacuating treatments were favoured, though older children might take the more aggressive remedies with less danger. Neither was there much alteration in the sorts of ingredients used in these treatments: herbs, fruits, and animal products, were the staples. This continuity is best illustrated through a direct comparison of medical recipes from texts published at either ends of the time frame. In his 1596 edition of *The childrens booke,* Thomas Phaer recommended an ointment for curing the 'swellyng of the navill' that contained 'spike or lavender', 'cleare turpentyne' and oil of sweet almonds. Over a century later, John Pechey described an identical treatment.[91] For helping children to sleep, Phaer suggested anointing the 'foreheade and temples...with oyle of vyolleets' and 'syrupe of poppye'; 108 years later, W. S. advised massaging the temples with 'Oil

---

[85] Hall, *Select observations,* 60.   [86] Van Diemerbroeck, *The anatomy of human bodies,* 47.
[87] Ibid. 151.   [88] Ibid. 37.   [89] Turner, *De morbis cutaneis,* 212.
[90] Van Diemerbroeck, *The anatomy of human bodies,* 13.
[91] Phaer, 'The Booke of Children', 183–4; Pechey, *A general treatise,* 136.

of Violets, or Juice of Poppies'.[92] These are by no means exceptional examples: many of the recipes for children's remedies are repeated across the period. The numbers of ingredients listed in the children's medical treatises varies from one to another, but this variation does not follow a chronological trend. For example, Phaer's book (1596) mentions approximately 170 medical substances, Pechey's treatise (1697), lists about 240, while W. S.'s text (1704), uses around 160. The lack of change over time may have arisen from the widespread view that traditional remedies were less hazardous than newer ones: when treating the tender bodies of children, it was preferable to use medicines that had been tried and tested over many years, than to risk using exotic new treatments, the properties of which were unpredictable. Contributing to the replication of advice over the period was the prevalence of plagiarism in medical writings.[93] Trends in trade may also explain the situation: Patrick Wallis has shown that while the overall volume of imported drugs rose over the course of the seventeenth century, the actual variety of substances changed very little.[94]

Nevertheless, a few minor differences can be observed between the earlier and later texts. These include the tendency of the later texts to mention slightly more frequently testaceous powders and chemical mixtures, substances promoted by chemical physicians. Likewise, these treatises occasionally include certain newly available ingredients, such as tea leaves, which were products of the expanding trade with the East.[95] The later authors were also more likely to recommend medicines that were made in pill form. For example, W. S. advised a 'Pill called Hierachum Agrico' for treating *'involuntary Pissing'*.[96] This author did not give instructions for the production of the pill, which implies that he may have expected his readers to buy it 'off-the-shelf' from an apothecary's shop.[97] The growing popularity of these remedies may therefore have been facilitated by the proliferation of apothecary shops and druggists in the period, which sold 'ready-made' medicines.[98]

The laity usually agreed with physicians that children should be given medicines. This is indicated by the fact that the majority of the personal memoirs and correspondence that mentioned the illness of a child also noted a medical treatment. Furthermore, of the total number of domestic recipe books consulted, 91 per cent contain recipes specifically intended for children.[99] In terms of the types of treatments advocated by laypeople, it seems that generally, they shared the hierarchy of preference favoured by the learned practitioners, as can be seen from a quantitative examination of the domestic recipe books. The most popular

[92] Ibid. (Phaer), 164; W. S., *A family jewel*, 53.
[93] Elizabeth Lane Furdell, *Publishing and Medicine in Early Modern England* (Woodbridge: 2002), 53.
[94] Patrick Wallis, 'Exotic Drugs and English Medicine: England's Drug Trade, *c.*1550–*c.*1800', *Social History of Medicine* (advanced access, 2011), doi: 10.1093/shm/hkr055, 1–27.
[95] Ibid.
[96] W. S., *A family jewel*, 62.
[97] See Nicholas Culpeper, *Culpeper's Complete Herbal* (Ware, 1995), 496.
[98] Patrick Wallis, 'London Apothecaries and Other Medical Retailers' 1580–1702', in Louse Hill Curth (ed.), *From Physick to Pharmacology: Five Hundred Years of British Drug Retailing* (Aldershot: 2006), 13–27, at 23.
[99] Thirty-seven out of the thirty-nine recipe books contained recipes specifically intended for children.

Types of treatment	Percentage of all treatments	Number of treatments (out of a total of 482)
Non-evacuating internal medicines	51.66	249
External medicines	28.42	137
Purges and clysters	15.35	74
Vomits, bloodletting, issues, and blisters	4.36	21

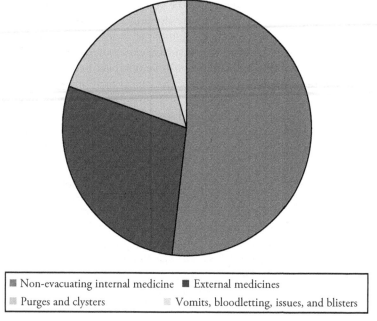

■ Non-evacuating internal medicine ■ External medicines
■ Purges and clysters   ▦ Vomits, bloodletting, issues, and blisters

Fig. 4. A table and pie chart to represent the popularity of various treatments in recipe books, compiled by author.

treatments were non-evacuating internal medicines: these made up just over half the total number of remedies for children contained within all the recipe books (249 of 482 remedies). The second most favoured type of physic was external medicine (ointments, plasters, poultices, and baths): this comprised just under 30 per cent of the total number of the treatments (137 of 482).[100] The third most common remedies were clysters and purges, which came to about 15 per cent of the recipes (74 of the 482). Finally, the least frequently recorded treatments were vomits, issues, bloodletting, and blisters, which made up just over 4 per cent (21 of 482). These statistics are represented in **Figure 4**.

[100] Pomata, *Contracting a Cure*, 132.

The diaries, autobiographies, and letters indicate that similar varieties of treatments were used, but, in significantly varying numbers, with vomits, blisters, bloodletting, and issues appearing more regularly than they had done in the recipe books. This conflicting evidence may stem from the fact that the vomits, bloodletting and so forth were considered to be more severe remedies, and therefore were more worthy of note in people's personal documents. Such remedies as ointments and baths may have been regarded as mundane, hence their comparative absence from these sources. Another reason might be that bloodletting and issues were surgical procedures, requiring no list of ingredients. Perhaps vomits required no ingredients either, because this form of evacuation could be initiated simply by putting a feather or finger to the back of the throat.[101] Alternatively, if the recipe books represent 'prescription', and the other sources, 'practice', the inconsistency between the two could have resulted from the tendency of parents to resort to more drastic treatments when faced with the desperate reality of a seriously ill child. Whatever the reason, both groups of source uphold the basic impression that the most favoured remedies were the external treatments and non-evacuating internal medicines, while the evacuative and surgical remedies tended to take second place. This is supported by the fact that laypeople often expressed reluctance to use the evacuative treatments. In 1638, Lady Denton wrote of her three-year-old great-grandson, 'I hope he shall have noe neede of an isshue'.[102] A few years later, Ralph Verney told his wife that their young daughter Pegg 'has been oftner troubled with her paine in her Ears', and that 'if it continues . . . she must have an ishu made in her neck and [be] . . . blooded, but I like not that. I hope those will bee not need[ed]'.[103]

Lay attitudes to the evacuative and surgical treatments varied according to the age of the child in question: parents and relatives were less reluctant to treat older children than young infants with these remedies. This is revealed in the personal documents, wherein the majority of the children who received these remedies were aged over about six or seven. Ten-year-old Samuel Smyth, for instance, was given a 'carduous vomit immediately upon his first complaint' of illness, while fourteen-year-old Samuel Jeake had a blister applied 'to my neck' in 1667 to drive away his headache.[104] Girls of this age as well as boys were likely to be treated with these remedies. The recipe books offer a similar impression: the Barrett family's purge for the smallpox was intended for 'a childe about 8. or 9. years old'. Likewise, Lady Grace Mildmay's 'gentle purging syrup' for epilepsy was suitable for children 'betwixt 3 and 10 years old' only.[105] The more positive attitude to treating older

[101] See p. 82 below.
[102] Verney (ed.), *The Verney Memoirs*, vol. 1, 217.
[103] BL, M.636/8, this manuscript is unfoliated (Verney papers on microfilm, 1646–50).
[104] Anton Bantock (ed.), *The Earlier Smyths of Ashton Court From their Letters, 1545–1620* (Bristol: 1982), 243; Samuel Jeake, *An Astrological Diary of the Seventeenth Century: Samuel Jeake of Rye,* ed. Michael Hunter (Oxford: 1988), 92.
[105] WL, MS 1071 (Barrett family, 'Select receipts', *c.* 1700), p 5; Lady Grace Mildmay, 'Medical Papers' in Linda Pollock, *With Faith and Physic: the Life of a Tudor Gentlewoman, Lady Grace Mildmay, 1552–1620* (1993), 114.

children with these treatments probably sprang from the assumption that they were physically and mentally stronger.

In short, learned and lay treatments of sick children seem to have been similar: the same sorts of medicines were thought most and least suitable for children, thus indicating that there was a shared awareness that children were physiologically different from adults, requiring gentler and safer treatments.[106]

ADAPTATIONS

This final section explores the various ways in which children's medicines were adapted to suit their special temperaments, thereby challenging the widespread historiographical assumption that the treatments of children and adults were the same. The underlying principle to all the adaptations was summed up by Harris in 1693: 'If we...do desire to lay any sure Foundation for the curing of Infants Diseases; we should chiefly eye their natural tenderness and weakness...the more gentle and safe these Remedies are which we administer, the event shall the more certainly answer our expectation'.[107] Thus medicines had to be made gentle and safe. This notion was reiterated across the early modern period by physicians from diverse theoretical perspectives.[108]

There were four main groups of adaptations: firstly, those which aimed at 'limiting the strength, quality and quantity of the remedy'.[109] The most common method was to reduce the dose.[110] Francis Glisson stated in 1651, 'It is obvious...that strong Vomits prescribed in a full quantity are not compatible to Children...It is necessary therefore that Vomits here prescribed be...administered in a lessened dose.[111] Chemical physicians agreed that 'It is safest' to give treatments 'in a little quantity...so the strength of the Medicine be tried without danger'.[112] Every type of medicine, evacuative and non-evacuative, needed to be altered in this way. Authors did not usually give precise measurements for the doses, but instead stated vaguely that 'less' should be administered to a child. The Galenic practitioner Jeremiah Love, for instance, advised that adults should drink 'a good draught' of his decoction for curing the scab and itch, but 'if a Child, less, as age

[106] This is at odds with Iris Ritzmann's findings—she states that purges and vomits were the most common treatments for children: 'Dedi Clysterem Purgantem', 179–80.
[107] Harris, *An exact enquiry*, 41.
[108] For example, Phaer, 'The Booke of Children', 166; Johnson, *Praxis medicinae reformata*, 34.
[109] J. S., *Paidon nosemata*, 44.
[110] Historians have occasionally recognized this kind of adaptation of children's medicines: Philip Rieder, 'Vivre et Combattre la Maladie', 234; S. Sandassie, 'Evidence-based medicine? Patient case studies in English surgical treatises, 1660–1700', *Journal of Medical Ethics; Medical Humanities*, 34 (2008), 11–18, at 13; Churchill, 'The Medical Practice of the Sexed Body', 18.
[111] Glisson, *A treatise of the rickets*, 326, 362.
[112] Sylvius, *Of childrens diseases*, 37.

doth require'.[113] Practitioners probably felt they could trust their readers to use their own discretion, basing the dose on the individual temperament of the patient. Doses were often graduated according to the child's age and size. Pemell suggested in 1653, 'If the child be of some reasonable growth, then you may give it... two drachmes to one ounce' of his medicine for curing constipation, but 'if it be young, you may give it half an ounce'.[114] The child's gender did not feature in these adaptations: girls and boys were given the same doses. This is significant because it represents another way in which children were distinguished from adults: women were often given smaller doses than men.[115] In clinical practice as well as prescription, doses were reduced for children. After treating the six-year-old son of one 'Mr *Cooper*' for worms, Dr van Diemerbroeck noted in his casebook, 'The dose of Mercury to be given to Children is 1 scruple', while the dose for 'elder People, 2 scruples'.[116]

The literate laity also gave children smaller doses of medicines. Sarah Hughes' recipe book, dated *c.* 1637, describes a treatment for the 'pin and web' of the eye: for adults, '16. or 20. slugs' had to be used, but for children 'a dozen [slugs] will serve'.[117] About forty years later, Elizabeth Hirst's 'Gascoins Powder', a remedy for the smallpox, was to be given to 'an Old body' in '10 granes', while 'to a child 7' grains.[118] Like the learned doctors, laypeople recognized the need to vary the dose according to the age and strength of the individual child. The Brumwich recipe book dated *c.* 1625 stated that 'a man' must 'Take 11 drops' of the 'spirit of Vitterell', while 'a child of 10 years old not above 6 or 7 drops', 'a child of 5 years old not above 4 drops', and finally 'a child of 3 years old not above 2 drops'.[119] Often, these graduated doses applied to older children and adolescents as well as infants, thus indicating that the concept of children's physic was extended to this age.[120] While it is likely that these dose reductions were applied in many cases, there were some occasions when in practice, this adaptation was not implemented. In 1647 Ralph Verney described the illness of his eight-year-old daughter Pegg: he bewailed, 'her Feavor began, & continued soe strong upon her that we were forced to Blood her 4 times in a fortnight with which cost her 24 ounces of Blood', adding that this was 'a strange proportion of blood for one of her age'.[121] Clearly, the impetus behind the decision to remove such a large quantity of blood was the

---

[113] Jeremiah Love, *The practice of physick... the nature and cause of most diseases* (1675), 9.

[114] Pemell, *De morbis puerorum*, 39.

[115] For example, Thomas Cartwright suggested giving a medicine for the plague to 'hym' (a man) in 'foure vnces', 'to a Woman but twoo vnces', and 'to children according to their age': *An Hospitall for the diseased* (1579), 6–7.

[116] Van Diemerbroeck, *The anatomy of human bodies*, 153.

[117] WL, MS 363, 144v (Sarah Hughes, 'Mrs Hughes her receipts', 1637).

[118] WL, MS 2840, 22r (Mrs Elizabeth Hirst, and others, collection of medical and cookery receipts, 1684–*c.* 1725).

[119] WL, MS 160, 27r (Anne Brumwich and others, 'Booke of Receipts or medicines', *c.* 1625–1700).

[120] For example, BL, Additional MS 72619, 123v–124v ('Book of recipes for the Trumbell's household', late seventeenth century).

[121] M.636/8, this manuscript is unfoliated (Verney papers on microfilm, 1646–50).

father's desperation; the fact he commented on the dose indicates that there was a general assumption that children's doses should be reduced.

Another way to limit the strength of medicines was to replace powerful ingredients with milder ones. Regarding purges, 'neither can there be any thing found that is naturally more unsafe and dangerous than *Aloes*' declared Harris, 'because of its intense *Heat*, and *fretting faculty*, which is most opposite to that tender Constitution' of children. He therefore recommended the use of rhubarb instead, reassuring his readers that 'there are none more innocent, and that are more agreeing with Infants, than the well known and very much used Rhubarb, which pleasantly and safely doth remove the Subject matter of the Feavers of those tender ones'.[122] Chemical remedies also had to be modified in this manner. William Salmon warned in 1692, '*Sulphur of Antimony*... must be given to Men, and not to Infants': children's medicines should contain alkali powders instead, such as cuttle-bone, egg-shells, and mother of pearl.[123] These metallic ingredients were avoided because they did not match the mild constitution of children: 'what natural Harmony can there be betwixt th[e] almost impenetrable hardness of Metals and the waxy Softness of the Constitution of Infants?'[124]

Laypeople also occasionally adapted medicines in this way. The Chantrell family's recipe for curing consumption instructed that 'common seeds and figgs bruised together' should be used in children, but 'to big people fresh Beefe and some time[s]... Garlick, [and] clay and viniger' could be added.[125] The strength of medicines could also be reduced through giving children weaker distillations of the mixtures. Sarah Hudson advised readers to 'every night, distill' a mixture of herbs 'in an ordinary still, with a gentle fire'; the resulting liquid should be 'divided into 2 or 3 sorts in severall glasses', and 'the weakest' part should be kept 'most for children'.[126]

Children were usually required to take their medicines less frequently than adults. In the 1560s, Ruscelli Girolamo noted that his medicine for the cough, which contained eggs and brimstone, should be taken 'before breakefast, five dayes together, if it be a man', but that 'if it be a childe three morninges'.[127] The same advice applied to surgical remedies: Sydenham stated that the pleurisy 'in adult Persons could be cur'd at... [the] expence... of 40 ounces of blood' over multiple sessions of bleeding, whereas 'for Children the Cure is commonly perfected by the opening of a Vein [only] once or twice', and removing just a small quantity of blood.[128] In medical practice as well as in the textbooks, this adaptation was mentioned: Richard Wiseman administered a one-month-old infant a purge 'Once in 4 or 5 days', whereas 'A Child of about 4 years' underwent the treatment

---

[122] Harris, *An exact enquiry*, 64, 124–5.

[123] William Salmon, *Medicina practica, or, practical physick* (1692), 80.

[124] Harris, *An exact enquiry*, 41.

[125] WL, MS 1558, 63r (Mary Chantrell and others, 'Book of receipts', 1690).

[126] WL, MS 2954, 28v (Sarah Hudson, 'Her book', 1678).

[127] Girolamo Ruscelli, *The thyrde and last parte of the secretes of the reverende Maister Alexis of Piemount* (1562), 38.

[128] Sydenham, *The compleat method*, 101.

'once in 3 or 4 days', and an adult, alternating days.[129] There is occasional evidence to suggest that the laity also treated children less frequently than adults. Grace Acton, in *c.* 1621, suggested that a mixture of 'honie', 'fysh oil', and 'lemons' should be given to grown persons 'every twoe hours' to cure the cough, but 'for a childe every 4 hours'.[130]

The strength of medicines was also attenuated by using fewer ingredients. To give a comparative example, in 1683 John Locke's purge for his adult patient, Mary Clarke, contained so many ingredients that he felt obliged to apologize for sending her 'soe long . . . a bill'. By contrast, he suggested that her young son should take a purge that consisted of 'manna dissolved in beere or posset drinke' alone.[131] Medicines composed of a select number of ingredients were considered milder and safer, because the properties and effects of the herbs could be more thoroughly understood and predicted.[132] Lay medicines also tended to be short and simple: the Evelyn recipe book recommended 'Groundsell leaves stamped and strained' for the 'Fretts in Childeren', while Johanna St John advocated the use of 'An emultion made with piony seeds . . . & Black cherry water' to cure children of convulsions.[133] Of course, it is true that the recipe books and medical treatises also recommended recipes of greater complexity for use in children, but generally, the shorter recipes were more likely to be given to the young than to adults.

The second group of adaptations related to the method of medicine administration. Instead of taking the medicine independently, the child had to be aided by adults. As explained by W. S. in 1704, 'Children are helpless, or not of Understanding to know what is necessary for their Health . . . and this I look upon to be the Parents Duty . . . with utmost Diligence, in exactly performing what is necessary, to the utmost of their Skill and Ability'.[134] To give an example, Thomas Sydenham stated that whereas an adult patient should 'anoint his Arms and Legs, with his own hand, for three nights together', in the case of children suffering from the rickets, the parent must 'anoint the Belly, and the parts under the short Ribs . . . every morning and evening . . . till the Child recover'.[135] It is probable that the laity also adhered to this arrangement, as can be inferred from the modes of address used in the recipe books: the authors usually addressed their readers as 'you', thus suggesting that their adult readers were expected to administer their own remedies. Mrs Elizabeth Hirst, for example, stated that her medicine for 'Wind Collick' should be taken 'when you perceive it coming upon you'.[136] By contrast, when referring to children, the authors usually instructed the adult to administer the treatment. To apply eye

---

[129] Wiseman, *Several chirurgical treatises,* 264–5.

[130] WL, MS 1, 4r (Grace Acton, collection of cookery and medicinal receipts, 1621).

[131] John Locke, *The Correspondence of John Locke,* ed. E. S. De Beer, 8 vols (Oxford, 1976–89), vol. 2, 587–8.

[132] Wear, *Knowledge and Practice,* 93–4.

[133] BL, Additional MS 78337, 6v (Evelyn papers, medical and culinary recipes, 1651–1700s); WL, MS 4338, 34r (Johanna St John Her Booke' 1680).

[134] W. S., *A family jewel,* 34.

[135] Sydenham, *The compleat method,* 69, 76.

[136] WL, MS 2840, 8r (Mrs Elizabeth Hirst and others, collection of medical and cookery receipts, 1684–*c.* 1725).

drops for 'sore Eyes', the Doggett family suggested getting 'some body' to 'hold the [child's] head back' and 'putt in a few dropps with a spoon'.[137]

Another way that medicine administration differed for children was in terms of physical positioning: grown patients usually lay on a bed or sat in a chair while undergoing treatment, whereas infants and small children were commonly held in somebody's lap. In the early eighteenth century, Turner noted that he placed his six-year-old patient 'upon the Nurse's Knee', 'against [her] Bosom' when dressing his head wound.[138] He had worried that the child would be 'froward' (irritable), and so asked the nurse 'keep his Head steady' and 'strongly supported' while carrying out the difficult procedure.[139] Holding the child in this manner may have also provided a degree of comfort during what was potentially a frightening or painful experience. Laypeople as well as doctors held sick children in their arms: in 1589, ten-year-old Jane Throckmorton was 'held in another woman's arms by the fireside' while she was ill of a diabolical illness.[140] More than a century later Frances Seymour mentioned that her seven-year-old daughter Betty, who 'has a sad cold... is half asleep upon my lap'.[141] It is not possible, however, to detect whether these laypeople were administering treatments while the children were being held.

Other differences in the way children's medicines were administered relate to particular treatments. Vomiting was usually induced in adults by swallowing a liquid that contained bitter ingredients. However, in children, a manual method was often preferred: 'Tis good to make the child vomit either by putting your finger in the throat of it, or by putting down a feather anointed with oyl, or by some other light and easie means', suggested Pemell in 1653.[142] The reason for this adaptation was that it was safer: whereas internal vomits might induce multiple evacuations, thus harming the tender body of the child, a manual method gave the practitioner exact control over the number of vomits. It also may have been easier to carry out, since little cooperation was needed from the child.

Another treatment that was administered differently in children was bloodletting: in adults, the usual places from which blood was taken were the arms, but in children, it had to be taken from the 'lower parts' of the body. '[C]hildren and such as are of tender years, it [is] not good to draw bloud out of the arme, but out of the inferior parts, as the thighes, hams, buttocks', advised Dr Edwards in 1652.[143]

---

[137] BL, Additional MS 27466, 43v ('Recipe-Book of Mary Doggett, 1682').

[138] Turner, *A remarkable case in surgery*, 8–11.

[139] Ibid. 8, 11, 34.

[140] '"The most strange and admirable discovery of the three Witches of Warboys...for betwitching of the five daughters of Robert Throckmorton" (1593)' printed in Philip Almond, *Demonic Possession and Exorcism in Early Modern England: Contemporary Texts and their Cultural Contexts* (Cambridge: 2004), 75–149, at 77.

[141] Isaac Archer, *Two East Anglian Diaries 1641–1729*, ed. Matthew J. Storey, Suffolk Record Society, vol. 36 (Woodbridge: 1994), 160–1; Frances Seymour, Countess of Hertford, *The Gentle Hertford: Her Life and Letters*, ed. Helen Hughes (New York: 1940), 78.

[142] Pemell, *De morbis puerorum*, 31. See also Eucharius Roesslin, *The byrth of mankynde, otherwise named the womans book*, trans. Richard Jonas (1613, first publ. 1540), 166.

[143] Edwards, *A treatise concerning the plague and the pox* (1652), 54. The Christian name of this author is unknown.

Bleeding from these lower regions 'doth not so much impaire the strength nor wast[e] the spirits, as that which is drawne in the upper parts', explained Simon Harward in his treatise on phlebotomy.[144] As was noted earlier, certain organs of the body were considered more 'noble' than others: since the arms were close to the heart and stomach it was best to take blood from the lower regions, which were further away from these sensitive organs. As well as applying to a different part of the body, the instrument used in the procedure differed: in grown-ups, a lancet was used to cut the vein, but in children, doctors recommended the use of leeches.[145] These creatures 'do draw out bloud by so small holes', that 'there is no danger of wasting any vital spirits' by taking away too much blood.[146] Furthermore, the sucking action of the leech was painless and therefore could be applied 'with ease' to the sensitive infant.[147] Theophile Bonet summed up this reasoning, stating that 'Both the inconvenience of pain . . . and of loss of strength by opening a Vein, may be avoided by applying of Leeches'.[148] Nonetheless, there were some occasions when doctors favoured the traditional method of the lancet over the leech. In a treatise published in 1674, Alius Medicus justified the use of a lancet to treat a four-year-old patient, 'young Mrs *Moore*', on the grounds that her illness was so serious that only 'the full stream of a Lancet' could help 'Nature' combat the distemper, since the remedy had to be 'proportionable to the Disease'. He believed that the disease would hardly 'notice . . . little barkings or bitings of . . . Leeches'.[149]

Doctors tried to make children's medicines 'grateful & pleasing to the sick Child, & such as . . . trouble not its Pallate'.[150] These adaptations challenge Roy and Dorothy Porter's generalization that 'Pre-modern medicine tasted foul'.[151] Foremost among these modifications was the substitution of unpleasant ingredients by substances of a more agreeable flavour. Pemell advised against the use of wormwood or scordium when treating children for worms, 'because these are so bitter, children will hardly take them'; instead, 'you may give them . . . the roots of grasse and mouseear with the juyce of Lemons or Citrons', which were more pleasant.[152] It was believed that children were particularly sensitive to bitter tastes: the 'pores' or 'teats' of their tongues (the regions responsible for taste), functioned most acutely.[153] In practice as well as in the learned treatises, doctors were careful to adapt children's medicines in this way. Wiseman noted that 'A Girl of about four years of age' who had been brought to him 'in a poor woman's arms in the very midst of Winter, the ground being covered with Snow', required a medicine 'to be well tasted', and therefore, he prescribed 'a small Ale' that was medicated with sarsaparilla (a trailing

---

[144] Simon Harward, *Harwards phlebotomy: or a treatise of letting of bloud* (1601), 56.
[145] Ibid. 56; J. S., *Paidon nosemata*, 50–1.
[146] Harward, *Harwards phlebotomy*, 56.   [147] J. S., *Paidon nosemata*, 50–1.
[148] Bonet, *A guide to the practical physician*, 329.
[149] Medicus, *Animadversions on the medicinal observations*, 112. Please note that the use of 'Mrs' for a young unmarried girl seems to have been a common convention in the early modern period—it may have been used in place of 'Mistress' or 'Miss'.
[150] Glisson, *A treatise of the rickets*, 344.
[151] Porters, *In Sickness and in Health*, 105.
[152] Pemell, *De morbis puerorum*, 43.
[153] Van Diemerbroeck, *The anatomy of human bodies*, 489–91.

vine).[154] It is significant that this doctor was prepared to alter the medicine of a poor child, for it might be expected that such care would have been reserved for patients who could pay their physicians generous fees. As children grew older, however, they were more likely to be given the less palatable medicines, on the grounds that they had the sense and courage to take what was necessary for their good. Children who 'are well grown', wrote Pechey, could be persuaded to take 'Aloes' and 'Hiera Picra' (a mixture of canella bark and honey), although young children 'will not take any such thing'.[155]

Occasionally, however, physicians did not remove the bitter ingredients, but instead compelled the child to take the medicine through use of force. In 1632 Gualtherus Bruele wrote that 'If children bee unwilling to receive bitter things, they must be forced thereto' by using 'a sirenge, and by that meanes conveyed into their mouthes, & body'.[156] Over half a century later, Theophile Bonet (1620–1689) echoed this advice, declaring that uncooperative children must be 'forced' through use of 'a Spoon' which was put between the teeth and a 'large Pipe', which was 'thrust . . . into the Mouth to the Jaws', so that the medicines could be 'poured in'.[157] However, these are the sole examples that could be found of this practice, which indicates that it may have been rare. Although the above doctors clearly intended to resort to force, when it came to everyday treatment, it seems likely that they did not. This is suggested by the fact that when Bonet's young son was sick of constipation and 'refused all internal Remedies', he did not coerce the child into taking it, but instead, used external physic.[158]

Where the use of unpalatable medicines was unavoidable, practitioners often tried to disguise the taste by putting the medicine into the child's normal food or drink. Sylvius declared, 'Knowing that children are nice [fussy], and can scarce be prevailed with to take even the smallest . . . doses' of bitter medicines, he suggested that 'these may be given in their milk or drink, they may be [the] better beguiled; scarce discerning them'.[159] Galenic authors also recommended this technique: in 1663 Louise Bourgeois Boursier stated 'you may give' the child 'a little of the pouder of *Diacarthamum* in the pap of an Apple' as a purge during the convulsions.[160] Doctors' casebooks confirm that this adaptation was carried out. Van Diemerbroeck recorded that 'The Son of Mr *Cooper*, about six or seven years old', who was infested with worms, was 'averse to all manner of Physick', and therefore he took the ingredient that was most unpleasant, quicksilver, and disguised it by adding 'Syrup of Limons'.[161]

Laypeople also took advantage of this technique. Mrs Elizabeth Hirst's herbal 'yellow water' had to be given in '2 spoonfulls of beare', for children, while adults

[154] Wiseman, *Several chirurgical treatises*, 137.   [155] Pechey, *A general treatise*, 123–4.
[156] Gualtherus Bruele, *Praxis medicinae, or, the physicians practice* (1632), 297.
[157] Bonet, *A guide to the practical physician*, 324.
[158] Ibid. 331.
[159] Sylvius, *Of childrens diseases*, 143.
[160] Louise Bourgeois Boursier, *The compleat midwife's practice* (1663), 232.
[161] Van Diemerbroeck, *The anatomy of human bodies*, 153.

could take the medicine neat.[162] This modification differed according to whether or not the child was weaned: for weaned children, the medicine could be added to any drink or food, but for sucking infants, the choice was limited to breast milk. The Jones' remedy for the falling sickness, for instance, 'fore a sucking Child' should be given 'in Womans Milk', while for older children it could be given in white wine.[163] Such an adaptation was intended to make the medicine as undetectable as possible. In addition to disguising the noxious taste, laypeople suggested giving pleasant drinks after the child had taken the medicine, in an attempt to counter any lingering bad taste. In the 1680s, Thomas Davies recommended that after the child had taken a remedy containing castor oil and piony, 'to take away the ill taste', they should be given 'a little beere posset drink or brest milk'.[164]

Another way to make medicine tasty was to 'give it sweetned with Sugar'.[165] Joan Thirsk has shown that although honey was the 'traditional sweetener', by the mid-seventeenth-century, sugar was becoming more fashionable, because it was regarded as a healthier food.[166] The sweetening of medicines was an adaptation that was used throughout the period: in the mid-sixteenth century, Phaer suggested that the powdered peony root for curing children from bladder stones should be mingled with 'as muche hony as shal be sufficient', but that if 'the child abhore hony, make it up with suger'.[167] A century later, Glisson advised adding 'some pleasant and agreable Liquor, or . . . candid Cherries' to his medicine on the grounds that the child 'delights . . . in such things'.[168] The reason so much emphasis was placed upon taste, according to Mauriceau, was to ensure the remedy 'do[es] not nausiat the Ventricle with such an ingrateful tast[e] and f[l]avour as may render an abhorrence from all future Medicaments'.[169] He also wished to 'please and comfort' the child, making patienthood as tolerable as possible.[170]

Laypeople as well as physicians sweetened children's medicines. In 1660, Abigail Harley told her brother-in-law Edward that his daughter had taken 'a drink of maidenhaire & violet leaves & hyslop' which she had 'swetened . . . with syrop of violets & sugar candy'.[171] Likewise, Anne Glyd's recipe 'Against the chin cough' instructed that the medicine should be taken with 'hony . . . or what the child likes best'.[172] Thus, lay practitioners were prepared to take into consideration the child's personal preferences. As well as adding ingredients to improve the taste, some laypeople sought to improve the smell. The Hughes family's recipe for 'A purge for

---

[162] WL, MS 2840, 40r (Mrs Elizabeth Hirst and others, collection of medical and cookery receipts, 1684–c. 1725).
[163] WL, MS 1340, 140v (Katherine Jones, Lady Ranelagh, collection of medical receipts, c. 1675–1710).
[164] BL, Egerton MS 2,214, 5v (Thomas Davies' medical recipes arranged in alphabetical order of common complaints', 1680).
[165] Salmon, *Medicina practica*, 40.
[166] Joan Thirsk, *Food in Early Modern England: Phases, Fads, Fashions 1500–1760* (London and New York: 2007), 234.
[167] Phaer, 'The Booke of Children', 184.
[168] Glisson, *A treatise of the rickets*, 328.
[169] Ibid, 327.
[170] Mauriceau, *The diseases of women*, 359.
[171] BL, Additional MS 70115, no folio number or pagination (Harley papers).
[172] BL, Additional MS 45196, 51r (Brockman Papers, 'Ann Glyd Her Book 1656').

Children', dated *c.* 1637, had to be tempered with 'soe much of cinnamon water as will mend the smell'.[173] While these adaptations were especially important when treating children, they were not exclusive to this age group: physicians and laypeople sometimes suggested adding sugar to adults' medicines as well.[174]

The fourth group of adaptations aimed to mitigate pain.[175] Historians have frequently claimed that pain relief 'was not a primary part' of medicine's 'rationale' during the early modern period.[176] However, when it came to children, this was not the case, for time and again, doctors stated that their priority was to 'First abate Pain'.[177] Eucharius Roesslin suggested that 'if the child have great paine and dolour' in the ears, then 'seeth Organie and Myrrhe with oyle Olive, and so beeing warme, put of it into the eares'.[178] This preoccupation with pain relief stemmed from the belief that pain was particularly damaging to children, owing to their extreme tenderness. To achieve the analgesic effect, certain ingredients had to be added, such as poppies or opium, the oil of roses, mallows, lettuce, fenugreek, and nightshade. '[P]ain must be mitigated', declared Pechey, by applying a plaster of 'Mallows boyled and bruised . . . Barley-meal . . . Lupins . . . Fenugreek [and] . . . Oyl of Roses' to the child's navel.[179] Some of these ingredients, such as opium, were only permitted in the form of external treatment, because they were considered too powerful to be taken inwardly by children.[180] The laity also placed great emphasis on the amelioration of pain. Arthur Corbett's recipe for the thrush in children's mouths states that 'If the mouth be very sore then in the sorest parte put on this powder of scarlet burned & all most as much alum burned'.[181] Likewise, Anne Glyd's recipe book suggested that 'if the sore' of St Anthony's Fire 'be very bad', it is necessary to 'anoint the place' with a 'warmed . . . ointment' containing elder shoots and butter. She added 'This ointment I have proved for a hott inflammation that my little girle Martha is Trubelled with some times espeachaly if shee hurt her selfe at any Time'.[182]

Another technique used to lessen pain was distraction.[183] Mauriceau suggested that infants suffering from painful teething should be given 'a Silver Coral,

[173] WL, MS 363, 115v (Sarah Hughes, 'Mrs Hughes her receipts', 1637). Richard Palmer has recognized the importance of smell in medicine: 'In Bad Odour: Smell and its Significance in Medicine from Antiquity to the Seventeenth Century', in W. F. Bynum and Roy Porter (eds), *Medicine and the Five Senses* (Cambridge: 1993), 61–8, at 64.

[174] For example, W. S., *A family jewel,* 54.

[175] For a history of pain relief in medicine, see Thomas Dormandy, *The Worst of Evils: The Fight Against Pain* (London and New Haven, CT: 2006).

[176] Roy Porter and Dorothy Porter, *Patient's Progress: Doctors and Doctoring in Eighteenth Century England* (Oxford: 1989), 163; Esther Cohen, 'Towards a History of European Physical Sensibility: Pain in the Later Middle Ages', *Science in Context,* 8 (1995), 47–74, at 70.

[177] Sennert, *Practical physick,* 263.

[178] Roesslin, *The byrth of mankynde,* 171.

[179] Pechey, *A general treatise,* 135–6.

[180] J. S., *Paidon nosemata,* 28–9.

[181] WL, MS 212, 85r (Arthur Corbett, collection of medical receipts, mid-seventeenth century).

[182] BL, Additional MS 45196, 77r (Brockman Papers, 'Ann Glyd Her Book 1656').

[183] Lisa Silverman has also noted the importance of distraction in the treatment of children, in: *Tortured Subjects: Pain, Truth, and the Body in Early Modern France* (Chicago: 2001), 138–9.

Fig. 5. The frontispiece of Francis Glisson, *De rachitide, sive morbo puerilli, tractatus* (Leiden: 1671). Image supplied by Light Incorporated.

furnish'd with small Bells, to divert the Child from the Pain it then feels'.[184] Another author stated, 'Tis very good to give a Child often new Play Things, to divert . . . him'.[185] **Figure 5**, from Glisson's treatise about rickets, shows a child in the background playing with a rattle—this may have functioned as a useful

---

[184] Mauriceau, *The diseases of women,* 343.   [185] *The nurse's guide* (1729), 54.

distraction. This method was also employed by the laity: in the early 1700s, the aunt of four-year-old Betty Egleton 'would often carry her to the Window' to watch 'some Children at Play in the Street', to 'divert her' from her pains.[186] Perhaps children were thought to be easier to distract than adults because their minds were more impressionable. When it came to treating older children, however, physicians were probably more inclined to use reasoned argument than distraction, on the grounds that the more rational minds of older children were capable of understanding that painful treatments could be beneficial. Dr William Brownrigg was able to persuade his 'very anxious' eleven-year-old patient, Jonathan Kelsick, to submit to some 'blistering vesicatories' by convincing him that 'the plaster would produce only slight blisters'.[187]

In addition to easing the pain of the illness, practitioners sought to mitigate the discomfort brought by the medical treatment. In the case of external remedies, this was achieved by administering the treatment with greater gentleness. When binding the limbs of crooked children, Felix Wurtz entreated practitioners not to apply splints 'too close... [nor] too hard': instead, they should be applied 'softly and gently', with 'good notice' being taken of any 'pains, redness, smartings' appearing around the joints.[188] Ointments also had to be applied in this manner. In 1710, Mauriceau suggested that the ulcers of the mouth could be 'gently rub'd' with a 'little Stick' that had been dipped in the ointment; he added, 'be... careful not to put them to too much pain, lest by irritating of them, an Inflammation be caus'd to augment the Malady'.[189] Laypeople as well as learned authors understood the great necessity of administering medicines with gentleness. The Brumwich recipe book, dated *c.* 1625, stated that an ointment for 'a younge child that hath a thrush in the mouth' should be anointed 'very sofly, not rubbing it' in order to cause minimum discomfort.[190] Likewise, the Hughes' recipe for 'a sore mouth' was to be 'softly anoint[ed] with your finger', avoiding any rubbing action.[191] The sense of compassion for children in all these writings undermines the notion that 'no allowances for their tender age' were made when treating children.[192]

The discomfort of the medical treatment could not always be assuaged, however. Pechey stated in 1697 that when children had 'scald head', 'you must... pull out the Hairs' of the head 'by the roots... A pitch Cap is ordinarily used for this purpose... they keep it on some days and afterwards pull it off with the Hairs'. He admitted that this was a 'severe' treatment, but could offer no advice as to how the pain could be mitigated.[193] Nevertheless, while it might not have been possible to lessen the physical pain of these treatments, practitioners sometimes did attempt to

---

[186] E. C., *Some part of the life and death of Mrs Elizabeth Egleton, who Died... 1705 in the fifth year of her age* (1705), 17.

[187] Brownrigg, *The Medical Casebook*, 55.

[188] Wurtz, 'An Experimental Treatise', 213–14.

[189] Mauriceau, *The diseases of women*, 340.

[190] WL, MS 160, 22r (Anne Brumwich and others, 'Booke of Receipts or medicines', *c.* 1625–1700).

[191] WL, MS 363, 166v (Sarah Hughes, 'Mrs Hughes her receipts', 1637).

[192] Payne, *With Words and Knives*, 96.

[193] Pechey, *A general treatise*, 57–8.

mitigate the *emotional* pain. Daniel Turner, upon the realization that he would need to apply a 'red hot' tobacco pipe to seal the wound in a child's neck, decided to conceal this from the child and nurse until the very moment of its application:

> [W]hile the Nurse's Head was turned another Way, and the Pipe heated...
> I suddenly clapt the End of it red hot as it was upon the Bleeding-Hole, which I
> just toucht, and threw away the Pipe, the Child not Crying so much.[194]

The combination of not anticipating pain, together with the speed with which the procedure was completed, made the child's experience tolerable. Implicit in this example is the assumption that the soul and body had a reciprocal relationship: the passions of the mind impacted on the experience of physical pain, so that when the mind was free from fear, the body sensed pain to a lesser degree.

Thus far, it has been argued that children's medicines were altered in various ways to make them more suitable for this tender age. It is important to point out that the modifications were not always implemented concurrently: sometimes just one or two sufficed. Furthermore, there were occasions when no adaptations were made at all. In the mid-sixteenth century, Ruscelli recommended pills containing hyssop and frankincense for curing coughs, and pronounced it 'a remedye very good, as well for yonge-children, as for olde folke'.[195] Over a century and a half later, Robert Johnson suggested a purge called '*Sal Mirabile*' which 'may be safely given to Men, Women, or Children, in all Diseases where purging is necessary'.[196] The most likely reason why these remedies were unaltered was because they were thought to be so safe that they could be taken by children in their exact forms. The motivation may also have been commercial: in the case of the practitioners who were advertising their own patented medicines, they may have sought to attract as many customers as possible by presenting their treatments as infallible cures for all ills and all patients. The fact the writers specified that both children and adults could take the medicine is in itself evidence of the existence of a concept of children's physic: writers took for granted that their readers would assume that the remedies could not be given in their identical form to all ages.

CONCLUSION

A concept of children's physic existed in early modern England: 'The Diseaes of Children . . . are cur'd in a different manner in them th[a]n they are in other Ages', declared J. S. in 1664.[197] Doctors and laypeople believed that sick children required medicines that had been specially adapted to suit their distinctive temperaments: remedies had to be made gentle, pleasant, and safe. Underscoring these adaptations was the belief that children were tender and sensitive beings, whose

---

[194] Turner, *De morbis cutaneis*, 340.
[195] Ruscelli, *The thyrde and last parte*, 7.
[196] Johnson, *Praxis medicinae reformata*, p. x.
[197] J. S., *Paidon nosemata*, 5.

minds and bodies were easily overwhelmed by painful or aggressive physic. What has emerged in this chapter is just how difficult children could be to treat: they were often 'froward' and uncooperative, unable to articulate their sufferings, and liable to die upon 'any small occasion'. However, these obstacles did not deter practitioners: an assortment of cunning, yet humane techniques, were employed to overcome the problems. The desire to make patienthood as agreeable as possible for children also testifies the compassionate attitudes of many physicians and laypeople to the sufferings of sick children.

Children were not treated in an identical manner: their remedies were modified according to their ages, strengths, and sizes. Childhood was thus a multifaceted, graduated phenomenon. Gender was rarely mentioned in the context of medical treatment: doctors and laypeople hardly ever differentiated their medicines according to whether the child was male or female. This was probably because the most important factor that was considered when prescribing a treatment was the patient's strength, and this was largely dependent upon the age, size, and weight of the child, rather than the sex.

The treatment of children altered very little across the early modern period: the same types of medicines were favoured, and a similar array of adaptations were implemented. Thus, the introduction of new medical theories, such as the chemical medicine of Franciscus Sylvius, does not seem to have brought about a transformation in the medical treatment of children. This finding confirms Wayne Wild's assertion that the basic remedies of physicians 'of all theoretical schools and speculative bent . . . were remarkably similar throughout the seventeenth and eighteenth centuries'.[198] Finally, we have seen that there was a degree of resemblance between the medicine of lay and learned practitioners, both in terms of the basic forms of treatment, and the ways in which these remedies were modified for children.

---

[198] Wild, *Medicine-by-Post*, 8, 19.

PART II

THE FAMILY'S PERSPECTIVE

3
'With Great Care and Pains':
Tending the Sick Child

This chapter explores the impact of caring for the sick child on the everyday life of the family. It asks how mothers, fathers, and other relatives were involved in the provision of care, and to what extent this involvement was socially, economically, and physically disruptive. The question of how the household was affected by the illness of family members has received only minor attention from historians despite the fact that it was almost a universal experience during the early modern period.[1] I show that while caring for young patients was often a time-consuming, costly, and exhausting undertaking for parents, it was also something they desperately wanted to do, and were prepared to carry out with unstinting commitment. Above all, the dedication with which parents tended their children demonstrates their great love for their offspring.

Through focusing almost exclusively on women's roles in domestic medicine, nursing, and childcare, historians have created the impression that men rarely played any part in these activities.[2] Some scholars have asserted that contemporary notions of masculinity simply would not have allowed a man to engage in such tasks as tending a sick child.[3] These views may derive from early modern conduct books, which distinguish clearly between male and female work, and link motherhood and housewifery with health provision. Nursing, for instance, grew out of childcare, while domestic physic sprang from food preparation.[4] This chapter will dispute these assumptions, showing that during serious illness, fathers were actively involved in the care of their children, thereby indicating that gender roles in this period were rather more flexible than has been acknowledged.[5]

---

[1] However there are a few exceptions, including the conclusion to Lucinda McCray Beier, *Sufferers and Healers: The Experience of Illness in Seventeenth-Century England* (1987), and Helena Wall, ' "My Constant Attension on My Sick Child": The Fragility of Family Life in the World of Elizabeth Drinker', in James Alan Marten (ed.), *Children in Colonial America* (2007), 155–67.

[2] See Introduction, footnote 14 for examples.

[3] Patricia Crawford, *Parents of Poor Children in England, 1580–1800* (Oxford: 2010), 122.

[4] Rebecca Tannenbaum, *The Healer's Calling: Women and Medicine in Early New England* (London and Ithaca, NY: 2002), 24.

[5] Some historians, however, have shown that men played a part in these fields—for example, Margaret Pelling, *The Common Lot: Sickness, Medical Occupations, and the Urban Poor in Early Modern England* (Harlow: 1998), 179–202, at 181–2; Lisa Wilson, ' "Ye Heart of a Father": Male Parenting in Colonial New England', *Journal of Family History*, 14 (1999), 255–74; Joanne Bailey, 'A Very Sensible Man': Imagining Fatherhood in England, c.1750–1830', *History*, 95 (2010), 267–92; Lisa Smith, 'The

Given the patriarchal nature of early modern society, and the vital importance of dynasty and inheritance, one might expect to find that elite parents devoted more attention to their sons than to their daughters.[6] Anthony Fletcher has implied that every aspect of childcare was gendered in some manner at this time, even if the actual standard of care was similar for girls and boys.[7] This chapter offers a different interpretation: it shows that during illness, families usually endeavoured to provide care of a comparable nature and quality for all their children, regardless of sex. This is not to deny that many other areas of children's lives were gendered. Rather, in certain contexts—such as severe illness—the importance of gender distinctions lessened.

An examination of parents' choices of medical practitioners will shed light on the relationships between laypeople and doctors. One of the earliest and most influential studies of doctor–patient relations was conducted by Nicholas Jewson in 1976. He argued that early modern patients possessed considerable authority over their doctors, being at liberty to accept or reject whatever treatments were advised; but from the late eighteenth century, patients came increasingly under the control of the medical profession.[8] This chapter will add to the historiography which challenges the teleological elements of Jewson's interpretation, while still upholding his assertion that laypeople did exert considerable power over their medical practitioners.[9] It will also be suggested that lay relationships with other types of practitioner besides physicians should be considered, because the 'medical marketplace' was pluralistic: the sick were treated by a range of practitioners.[10]

The first part of this chapter outlines the various elements of care provided to ill children, demonstrating the eclectic nature of early modern patient care. The second part then examines the roles of family members and other individuals in the provision of this care, drawing particular attention to the actions of fathers.

Relative Duties of a Man: Domestic Medicine in England and France, ca. 1685–1740', *Journal of Family History*, 31 (2006), 237–56. Smith is currently preparing a book on this subject.

[6] See Sara Mendelson and Patricia Crawford, *Women in Early Modern England, 1550–1720* (Oxford: 2003, first publ. 1998), 84; Barbara Hanawalt, *Growing Up in Medieval London: the Experience of Childhood in History* (Oxford and New York: 1993), 58–9; Lawrence Stone, *The Family, Sex and Marriage in England 1500–1800* (London and New York:, 1977), 87.

[7] Anthony Fletcher, *Growing up in England: The Experience of Childhood 1600–1914* (London and New Haven, CT: 2008).

[8] Nicholas Jewson, 'The Disappearance of the Sick Man from Medical Cosmology 1770–1870', *Sociology*, 10 (1976), 225–44.

[9] For example Elborg Forster, 'From the Patient's Point of View: Illness and Health in the Letters of Liselotte Von Der Pfalz (1652–1722)', *Bulletin of the History of Medicine*, 60 (1986), 297–320; Roy Porter (ed.), *Patients and Practitioners: Lay Perceptions of Medicine in Pre-Industrial Society* (Cambridge: 2002, first publ. 1985); Dorothy Porter and Roy Porter, *Patient's Progress: Doctors and Doctoring in Eighteenth Century England* (Oxford: 1989); Michael Stolberg, 'Medical Popularization and the Patient in the Eighteenth Century', in Willem De Blécourt and Cornelie Usborne (eds), *Cultural Approaches to the History of Medicine: Mediating Medicine in Early Modern and Modern Europe* (Basingstoke: 2004), 89–107, at 95.

[10] The historiography of the 'medical marketplace' has been summarized by Mark Jenner and Patrick Wallis in ch.1 of their edited volume, *Medicine and the Market in England and its Colonies, c.1450–c.1850* (Basingstoke: 2007).

Finally, the third section investigates the family's emotional and physical experiences of tending the sick child.

THE TASKS OF CARE

An essential, unchanging element of children's care was nursing. Contemporaries often associated this word with the rearing of children, as is evident from such terms as 'nurse-maid', 'nursery', and 'wet nurse'.[11] However, it was also used to denote the task of tending the sick, and it is to this meaning that this chapter refers. The most important role of the nurse was to keep watch over the patient; so crucial was this task, nursing was often called 'keeping' or 'watching'.[12] In cases of serious illness, great significance was attached to staying with the child at all times, through the day and night. The Anglican clergyman Isaac Archer recorded that he 'sate by' his six-year-old daughter Frances and 'helpt it all night' during her illness in 1679.[13] Usually nurses sat by the child's bed to carry out this duty, although in the case of infants and young children, they often cradled their charges in their arms. While watching, nurses were expected to pay close attention to the child's symptoms, reporting any alarming alterations to the child's family or doctors. One midnight in 1698, the nurse of baby Nancy Henry noticed that her little charge 'looked ill' and 'breath'd shorter and shorter', and therefore quickly awoke her master and mistress.[14] The symptoms mentioned most regularly by nurses related to the patient's temperature, breathing, appearance, sleeping patterns, and pains.[15] Nurses were also responsible for attending to the patient's dressings. In 1647, Ralph Verney told his uncle that he dressed the ulcer of his eight-year-old daughter Pegg 'night and day 4 times every 24 hours'.[16] Finally, nurses were supposed to provide emotional support to patients, by offering words of encouragement and sympathy. When fourteen-year-old Susanna Bicks contracted the plague in 1664, her father told her, 'be [of] good comfort my Child for the lord will be near to thee and us, under this heavy and sore Trial, he will not forsake us'.[17]

A further component of patient care was prayer: parents, relatives, and friends prayed earnestly for the child's recovery, and salvation in the event of death.[18] Elizabeth Egerton, the countess of Bridgewater, besought 'God, and...thy sonne...to heale' her daughter Frances 'from her great paine & sicknesse...have

[11] Margaret Pelling, 'Nurses and Nursekeepers: Problems of Identification in the Early Modern Period', in her, *The Common Lot*, 179–202, at 180.
[12] Jeremy Boulton, 'Welfare Systems and the Parish Nurse in Early Modern London, 1650–1725', *Family and Community History*, 10 (2007), 127–51, at 127; Tannenbaum, *The Healer's Calling*, 29.
[13] Isaac Archer, *Two East Anglian Diaries 1641–1729*, ed. Matthew J. Storey, Suffolk Record Society, vol. 36 (Woodbridge: 1994), 160–1.
[14] BL, Additional MS 42,849, fol. 27r (Henry family letters).
[15] Guildhall Library, London, MS 204 ('A Record of the Mercies of God: or A Thankfull Remembrance', [his pagination] 183, 404, 406, 409, 421–2, 432–4, 467).
[16] BL, M.636/8, this manuscript is unfoliated (Verney papers on microfilm, 1646–50).
[17] James Janeway, *A token for children. The second part* (1673), 49.
[18] Houlbrooke, *Death, Religion and the Family*, 163.

mercy of her in the world to come, to make her one of thy Elect in Heaven'.[19] The rationale for this form of therapy was the providential origin of sickness: God was responsible for bringing illness, and therefore He was capable of revoking it.[20] The Bible confirmed the efficacy of prayer, stating that when the 'elders of the church pray' over the patient, 'the prayer will make the sick person well'.[21] Prayer and medicine were not incompatible, but could be used concurrently or consecutively. In 1720, the medical practitioner James Clegg 'made use of many [medical] means to procure' his infant son's 'ease[,] and followed the use of them with earnest prayers for success'.[22] In fact, many believed that without prayer, medicine could not work: it was necessary for the patient to first seek God's forgiveness before He would allow the medicine to take effect. As the astrologer-physician Simon Forman declared in 1597, 'sickness coms from god... ther[e] is noe way but prayer unto god & repentance first. That the finger of god may be taken from [the patient], or ells no medison will prevaille'.[23] In cases of illness caused by possession, prayer was especially important, since Protestants believed that this, combined with fasting, was the only legitimate means of defeating an evil spirit.[24]

The use of prayer presents some interesting theological tensions: according to the doctrine of predestination, the Lord had already decided the outcome of illness, and as such, the degree to which Christians could influence their condition through prayer was questionable. One could argue, that by believing in the instrumentality of prayer, people were implying that God was capable of changing His mind. Alexandra Walsham has highlighted these instances of theological inconsistency, suggesting that at moments of emotional crisis, 'thorny' doctrinal niceties could easily be forgotten.[25] Perhaps the tensions arise from a greater ambivalence within Christianity itself, between the two crucial doctrines of free will and predestination.[26]

Prayer seems to have been an unchanging element of children's care, for it is mentioned frequently in the primary documents across the early modern period. There is little evidence to show that by the 1690s, people had 'turned from praying for spiritual physic to paying for medicines when struggling with grave illness'.[27]

---

[19] BL, Egerton MS, fol. 18–23 (Elizabeth Egerton, 'True coppies of scertaine loose Papers left by the Right honourable Elizabeth Countesse of Bridgewater, Collected and Transcribed together here since her Death Anno Dm 1663).

[20] David Harley, 'Spiritual Physic, Providence and English Medicine, 1560–1640', in Ole Peter Grell and Andrew Cunningham (eds), *Medicine and the Reformation* (1993), 101–17, at 104.

[21] James 5:14–15, KJV.

[22] James Clegg, *The Diary of James Clegg of Chapel-en-Frith 1708–1755*, vol. 1 (1708–36), ed. Vanessa S. Doe, Derbyshire Record Society, vol. 5 (Matlock: 1978), 12.

[23] Cited by Lauren Kassell, *Medicine & Magic in Elizabethan London* (Oxford: 2009, first publ. 2005), 149.

[24] Michael MacDonald (ed.), *Witchcraft and Hysteria in Elizabethan London* (1991), p. xx.

[25] Alexandra Walsham, *Providence in Early Modern England* (Oxford: 2003, first publ. 1999), 152–3.

[26] Philip Almond has drawn attention to other ambivalences in Christianity in his edited volume, *Demonic Possession and Exorcism in Early Modern England: Contemporary Texts and their Cultural Contexts* (Cambridge: 2004), 14.

[27] Ian Mortimer, *The Dying and the Doctors: The Medical Revolution in Seventeenth-Century England* (Woodbridge and Rochester, NY: 2009), 2.

Admittedly, the sources used in this research were products of the religious elites, and therefore prayer is likely to feature at any given point in the chronology. However, since the difference between the beliefs of puritans and the rest of society was one of 'temperature rather than substance', it does seem probable that prayer remained important in the population at large.[28] This has been confirmed by W. M. Jacob, who has found 'overwhelming' evidence to indicate that prayer continued to be essential throughout the eighteenth century across a wide spectrum of society.[29]

Another element of patient care was medicine, but since this has already been discussed in the previous chapter, it will only be briefly summarized here. As revealed in the various medical and lay sources, the most common types of treatments given to children were non-evacuating internal medicines, clysters, external physic, and environmental medicine. Older children were more likely than younger children to be treated with surgical and evacuative treatments. The principle behind medicine was usually Galenic: it was designed to oust the noxious humours that had been responsible for the disease. This thinking fitted comfortably with the providential model of disease causation: God was thought to bring disease through natural means, and therefore health could be restored through natural methods.[30]

The overall propensity of children to take medicine does not seem to have changed between the late sixteenth and early eighteenth centuries: the personal documents and doctors' casebooks suggest that treatments were given regularly. This is at odds with the findings of certain recent studies, which have argued that the consumption of medicines rose exponentially during the period. Patrick Wallis, for instance, has traced an expansion in the importation of drugs into England, as shown in port books and customs accounts.[31] Likewise, Ian Mortimer has noticed an increasing incidence of medical expenses in people's probate documents, which were incurred by the purchase of medicines from physicians during final illnesses.[32] A possible reason why no comparable trend has been detected in my research, is that I have included medicines that were made from 'home-grown' ingredients, and were administered for free by family members, as well as those given by physicians. Since 'kitchen physic' was considered to be especially suitable for children, its prevalence in the sources probably adds to the impression that medicine was a constant feature of children's care across the period.

[28] Walsham, *Providence*, 2.
[29] W. M. Jacob, *Lay People and Religion in the Early Eighteenth Century* (Cambridge: 1996), 9, 14, 225.
[30] David Harley, 'The Theology of Affliction and the Experience of Sickness in the Godly Family, 1650–1714: The Henrys and the Newcomes', in Ole Peter Grell and Andrew Cunningham (eds), *Religio Medici: Medicine and Religion in Seventeenth-Century England* (Aldershot: 1996), 273–92 at 280–1.
[31] Patrick Wallis, 'Exotic Drugs and English Medicine: England's Drug Trade, c.1550–c.1800', *Social History of Medicine* (advanced access, 2011), doi:10.1093/shm/hkr055, 1–27.
[32] Ian Mortimer, 'The Triumph of the Doctors: Medical Assistance to the Dying, c.1570–1720', *Transactions of the Royal Historical Society*, 15 (2005), 97–116.

There is less information available concerning the medicines provided to children from lower down the social scale, but it does seem likely that they were treated. Elite gentlewomen often administered remedies to poor children out of charity. In 1599, Lady Margaret Hoby 'dressed a poor boy's leg', and then treated the hand of one of her young servants 'that was very sore'.[33] Local authorities also ensured that poor children were seen by practitioners, as Margaret Pelling has shown in her study of early modern Norwich.[34] The motivation for this provision was partly financial: if children were not cured, they would become even greater drains on the local poor rates, since they would be unable to work.[35]

An element of care that may have been regarded as more important than all the others was helping the child to prepare spiritually for death.[36] This was the process through which the mortally ill tried to reach a state of assurance of their eternal salvation. It involved various acts of piety, such as repentance, prayer, and Bible-reading.[37] Through exhibiting religious devotion, the dying person demonstrated his or her inward faith, which in turn was evidence of God's grace, and in effect, of salvation after death. This process was therefore essential both for the dying and for their families, because it offered the consolation of heaven and the prospect of heavenly reunion.[38] Of course, according to the doctrine of predestination, no amount of piety on the sickbed could influence the afterlife of the dying Christian, since such matters had been predetermined by the Almighty. But in practice, people hoped that they still held some sway over their salvation, perhaps considering that God had foreseen their godly conduct.[39] Although the ultimate responsibility for the preparation for death lay with sick people themselves, in reality, great dependence was placed upon family members and friends to guide the process.[40] This support was especially necessary in the case of children, since the religious education of the young fell to parents.

The most direct method by which parents helped their children to prepare for death was by asking them if they were ready to die. When eleven-year-old John Harvy was smitten with the plague in 1673, his mother asked him 'whether he were willing to die, and leave her', to which he answered 'yes, I am willing to leave you, and go to my heavenly Father'.[41] This question was vital because it provided dying

---

[33] Margaret Hoby, 'Diary of Lady Margaret Hoby', in Charlotte Otten (ed.), *English Women's Voices 1450–1700* (Florida: 1992), 186.

[34] Pelling, *The Common Lot*, 75.

[35] Ibid. 105–33.

[36] Lucinda McCray Beier, 'The Good Death in Seventeenth-Century England', in Ralph Houlbrooke (ed.), *Death, Ritual and Bereavement* (London and New York: 1989), 43–61, at 49, 59.

[37] See Ralph Houlbrooke, *Death, Religion and the Family in England, 1480–1750* (Oxford: 1998), chs 3, 6, and 7.

[38] Ibid. 162, 183–4; Ralph Houlbrooke, 'Death in Childhood: the Practice of the Good Death in James Janeway's "A Token for Children" ', in Anthony Fletcher and Stephen Hussey (eds), *Childhood in Question: Children, Parents and the State* (Manchester: 1999), 37–56.

[39] Houlbrooke, *Death, Religion, and the Family*, 154. See Dewey D. Wallace, Jr, *Puritans and Predestination: Grace in English Protestant Theology, 1525–1695* (North Carolina: 1982).

[40] Lucinda M. Becker, *Death and the Early Modern Englishwoman* (Aldershot and Burlington, VT: 2003), 32.

[41] Janeway, *A token for children*, 85.

children with the opportunity to express their soteriological confidence, which in turn was the most widely recognized sign of salvation. Young children as well as older children, and girls as well as boys, were questioned in this way. Four-year-old Mary Stubbs was asked 'Whether she was willing to die and go to Heaven' during her illness in the 1680s, to which her reply was '*Go to Heaven, but no[t to] die*'. Her parents continued to question her until she was able to answer with more confidence that 'She would die and go to Jesus Christ'.[42] Although this practice might seem cruel today, in the early modern period, it was considered quite the opposite: parents desperately wanted their children to be able to overcome any doubts about salvation, so that they could die happy and confident about heaven.[43] To this end, parents and relatives offered reassurance about salvation to those children who were unconvinced. When Sarah Savage's granddaughter Betty expressed anxiety about death in 1723, her mother told her that 'thou art going to thy dear father'; the girl then told her family with greater assurance, 'I am going to my *dear Jesus*'.[44] Other ways to aid children's preparation for death included talking about sin, and urging prayer and repentance. Seven-year-old John Martindale, when 'very ill' in 1659, was asked by his mother 'what he would do': he responded that 'he would pray, and accordingly he did'.[45] Finally, parents read passages from the Bible, and asked their children to repeat or recite the Scripture or catechisms. In 1665, Matthew Henry asked his five-year-old son John to repeat 'the 4th commandment'.[46] The examples above span the whole of the early modern period, thereby indicating the continuing importance of the preparation for death.[47]

Not all children were able to prepare for death, however. When illness caused delirium, or was very sudden, the process was impeded. This was the case for Sarah Savage's daughter in 1714: the girl was so 'insensible' that her family feared she 'sh[oul]d dye in . . . sad Circumstances', not being able to say 'Lord have mercy on me' nor carry out any of the other religious actions.[48] Some scholars have suggested that poorer, uneducated families may not have been 'sufficiently pious' to ensure the performance of these religious duties.[49] However, Christian beliefs about the afterlife were pervasive at this time, and therefore it is likely that a degree of concern

---

[42] William Bidbanck, *A present for children. Being a brief, but faithful account of many remarkable and excellent things utter'd by three young children* (1685), 37.

[43] Houlbrooke has also acknowledged this point in his chapter 'Death in Childhood', 43.

[44] Sarah Savage, *Memoirs of the Life and Character of Mrs Sarah Savage*, ed. J. B. Williams (1821), 203–6.

[45] Adam Martindale, *The Life of Adam Martindale*, ed. Richard Parkinson, Chetham Society, vol. 4 (Manchester: 1845), 108–9.

[46] Philip Henry, *The Diaries and Letters of Philip Henry of Broad Oak, Flintshire, A. D. 1631–1696*, ed. M. H. Lee (1882), 205.

[47] Jonathan Barry agrees that 'Interest in . . . the death-bed scene remained intense' in the eighteenth century: 'Piety and the Patient: Medicine and Religion in Eighteenth Century Bristol', in Porter (ed.), *Patients and Practitioners*, 145–75, at 172.

[48] Bodleian Library, Oxford, MS Eng. Misc. e. 331 [her pagination] 24 (Diary of Sarah Savage, 1714–23).

[49] Linda Pollock, 'Parent–Child Relations', in David Kertzer and Marzio Barbagli (eds), *Family Life in Early Modern Times, 1500–1789* (London and New Haven, CT: 2001), 191–220, at 202.

was shown for the child's salvation among all levels of society.[50] This is supported by evidence from popular ballads, documents that were accessed by even the destitute poor: they are littered with references to the preparation for death.[51] For instance, *The children's example* (1700) tells the story of the little daughter of one Mrs Johnson, who prepared for death 'like one divine'.[52] Although we cannot assume that the religious content of these texts 'unambiguously reflected and conditioned' the practices of the people who perused them, the fact that they sold in great numbers does suggest that their consumers were at least partially interested in the ideas that they espoused, including notions about the preparation for death.[53] This has been confirmed by Margaret Spufford, who has shown that one of the most popular subjects of 'penny godlinesses' (cheap religious books), was death.[54] Poor children who were particularly likely to have engaged in the process of preparation for death were those who were fostered by puritans. Janeway's collection of children's biographies describes the death of 'A Very poor Child' from Newington Butts, who had been 'taken up from begging' by a godly neighbour in 1671. When he fell ill, the neighbour encouraged him to repent his sins, pray, and realize the 'joy and assurance of God's love'.[55] A similar story is told in the autobiography of Alice Thornton: her father had 'taken for charitie' a nine-year-old boy called Frank Kelly. During his fatal illness from smallpox in 1642, he was 'full of sweete expressions [and] acts of religion'.[56]

The final component of children's care involved visits from relatives, friends, and neighbours. Sick-visiting was considered a vital Christian duty: visitors offered moral and practical help, and in return were reminded of their own mortality.[57] The tasks which visitors carried out included prayer, nursing, and medicine manufacture.[58] An assortment of individuals visited the sick. In 1689, John Evelyn went to see his grandson, who had 'falln ill of a scarlet feaver'.[59] Siblings who were living away from one another often returned to visit their sick brothers and sisters: when Lady Lisle's daughters Frances and Philippa were ill of agues, their younger brother 'Master Basset' journeyed from school to visit them.[60] Friends and neighbours also partook in this task: Sarah Savage recorded in 1694 that she visited 'Mr Becket', who had 'Two sons not well'.[61] Clergymen were especially frequent visitors during sickness, perhaps because they were

---

[50] Walsham, *Providence*, 327–31.
[51] See Ian Green, *Print and Protestantism in Early Modern England* (Oxford: 2000), 466–9.
[52] *The children's example* (1700).
[53] Walsham, *Providence*, 38.
[54] Margaret Spufford, *Small Books and Pleasant Histories* (1981), 197–203.
[55] James Janeway, *A token for children being an exact account of the conversion, holy and exemplary lives and joyful deaths of several young children* (1671), 70–1.
[56] Alice Thornton, *The Autobiography of Mrs Alice Thornton*, ed. Charles Jackson, Surtees Society, vol. 62 (1875) 34–5.
[57] Roy Porter and Dorothy Porter, *In Sickness and in Health: The British Experience, 1650–1850* (1988), 195.
[58] McCray Beier, 'The Good Death', 56.
[59] John Evelyn, *John Evelyn's Diary: A Selection*, ed. Philip Francis (1963), 916.
[60] Muriel St Clare Byrne (ed.), *The Lisle Letters*, 6 vols (Chicago: 1981), vol. 5, 296–7.
[61] Savage, *Memoirs of the Life*, 156.

considered best qualified for helping the sick improve their spiritual states. Reverend Henry Newcome visited sick people almost every day, including children from a range of socio-economic backgrounds.[62] Sick-visitors came in greatest numbers when the child was suffering from a particularly gruesome or unnatural illness. In 1595, the possessed girl Jane Ashton from Lancashire was visited by up to fifty visitors on one single day.[63]

Sick-visiting did not always take place, however. As Ralph Houlbrooke has noted, relatives and friends sometimes 'preferred to avoid the harrowing spectacle' of the sickbed.[64] If the patient was suffering from an acutely infectious disease, visitors were often deterred.[65] When plague broke out in his household in 1665, Richard Kidder lamented, 'My neighbours durst not come near, and the provisions which were procured for us were laid at a distance upon the Green'.[66] Historians have explored the social impact of epidemics, showing that plague was especially destructive to local community networks because 'the impulse to preserve self and family necessarily triumphed over other loyalties and obligations', such as visiting sick neighbours.[67] Nevertheless, even when children were not visited, they frequently received tokens of their relatives' concerns. Sixteen-year-old son William Paston sent his younger brother a 'fine knife' during his ague in 1626.[68]

In sum, sick children received an eclectic mix of care throughout the period, which included medical, spiritual, and social elements. In particular, nursing and prayer were of unquantifiable importance, and yet both forms of care have often been overlooked in the historiography.[69]

THE PROVIDERS OF CARE

Nursing was usually performed by mothers. In 1603, the sickly infant Simonds D'Ewes was tended 'with great care and pains' by his mother for five months following his birth.[70] Roughly seventy years later, Elizabeth Walker 'was not from'

---

[62] Henry Newcome, *The Autobiography of Henry Newcome,* ed. Richard Parkinson, Chetham Society, vol. 26 (Manchester: 1852).

[63] John Darrel, *A true narration of the strange and grevous vexation by the Devil, of 7. persons in Lanchashire* (1600), 13.

[64] Houlbrooke, *Death, Religion and the Family*, 193.

[65] David Gentilcore, 'The Fear of Disease and the Disease of Fear', in William Naphy and Penny Roberts (eds), *Fear in Early Modern Society* (Manchester and New York: 1997), 184–208, at 196.

[66] Richard Kidder, *The Life of Richard Kidder D. D. Bishop of Bath and Wells Written by Himself,* ed. Amy Edith Robinson, Somerset Record Society, vol. 37 (1924), 15.

[67] Paul Slack, *The Impact of Plague in Tudor and Stuart England* (Oxford: 1990), 20.

[68] Paston, *The Correspondence of Lady Katherine Paston, 1603–1627,* ed. Ruth Hughey, Norfolk Record Society, vol. 14 (1941), 90.

[69] Some scholars have now shown an interest in prayer and nursing, including Grell and Cunningham (eds), *Religio Medici*; John R. Hinnells and Roy Porter (eds), *Religion, Health, and Suffering* (and New York: 1999); R. Dingwall, A. M. Rafferty, and C. Webster, *An Introduction to the Social History of Nursing* (1988); Pelling, 'Nurses and Nursekeepers'; Boulton, 'Welfare Systems'.

[70] Simonds D'Ewes, *The Autobiography and Correspondence of Sir Simonds D'Ewes, Bart.,* ed. J. O. Halliwell, 2 vols (1845), vol. 1, 24.

her thirteen-year-old daughter 'but one night'.[71] Children often wanted to be nursed by their mothers: in 1677, fifteen-year-old Susanna Whitrow from London 'would hardly suffer her Mother to be from her, if she could help it'.[72] The tendency of mothers to nurse their ill children supports the work of gender historians who have firmly linked nursing and childcare with women.[73] However, wealthy mothers often took supervisory roles, spending some of their time nursing, but also enlisting the help of servants. The Hertfordshire gentlewoman Brilliana Harley saw her son Tom 'twes or thrise a day', and in the meantime, the maid, 'Blechly' took care of him.[74]

According to Margaret Versluysen, fathers were rarely involved in nursing in the early modern period.[75] Perhaps this assumption is unsurprising, since contemporaries often associated nursing with women. Ralph Verney warned his adult son against nursing his own children, on the grounds that 'tis not a Man's employment, but Woemen's work, & they both understand it & can performe it much better than any Man can doe. A good nursekeeper is better then Ten men'.[76] As Patricia Crawford has commented, an 'Englishman's masculinity' would have made the physical care of children a 'questionable' task.[77] However, in practice, fathers were often involved in the nursing of their children. Simonds D'Ewes 'was near' his two-year-old son Clopton 'all the time' during his illness in 1635.[78] Likewise, John Vernon looked after his twelve-year-old son Caleb in 1665: he spent several weeks by his bedside, even breakfasting in the same room.[79] Fathers nursed daughters as well as sons: in the 1680s, eight-year-old Sarah Camm, ill of smallpox, 'lay . . . in her Fathers arms', and thanked him for taking '*great pains with me in my Sickness*'.[80] These examples contradict the historiographical notion that female patients were nursed 'almost exclusively' by women, and that fathers had little to do with the physical care of children.[81] Fathers themselves did not always regard nursing as a feminine activity: on the contrary, when the child was suffering from a particularly distressing or dangerous illness, they sometimes hinted that it required courage

---

[71] Elizabeth Walker, *The vertuous wife: or, the holy life of Mrs. Elizabeth Walker*, ed. Anthony Walker (1694), 111.

[72] Rebecca Travers, *The work of God in a dying maid . . . Susanna Whitrow* (1677), 13.

[73] For example, Mendelson and Crawford, *Women in Early Modern England*, 224–5; Tannenbaum, *The Healer's Calling*, 31; Crawford, *Parents of Poor Children*, 128.

[74] Brilliana Harley, *Letters of the Lady Brilliana Harley*, ed. Thomas Taylor Lewis (1853), 120.

[75] Margaret Connor Versluysen, 'Old Wives' Tales? Women Healers in English History', in Celia Davies (ed.), *Rewriting Nursing History* (1980), 175–99. See also, Patricia Crawford and Laura Gowing (eds), *Women's Worlds in Seventeenth Century England: A Sourcebook* (2000), 187.

[76] Frances Verney (ed.), *The Verney Memoirs, 1600–1659*, 2 vols (1925, first publ. 1892), vol. 2, 376.

[77] Crawford, *Parents of Poor Children*, 122.

[78] D'Ewes, *The Autobiography*, vol. 2, 145.

[79] John Vernon, *The compleat scholler; or, a relation of the life, and latter-end especially, of Caleb Vernon* (1666), 54.

[80] Thomas Camm, *The admirable and glorious appearance of the eternal God . . . through a child . . . upon her dying bed* (1684), 6.

[81] The quotation is from Tannenbaum, *The Healer's Calling*, 29; others who agree include Ralph Houlbrooke, *The English Family 1450–1700* (1984), 185, and Crawford, *Parents of Poor Children*, 243.

and rationality, attributes associated with masculinity. Isaac Archer recorded that he 'was almost always'with his six-year-old daughter Frances during her fatal illness in 1679 because 'My wife could not helpe her through griefe'.[82] He implied that his wife was unable to cope with the terrifying spectacle of her dying child, perhaps due to the weakness of the female sex. It is possible, therefore, that rather than undermining a man's masculine identity, nursing may have actually served to enhance it.

Nonetheless, fathers did not always nurse their children. When Adam Martindale's seven-year-old son John fell ill of the smallpox in 1659, he was 'gone to Chester', though as soon as he heard this news, he decided to 'go home that night'.[83] During the Civil Wars, Ralph Verney was not able to nurse his son Jack because he was in exile in France; however, he showed great concern for this child, regularly asking his wife 'if Jacks leggs are weake, or crooked, or Both; and in what part'.[84] Even so, the evidence that some fathers were involved in the care of their sick children indicates that we must recognize the flexibility of gender roles at this time.

Sometimes parents delegated the nursing of their sick children to other individuals, including aunts, uncles, and grandparents. In 1632, Sir Gilbert Gerard sent his son Francis, who was ill of an ague, to his brother's house, where he was nursed by his aunt and uncle. The anxious father admitted that he 'would willingly have him home', but that he feared the 'aier . . . will doe him [no] good'.[85] Another father, Sir Thomas Barrington, sent his son Oliver to the child's grandmother's home in 1628, because he knew that the child would be 'quickly refresht' when he was near her 'affectionate and tender eye'.[86] Thus, care arrangements seem to have been motivated by a desire to do what was in the best interest of the child, and can be taken as evidence of parental love. Pragmatism also played a part in these decisions: Anne Clavering 'nurse[d] dear Betty', her twelve-year-old half-sister, because the child's parents were both dead.[87] Given the high rates of parental death, this arrangement was probably common.[88] Another member of the Clavering family, the schoolboy James, was looked after by his uncle John Yorke when he fell sick in the 1720s. The boy's family decided to keep him at his uncle's house, rather than send him home, because 'he [would] scarce be able to undergo a long journey . . . in the stage coach'.[89]

Non-relatives also played a role in the nursing of sick children. In the case of infants, they were often tended by wet nurses away from the family home. When baby Samuel Wallington became 'consumed and wasted' in 1632, he was 'put forth to nurse into the country' because the air was thought to be therapeutic.[90] While infants were under the care of these women, parents often maintained a keen

---

[82] Archer, *Two East Anglian Diaries*, 156.

[83] Martindale, *The Life of Adam Martindale*, 108–9.

[84] BL, M.636/8, this manuscript is unfoliated (Verney papers on microfilm, 1646–50).

[85] A. Searle (ed.), *Barrington Family Letters, 1628–1632* (1983), 230.

[86] Ibid. 39–40.

[87] James Clavering, *The Correspondence of Sir James Clavering*, ed. Harry Thomas Dickinson, Surtees Society, vol. 178 (Gateshead: 1967), 51.

[88] See Ch. 6, footnotes 207–8.

[89] Clavering, *The Correspondence*, 160.

[90] Guildhall Library, London, MS 204, [his pagination], 432 ('A Record of the Mercies of God: or A Thankfull Remembrance' by Nehemiah Wallington).

interest in their health, thus confirming that wet nursing was not a sign of parental indifference.[91] In 1709, Sarah Johnson from Litchfield visited her sickly infant Samuel 'every day . . . and often left her fan or glove behind her, that she might have a pretence to come back unexpected'.[92] Older children were also nursed by non-relatives in certain situations. If they became ill at school, for example, tutors or hired sick-keepers were often enlisted. The schoolboy James Basset who was suffering from an eye illness while at school, told his mother that he had been sent to the 'lodging of Monsieur le Gras', a tutor, to be nursed.[93] Upon hearing about the child's illness, parents often hurried to collect the child.[94] However, if the illness was not too serious, families sometimes decided to leave their children at school, in order to minimize the disruption to their education. This was the case for one of Ralph Verney's correspondents, who decided it was best for her son to stay at school because 'should I take him home his littill larning would sure be lost, which would be an inevetabill ruing to him'.[95]

Children from the lower social echelons, who were employed as labourers, servants, and apprentices, were probably cared for by their masters or employers when they fell ill.[96] This was because these individuals acted in *loco parentis*, providing for the physical welfare of their charges. Apprentices often lived far away from their own families, so it was not feasible for them to return home to be nursed.[97] Younger children, who were still living at home, were probably cared for by their mothers.[98] After the death of her child, a poor woman called Dorothy Hixon told the coroner that she 'took up the child . . . and . . . tended it all night'.[99] In the case of children living in urban areas, nursing was sometimes performed by 'parish nurses', as Jeremy Boulton has shown.[100] These nurses were employed by local authorities to provide care to the sick and disabled, including children. For example, 'Nurse Pomfrett' tended two pauper children in her house for 'a month in the small pox' in 1724.[101] Children might also be nursed in an institutional setting: in 1621, a 'Children's Hospital' was established in Norwich, for the 'keeping, bringing up, and teaching' of poor children. The hospital's founder, Thomas Anguish, explicitly stated that those children with 'grievous diseases' should be nursed by especially appointed watchers.[102] Likewise, the 'General Nursery' in

---

[91] Stone, *The Family, Sex and Marriage*, 65, 83.

[92] Samuel Johnson, *An Account of the Life of Dr Samuel Johnson, from his Birth to his Eleventh Year, Written By Himself* (1805), 12.

[93] St Clare Byrne (ed.), *The Lisle Letters*, vol. 4, 493.

[94] For example, D'Ewes, *The Autobiography*, vol. 1, 28.

[95] Verney, *The Verney Memoirs*, vol. 2, 229.

[96] Ilana Ben-Amos, *Adolescence and Youth in Early Modern England* (1994), 113; Pelling, *The Common Lot*, 123–8.

[97] Pelling, *The Common Lot*, 126–7.

[98] Crawford, *Parents of Poor Children*, 128.

[99] Cited by Garthine Walker, 'Just Stories: Telling Tales of Infant Death in Early Modern England', in Margaret Mikesell and Adele Seeff (eds), *Culture and Change: Attending to Early Modern Women* (Newwark, NJ: 2003), 98–115.

[100] Boulton, 'Welfare Systems', 127–51.

[101] Ibid. 133.

[102] Pelling, *The Common Lot*, 112–13.

Middlesex, which housed orphaned children, employed 'an old Nurse, to take care of all Sick and Weak Children' in the 1680s.[103] From the late seventeenth century, these institutions were becoming increasingly common.

Turning from nursing to medicine administration, a range of individuals were responsible for this task. Mothers played a crucial role. Elizabeth Walker placed 'five or six spoonfuls' of 'Oil of Sweet-Almonds' in a silver cup, which her child took in 1671.[104] Jane Josselin provided 73 per cent of the medicines mentioned in her husband's diary.[105] Mothers also took an active role in the manufacture of these substances, as is evident in the many domestic recipe books kept by housewives for use within the home. Among the ingredients stored by Elizabeth Freke in her cupboards for this purpose, were '2 quarts of sirrup of bulles' for easing stomach pains, and '1 quart of sirrup of issop', for treating lung conditions.[106] The provision of medicines by mothers continued over the course of the early modern period.[107] There is little evidence to suggest that by the late 1600s, kitchen physic had been replaced by 'professional' medicine.[108]

Fathers as well as mothers administered medicines to children. In 1647 Ralph Verney laid 'a thick plaster' to his daughter Pegg's ear, which was made out of 'milke, grated white bread and the yolke of an Egg and saffron with oyle of sweet almonds poured uppon it'.[109] His detailed knowledge of the ingredients suggests that he had had some involvement in the medicine's production. Likewise, John Vernon was 'in great care' for his twelve-year-old son Caleb in 1665: when the boy grew breathless, he ran downstairs to fetch some remedies for his relief, and 'applied to his Lips and palms of his Hands . . . inoffensive revivers in a small quantity'.[110] Sometimes fathers hinted that medicine administration was a joint effort between husbands and wives. Ralph Josselin wrote 'wee applied . . . 3 spoonefuls of juyce of red fennel clarified with 6 spoonfulls of beare and swetned' to his seven-year-old daughter in 1652, implying that his wife Jane had helped him.[111] Historians have frequently 'overlooked men's roles within the home with respect to domestic medical activities', possibly because they have assumed that the ideology of masculinity was incompatible with this role.[112] However, some contemporaries did not think this was the case. The diplomat and philosopher Edward Herbert declared, 'It will become a gentleman to have some knowledge in Medicine . . . it will become him also to know not only the ingredients but Doses of certain . . . .

---

[103] *An account of the general nursery, or colledg of infants* (1686), 4.

[104] Walker, *The vertuous wife*, 104–5.

[105] Mary Lindemann, *Medicine and Society in Early Modern Europe* (Cambridge: 2006, first publ. 1999), 201.

[106] Elizabeth Freke, *The Remembrances of Elizabeth Freke*, ed. Raymond Anselment, Camden Fifth Series, vol. 18 (Cambridge: 2001), 328.

[107] Lindemann, *Medicine and Society*, 199.

[108] Mortimer, 'The Triumph of the Doctors', 109; idem. *The Dying and The Doctors*.

[109] Verney, *The Verney Memoirs*, vol. 1, 376.

[110] Vernon, *The compleat scholler*, 53, 75.

[111] Ralph Josselin, *The Diary of Ralph Josselin 1616–1683*, ed. Alan Macfarlane (Oxford: 1991), 281.

[112] Smith, 'The Relative Duties of a Man', 237.

medicines'.[113] Thus once again, it seems that ideas about gender roles within the family need to be revised.

Members of the extended family also provided medical treatments to ill children. In 1632, the daughter of Sir William Masham was offered some of her aunt's 'water for the eyes' when her eyes were sore.[114] Outside the family, the assistance of elite gentlewomen was often enlisted. In 1645, the Josselin parents 'went to . . . Lady Honywoods who gave us divers things' for their sick daughter, eight-year-old Mary.[115] These women treated children from a range of socio-economic backgrounds, including the very poor.[116] Occasionally, the services of gentlemen were also solicited.[117] In 1724, the Norfolk architect John Buxton told his fourteen-year-old son Robert that 'S[i]r Ben[jami]n Wrench . . . says you may take 15 grains of rhubarb in powder' to purge his corrupt humours.[118] Parents' attitudes to these 'elite–lay' practitioners were mixed: on the one hand they admired their benevolence, as was suggested by Lady Anne Halkett, who praised Sir Thomas Gore for studying 'phisike more for devertisement than gaine'.[119] On the other hand, parents believed these practitioners were fallible: this is suggested by the fact that they were prepared to reject any treatments that they judged unsuitable. When Lady Honywood told Jane Josselin that her son needed an issue to cure him of his consumption, Jane disagreed, stating that she 'hath no minde' to such a treatment because she believed he was actually suffering from rickets.[120]

Men and women lower down the social scale acted as medical practitioners for sick children, including midwives and wet nurses. The treatments prescribed by these individuals were often regarded as especially suitable for children because they were usually simple and gentle.[121] When Katherine Newcome obtained an ointment for worms from 'one Mrs Shore', her husband wrote approvingly, 'It was nothing but walnut leaves . . . boiled in fresh butter', and yet it worked remarkably.[122] Sometimes parents believed these practitioners were better qualified for treating children than physicians because they were more experienced. Ralph Verney beseeched his wife to 'give the child no physick but such as midwives and old women [prescribe] . . . for assure yourselfe they by experience know better then [sic] any phisition how to treat such infants'.[123] At another time, this same father admitted that he had obtained the services of a horse-smith to treat his two

[113] Edward Herbert, *The Life of Edward, First Lord Herbert of Cherbury written by himself*, ed. J. M. Shuttleworth (1976), 21–2.

[114] Barrington, *Barrington Family Letters*, 232.

[115] Josselin, *The Diary*, 41.

[116] Hoby, 'Diary of Lady Magaret Hoby', 186.

[117] Ronald Charles Sawyer, 'Patients, Healers, and Disease in the Southeast Midlands, 1597–1634' (unpubl. PhD thesis, University of Wisconsin, 1986), 185.

[118] John Buxton, *John Buxton, Norfolk Gentleman and Architect: Letters to his Son, 1719–1729*, ed. Alan Mackley, Norfolk Record Society, vol. 69 (Norwich: 2005), 50.

[119] Anne Halkett, *The Autobiography of Anne Lady Halkett*, ed. John Gough Nichols, Camden Society New Series, vol. 13 (1875–76), 31.

[120] Josselin, *The Diary of Ralph Josselin*, 186.

[121] Rebecca Tannenbaum agrees, in her book, *The Healer's Calling*, 14.

[122] Newcome, *The Autobiography*, 43.

[123] Verney, *The Verney Memoirs*, vol. 1, 262.

youngest children because 'he gives you as rationall an Accompte for what hee doth, as any Phisitian that I ever yett mette withal'.[124] Thus it seems likely that families regarded these more humble practitioners with considerable respect.

Few of the sources mentioned the use of 'cunning' men or women, astrologers, or white witches. This may have been because puritan families avoided these individuals on the grounds that their practices were superstitious. Had they consulted cunning folk, it is likely that they would have preferred not to divulge such disreputable practices in their personal documents, for fear of censure.[125] Nevertheless, it is possible that some of the aforementioned practitioners, such as Mrs Shore, were considered by certain members of the community to be of this variety, but during serious illness, their services were obtained anyway. Charles Ronald Sawyer supports this notion, stating that at times of mortal illness, families may have 'refused to consider . . . cunning men and women as lawbreakers'.[126] The boundary between authorized and unauthorized practitioners was sufficiently blurred to allow laypeople the flexibility to consult whoever they wished.[127] While the personal documents do not contain much evidence about the use of these practitioners, the possession cases are more forthcoming. In 1661, the father of the adolescent James Barrow, 'made use' of an astrologer called John Hubbard, who proceeded to treat the boy with a variety of charms. The father later emphasized that this decision was a last resort, resulting from his 'great extremity'.[128] Parents' abandonment of their usual moral codes for the sake of their child's recovery reveals their love for their offspring. However, occasionally parents did refuse to endorse the superstitious treatments of these practitioners. In 1683, Oliver Heywood described the strange illness of a twelve-year-old boy, Abraham Higson. The boy's parents consulted 'one Dr Thornton', who advised them to have his urine 'tried by fire'—a charm which involved making a 'cake or loaf' of his urine and wheat meal, and then burning the mixture. The boy's mother told Heywood she was 'afraid to offend god' by this charm, and Heywood agreed, telling her he 'utterly dislik'd it'.[129]

A recent study has shown that the seventeenth century witnessed a dramatic rise in the employment of physicians at times of serious illness.[130] Certain scholars have asserted that before the eighteenth century, it was rare for elite doctors to be called to the aid of a child.[131] The sources examined in my research indicate that

---

[124] Ibid. vol. 2, 128.
[125] David Harley believes that 'The godly preferred learned medicine', and avoided 'magical medicine', in his chapter 'The Theology of Affliction', 280.
[126] Sawyer, 'Patients, Healers, and Disease', 148.
[127] Barbara Duden, *The Woman Beneath the Skin: A Doctor's Patients in Eighteenth-Century Germany*, trans. Thomas Dunlap (Cambridge, Mass.: 1991), 78.
[128] John Barrow, 'A true Relation of the wonderful Deliverance of Hannah Crump', in John Barrow, *The Lord's arm stretched out in an answer of prayer: or a very relation of the wonderful deliverance of James Barrow* (1664), 17–20, at 11.
[129] Oliver Heywood, *The Rev. Oliver Heywood, B. A: His Autobiography, Diaries, Anecdote and Event Books*, ed. Horsfall Turner, 4 vols (1883), vol. 4, 55–6.
[130] Mortimer, 'The Triumph of the Doctors'.
[131] Roy Porter, *Patient's Progress*, 183; Broomhall, *Women's Medical Work*, 179.

physicians *were* consulted for the treatment of children before the 1700s. It is less clear, however, whether there was an increase in the overall tendency of parents to consult doctors as time progressed. Certainly, parents and relatives mentioned their dealings with these practitioners throughout the early modern period, but whether or not such individuals were actually qualified physicians is undetectable, since this occupational label was used loosely. What is more evident is that the circumstances which led parents to contact these elite practitioners, do *not* appear to have changed over the period: they were usually sought only after the domestic medicine had failed—medicine operated on a 'hierarchy of resort'.[132] In 1709, the surgeon and physician Daniel Turner saw 'One of my Neighbour's Sons, a Lad about eight or nine Years old' who was suffering from a sore scalp. The boy had initially been treated with 'all the good Wives Remedies', but after a few months of no improvement, he was 'brought . . . and committed to my Care'.[133] Examples of this kind demonstrate that even in the eighteenth century, parents continued to consult an eclectic array of lay and learned practitioners.

It was not uncommon for parents to employ several physicians simultaneously, especially if the illness became very serious. In 1697, Lady Russell's adolescent son became 'so sick and so ill' of the smallpox that she 'sent for more doctors'.[134] The total number of physicians consulted could be large: Elizabeth Walker noted that during the 'great Fit' of her daughter in 1671, she 'Had the Advice of eight or nine Physicians from *London* and *Chelmsford*'.[135] These findings support Mary Lindemann's assertion that 'early modern people were medically promiscuous'.[136] Multiple consultations were managed in several ways: often, one doctor would visit the sick child, while another was consulted by letter. John Hervey and his wife wrote to 'Doctor Clopton' in 1719, asking him to check over the other doctor's prescription to reassure them that 'there is nothing in it but what is proper'.[137] Alternatively, the practitioners visited the child together, offering their various prescriptions, and allowing the family to decide which course to take. This was the case for nine-year-old Adam Martindale in 1632: the advice of several 'skilful men' was requested for the cure of an 'ugly dry scurfe' that was 'eating deep' into his body: they presented three different treatment options.[138]

The practice of consulting several physicians concurrently sheds light on lay-people's attitudes to these practitioners: they were regarded as potentially useful but fallible.[139] It was hoped that if the opinions of enough doctors were collected, their overall value would hold more weight, and their faults would be exposed.

---

[132] Margaret Pelling, *Medical Conflicts in Early Modern London: Patronage, Physicians, and Irregular Practitioners, 1550–1640* (Oxford: 2003), 249–51.

[133] Daniel Turner, *De morbis cutaneis, a treatise of diseases incident to the skin* (1714), 153.

[134] Rachael Wriothesley Russell, *Letters of Rachel, Lady Russell*, 2 vols (1853, first publ. 1773), vol. 2, 67.

[135] Walker, *The vertuous wife*, 104.

[136] Lindemann, *Medicine and Society*, 199.

[137] John Hervey, *Letter-Books of John Hervey, First Earl of Bristol*, ed. S. H. A. Hervey, 3 vols, (Wells: 1894), vol. 2, 72.

[138] Martindale, *The Life of Adam Martindale*, 19–21.

[139] Porter, *Patient's Progress*, 13.

Parents and relatives were critical of their physicians, and were prepared to decline a treatment if they believed that it was inappropriate. Ralph Verney challenged his doctor's advice to 'dry . . . upp' the oozing swelling on his son's leg using 'Betane flower' in 1647. He declared that he would 'not doe it' because he believed that it was a good thing that the corrupt matter was leaving the child's body naturally.[140] Attitudes were not always so critical, however: many parents trusted their doctors implicitly. 'I shall alwaies think them safe in your skill and care', wrote Lady Elizabeth Hervey to Dr Clopton in 1718 during the illness of one of her daughters.[141] Parents often held one particular doctor in especially high esteem, and valued his opinions over those of others. Ralph Verney always verified the medical prescriptions of other practitioners with his favourite doctor, whom he called, 'the honest doctor'.[142] The ingratiating tone of parents' letters to these revered doctors conveys their respect: Mrs B. Boyle asked her physician, Sir Hans Sloane, for his 'Directions' regarding her young daughter, stating that 'noe body among the thousands you doe good to can be more sencable of your Favours than' she.[143] The fact that families frequently consulted physicians, and often accepted their treatments, is also evidence of their more positive views of these practitioners. In short, the relationships between laypeople and their doctors were characterized by a complex mix of trust and distrust, defiance and submission.[144]

Poorer children were also treated by elite practitioners on some occasions. Doctors frequently mentioned treating these patients in their casebooks: Richard Wiseman, for instance, attended 'A Girl of about four years of age' who had been brought to him 'in a poor woman's arms in the very midst of Winter, the ground being covered with Snow'.[145] Afterwards, the girl's parents consulted another physician about 'their own healths, and discoursing of the Child's Cure, he perswaded them' to take another course of treatments and to 'decline' his own. Thus, even the poor were able to obtain the services of several physicians at once, picking the treatments they preferred. It is questionable whether this was a common experience, but it is nevertheless a useful reminder that the poor may have had more options than might be expected. Incidental information from the Proceedings of the Old Bailey supports this assertion. In 1680, a bailiff attempted to 'Arrest a poor man for a Debt'; he dragged the man out of the house with 'barbarousness'. The man's little daughter, witnessing this cruelty, 'cryed out', and the bailiff then hit the child with a 'great Cudgel'. The family obtained the 'help of a surgeon', by which means she 'recovered to life', but later languished and died.[146] As well as demonstrating that even the indebted poor might be treated by medical

[140] BL, M.636/8, this manuscript is unfoliated (Verney papers on microfilm, 1646–50), a letter dated 24 November 1647.

[141] Hervey, *Letter-Books,* vol. 2, 72.

[142] BL, M.636/8, this manuscript is unfoliated (Verney papers on microfilm, 1646–50), a letter dated 9 February 1648.

[143] BL, Sloane MS 4034, fol. 240r (Correspondence of Sir Hans Sloane 1720–30).

[144] Porter, *Patient's Progress,* 58–66, 87, 210.

[145] Richard Wiseman, *Several chirurgical treatises* (1686, first publ. 1676), 137.

[146] OBP, reference: t16800526-6 (accessed 14 January 2011).

personnel, this vignette reveals the love and sympathy of a poor child for her father, and challenges the notion that it is impossible to uncover poor children's feelings about their parents.

Other sources that confirm that poor children were treated by doctors are the records of the Poor Law. The sixteenth-century religious reformer William Marshall advised local authorities to 'assigne certeyn Phisicians and Surgeons to loke unto and remedie' the diseases of 'sicke and sore persones'.[147] One town that enacted Marshall's advice was Norwich: in the 1570s a variety of learned doctors were contracted to treat sick children, at the charge of the local authorities.[148] These practitioners treated children at home, or in an institutional setting, as is revealed in published accounts of workhouses from the late seventeenth century. The workhouse in Bishops-gate Street in London, for example, devoted several rooms to the care of sick children by 'Physicians, Surgeons, and Apothecaries'.[149] Nevertheless, some institutions sought to avoid the high costs incurred by elite practitioners: the workhouse at Chelmsford, Essex, claimed that the sickness of eleven inmates from smallpox 'cost the Parish not one shilling' because 'they all did well with the Kitchen Physick' given by the workhouse staff.[150]

THE FAMILY'S EXPERIENCE OF CARE

For the family, the most striking impact of care was the sheer time and effort it took. Medicine manufacture was particularly time-consuming: many different ingredients had to be found or purchased, and complex instructions for the actual making of the medicines had to be followed. The Trumbell family's recipe for 'plague water' required carers to,

> Take Egremony Rue Wormwood, sollendin, Angelica Sage, Tormentil ... Scabius, Baume, Mugwort, Pimpernell, Spermint, Scordium or Scordus, Cardus, Dragons, Fetherfew, Galiga, Rosasolis, Lilly of thevally, Marygold flowers, Barage flowers, Cowslip flowers, Pancy flowers, of each of these a quarter of a pound. Fenell seeds, Coriander seeds and Anniseeds, Cardimum seeds of each an ounce, half a pound of Rosmary Ledoary or Zedaree halfe an ounce Scorzonera a handfull, shred the herbs small ... putt them into an earthen pott well glazed, then put into the pott 3 gallons of Sack & then cover it & past it up very close let it stand 8 or 9 dayes, then put it into the still & add to it 2 ounces of fine Methridate 3 ounces of Venice Treacle, of Cinnamon, Cloves & Nutmegs of each halfe an ounce & still it gently.[151]

The tasks involved in concocting medicines, such as boiling and re-boiling, straining and sieving, and shaking and stirring, could be physically arduous, as well as

[147] Cited by Pelling, *The Common Lot*, 81.
[148] Ibid. 114.
[149] *An account of several work-houses for employing and maintaining the poor* (1725), 4.
[150] Ibid. 63.
[151] BL, Additional MS 72619, fol. 111v ('Book of recipes for Trumbell's household', late seventeenth century).

tedious, to carry out.[152] Likewise, the administration of medicine took much time, and often had to be repeated over a long period. Arthur Corbett's ointment for children suffering from rickets had to be massaged into the child's chest and stomach for one whole hour every 'morning & evening' during all the months of spring, and repeated every year until the child was cured.[153] Of course, there may have been some occasions when parents did not keep strictly to the recipe—they may have skipped over some procedures, or left out certain ingredients. Furthermore, children's remedies were not always complicated: as we saw in the previous chapter, they were often short and simple, consisting of two or three ingredients alone. Johanna St John's recipe for curing epilepsy contained only 'piony seeds of single Piony & Black cherry water'.[154] Young patients were usually required to take their medicines less frequently than adults. These features of children's physic, which were motivated by concerns about safety, probably made the manufacturing and administrating processes easier and quicker in some instances. Time could also be saved by purchasing 'ready-made' medicines 'off-the-shelf' from apothecary shops, especially towards the end of the seventeenth century.[155]

Nursing was also time-consuming: in cases of serious illness, it was carried out through day and night.[156] Likewise, prayer could take much time, particularly in cases of chronic illness or diabolical possession, for during these afflictions it was not uncommon for parents to devote whole days to prayer. In September 1663, the father of thirteen-year-old James Barrow 'set apart' three entire days from sunrise to when 'the Sun went down' for the seeking of 'the Lord in behalf of my Child'.[157] This lengthy prayer was not confined to boys: parents were just as willing to devote prayer days to their daughters. In December 1602 Mary Glover's family invited twenty-four people to attend a day of 'prayer and fasting' in an attempt to persuade God to recover her.[158]

This time-consuming care prevented family members from undertaking their normal duties and excursions. In 1632, Lady Barrington wrote to her grandmother to apologize for not being able to visit her; the reason she gave was, 'my litle one which is il'.[159] Fathers as well as mothers were affected in this way. Ralph Verney told his friend Mrs Cockrain that he had 'intended to have been with' her 'before this time, but...my Boy Mun hath been ill'.[160] Sometimes parents urged one

---

[152] Jennifer Stine, 'Opening Closets: The Discovery of Household Medicine in Early Modern England' (unpubl. PhD thesis, Stanford University, 1996), p. iv.

[153] WL, MS 212, fol. 64r (Arthur Corbett, collection of medical receipts, mid-seventeenth century).

[154] WL, MS 4338 fol. 34r ('Johanna St John Her Booke' 1680).

[155] Porter, *Patient's Progress*, 47–8.

[156] Tannenbaum, *The Healer's Calling*, 29.

[157] John Barrow, *The Lord's arm stretched out in an answer of prayer, or, a true relation of the wonderful deliverance of James Barrow* (1664), 13–17.

[158] John Swan, ' "A True and Briefe Report, of Mary Glovers Vexation" (1603)', in Philip Almond (ed.), *Demonic Possession and Exorcism in Early Modern England: Contemporary Texts and their Cultural Contexts* (Cambridge: 2004), 291–330, at 298–307.

[159] Barrington, *Barrington Family Letters*, 223.

[160] BL, M.636/8, this manuscript is unfoliated (Verney papers on microfilm, 1646–50; a letter dated 1 December 1647).

another to stay at home to care for the sick child: in 1624, the artist Sir Nathaniel Bacon begged his wife 'not [to] hasten your cominge hither; for your presence may better be spared here than there'.[161] Implicit in this statement is the idea that the mother's presence would be therapeutic to the child, or that the child actually preferred being cared for by his mother. Being confined to the house could be frustrating, as Thomas Barrington found: in 1632, he complained that the 'interruptoions and delayes' occasioned by the illness of his daughter Lucy had caused his 'patience and best judgement' to be 'extended to theire best'.[162] Parents feared that if they were to leave the house, their child might deteriorate while they were absent. Joan Everard wrote that she was unable to visit her mother because 'My child has bene very ille againe which mak[e]s me fearfull to stir from hir'.[163]

An activity regularly disrupted by the tasks of care was letter-writing. Ralph Verney wrote in 1644 to his correspondent, 'I have scarce time to tell you now' about his news because 'poore Mun & Peg are Both in there Bedds' with smallpox.[164] Relatives used the child's sickness as an excuse for their failure to reply promptly to their correspondents. In 1632, Sir Gilbert Gerard informed his correspondent, Lady Joan Barrington, that, 'I have bine too long silent, having forborne to send [a letter] during my newphrew['s] ... sicknes'.[165] It was not only a lack of time that prevented family members from writing letters: part of the problem was that they were experiencing such anxiety over their child's illness that they were unable to focus on anything else. In 1626, Lady Katherine Paston bewailed that she had 'had pen in hand' to begin a letter to one of her children, but that her son's illness 'prevented me at that time, and made me unfit for any thinge'.[166] The widespread use of this excuse suggests that it was considered an acceptable and natural consequence of child sickness. Amanda Vickery has commented on this tendency for childhood illness to make parents 'poor correspondents', stating that mothers in particular 'could not be spared from the bedside' to write their letters.[167] Lower down the social scale, caring for sick children prevented parents from undertaking their paid employments.[168] In the 1660s, a widow called Mary Lapworth told Christ's Hospital that her son had 'such violent convulsions that she dare not absent her selfe from him because he throws himself in the fire and burnes himselfe'.[169] It must have been especially difficult for single mothers to cope

---

[161] [Cornwallis], *The Private Correspondence of Jane Lady Cornwallis, 1613–1644*, ed. Lord Braybrooke (1842), 92.

[162] Barrington, *Barrington Family Letters*, 243–4.

[163] Ibid. 58.

[164] BL, M.636/6, this manuscript is unfoliated (Verney papers on microfilm, 1646–50; a letter dated 27 December 1644).

[165] Barrington, *Barrington Family Letters*, 230.

[166] Paston, *The Correspondence*, 88.

[167] Amanda Vickery, *The Gentleman's Daughter: Women's Lives in Georgian England* (London and New Haven, CT: 2003, first publ. 1998), 117.

[168] Joanne Bailey, ' "Think Wot a Mother Must Feel": Parenting in English Pauper Letters, *c*.1760–1834', *Family & Community History*, 13 (2010), 5–19, at 9.

[169] Cited in Crawford, *Parents of Poor Children*, 128.

with the burdens of nursing, since it impeded their sole means of economic survival, paid work.[170]

Tending the sick child disrupted servants' work. Lady Barrington complained that she would have liked her servant 'Smyth' to have waited upon her mother, but her daughter 'Lucy[,] falling extream sick' forced her to 'stay him'.[171] The idea that a male servant might be involved in the care of an ill child challenges contemporary and current notions about the gendered nature of servants' work.[172] Nevertheless, it is not clear what role this servant played in the care of the child—it may have been that the extra work created by sickness necessitated the help of Smyth in other household tasks. Sometimes servants became infected with the child's illness. In the early eighteenth century, the Batton family complained that six servants, including 'Four men and two Maids' were 'all seiz'd at Once' with the disease of two-year-old Mary. The doctor, Charles Maitland, believed that the rapid spreading of the illness had resulted from the servants' tendency to 'Hug and Caress the Child'.[173] This case indicates that emotional bonds could form between children and household servants, and suggests once again that male servants may have played a part in the care of sick children.[174]

Perhaps the most burdensome consequence of care-giving was physical and emotional exhaustion. Prayer was carried out with passion, and caused considerable mental fatigue. Isaac Archer 'wrestled with God with much earnestnes for the child's life, so as I never was in such anguish before'.[175] The use of words associated with combat, such as 'battle', 'fight', and 'wrestle' convey the arduous experience of prayer. This is also suggested by the tendency of parents to shed tears during prayer. Ralph Josselin confessed that when his 'dear sonne was ill' in 1651, he 'creid to my god with teares for him'.[176] Prayer may have been one of the few contexts in which tears were considered acceptable in males, since crying was seen as a sign of the Christian's earnestness.[177] Indeed, there is sometimes a sense that tears were necessary for eliciting God's mercy—they 'held a near mechanical efficacy'.[178] The task of preparing the child for death was possibly even more emotionally tiring, because this process forced parents to confront the possibility of their children's mortality. This was the case for the mother of eleven-year-old John

---

[170] Ibid. 128.

[171] Barrington, *Barrington Family Letters*, 245.

[172] For example, Jane Whittle, 'Servants in Rural England c.1450–1650: Hired Work as a Means of Accumulating Wealth and Skills Before Marriage', in Amy Louise Erickson and Maria Agren (eds), *The Marital Economy in Scandinavia and Britain, 1400–1900* (Aldershot: 2005), 89–110 at 91.

[173] BL, Sloane MS 4034, fol. 19r (Correspondence of Sir Hans Sloane 1720–30).

[174] Historians have rarely examined the relationships between children and servants—for example, Tim Meldrum's book, *Domestic Service and Gender, 1660–1750: Life and Work in the London Household* (Harlow: 2000), contains a chapter on 'Household Relations', but most of this is about relationships between servants and masters/mistresses.

[175] Archer, *Two East Anglian Diaries*, 150.

[176] Josselin, *The Diary of Ralph Josselin*, 262.

[177] See C. F. Otten, 'Women's Prayers in Childbirth in Sixteenth-century England', *Women and Language*, 16 (1993), 18–21; Philip Carter, 'Tears and the Man', in Sarah Knott and Barbara Taylor (eds), *Women, Gender, and Enlightenment* (New York: 2005), 156–73.

[178] Walsham, *Providence*, 150.

Harvy in the 1660s: upon asking her boy whether he was willing to die, she 'burst forth into tears', and when he then uttered statements of resignation to death, 'all this did rather increase than allay his Mothers grief'.[179]

The exhaustion of nursing an ailing child was sometimes so extreme that contemporaries believed it could make family members ill. In 1650, Dr Thomas Willis attributed the death of his forty-year-old patient to her having 'spent many sleepless nights nursing a sick child'.[180] Over half a century later, the Yorkshire vicar John Brockbank wrote that his wife 'has been sometime indisposed[,] which we believe was occasioned by the paines shee took with her son [who] requires a great deal of attendance [that] . . . is allmost above her strength'.[181] Especially vulnerable were parents who had been unwell prior to the sickening of their children, or who lacked the help of servants. Isaac Archer noted that the 'feaver of wormes' of his 'boy Will' in 1675, had made his wife, who had already 'bin very sick', much worse.[182] Jane Josselin, who had no maids to assist her, became 'sickely with toiling' over their baby son, recorded her husband Ralph in 1649.[183] The sources provide fewer examples of fathers suffering in this way: perhaps this is evidence that their roles were less intensive than those of mothers. Nevertheless, men did show signs of severe exhaustion. John Brockbank was so 'overcome for want of sleep' from nursing his son in 1687 that he laid his 'head on the [child's] bed' and let 'sleep c[o]me upon me'.[184]

Caring for the sick child could be expensive. When Lady Elizabeth Bradshaigh's two grandsons caught the smallpox in 1687, she complained that the total cost incurred to pay for 'the doctors and people to watch with them, and the [a]pothecary's bill', amounted to 'near twenty pounds'. She added, 'to save the pretty boys' lives, I am content to do anything'.[185] Considering that the average wage of a skilled craftsman in the late seventeenth century was fifty-four pounds a year, this price seems considerable.[186] The cost of hiring a nurse was particularly high when the patient's distemper was especially unpleasant or infectious.[187] The smallpox was one such disease: in 1673, it cost the Fleming family one shilling and six pence to pay a maid to tend 'Alice & Barbara in the small pocks'.[188] Nurses had to dress the repugnant pustules of the smallpox over several weeks, so it is not surprising that it incurred higher fees.[189]

[179] Janeway, *A token for children* (part 2), 85–6.
[180] Thomas Willis, *Willis's Oxford Casebook (1650–52)*, ed. Kenneth Dewhurst (Oxford: 1981), 79–80.
[181] Thomas Brockbank, *The Diary and Letter Book of the Rev. Thomas Brockbank 1671–1709*, ed. Richard Trappes-Lomax, Chetham Society New Series, vol. 89 (Manchester: 1930), 290.
[182] Archer, *Two East Anglian Diaries*, 150.
[183] Josselin, *The Diary of Ralph Josselin*, 186.
[184] Brockbank, *The Diary and Letter Book*, 5–7.
[185] Cited in Sir Arthur Wynne Morgan Bryant (ed.), *Postman's Horn: an Anthology of the Family Letters of Later Seventeenth Century England* (1946), 19.
[186] This figure has been calculated from the data provided by Doreen Nagy in her book *Popular Medicine in Seventeenth-Century England* (Ohio: 1988), 21.
[187] Jeremy Boulton, 'Welfare Systems', 134.
[188] [Fleming], *The Flemings in Oxford*, ed. John Richard Magrath, Oxford Historical Society, vol. 44 (Oxford: 1904), 466.
[189] Boulton, 'Welfare Systems', 134.

Medicine could also be costly, since physicians were at liberty to demand considerable amounts for their consultations, especially if the family was wealthy. Doreen Nagy has estimated that London physicians charged between six shillings eight pence, and ten shillings for one visit, a fee 'well beyond the means of all but a small group of prosperous patients'.[190] Doctors outside London may have charged less. Dr John Symcotts, for example, requested two shillings and six pence for consultations.[191] Yet, when one considers that Symcotts usually visited his patients several times, the price would have soon mounted up.[192] On top of the physicians' fees, were the apothecaries' bills. In the 1680s, William Blundell complained that 'the apothecary's bill especially, is like to be somewhat' for the young boy he was looking after, although he did not provide a figure.[193] Even when families made their own medicines, the cost was not insignificant: Lady Grace Mildmay recorded spending a total of six pounds, eleven shillings, and nine pence on various ingredients. When compared against Mildmay's yearly expenditure of 130 pounds, this price seems high.[194] Ingredients that had to be imported, such as musk, opium, and ginger, were especially expensive.[195] Chronic illnesses were among the most costly to treat because the necessary remedies had to be purchased repeatedly. John Evelyn bemoaned that the total cost of rectifying his son John's crooked leg was almost '150 pounds' in 1662.[196] Similarly expensive was the treatment for the King's Evil, which involved sending the patient to London to be touched by the monarch: Ralph Verney complained that the little girl under his care, Mary, incurred 'excessive rates' because of the costs of 'Clothes, lodging and diet', and travel.[197]

Among the poorer groups, the cost of medical care could be crippling: it 'further drained the family's savings and resources, as well as impeding mothers from undertaking gainful employment'.[198] The impact of these costs becomes clear when one examines the income and expenditure of poor families at this time. Keith Wrightson and David Levine have estimated that the annual income for a labouring family in Terling, Essex, was fifteen pounds and twelve shillings. The total cost of food, clothing, rent, and fuel for a couple with three children was thirteen pounds and fourteen shillings per annum. It is evident from these figures that there was little margin for the costs of medicine.[199] Despite the financial straits

---

[190] Nagy, *Popular Medicine*, 21.

[191] Ibid. 22.

[192] For example, in 1636 John Symcotts visited fourteen-year-old Elizabeth Burgoyne at least six times: John Symcotts, *A Seventeenth Century Doctor and his Patients: John Symcotts, 1592?-1662*, eds F. N. L. Poynter and W. J. Bishop, Bedfordshire Historical Record Society, vol. 31 (Streatley: 1951), 60–1.

[193] William Blundell, *Cavalier: Letters of William Blundell to his Friends, 1620–1698*, ed. Margaret Blundell (1933), 269–70.

[194] Linda Pollock, *With Faith and Physic: the Life of a Tudor Gentlewoman, Lady Grace Mildmay, 1552–1620* (1993), 103.

[195] Ibid. 103.

[196] Evelyn, *John Evelyn's Diary*, 436–7.

[197] Verney, *The Verney Memoirs*, vol. 1, 509.

[198] Crawford, *Parents of Poor Children*, 128.

[199] Keith Wrightson and David Levine, *Poverty and Piety in an English Village: Terling, 1525–1700* (New York: 1979), 41–2, cited in Crawford, *Parents of Poor Children*, 126.

faced by the poor, there is evidence to show that parents did manage to provide their offspring with medicines. A lowly widow from Covent Garden undertook extra needlework on top of her usual labour to earn enough money to pay for the physician's treatment of her son's sores.[200] Such cases challenge Lawrence Stone's assertion that poor parents were indifferent to their children.[201]

Care was not always so expensive, however. Nurses were often family members or friends who were performing this task out of love or neighbourliness, charging no fee. Even when nurses were paid, the costs for tending sick children were often quite low compared to the amount spent on adults. Jeremy Boulton has estimated that in *c.*1724, it cost about four shillings to nurse an adult for one week, whereas for infants and children, the price was halved.[202] The expense of medicine was also lower when families and friends were involved in the manufacturing processes, for many of the ingredients could be gathered without charge from the kitchen or local meadow.[203] This is implied in Nicholas Culpeper's *Complete herbal*, which states that the herbs needed to make most of his medicines were 'so familiar' that 'every boy that can eat an egg knows it'.[204] Families and friends also exchanged medicines free of charge. In 1645, Jane Josselin visited her friend Lady Honywood, who 'gave us divers things' for her three-year-old daughter Mary, including a special oil.[205] Furthermore, parents could favour cheaper alternatives if faced with expensive treatments. When ten-year-old Hannah Martindale developed rickets, her father considered, 'Some would have us carry her to the Bath; but, besides that the charge was very great, and would much lessen her little portion that I intended her'. He added that his 'honest and able' doctor friend believed spas would do his daughter no good.[206] For the poor, doctors often provided medical remedies free of charge, and many children received treatments that had been paid for by the local authorities, or given out of charity by gentlewomen.[207]

When medicines were found to be ineffective, parents and relatives expressed great frustration and distress. In 1538, Lady Lisle's daughter had been 'sore sick for more than five weeks of a fever'; she complained that that she 'neither knew nor can find remedy to heal her thereof'.[208] Over a century later, Oliver Heywood gave his seven-year-old son two 'clisters...w[hi]ch wrought not according to expectation'.[209] These reactions shed doubt on the view that disappointment over medical failure is a modern development.[210] Sometimes medicine was not only found to be ineffective, but in fact seemed to make the illness worse. In 1636, Simonds D'Ewes blamed the renewed 'fits of convulsions' of his two-year-old infant on the 'issue'

---

[200] Ibid. (Crawford),128.

[201] Stone, *Family, Sex and Marriage*, 65.

[202] Boulton, 'Welfare Systems', 133–4.

[203] Tannenbaum, *The Healer's Calling*, 26.

[204] Nicholas Culpeper, *Culpeper's Complete Herbal* (Ware: 1995), 274.

[205] Josselin, *The Diary of Ralph Josselin*, 41.

[206] Martindale, *The Life of Adam Martindale*, 214–15.

[207] Pelling, 'Child Health as a Social Value'.

[208] Lisle, *Lisle Letters*, vol. 5, 215.

[209] Heywood, *The Rev. Oliver Heywood*, vol. 1, 203–4.

[210] Porter, *Patient's Progress*, 210.

that had been used 'violently and unskilfully' by the doctor.[211] Evacuative medicines were thought to be especially risky, because they could 'work' too violently,
making the patient weaker. After giving his two children purging medicine in 1650,
Ralph Josselin 'trembled' with fear as they were 'sick even to death'.[212] A few
decades later, Mary Jervoise complained that the vomit she had administered to
her daughter Lucy made her the 'sickest creatur' she had ever seen, vomiting from
'5 a clocke this morning . . . [until] past 6 att night'. The anxious mother lamented,
'[if the medicine] duse nott sease working I fear it will bee very sad'.[213]

Parents found it upsetting observing the pain that the medical treatments caused
their offspring. In 1714, the surgeon Daniel Turner noted that the parents of his
young patient were 'affrighted' because their daughter 'cry'd . . . day and Night'
from the pain of the tight band he had tied around a growth on her eye-lid: they
demanded that Turner 'slacken'd' the band, because she 'could bear it no longer'.[214] Another of his patients, 'a Lad about eight or nine Years old', was treated
with strong plasters to remove a 'stubborn' scab from his head: the medicine made
the scalp 'swelled and inflam'd', and in response, the boy's parents 'murmur'd that
I had put him to much Pain, and made the Place more raw, as they called it, than it
was before'.[215] Some parents became so distressed at the prospect of the child's
painful treatment that they could not bear to watch it. This was the case for the
Northamptonshire gentlewoman Judith Isham in the early 1600s: 'being full of
tender compasation' for her daughter, she 'went into the next rome because she
could not [bear to] see her missery' of having her broken thighbone reset.[216]

Similarly stressful was the task of preparing the sick child spiritually for death.
Godly parents were intensely aware that a failure to help their children reach a state
of assurance about their salvation might affect their eternal future. James Janeway's
'instruction to parents' on the religious teaching of children reveals the immense
pressure put on parents:

> Are the Souls of your Children of no value? Are you willing that they should be
> Brands of Hell? Are you indifferent whether they be Damned or Saved? Shall the
> Devil run away with them without controul? Will not you use your utmost endeav-
> our to deliver them from the wrath to come? . . . whatever you think of them, Christ
> doth not slight them; they are not too little to dye, they are not too little to go to
> Hell.[217]

Janeway wanted parents to realize that salvation was not guaranteed for children,
impressing upon them the urgent need to instruct their offspring in religious

---

[211] D'Ewes, *The Autobiography*, vol. 2, 143–4.
[212] Josselin, *The Diary of Ralph Josselin*, 207.
[213] Hampshire Record Office, Winchester, 44M69/F6/1/2, letter number 18, no folio number
(a letter dated 26 April 1684).
[214] Turner, *De Morbis Cutaneis*, 127.
[215] Ibid. 153.
[216] Elizabeth Isham, '*My Booke of Rememenberance*': [sic] *The Autobiography of Elizabeth Isham*,
ed. Isaac Stephens; PDF file on the internet, website address: http://history.ucr.edu/people/grad_
students/stephens/TheAutobiography.pdf, [pp.] 10–11 (accessed June 2009).
[217] Janeway, *A token for children* (part 1), 'to the teachers of children'.

matters, including the preparation for death. Since the only true source of consolation for bereaved parents was the prospect of heavenly reunion, it is not surprising that they found the preparation process to be stressful. This is demonstrated in the biography of four-year-old Mary Stubbs from Norfolk: at the beginning of her sickness in the early 1680s, she 'shewed a great dislike, and would be very angry' whenever her family tried to talk to her about death. Her parents were 'discouraged' by her response, and felt 'greatly concerned for the everlasting Good and Happiness of the Soul of this their Child'.[218]

Thus far, the family's experience of care seems to have been largely negative. This may be slightly misleading, for there was also a more positive side. Most parents derived a degree of hope from the use of medicine. Remedies that 'wrought well' by purging the body were often regarded as effective, even if they did not cure the child. This was because Galenic medical theory taught that illness was caused by corrupt or unbalanced humours, and therefore would be removed by the evacuation of these fluids.[219] When Brilliana Harley's adolescent son Tom 'tooke a vomit' in 1641, she noted approvingly, it 'rought very well with him, and I hope he will be much better for it'.[220] About forty years later, Sir Thomas Browne declared that the medicine, 'Scillit', made his infant granddaughter 'very sick', and concluded it was 'a good medicine'.[221] Frequently, medicines not only 'wrought well', but were actually believed to be capable of bringing about a complete recovery. Following the 'meanes used' by the physicians in 1632, Sir Thomas Barrington noted that his daughter Lucy 'is now resonably well amended'.[222] Domestic recipe books also reveal this optimistic attitude to physic, since they regularly state that particular recipes are guaranteed to cure the illness: Bridget Hyde's 'Dyet drink for the Rickets', for example, was pronounced 'an infallible cure for the rickets'.[223] Parents from lower down the socio-economic scale shared this experience. In 1714, a wigmaker called William Clarke certified that when his child had been 'violently afflicted with Pain . . . by the Breeding of Teeth', he had used a 'famous Remedy' from the surgeon Mr Perronet, which occasioned the 'happy Preservation' of his infant.[224] The above examples seem to discredit the common historiographical assumption that people did not actually expect to be cured by their medicines.[225]

The use of prayer also inspired hope of recovery. In 1683, Oliver Heywood believed that the 'strange' illness of twelve-year-old Abraham Higson, the son of a friend, could be cured by nothing except 'fasting and prayer'.[226] In the historiography of medicine, prayer has sometimes been treated as a marginal, second-rate

---

[218] Bidbanck, *A present for children*, 43–4.

[219] Porter, *In Sickness and in Health*: 105, 266; McCray Beier, *Sufferers and Healers*, 170; Gianna Pomata, *Contracting a Cure: Patients, Healers, and the Law in Early Modern Bologna* (London and Baltimore, MD: 1998),131.

[220] Harley, *Letters of the Lady Brilliana*, 122.

[221] Browne, *The Works*, 207.

[222] Barrington, *Barrington Family Letters*, 243.

[223] WL, MS 2990, 63r ('Madam Bridget Hyde her receipt book', 1676–90).

[224] OBP, reference: a17140630-1 (accessed 14 January 2011).

[225] Beier, *Sufferers and Healers*, 5.

[226] Heywood, *The Rev. Oliver Heywood*, vol. 2, 54–6.

response to sickness.[227] This is misleading, because many people in this period believed passionately in the instrumentality of prayer. Following the death of one son and the illness of another, Mary Carey declared in 1649, 'Prayer mercies are certain mercies; they are mercies in promise, we may rely on them, they cannot fail'.[228] She drew on Biblical passages to support this conviction, including, 'If his people call, the LORD shall answer; if they cry he shall say, here I am. He is a GOD hearing prayer', and, 'Call upon me in the day of trouble, I will deliver thee. Ask what you will and it shall be done unto you'.[229] Likewise, when praying for the recovery of two young daughters from the plague in 1678, Isaac Archer called to mind the power of Christ, 'who had diseases at his command', and who had, in Luke, 'rebuke[d] the fever in Peter's wive's mother, and it left her'.[230] By this time, four of his other children had already died. The fact that these parents maintained their faith in prayer even though they had had previous experience of child death demonstrates the immense trust of some early modern Christians.

A more optimistic perspective is also provided by the evidence that parents invariably wanted to care for their sick children, and were often extremely unhappy if they were unable to do so. In 1719 Lady Elizabeth Hervey was away from home at the time of her daughter Betty's illness: she wrote to her husband telling him that she had been so 'overwhelmd [and set] . . . into such a passion of crying', that the lady with whom she was staying showed 'much tender compassion to my distress', and told her that she should 'go away to day' to see her child 'rather then . . . see me suffer so much, being truly sinceable what it was to be from a sick child'.[231] This mother implied that being absent from an ill child was a notorious cause of distress in parents, widely recognized by contemporaries. Parents also enjoyed being with their children, valuing their company in spite of illness. 'You would be much pleased with his Company', wrote Mary Verney to her husband, about their seven-year-old son Jack, who had the rickets in 1647. He 'is . . . soe fond of the name of his father and mother', she added happily.[232] Likewise, John Vernon recalled the 'very gracious converse' he had enjoyed with his ill son, twelve-year-old son Celeb, as he sat next to him wrapped 'in warm Blankets' and propped up by pillows.[233] Parents' letters abound in expressions of love for children's company. For example, Anne Dormer told her sister that her 'deare Fanny and little Clem are all the pleasure to me that two sweete natured towardly children can be'.[234]

---

[227] There are some exceptions, however, including Grell and Cunningham (eds), *Religio Medici;* Walsham, *Providence.*

[228] Mary Carey, *Meditations from the Note Book of Mary Carey, 1649–1657,* ed. Sir Francis Meynell (Westminster, 1918), 29–31.

[229] Ibid. 29–31.

[230] Luke 4:38, Archer, *Two East Anglian Diaries,* 156.

[231] Hervey, *Letter-Books,* vol. 2, 109.

[232] Verney, *The Verney Memoirs,* vol. 1, 379.

[233] Vernon, *The compleat scholler,* 40.

[234] BL, Additional MS 72516 (Trumbell papers, the letters of Anne Dormer).

CONCLUSION

The family's experience of caring for a sick child was summed up neatly by the gentleman Amyas Poulett in the 1650s: 'Wee [are] . . . imployed to the unfavouryst of employments—tending the sick with whom our house is so furnisht'.[235] Care was often exhausting, time-consuming, and costly. However, the arduous sides to care were balanced by the fact that parents and relatives had a deep-seated desire to be involved in the care of their offspring: it was clearly something they wanted to do. This devoted care demonstrates the close emotional bonds between children and their relatives, and once more challenges Lawrence Stone's interpretation of family relationships.[236]

The care of sick children was eclectic: it encompassed spiritual, social, and medical elements. Perhaps the history of early modern medicine should actually be called the history of sickness or health-care, because this way, it would include all these non-medical, and yet extremely important, elements. There is little evidence of any major change over time regarding the fundamental ingredients of children's care: prayer, domestic and 'professional' medicine, nursing, preparing for death, and sick-visiting continued throughout the centuries. Across the period, children were treated by an array of medical practitioners, from elite physicians to humble horse-smiths: laypeople were medically promiscuous.[237] Attitudes to these various practitioners were mixed: they were regarded as potentially helpful, but also fallible.

Contrary to common opinion, early modern men and women did not adhere rigidly to the prescribed spheres of masculine and feminine activity while their children were ill. During these anxious times, the boundaries delineating gender roles became blurred, and mothers, fathers, aunts, uncles, and grandfathers and grandmothers, came to one another's aid. Perhaps when faced with the desperate reality of a sick child, the niceties of gender prescriptions seemed unimportant. This finding seems to challenge the widespread view that elite and middling fathers contributed little to the actual physical care of their children.[238] Neither did gender appear to have had much impact on the experiences of the sick children themselves: it seems that families strove to provide a similar array and standard of care for all their offspring, including sons and daughters.

[235] Anon Bantock (ed.), *The Earlier Smyths of Ashton Court From their Letters, 1545–1741* (Bristol, 1982), 197.
[236] See Introduction, footnote 15.
[237] This point has been made also by Iris Ritzmann in 'Children as Patients in German-Speaking Regions in the Eighteenth Century', in Anja Müller (ed.), *Fashioning Childhood in the Eighteenth Century: Age and Identity* (Aldershot and Burlington, VT: 2006), 25–32, at 29–30.
[238] Crawford, *Parents of Poor Children*, 243.

4

'Wrackt Betwixt Hopes and Fears':
Parents' Emotions

Must my lov'd Daughter too be snatch'd away,
Must she so soon the Call of Fate obey?
Methinks I still her dying Conflict view,
And the sad Sight does all my Grief renew:
Rack'd by Convulsive Pains she meekly lies,
And gazes on me with imploring Eyes,
With Eyes which beg Relief, but all in vain,
I see, but cannot, cannot ease her Pain:
She must the Burthen unassisted bear,
I cannot with her in her Tortures share:
Wou'd they were mine, and she stood easie by;
For what one loves, sure t'were not hard to die.
See, how she labours, how she pants for Breath,
She's lovely still, she's sweet, she's sweet in Death.[1]

This chapter explores mothers' and fathers' emotional responses to the pains, sufferings, and deaths of their sons and daughters. While many historians have investigated parents' emotional responses to children's deaths, very few have focused explicitly on their experiences of illness itself.[2] It is argued that parents

[1] Mary Chudleigh, 'On the death of my dear daughter Eliza Maria Chudleigh', in her *Poems on several occasions* (1713), 95.
[2] For example, Raymond Anselment, *The Realms of Apollo: Literature and Healing in Seventeenth-Century England* (Newark, NJ and London: 1995), 49–90; Robert Woods, *Children Remembered: Responses to Untimely Death in the Past* (Liverpool: 2006); Anne Laurence 'Godly Grief: Individual Responses to Death in Seventeenth-Century Britain', in Ralph Houlbrooke (ed.), *Death, Ritual, and Bereavement* (London and New York: 1989), 66–71; Ralph Houlbrooke, *Death, Religion and the Family in England, 1480–1750* (Oxford: 1998), 234–8; Anthony Fletcher, *Growing up in England: The Experience of Childhood 1600–1914* (London and New Haven, CT: 2008), 81–93; Elizabeth Clarke, '"A Heart Terrifying Sorrow": the Deaths of Children in Seventeenth-Century Women's Manuscript Journals', in Gillian Avery and Kimberley Reynolds (eds), *Representations of Childhood Death* (Basingstoke: 2000), 65–86. The exceptions include Helena M. Wall, '"My Constant Attension on My Sick Child": The Fragility of Family Life in the World of Elizabeth Drinker', in James Alan Marten (ed.), *Children in Colonial America* (2007), 155–67; Linda Pollock, *Forgotten Children: Parent-Child Relations from 1500 to 1900* (Cambridge: 1983), 124–40; Amanda Vickery, *The Gentleman's Daughter: Women's Lives in Georgian England* (London and New Haven, CT: 2003, first publ. 1998), 117–21; Rudolf Dekker, *Childhood, Memory and Autobiography in Holland from the Golden Age to Romanticism* (Basingstoke: 1999), 26, 35; Isabelle Robin-Romero, 'L'Enfant Malade dans les Écrits Privés du XVIIIe', *Histoire Économie et Société,* 22 (2003), 469–86.

endured a mixture of torturous emotions when their children were ill or dying, including fear and hope, anxiety and guilt, and sorrow and grief. If the child showed signs of recovery, however, these sad feelings were normally superseded by perhaps the happiest of all emotions, joy and relief. Medical historians have largely overlooked this positive outcome of illness, instead dwelling on the 'universal sickness, suffering and woe' experienced by people in the past.[3] All these emotional responses, including the joy and the grief, testify to the intensity of parental love, thereby adding weight to Anthony Fletcher's assertion that 'parental . . . affection was constant, powerful, and virtually invariable' across the early modern period and beyond.[4] It is also shown that while the illnesses and deaths of children could be devastating to parents, the Christian doctrines of salvation and providence provided a measure of comfort. This cathartic side to Protestantism remained important throughout the early modern period.

An underlying theme in this chapter is gender. Historians have often implied that mothers' grief upon the deaths of children may have been more intense than the grief suffered by fathers, owing to the close maternal bond between infants and their mothers, and the contemporary assumption that women were naturally more emotional than men.[5] This chapter will suggest that these gender differences may have been overstated, agreeing with Patricia Phillippy that 'generally speaking . . . men were subject to grief as profound as their wives' at child loss'.[6] Fathers loved their children deeply, and mourned their deaths.[7] Another gender issue concerns the link between grief and the child's sex. The historiography has often suggested that sons were mourned more keenly than daughters, owing to the patriarchal values of society, and the concerns about dynasty.[8] Here, it is shown that there is little concrete evidence to support this view: the sufferings and deaths of children of both genders provoked comparable expressions of distress in parents.

---

[3] Roy and Dorothy Porter, *In Sickness and in Health: The British Experience, 1650–1850* (1988), 1–2.

[4] Fletcher, *Growing Up*, 81.

[5] Michael MacDonald, *Mystical Bedlam: Madness, Anxiety and Healing in Seventeenth-Century England* (Cambridge: 1981), 84; Margaret Angela Thomas, 'Parent-Child Relationships and Childhood Experiences: the Emotional and Physical Aspects of Care for Children in Early Modern Britain, 1640–1800' (unpubl. PhD thesis, University of Reading, 2000), 191, 194; Lucinda Becker, *Death and the Early Modern Englishwoman* (Aldershot and Burlington, VT: 2003), 138.

[6] Patricia Phillippy, ' "I Might Againe Have Been the Sepulcure": Paternal and Maternal Mourning in Early Modern England', in Jennifer Vaught (ed.), *Grief and Gender, 700–1700* (Basingstoke and New York: 2003), 197–214, at 203. Avery and Reynolds make a similar statement in, *Representations of Childhood Death*, 2.

[7] Joanne Bailey agrees about the importance of paternal love, but for the later period: 'A Very Sensible Man': Imagining Fatherhood in England, c.1750–1830', *History*, 95 (2010), 267–92.

[8] Historians who have suggested grief for sons was greater include Houlbrooke, *Death, Religion and the Family*, 234 and his article, 'Royal Grief in England, 1485–1640', *Cultural and Social History: The Journal of the Social History Society*, Special Issue: Passions and the Legitimacy of Rule from Antiquity to the Early Enlightenment, 2 (2005), 63–79, at 78; Keith Thomas, *The Ends of Life: Roads to Fulfilment in Early Modern England* (Oxford: 2009), 218.

A question that preoccupies historians of emotions is whether it is ever possible to 'capture, identify or convey affective experiences' of people in the past.[9] Fay Bound Alberti has stated that while 'we can chart and analyse the language used to describe somatic experience... we cannot access experience itself'.[10] This is because the primary sources only provide 'a series of representations *about* emotion that survive in textual form', rather than evidence of the emotions themselves.[11] Contemporaries were 'performing' their feelings in specific cultural contexts, and consequently, their emotional expressions were shaped by the conventions prevailing in these situations.[12] Contributing to the difficulty of accessing emotions is the fact that emotions are 'incoherent biological states' which 'resist... easy or adequate verbalization'.[13] Nevertheless, some scholars have taken more confident standpoints, arguing that any person articulating an emotion had to do so in a way that could be 'understood by both writer and recipient', and therefore, the representation of an emotion 'expressed a reality', even though it was 'embedded in social and cultural constructs'.[14] This chapter demonstrates that although emotions can never be accessed in an unmediated form, it is possible occasionally to catch a glimpse of the feelings of people from the past.

Before examining parents' emotional responses, it is necessary to set out how emotions were understood in the early modern period. At this time, the word 'emotion' was not used: instead, people referred to the 'passions' of the soul.[15] In 1621, F. N. Coeffeteau defined 'passion' as 'no other thing, but a motion of the sensitive appetite, caused by the apprehension or imagination of good or evill, the which is followed with a change or alteration of the body'.[16] The 'sensitive appetite' was the middle part of the human soul: it controlled the powers of perception and some of the passions.[17] By 'motions', Coeffeteau meant an actual physical movement in the body: the sensitive soul was able to detect when a situation was likely to be harmful or beneficial to the person, and respond by 'agitating' the humours of the body, sending them to various organs in order to instigate an appropriate response, such as fight or flight. The passions were therefore products of an intangible soul, and yet they themselves were understood to be physical entities,

[9] Fay Bound Alberti, 'Emotion in Early Modern England, 1660–1760: Performativity and Practice at the Church Courts of York' (unpubl. DPhil thesis, University of York, 2000), 4. See Barbara Rosenwein, 'Worrying about Emotions in History', *American Historical Review*, 107 (2002), 821–45, for a review of the historiography of emotions.
[10] Fay Bound Alberti, *Medicine, Emotion and Disease, 1700–1950* (Basingstoke and New York: 2006), p. xvii.
[11] Ibid. p. xvii.
[12] Alberti has coined the term 'performativity' to describe this process, in 'Emotion in Early Modern England'.
[13] Graham Richards, 'Emotions into Words—or Words into Emotions?', in Penelope Gouk and Helen Hills (eds), *Representing Emotions: New Connections in the Histories of Art, Music and Medicine* (Aldershot and Burlington, VT: 2005), 36–49, at 49.
[14] Lisa Smith, '"An Account of an Unaccountable Distemper": the Experience of Pain in Early Eighteenth-Century England and France', *Eighteenth-Century Studies*, 41 (2008), 459–80, at 461.
[15] See Thomas Dixon, *From Passions to Emotions: The Creation of a Secular Psychological Category* (Cambridge and New York: 2003).
[16] F. M. Coeffeteau, *A table of humane passions* (1621), 2.
[17] See p. 41 for a discussion of the human soul.

very much linked to the bodily humours.[18] Certain humours engendered particular passions, and vice versa.[19] Of crucial importance in discussions of the passions was the heart: the agitated humours would travel

> from the heart, disperse themselves throughout the ... body ... in motions of joy ... the heart melts with gladness. In ... sorrow and trouble, it shrinks up and freezeth with griefe. In those of choler ... it is inflamed and ... on fire. In those of feare, it growes pale and trembling.[20]

Thus, each emotion caused a different physical effect. In contrast with modern ideas, the passions in the early modern period were depicted as tangible liquids that flowed through the body, bringing trembling, heat, and cold. Like the humours that caused disease, the passions needed to be tempered, purged, and controlled.[21] By examining parents' emotional responses to children's illnesses, this chapter explores early modern ideas about the emotions, and investigates the ways people understood, defined, and imagined their passions. It supports Gail Kern Paster's thesis that the emotions were regarded as fluids that 'flood[ed] the body not metaphorically but literally'.[22]

The chapter is divided into three, with each part examining a different aspect of parents' experiences: children's physical suffering; the providential origin of sickness; and the anticipation and occurrence of death.

WITNESSING THE CHILD'S PAIN

One of the most obvious reactions to the sufferings of children was pity.[23] When the adolescent William Somers was 'continually torne in very fearful manner and disfigured' during his diabolical convulsions in 1596, his family were 'astonished ... with the grevyoues sight', and 'affected in the bowels of compassion towards hym'.[24] The sufferings of daughters as well as sons provoked this response: in the 1640s, the parents of eleven-year-old Margaret Muschamp could not 'look at her without compassion'.[25] Pity and compassion were commendable, unlike so many

[18] See Gail Kern Paster, *Humoring the Body: Emotions and the Shakespearean Stage* (Chicago: 2004) for an analysis of the relationship between the humours and the passions.
[19] Coeffeteau, *A table of humane passions*, 24–6.
[20] Ibid, 11–12, 16–17. See Fay Bound Alberti, *Matters of the Heart: History, Medicine, and Emotion* (Oxford: 2010).
[21] See Dixon, *From Passions to Emotions*, 25; Linda Pollock, 'Anger and the Negotiation of Relationships in Early Modern England', *The Historical Journal*, 47 (2004), 567–90; Lynda Ellen Stephenson Payne, *With Words and Knives: Learning Medical Dispassion in Early Modern England* (Aldershot: 2007), 62, 66.
[22] Kern Paster, *Humoring the Body*, 17.
[23] For a discussion of the sympathy evoked by witnessing pain, see Joanna Bourke, *Pain and the Politics of Sympathy, Historical Reflections, 1760s to 1960s: Inaugural Address* (Utrecht, 2011), 27–33.
[24] John Darrel, *A true narration of the strange and grevous vexation by the Devil, of 7. persons in Lanchashire* (1600), 19–20.
[25] Mary Moore, '"Wonderful Wonderful News from the North. Or, a true relation of the sad and grievous torments, Inflicted on the Bodies of three Children of Mr George Muschamp, late of the County of Northumberland, by witch-craft" (1650)', in Philip Almond (ed.), *Demonic Possession and*

of the other passions: they would move and 'stir up' humans 'for the service of virtue'.[26]

The spectacle of suffering evoked 'more than pity and empathy' in onlookers: it caused acute emotional pain.[27] In 1647, Ralph Verney wrote several letters to his uncle, Dr William Denton, about the long illness of his eight-year-old daughter Pegg. He lamented:

> Poore childe you doe not know what miserie she hath endured . . . she having a great deflustion in her cheeke w[hi]ch tortured her both night & day, wee searched the mouth & found the Cankers [ulcers] . . . she comonly goes to stoole 16, 18, or 20 times in 24 howors . . . w[h]ich hath brought [her] soe weake that she cannot turne her selfe in her Bed . . . But alas this is not all, [the] poore childe she suffers strangely . . . the eye lids swell very much . . . oh Dr I am so full of affliction that I can say noe more but pray for us.[28]

This extract, which exposes the harrowing realities of seventeenth-century illness, reveals the emotional devastation caused by witnessing a child in pain: Ralph Verney felt completely overwhelmed with distress—'full of affliction'. See Figure 1, page 22, for a reproduction of one of the letters. Other terms used by parents to describe their feelings include 'great grief', 'filled with care and sorrow', and 'sadness of heart'. These linguistic choices indicate that extreme passions were located in the heart, and were experienced as liquids that saturated and choked the body and soul. Contemporary definitions of the nouns 'sorrow', 'grief,' and 'affliction' referred to 'intense suffering'.[29] Unlike today, 'grief' was not associated exclusively with bereavement, but in fact, applied to any acute mental or physical pain.[30]

The distress caused by witnessing the pains of children probably transcended socio-economic divides. Patricia Crawford and Joanne Bailey have shown that poor parents experienced 'intolerable anguish' when observing the agony of offspring.[31] Although speaking in reference to hunger rather than illness, both conditions involve suffering. Popular ballads convey powerfully the distress caused by witnessing the hunger of children. *A true sence of sorrow* (1671–1702), for example, describes the plight of a poor Yorkshire father who, 'with many a Tear', confessed to his family 'I have no money to buy us Bread'. His children 'sadly made their

---

Exorcism in Early Modern England: Contemporary Texts and their Cultural Contexts (Cambridge: 2004), 363–90, at 365.

[26] Thomas Wright, *The passions of the minde* (1630, first publ. 1601), 17.

[27] Lisa Silverman, *Tortured Subjects: Pain, Truth, and the Body in Early Modern France* (Chicago and London: 2001), 149.

[28] BL, M.636/8, this manuscript is unfoliated (Verney papers on microfilm, 1646–50; letters dated 8 September to 13 October 1647).

[29] See Woods, *Children Remembered*, 173.

[30] Michael Schoenfeldt, 'Aesthetic and Anesthetics: the Art of Pain Management in Early Modern England', in van Jan Frans Dijkhuizen, and Karl A. E. Enenkel, (eds), *The Sense of Suffering: Constructions of Physical Pain in Early Modern Culture*, Yearbook for Early Modern Studies, vol. 12 (Leiden and Boston: 2008), 19–38, at 29–30.

[31] Crawford, *Parents of Poor Children*, 121; Joanne Bailey, '"Think Wot a Mother Must Feel": Parenting in English Pauper Letters, c.1760–1834', *Family & Community History*, 13 (2010), 5–19, at 12–13.

complaint, their little hands they wrung'; seeing his children's pain, he was filled with 'Grief and Care, almost Dispair'.[32]

Occasionally fathers implied that their wives' emotional distress was greater than their own. Upon hearing the 'sad groans' of his dying infant in 1669, the clergyman Isaac Archer lamented, 'Our grieffe was great, but I was better able to beare it than my deare wife'.[33] Similarly, Simonds D'Ewes noted that the absence of his wife, Anne, at the time of their two-year-old son's illness in 1636 'ministered some comfort to me, being glad that she was absent from those terrors and dolours I had been sensible of, which would even [more] have oppressed her tender heart'.[34] Men attributed their wives' greater emotional pain to the sensitivity and fragility of the female sex. Such a notion was in keeping with the contemporary association between women and emotion: it was thought that females' moist humours partially incapacitated their rational souls, leaving their passions unrestrained.[35] As the Dutch physician Levinus Lemnius asserted, 'women are subject to all passions . . . this proceeds from weaknesse of mind . . . she cannot rule her passions . . . or stand against them with force of reason and judgment'.[36] At first glance the examples above seem to confirm Michael MacDonald's assertion that 'men . . . found it easier to protect themselves from unbearable sorrow by remaining emotionally aloof from their children'.[37] However, these fathers were not denying their own sadness, for as many of the above extracts testify, the distress of both parents was profound. What is perhaps more likely, is that these men were using their diaries and autobiographies as forums for 'self-fashioning', mentioning their wives' grief as a way of constructing their own masculine identities, and reminding themselves of the necessity of manly self-control.[38] It was 'uncomly and womanish' for men to indulge in 'wommanish kinde of wayling and shricking'.[39] Thus, rather than interpreting men's comments as evidence of a difference between the intensity of maternal and paternal grief, they should be seen as manifestations of the powerful cultural pressures under which males lived during the early modern period, consequences of patriarchy.[40]

[32] *A true sence of sorrow* (1671–1702).
[33] Isaac Archer, *Two East Anglian Diaries 1641–1729*, ed. Matthew J. Storey, Suffolk Record Society, vol. 36 (Woodbridge: 1994), 120.
[34] Simonds D'Ewes, *The Autobiography and Correspondence of Sir Simonds D'Ewes, Bart.*, ed. J. O. Halliwell, 2 vols (1845), vol. 2, 145.
[35] Shepard, *Meanings of Manhood*, 76.
[36] Levinus Lemnius, *The secret miracles of nature* (1658, first publ. 1559), 273–4.
[37] MacDonald, *Mystical Bedlam*, 84.
[38] The idea of 'self-fashioning', first developed by Stephen Greenblatt, is now regularly applied in a context of gender—for example, Elizabeth Foyster, *Manhood in Early Modern England: Honour, Sex, and Marriage* (1999), 28–30, 55–8. On men and self-control see Vaught, *Masculinity and Emotion*, 2; Kern Paster, *Humoring the Body*, 79.
[39] Andreas Hyperius, *The practice of preaching* (1577), cited in Jennifer Vaught, *Masculinity and Emotion in Early Modern English Literature* (Aldershot: 2008), 2.
[40] Historians are increasingly aware that men as well as women could be 'victims of patriarchy': Alexandra Shepard, 'From Anxious Patriarchs to Refined Gentlemen? Manhood in Britain, circa 1500–1700', *Journal of British Studies*, 44 (2005), 281–95, at 283–4.

Theologians condoned fathers' expressions of grief during their children's illnesses, implying that this was one of the few contexts in which untrammelled
passion in males was permissible. In 1680, John Owen preached on 2 Samuel 12,
verses 15–23, the passage about the sickness of David's child:

> David's sorrowing for his Child when he saw it in pain . . . was but a reasonable
> passion, becoming him as . . . a Father, whose Bowels . . . must . . . move and yearn
> over a sick and languishing Child . . . he saw it restless, and tumbling up and down
> for ease . . . He saw the Child lie panting and heaving, and bemoaning it self with sighs
> and groans that were unutterable . . . how could a Father forbear weeping and making
> great Lamentations . . . Would it not melt a heart of stone, and draw tears from
> a marble to behold such a spectacle of pain and misery? And therefore David's taking
> on so heavily for his Child in time of its sickness, was very reasonable.[41]

Owen's empathetic reading of the biblical passage indicates that he saw it as entirely
justifiable for fathers (and mothers) to grieve whilst their children were suffering
pain. However, as will become apparent below, whilst theologians may have been
willing to defend the expression of grief during the child's illness, they were less
tolerant of this response after the child's death.

Certain aspects of illness were particularly distressing to parents. One was the
sound of the child's moans and cries. In 1652, eleven-year-old Martha Hatfield
contracted a disease of the spleen: her 'doleful cries' filled the 'ears of her dear
relations' with 'extram sadness', and were 'very grievous and afflictive to the spirits
of all that heard her'.[42] During the illness of his baby daughter Mary a few years
later, Isaac Archer bewailed, 'Oh what a griefe it was to mee to heare it groane, to
see it's [sic] sprightly eyes turne to mee for helpe in vaine!'[43] Parents' responses were
not affected by the child's gender or age—the cries of sons and daughters, babies
and adolescents, provoked similar expressions of grief. Another feature of illness
that was especially upsetting was the 'convulsion fit'. In 1700, Charles Trelawny
lamented that his infant 'is at this minute upon the Rack w[i]th convulsion fitts,
w[hi]ch makes the mother almost mad'.[44] So horrible was the sight of her afflicted
child this woman's mental health was affected. When the convulsions were of
a supernatural character, caused directly by Satan, parental dolour was greatly
exacerbated. In 1602, fourteen-year-old Mary Glover was diagnosed with diabolical
possession:

> Now . . . Satan appalled her senses . . . her eyes fearfully turned upward, her tongue
> black and curled inward, her countenance ugly and distorted, her mouth excessively
> wide, gaping . . . her head tossed from one shoulder to another . . . so far writhed to the
> one side . . . that I feared it would have so remained . . . At this time the Father . . .

---

[41] John Owen, *Immoderate mourning for the dead, prov'd unreasonable* (1680), 1–2, 26–9.
[42] James Fisher, *The wise virgin, or, a wonderfull narration of the hand of God . . . in afflicting a childe of eleven years of age* [Martha Hatfield] (1653), 138–41.
[43] Archer, *Two East Anglian Diaries,* 120.
[44] BL, Additional MS 28052, fol. 100r (Domestic correspondence of the Godolphin family, 1663–1782).

roared right out with abundance of tears in the disquietness of his mind and anguish of his heart.[45]

The idea that one's child had been taken over by the Devil was obviously a terrifying prospect in itself, but adding to parent's anguish was the belief that the symptoms inflicted by Satan were especially gruesome: possessed children appeared strangely disfigured, their bodies and faces transformed beyond recognition. A comparable natural distemper that caused disfigurement was the smallpox, for this disease could render the victim scarcely recognizable owing to the density of the pustules on the face.[46] 'Their faces are very full of sores', lamented Joan Thynne to her husband John in 1602. 'I can[not] without mourning look upon her', she added, about her daughter Doll.[47] Given the importance of beauty in females, it might be expected that this consequence of illness would have caused greater distress when it affected daughters, than sons.[48] However, this was not the case: Lady Elizabeth Bradshaigh complained, 'in all my life I never saw any so full . . . of the scar' as her grandson Harry. 'They will mar his pretty face', she bewailed.[49] Even more distressing than the disfigurement brought by illness, was the gradual wasting of the child's body, for this signalled that recovery was unlikely. In the 1650s, Amyas Poulett bewailed that his little nephew was 'the leanest and saddest spectacle that ever was beheld'.[50] Just how emaciated the child could become is revealed in John Vernon's account of the illness of his twelve-year-old son Caleb in 1665: after nine months of 'consumption', the boy was so thin that he was not able to endure 'so much as a Doubet or Gown upon him, his bones were so bare'. His thigh measured 'not full four inches' in circumference.[51]

As well as eliciting pity and grief, the child's symptoms and sufferings could provoke repugnance. This response was especially likely when the condition involved decomposing flesh, oozing cysts, or vomiting. In 1725, John Yorke recorded that his young nephew James, 'daily . . . throw[s] up the ulcerous humour, which is so nauseous that . . . [it] is past enduring the room . . . [James] can scarce bear the stench himself'.[52] Similarly revolting for relatives, was coming directly into contact with the bodily fluids of the child. In 1602, Mary Glover vomited

[45] John Swan, '"A True and Briefe Report, of Mary Glovers Vexation" (1603)', in Almond (ed.), *Demonic Possession*, 291–330, at 315–17.

[46] See David Shuttleton, 'A Culture of Disfigurement: Imagining Smallpox in the Long Eighteenth Century', in George Sebastian Rousseau (ed.), *Framing and Imagining Disease in Cultural History* (Basingstoke: 2003), 68–91.

[47] [Thynne], *Two Elizabethan Women: Correspondence of Joan and Maria Thynne 1575–1611*, ed. Alison D. Wall, Wiltshire Record Society, vol. 38 (Devizes: 1983), 22–3.

[48] Isobel Gundy has argued that 'smallpox discourse was gendered', in her article, 'Medical Advance and Female Fame: Inoculation and its After-Effects', *Lumen*, 13 (1994), 13–42, at 15.

[49] Sir Arthur Wynne Morgan Bryant, *Postman's Horn: An Anthology of the Family Letters of Later Seventeenth Century England* (1946, first publ. 1936), 19.

[50] Anon Bantock (ed.), *The Earlier Smyths of Ashton Court From their Letters, 1545–1741* (Bristol: 1982), 197.

[51] John Vernon, *The compleat scholler; or, a relation of the life . . . of Caleb Vernon* (1666), 39.

[52] James Clavering, *The Correspondence of Sir James Clavering*, ed. Harry Thomas Dickinson, Surtees Society, vol. 178 (Gateshead: 1967), 158–60.

'abundance of froth or foam, whereof some did light on the face of one that kneeled by, in such a way that his wife was moved to cast him her hankerchief to wipe it off'.[53] One might ask how parents coped with these disgusting elements of sickness. Lynda Payne has argued that anatomists and surgeons dealt with the 'nausea, loathing, and foetor' of their work by learning 'medical dispassion'—a term meaning emotional disengagement.[54] However, for parents it was probably their deep love for their offspring that enabled them to overcome any sense of revulsion, rather than dispassion.

When children appeared not to be in pain, or were 'patient' and did not complain, parents responded with relief. In May 1650, eight-year-old Mary Josselin was gravely ill: her father consoled himself with the thought that 'she rests free from much paine wee hope in regard shee maketh no dolour'.[55] Several decades later, Isaac Archer deduced that his five-year-old son William 'felt nothing' because he was 'senseless all the time . . . having little violent paines that we knew of'.[56] These parents were acutely aware of their children's sensation of pain, and were relieved when they could find evidence to indicate that their suffering was slight.

Closely tied to parents' appreciation of the absence of pain, was their commen-dation of the child's patient endurance of suffering. In the 1660s, Reverend Philip Henry praised his five-year-old son John for his patience: 'not a wicked word nor once taking the name of God in vain', his only complaint was 'O dear'.[57] Likewise, William Bidbanck, the author of a number of children's biographies, commended one girl of two for 'keep[ing] in her Groans' even 'in . . . her great Weakness and Pain'.[58] The reason patience elicited such positive responses was that it signified 'a voluntary yielding to what ever Afflictions *God* is pleased to inflict upon us . . . perswading us not to murmur, or repine at any thing *God does*'.[59] The acceptance of suffering without complaint was regarded as a religious virtue: it demonstrated the person's submission to God's will, which in turn was often regarded as evidence of the sick person's likely salvation after death. It is therefore understandable that parents were pleased if they could find evidence of such a response in their children.

Parental approval of patience is not, however, evidence of their disapproval of the expression of pain. Clearly, parents expected children to complain: such a response was considered entirely natural. When four-year-old Mary Stubbs expressed loathing for her pains during her illness in 1683, her family responded sympatheti-cally, saying 'no wonder, considering her violent Pain, and long Affliction'.[60] Nonetheless, when children did manage to endure pain, 'without schreekes, or

---

[53] Swan, 'A true and briefe Report', 316–17.
[54] Payne, *With Words and Knives*, 17–18, 84–7.
[55] Josselin, *The Diary of Ralph Josselin*, 203.
[56] Archer, *Two East Anglian Diaries*, 150–2.
[57] Philip Henry, *The Diaries and Letters of Philip Henry of Broad Oak, Flintshire, A. D. 1631–1696*, ed. M. H. Lee (1882), 198.
[58] William Bidbanck, *A present for children. Being a brief, but faithful account of many remarkable and excellent things utter'd by three young children* (1685), 34.
[59] Richard Allestree, *The art of patience* (1694, first publ. 1684), 2.
[60] Bidbanck, *A present for children*, 68.

sobs or sad groanes', parents obviously admired their offspring.[61] These attitudes to the expression of pain do not seem to have varied according to the sex of the child: patience in girls as well as boys was commended. Isaac Archer, for instance, praised his six-year-old daughter Frances for her patience, saying, 'She . . . did not complaine', and only said 'I would beare it if I could'.[62] Similarly, boys' complaints of pain do not appear to have elicited any censure. When thirteen-year-old Thomas Darling was heard 'gro[a]ning verie pitifully' and 'crying out' in pain in 1596, his parents did not admonish him, but rather, were 'moved' to 'commiseration and pittie, for the childes so distressed estate'.[63] This apparent parity in attitudes contradicts contemporary gender ideals, according to which males were expected to display a 'courageous endurance of physical pain', whilst girls might show greater distress, owing to their weakness.[64] Perhaps this situation arose from the understanding that children—boys as well as girls—were more sensitive to pain than adults, and therefore both sexes were permitted to complain of their pains.[65] It may not have been until the age of adolescence or young adulthood that males were subjected to the same demands for manly fortitude as adult males. This is implied in the biography of twelve-year-old Charles Bridgeman: when he was asked about his pains in 1632, he replied, 'being but a Child' they were hard to 'endure', for 'these pains may stagger a strong man'.[66] Nonetheless, when boys succeeded in withstanding pain with little complaint, parents often used gendered vocabulary in their praise, which indicates that even at a young age, the ideology of masculinity was important. The MP John Campbell commended his six-year-old son Pryce for his bravery by exclaiming, 'I am very glad you are so much a Man'.[67]

THE PROVIDENTIAL ORIGIN OF SICKNESS

'Providence' was the Christian doctrine of causation which held that God was behind all happenings on Earth, from the 'eruption of a volcano' to the 'falling of a sparrow'.[68] Although the purposes of the Almighty were always benevolent, His providences could be both negative and positive, encompassing such things as disease and famine, but also prosperity and recovery from illness.[69] The doctrine

---

[61] Josselin, *The Diary of Ralph Josselin*, 113–14.

[62] Archer, *Two East Anglian Diaries*, 160–1.

[63] I. D., *The most wonderfull and true storie, of a certain witch . . . as also a true report of the strange torments of Thomas Darling, a boy of thirteene yeres of age* (1597), 2–3, 6–7, 12.

[64] Foyster, *Manhood in Early Modern England*, 31. Similar statements are made by Roselyne Rey, *The History of Pain*, trans. Louise Elliot Wallace, J. A. Cadden, and S.W. Cadden (London and Cambridge, Mass.: 1998, first publ. 1993), 86–7; Esther Cohen, 'The Animated Pain of the Body', *American Historical Review*, 105 (2000), 36–68, at 38.

[65] See Ch. 1 for a discussion of medical ideas about children's sensitivity to pain.

[66] James Janeway, *A token for children being an exact account of the conversion, holy and exemplary lives and joyful deaths of several young children* (1671), 46.

[67] Carmarthen Record Office, Cawdor 128 (letters from John Campbell, 1733–36: no folio number: Bundle 1: John Campbell to Pryce Campbell).

[68] See Alexandra Walsham's *Providence in Early Modern England* (Oxford: 2003, first publ. 1999).

[69] John Calvin, *The Institutes of Christian Religion* (1559; first publ. 1536), 173.

was most conspicuously embraced by puritans, but as Alexandra Walsham has shown, its most basic tenets were probably shared by the unlearned laity.[70] Since the majority of the families in the sources used here were puritan, it is important to ask how this doctrine affected their emotional responses to children's illnesses. Until recently, historians have usually taken pessimistic views of the emotional impact of providence and other related Christian doctrines, arguing that they evoked feelings of guilt and 'inner loneliness' in Christians.[71] John Stachniewski asserted that many aspects of Protestantism were 'repellent' and 'punishing', creating 'incalculable... volume[s] of despair' in Christians.[72] Recently, however, scholars have offered more balanced views, demonstrating that whilst providence 'was capable of precipitating self-loathing, melancholy, and debilitating despair', it also enabled its believers to exhibit 'stoical courage and patience' in the face of misfortune.[73] The following discussion supports the latter interpretation, showing that providence was simultaneously comforting and corrosive to the morale. It also asserts that the providential view of illness endured throughout the whole of the early modern period. This is significant because scholars have sometimes argued that after the Restoration, this doctrine was invoked less frequently by contemporaries, on the grounds that it had become tainted by associations of religious enthusiasm.[74]

Arguably the most distressing response to the providential origin of children's distempers was guilt. During the illness of her daughter Frank in the 1640s, Elizabeth Egerton confessed to God, 'my poore afflicted infant... now feeles the Rodd of thy displeasure, for the sinnes of her parents'. She beseeched the Lord to 'lay not my sinnes to her innocent charge'.[75] Roughly eighty years later, Dr James Clegg regarded the fatal illness of his infant Ebenezer as 'A token' of God's 'displeasure', admitting, 'I am conscious that I have for some time past been very careless of my heart and in my conversation very loose and carnall'.[76] John Owen explained why the parent had 'a great deal of reason... to be troubled' in this way:

> [T]he sickness of his Child... being sent as a punishment for his own personal sin; and therefore when he saw it in misery and pain, and great anguish, and considered that it suffered all this principally for his sake, and that he had the greatest hand in bringing all

---

[70] Walsham, *Providence*, 2, 331.

[71] See Introduction, footnote 21 for this historiography.

[72] John Stachniewski, *The Persecutory Imagination: English Puritanism and the Literature of Religious Despair* (Oxford: 1991), 2, 5–6.

[73] Walsham, *Providence*, 20; David Harley, 'The Theology of Affliction and the Experience of Sickness in the Godly Family, 1650–1714: The Henrys and the Newcomes', in Ole Peter Grell and Andrew Cunningham (eds), *Religio Medici: Medicine and Religion in Seventeenth-Century England* (Aldershot: 1996), 273–92, at 283.

[74] See Introduction, footnote 31.

[75] BL, MS Egerton 607, pp. 131–4 ('True coppies of scertaine loose Papers left by the Right honourable Elizabeth Countesse of Bridgewater, Collected and Transcribed together here since her Death Anno Dm 1663').

[76] James Clegg, *The Diary of James Clegg of Chapel-en-Frith 1708–1755*, vol. 1 (1708–36), ed. Vanessa S. Doe, Derbyshire Record Society, vol. 5 (Matlock: 1978), 14.

this trouble and sorrow upon it . . . How could he do otherwise than lay the sickness of it to heart, and take on bitterly.[77]

Thus, the sickness of children was a punishment for parental sin: no wonder therefore, that parents felt guilt when they witnessed their child's pains. It was the duty of parents to identify the particular transgressions which had provoked God's wrath, so that they could seek forgiveness and the child's recovery. 'O that I could now be so under the correcting hand of my heavenly father', bewailed Philip Henry at the sickening of his five-year-old son John in the 1660s. '[L]ord wherefore is it that thou contendest, show mee, show mee . . . my heart bleeds, lord have mercy', he pleaded.[78] A sense of desperation pervades his words, as he wrestled with God to discover the sins that had caused his son's illness. The image of the bleeding heart conveys his great emotional pain, and confirms Gail Kern Paster's assertion that while in the 'throes of various passions' the heart was thought to undergo physical changes which 'could not be witnessed directly' but 'could be felt'.[79] Mothers as well as fathers examined their souls in this way, desirous to detect which sins were to blame. During the illness of her adolescent daughter in 1674, Elizabeth Walker beseeched the Lord to 'shew me in particular why thou contendest with me . . . give me to know . . . the forfeiting cause on my part, which mov'd thee to smite with so severe a stroke'.[80] It was not just members of the social elites who were vulnerable to guilty feelings: Patricia Crawford has predicted that among the poor, the deaths of children 'could convey a harsh reprimand for sins'.[81] This was because providentialism was 'not a marginal feature of the religious culture of early modern England, but part of the mainstream, a cluster of presuppositions which enjoyed near universal acceptance'.[82]

A great variety of sins were blamed for eliciting God's wrath. In 1646, the Countess of Warwick, Mary Rich, was 'beyond expression struck' by the illness of her three-year-old son, writing that her 'conscience told me it was for my backsliding' and neglect of 'taking after the service of God'.[83] Around the same time, Henry Newcome believed that his decision to socialize with friends one evening rather than attend to his family's spiritual welfare caused 'the Lord . . . to manifest his displeasure' through the sickening of his daughter Betty.[84] A sin commonly mentioned by parents was 'over-loving' their child: 'God . . . saw we loved it too well, and took it away; God knew how much time it stole from mee, which I ought better to have spent and so hath warned mee of my duty!' cried Isaac Archer after the death of his baby girl in 1669.[85] Other sins identified by parents were

---

[77] Owen, *Immoderate mourning*, 15–22.

[78] Henry, *The Diaries and Letters*, 198.

[79] Kern Paster, *Humoring the Body*, 12–13.

[80] Elizabeth Walker, *The vertuous wife: or, the holy life of Mrs Elizabeth Walker*, ed. Anthony Walker, (1694), 112–13.

[81] Crawford, *Parents of Poor Children*, 129.

[82] Walsham, *Providence*, 2–3, 20.

[83] Mary Rich, *Autobiography of Mary Countess of Warwick*, ed. Croker Crofton (1848), 17–18.

[84] Henry Newcome, *The Autobiography of Henry Newcome*, ed. Richard Parkinson, Chetham Society, vol. 26 (Manchester: 1852), 73–4.

[85] Archer, *Two East Anglian Diaries*, 120.

drowsiness during prayer, neglect of self-examination, and self-love.[86] The list was endless: it must have been both frustrating and terrifying to know that the slightest lapse could bring about the child's illness, and possibly death. The tendency of parents to blame themselves persisted into the eighteenth century, thus indicating that the belief in providence was deeply ingrained.

As well as being responsible for precipitating the supernatural cause of illness, parents were often blamed for the natural or secondary causes. Medical practitioners were chief among those who blamed parents, and particularly mothers. Dr Thomas Willis criticized one mother, Mrs Bodily, for having 'carelessly exposed' her little infant 'to cold air', which brought on the measles. To make matters worse, this mother was then accused of 'greatly fostering' the ailment through her 'excessive grief and sadness', which 'infected' her breast milk with 'a melancholy juice'.[87] Thus, somewhat ironically, the already distressed mother now had to blame herself for her infant's deterioration: her sense of guilt can only be imagined. This tendency to blame the mother rather than the father was a consequence of contemporary medical theories of disease causation in children: many of the causes of disease in infants were related to the mother, including her impure breast milk and menstrual blood.[88] Fathers, by contrast, were only blamed occasionally.

Nevertheless, parents themselves rarely blamed one another for children's diseases: they usually preferred to point the finger at other individuals or circumstances. In 1677, Edward Lake accused 'Mrs Chambers and Mrs Manning', his child's dry nurses, of 'struck[ing] in the humour which broke forth under his arm and at his navel, instead of putting a cole leaf to draw it out'.[89] Similarly, Simonds D'Ewes blamed his two-year-old's rickets on the bad milk of his 'proud, fretting, ill-conditioned' wet nurse.[90] The tendency of fathers to not blame their wives is indicative of the loving relationships between many couples. By dwelling on these secondary causes instead of the primary, providential cause, parents may have been able to allay their feelings of guilt. Indeed, some historians believe that this need to mitigate guilt may have been the motivation for many witchcraft accusations, since witches were convenient scapegoats for the illnesses of children.[91] When the Throckmorton girls fell sick of a strange distemper in the 1580s, their uncle was convinced that one 'Mother Samuel', a witch, was the cause. He was furious with the woman, declaring 'he hoped one day to see her burned at a stake . . . And that he himself would bring fire and wood, and the children would blow the coals'.[92] This relative may have found it more palatable to direct his anger at the witch than at the

---

[86] Ann Hulton, 'The Memoirs of Mrs Anne Hulton, Youngest Daughter of the Rev. Henry Hulton', ed. [and narrated] Matthew Henry, in Sarah Savage, *Memoirs of the Life and Character of Mrs Sarah Savage* (1821), 325–6.

[87] Thomas Willis, *Willis's Oxford Casebook (1650–52)*, ed. Kenneth Dewhurst (Oxford: 1981), 141.

[88] Disease causation is discussed in Ch. 1.

[89] Edward Lake, *Diary of Dr Edward Lake, Chaplain and Tutor to the Princesses Mary and Anne, 1677–1678*, ed. Henry Ellis, Camden Miscellanies, vol. 1 (1847), 5–31, at 15.

[90] D'Ewes, *The Autobiography*, vol. 2, 143–4.

[91] Keith Thomas, *Religion and the Decline of Magic* (1991, first publ. 1971), 648.

[92] '"The most strange and admirable discovery of the three Witches of Warboys . . . for betwitching of the five daughters of Robert Throckmorton" (1593)', in Almond (ed.), *Demonic Possession*, 75–149, at 91.

children's parents. Although in theological terms the natural and diabolical causes of illness did not cancel out the providential cause, in practice these doctrinal tenets could be overlooked.

Besides guilt, the providential origin of children's distempers sometimes caused parents to feel angry with God, or 'divinely victimized'.[93] Following the death of his little son William in 1675, Isaac Archer cried, 'How am I man of sorrowes! My troubles are multiplied upon mee! God hath written bitter things against mee, the poison of his arrows is ready to drink up my blood, and spirit'.[94] The use of exclamation marks, punctuation rarely used in Archer's diary, reflects the intensity of his feelings. His reference to the arrows of God was probably inspired by Job 6, verse 4: 'For the arrows of the Almighty are within me, the poison whereof drinketh up my spirit: the terrors of God do set themselves in array against me'. Job had uttered these words following a series of dreadful providences. Possibly, by using Job's statement, Archer was seeking to legitimize his emotions: although the Lord had criticized Job's resentment, He had pronounced him 'a perfect and upright man'.

Anger at God was especially likely when several misfortunes had occurred simultaneously or in close succession. In the space of seven years, Ralph Verney had lost his 'good and carefull parents, 2 parts of 3 of my innocent children, and my best and beloved Brother', 'and yet I thanke God I was not quite forsaken', for his much loved wife was still alive: 'But alas, what shall I now doe! For . . . I . . . am now deprived of her'. The accumulation of these tragedies made Ralph Verney feel bitter against God, lamenting 'What course shall I take to reconcile my selfe unto my Maker, & divert the Dreggs of his Fury from mee? He hath covered mee with ashes, filled mee with Bitternesse & made mee drunken with wormwood'.[95] There are fewer examples of anger in the sources than there are of guilt: this may be because guilt was seen as an appropriate, virtuous response to affliction, whereas resentment was regarded as sinful. As John Flavel noted, 'to swell with secret discontent and have hard thoughts of God . . . O this is a vile temper'.[96] Given this attitude, it is likely that parents tried to suppress their feelings of anger. Perhaps the reason even fewer mothers expressed anger than fathers was that such a response would have been incompatible with the contemporary ideology of femininity, which celebrated the qualities of meekness and patience.[97]

The emotional impact of providence was not entirely negative, however. The doctrine could also be a source of comfort, helping parents cope with the distress occasioned by the sickness or death of a child. This was because it was believed that however painful the affliction, God's purposes were always benevolent, intended for the spiritual good of the sufferer. During the sickness of her infant Robert in

---

[93] Stachniewski, *The Persecutory Imagination*, 93.
[94] Archer, *Two East Anglian Diaries*, 150–2.
[95] Frances Verney (ed.), *The Verney Memoirs, 1600–1659*, 2 vols (1925, first publ. 1892), vol. 1, 453.
[96] John Flavel, *A token for mourners* (1674), 35–6.
[97] Pollock, 'Anger and the Negotiation'.

1649, Mary Carey consoled herself with the thought, 'it is God's will . . . God is wise and knows best, God is loving and therefore did it'.[98] Roughly half a century later, Matthew Henry concluded that though his baby daughter Nancy was ill, 'It is well for . . . God . . . is neither unwise nor . . . unkind . . . that [which] Hurt doth our Souls good'.[99] Thus, parents were eased by the notion that the child's sickness was sent by a loving God, for their spiritual benefit. To make the principle of benevolent affliction understandable, theologians used the metaphor of fatherly chastisement. Richard Allestree explained, 'if we . . . know how loving and beneficical Correction [is] to our Children, how much more shall our Father which is in Heaven, [k]now how to chastise us for our Advantage?'[100] The reference to correction tapped into the entrenched cultural notion of positive pain. Parents were familiar with the idea that 'he who hateth his son spareth the rod', and sought to apply this principle to their own afflictions.[101] As Sarah Savage declared, 'God is teaching me by his rod'.[102] By regarding children's illnesses as punishments from the Lord, parents became like children: all Christians, including parents, were children of God, and in no context was this more apparent than when they were being chastised by their heavenly Father.

Providential affliction was regarded as beneficial in a number of ways. Firstly, 'Hurt weans us from the world, and makes Death and the Grave familiar to us'.[103] It was believed that without suffering, humans would grow overly attached to their earthly pleasures, and fail to give sufficient thought to God. As Winefrid Thimelby explained during the illness of her young niece Kate, 'had she health, I shuld fynd too much comfort in this world's banishment', and therefore 'God Allmigtes wisedome shynes' through her sickness.[104] The illness or death of a child was a useful means by which parents' love for heaven could be augmented, and their devotion to the earth, lessened. 'A bitter portion indeed . . . yet it was wholesome . . . for where a man's treasure is, there is his heart: now that our child is gone to heaven, our heart will be there', declared Nehemiah Wallington after the death of his three-year-old son in 1628.[105]

Providential pain could also 'awaken and reform' Christians, making them aware of their sins, and inspiring them to live more piously.[106] After the death of his baby daughter Sarah in 1713, the wigmaker Edmund Harrold wrote, 'I beg it . . . would influence me to come to an universall reformation of my life for the time to come, that I may repent, and forsake the evill of my ways, and live soberly, righteously,

[98] Mary Carey, *Meditations from the Note Book of Mary Carey, 1649–1657*, ed. Sir Francis Meynell (Westminster: 1918), 14.

[99] BL, Additional MS 42,849, fol. 27r (Henry family letters).

[100] Allestree, *The art of patience*, 14–15.

[101] Thomas Case, *Correction instruction, or a treatise of afflictions* (1653, first publ. 1652), 272–4.

[102] Savage, *Memoirs of the life*, 70–2.

[103] BL, Additional MS 42,849, fol. 27r (Henry family letters).

[104] Arthur Clifford (ed.), *Tixall Letters: or, The Correspondence of the Aston Family*, 2 vols (1815), 27.

[105] Guildhall Library, London, MS 204, pp. 421–2.

[106] Clegg, *The Diary of James Clegg*, 13.

and godily in this world'.[107] Since the child's illness was a punishment for parental sin, it made sense for them to respond in this way: they hoped that a reformed life would persuade God to recover their child. Often, parents listed the improvements that they would make to their lives, hoping to bargain with God for the child's preservation. James Clegg resolved to 'Be more . . . bent against all sin . . . more diligent in reading, studying, praying and writing . . . more loving and peaceable meek and patient in my behaviour to my wife'.[108]

Another purpose of affliction was to refine the sufferers' faith 'as gold is tried in the furnace'.[109] In the 1620s, Nehemiah Wallington declared, 'God doeth prove and trieth us whither wee will sticke as fast to him in adversity as in properity'.[110] The most famous Biblical story about the trial of faith was the story of Job. This man, who 'feareth God, and escheweth evil', was afflicted in numerous ways by God: his children were killed, his cattle burned, and his body covered in boils. These afflictions were sent by God as a test, to prove to Satan that Job would not 'curse to thy face' as soon as he was 'touched' by the Lord's hand.[111] Parents commonly cited this scriptural passage at their child's death. Upon the 'sad newes' of his 'litle girle's death' in 1682, Isaac Archer sought desperately to 'Remember Job's case!' He declared, 'the Lord vouchsafe to try me, like Job, to see my patience and constancy!'[112] By regarding children's illnesses as tests of faith rather than punishments for sin, parents were aligning themselves with Job, thereby elevating their own moral statuses, and displacing guilt.

Taken together, the purposes of affliction outlined above were thought to improve the Christian's soteriological chances. In 1695, Ann Hulton wrote that 'God hath of late been proving and trying me' by taking away her nine-day-old infant, 'to do me good in my latter end'.[113] Through reference to her 'latter end', Hulton was implying that her earthly suffering would impact on her salvation. This notion was not endorsed in orthodox Protestant theology: the doctrine of predestination held that no matter how religiously a person lived, or how much they were afflicted, their eternal destiny was already decided by the Almighty.[114] Nonetheless, in practice, people hoped that they could influence their eternal future.

One reason why providentialism has been interpreted so negatively in the historiography is that historians have focused on people's responses to afflictive providences. This is rather misleading, because life encompassed joys as well as sorrows, was 'checquered with . . . mercies and miseries'.[115] When the Almighty

---

[107] Edmund Harrold, *The Diary of Edmund Harrold, Wigmaker of Manchester 1712–15*, ed. Craig Horner (Aldershot: 2009), 67.

[108] Clegg, *The Diary of James Clegg*, 13–14.

[109] Case, *Correction instruction*, 49–50.

[110] Guildhall Library, London, MS 204, p. 209.

[111] Job 1:1, 11 (KJV); the full story of Job is told in Job 1–42.

[112] Archer, *Two East Anglian Diaries*, 166–7.

[113] Hulton, 'The Memoirs of Mrs Anne Hulton', 291.

[114] Dewey D. Wallace, *Jr, Puritans and Predestination: Grace in English Protestant Theology, 1525–1695* (North Carolina: 1982), 6.

[115] Adam Martindale, *The Life of Adam Martindale*, ed. Richard Parkinson, Chetham Society, vol. 4 (Manchester: 1845), 217.

sent positive providences ('mercies'), people responded with joy, since these divine interventions demonstrated God's love. Such happy responses were particularly evident in the context of children's recoveries from illnesses. Alice Thornton wrote, 'oh that our hearts weare inlarged in thankfullnesse to the great Lord our God for the preservation' of her fourteen-year-old daughter Nally.[116] Thus, happy as well as sad emotions were located in the heart, and were thought to have physical effects. The divine recovery of children served to bolster parents' faith in prayer. In 1675, Elizabeth Mordaunt 'Praise[d] the Lord...for his mercy...he hathe not refused the request of my Lipes, but hathe herd, and granted [my] humble desir[e]'.[117] God's 'special deliverances' were cherished because they revealed the more compassionate side to their deity's character. Lady Russell declared, 'It hath pleased the Author of all Mercies to give us some glimpse and ray of his compassions in this dark day of my calamity [with] the child beeing exceedingly better'.[118] Such instances of mercy improved parents' relationships with God, sparking feelings of love.

THE ANTICIPATION AND OCCURRENCE OF DEATH

For those unfortunate parents who had already experienced child loss, fears of death were often triggered by the onset of the illness. In 1681, Isaac Archer lamented, 'every litle illnes makes us feare the worst, having had so many instances of God's severity'.[119] Six of Archer's eight children had died. For other parents, it was the violence of the symptoms that presaged death. In 1648, Jane Josselin became convinced that her baby Ralph would die because 'the sicknes was very strong' and 'it was a very sicke child indeed'.[120] Parents also looked out for more specific symptoms of death. Philip Henry recorded the 'intermittent pulse, blacknes of nayles' and 'shortnes of breath' of his five-year-old son John, acknowledging that these were 'many symptoms of Death'.[121] Especially frightening was the movement of the eyes during death: Nehemiah Wallington recorded that his son John did 'cast up the white of his eyes much like one that is dying which was very wofull to the Father and Mother and the rest of the beholders'.[122] Laypeople identified the same signs of death that were mentioned in learned medical treatises.[123] Lower down the social scale, parents also seem to have known when their children were dying. A deposition from the Northern Assizes in 1656 states that a beggar

---

[116] Alice Thornton, *The Autobiography of Mrs Alice Thornton*, ed. Charles Jackson, Surtees Society, vol. 62 (1875), 158–9.

[117] Elizabeth Mordaunt, *The Private Diarie of Elizabeth Viscountess Mordaunt* (Duncairn: 1856), 171–2.

[118] Rachael Wriothesley Russell, *Letters of Rachel, Lady Russell*, 2 vols (1853, first publ. 1773), vol. 1, 140.

[119] Archer, *Two East Anglian Diaries*, 164.

[120] Josselin, *The Diary of Ralph Josselin*, 112–14.

[121] Henry, *The Diaries and Letters*, 198.

[122] Guildhall Library, London, MS 204, p. 406.

[123] See Francis Bacon, *Historie naturall and experimentall, of life and death* (1638), 344–69.

woman from West Riding, Katherine Tabott, suspected that her ill child 'was not like[ely] to live one hour [more]'. She was proved correct, for the infant died shortly afterwards.[124] The poor may have been especially familiar with the signs of death, due to the higher rates of mortality.

While there were still signs that the child might recover, parents expressed hopes mixed with fears. In 1601, Joan Thynne told her husband John that their daughter, Doll, 'is much better than she was, but not yet well . . . I fear the worse but I hope the best'.[125] Sixty years later, Philip Henry recorded that he was 'full of cares & fears' for his 'dear Child', feeling 'betw[een] hope & fear'.[126] The experience of these emotions could be agonizing: Abigail Harley told her husband that she was 'wrackt between hop[e]s and fears' for her infant Brian.[127] The reference to the rack conveys the horrible sensation of these emotions: parents felt as though their minds were being stretched between the dichotomous passions of hope and fear. In early modern philosophy these two emotions were defined in relation to one another, since they were regarded as polar opposites.[128] Whereas hope 'tends always to that which is good', fear 'hath for the object the evill wherewith man is threatned'.[129] These passions were inextricably linked: one could not be felt without the other, for '*Hope* is always mixt with some feare, by reason of the obstacles which present themselves, and may hinder mans enjoying of the good hee hopes for'.[130]

When death finally arrived, parents experienced intense emotional pain or 'grief'. Grief was defined as '*a violent* passion *of the Soule, entertained by some sensible discontent . . . a torment of the mind*'.[131] As has already been noted, grief was not an emotion exclusively associated with bereavement: it referred to any extreme emotional (or physical) suffering. Nonetheless, it did carry strong connotations of loss and mourning, which indicates that it was linked particularly with death.[132] The nature and expression of grief seems to have gradually altered as time elapsed after the child's death: an analysis of these 'stages of grief' will provide further insights into parents' emotional experiences, while also revealing more about the meanings of the passions in the early modern period.

Grief and bereavement began when parents realized their child was dying. 'I went to my bed at night, but was raised up with the dolour of my wife, that Mary was dying', wrote Ralph Josselin, about his eight-year-old daughter.[133] Historians have commented on this tendency for grief to begin before the person had died: Lucinda Becker has termed this phase 'pre-mourning'.[134] So upsetting

---

[124] Cited by Patricia Crawford and Laura Gowing (eds), *Women's Worlds in Seventeenth-Century England: A Sourcebook* (2000), 118–19.
[125] [Thynne], *Two Elizabethan Women*, 19.
[126] Henry, *The Diaries and Letters*, 256.
[127] BL, Additional MS 70115, this manuscript is unfoliated (Harley papers).
[128] Coeffeteau, *A table of humane passions*, 514–15.
[129] Ibid. 515, 524.
[130] Ibid. 517.
[131] Coeffeteau, *A table of humane passions*, 318–19.
[132] One of the definitions given by the OED Online is 'Deep or violent sorrow, caused by loss'.
[133] Josselin, *The Diary of Ralph Josselin*, 202.
[134] Becker, *Death and the Early Modern Englishwoman*, 137.

was the sight of the dying child, the image often became forever seared on the parent's memory. 'Remember dying looks and parting sigh', bewailed James Clegg at the death of his twelve-year-old daughter Margaret in 1723.[135] This initial grief was often expressed through tears rather than words: when John Vernon observed his twelve-year-old son's 'alteration in countenance', he 'gushed out into tears', sensing that death was imminent.[136]

The next stage of grief occurred in the minutes, hours, and days after the child's death, and was labelled 'distraction' by contemporaries. In 1647, Mary Verney lost two children in close succession, eight-year-old Pegg and baby Ralph. At this time, Mary was living apart from her family: her husband had moved temporarily to France with their children, to avoid certain punitive measures that had been imposed on the Verneys by parliament in the Civil War. Mary was in the middle of writing to her husband when she heard about her children's deaths. The surviving letter provides an exceptionally rare, and heartrending insight into the experience of early grief. She wrote, 'Since I writt this, I have received the sad nues of toe of our deare chilldrens death, which affliction Joyned with being absent from thee is without Gods great Marcy to me a heavier burthen then can be borne by thine

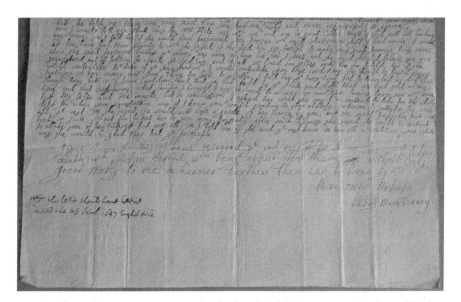

Fig 6. A letter from Mary Verney to her husband Ralph Verney, 28 October 1647; by kind permission of Sir Edmund Verney, and with the assistance of the archivist, Mrs Sue Baxter.

---

[135] Clegg, *The Diary of James Clegg*, 20.
[136] Vernon, *The compleat scholler*, 73.

owne unhappy Mary'.[137] The handwriting, rather than the words, conveys her extreme torment: it changes from its neat, small italic style, to a larger scrawl (see **Figure 6**). A member of Mary's household reported that the tragic news 'did much afflict and distract her, soe that she spake idly for two nights and sometimes did not know her frends'.[138]

Fathers as well as mothers experienced distracted grief. Nehemiah Wallington admitted that he was 'much disstrackted in my mind and could not be comforted', at the death of his three-year-old daughter Elizabeth from the plague in 1625.[139] 'Distraction' was a form of grief that verged on mental illness: it was characterized by periods of delirium, weeping, and sighing. When Simonds D'Ewes' baby son 'had given up the ghost', he 'could not refrain from many tears, sighs and mournings', while his wife 'instantly fell a-shaking, and scarce being able to speak in respect of the abundance of tears that issued from her intermixed with many sobs'.[140] Early modern physicians believed that weeping had 'a deeply therapeutic function':[141]

> Tears...disperse heavinesse: yea wee finde many times in our bitterest griefes, that teares diminish our paine, and mollifie our miseries...when wee powre forth teares, we cast out that which afflicts us, & emptying the humor which oppresseth us.[142]

Tears were thus associated both with the humours and the passions, providing a link between the spheres of body and mind: like the humours that caused bodily disease, the emotions needed to be purged.[143] During this stage of distracted grief, parents often found it difficult to speak, think, or engage in any activity. Immediately after the death of the aforementioned Pegg, Mary Verney told her husband, 'My dearest hart, I was in soe much affliction for the losse of my deare children... that I was nott in a condition to wright or doe anthing elce and truly att present I am soe weake that I am scarse able to goe upp and downe my chamber'.[144] Contemporaries were familiar with the debilitating nature of grief: they attributed it to the fact that 'all the powers of our soule' were 'busied in the functions' of this passion, so that the soul 'cannot attend any thing else'.[145]

In the weeks and months following the death, the initial 'distraction' seems to have been gradually superseded by a more composed, but equally unbearable sadness. These feelings could be so painful that parents found it difficult to imagine emotions of a more unbearable nature. 'I am nott able to say one word more but that at this time there is nott a sadder creature in the world than thine

---

[137] MS 636/8, this manuscript is unfoliated (Verney papers on microfilm, 1646–50, a letter dated 28 October 1647).

[138] Verney (ed.), *The Verney Memoirs,* vol. 1, 382.

[139] Guildhall Library, London, MS 204, p. 209.

[140] D'Ewes, *The Autobiography,* vol. 2, 45–6, 147.

[141] Schoenfeldt, 'The Art of Pain Management', 34.

[142] Coeffeteau, *A table of humane passions,* 348–9.

[143] See Tom Lutz, *Crying: the Natural and Cultural History of Tears* (New York: 1999).

[144] Verney (ed.), *The Verney Memoirs,* vol. 1, 382.

[145] Coeffeteau, *A table of humane passions,* 330–1.

owne Deare M', wrote Mary Verney to her husband a month after the death of her two children.[146] Following the death of his two-year-old in 1636, Simonds D'Ewes declared, 'myself and my dear wife [are] the saddest and most disconsolate parents that ever lost so tender and sweet an infant'.[147] The powerful sadness occasionally sparked suicidal feelings in parents. Mary Carey's 'heart-terrifying' sorrow caused her to have 'some hideous temptation' after the death of her children.[148] Siblings may have also experienced these temptations: after the death of seven-year-old John Martindale in 1659, his sister Mary 'seemed utterly to despise life, and would frequently talk of heaven and being buried by him'.[149] The intensity of grief led many parents to suppose that their physical or mental health would be affected.[150] Learned authors propagated the notion that grief could affect the body: 'grief... doth... produce fearefull effects upon our bodies: for that it is a malign, colde and dry Passion, which... consumes our forces, causeth our heart to languish, and makes our life short, but extreamly miserable'.[151] To ease their emotional pain, parents tried to verbalize their feelings, hoping that this would purge their minds and bodies of some of their grief. 'I am soe full of griefe... that I must needes vent some part of it to thee', wrote Ralph Verney to his wife two months after their children's deaths.[152] Words thus functioned in a similar way to tears, providing a release to the painful passions.[153]

In the months and years following the child's death, parental sorrow often persisted, though it may have lost some of its sharpness. Three years after the death of their son John Brockbank, his parents were still 'mightily broke'. The grandfather informed the dead boy's brother Thomas 'you wo'd scarce know your dear Mother if You saw her', implying that her grief had produced an ageing effect.[154] Certain situations could rekindle the painful remembrances. The Verney parents were asked if they could look after a friend's little girl: Mary replied, 'Since itt has pleased god to take away... my deare gerle' Pegg, 'I cannot have patience to lett any Bodies elces [daughter] dwell with me[,] for the sight of them in my owne howse would butt make my wound dayly bleed afresh'.[155] Her husband agreed, saying 'It would renew your griefe, and breake my hart, for I confesse noe creature knew how much you loved that poore childe'.[156] As well as revealing the mutual

---

[146] Verney (ed.), *The Verney Memoirs*, vol. 1, 384.

[147] D'Ewes, *The Autobiography*, vol. 2, 108.

[148] Carey, *Meditations from the Note Book*, 31–2.

[149] Martindale, *The Life of Adam Martindale*, 108–9.

[150] See MacDonald, *Mystical Bedlam*, 72–3.

[151] Coeffeteau, *A table of humane passions*, 332–3.

[152] Verney (ed.), *The Verney Memoirs*, vol. 1, 385.

[153] See Michael Schoenfeldt, '"Give Sorrow Words": Emotional Loss and the Articulation of Temperament in Early Modern England', in B. Dufallo and P. McCracken (eds), *Dead Lovers: Erotic Bonds and the Study of Premodern Europe* (Ann Arbor, MI: 2007), 143–64.

[154] Thomas Brockbank, *The Diary and Letter Book of the Rev. Thomas Brockbank 1671–1709*, ed. Richard Trappes-Lomax, Chetham Society New Series, vol. 89 (Manchester: 1930), 12.

[155] BL, M.636, this manuscript is unfoliated (Verney papers on microfilm, 1646–50, a letter dated 18 November 1647).

[156] Verney (ed.), *The Verney Memoirs*, vol. 1, 395.

love and understanding between this couple, the images of the bleeding and broken hearts confirm the idea that the passions were thought to be tangible liquids which seeped from the heart. Sometimes, parents felt they would never be entirely free from sadness: 'she never much enjoyed herself [again] since the death of her eldest daughter', lamented Ann Fanshawe about her grieving sister.[157] Fathers' grief could be equally enduring. 'Here ends the joy of my life, & for which I go even mourning to the grave', bewailed John Evelyn after the decease of his five-year-old son Richard in 1658.[158]

Both mothers and fathers experienced profound grief upon the deaths of their children. Indeed, parents themselves often believed their emotional distress was of equal intensity. Robert Sidney told his wife, 'your grief must be as much as mine' after the death of his daughter Philipa.[159] Conduct literature expected men as well as women to feel great sadness in this context: one writer stated that 'to barre' the father 'from lamenting & sorrowing...were as unreasonable, as to chide a *Man,* for shewing himselfe sensible when a Tooth is drawne...And therefore I blame you not to melt, yea, to ake, and to be sore of such a wound' as the death of a child.[160] However, whilst the intensity of the feelings may have been the same for both parents, the extent to which they expressed these emotions sometimes did vary. 'I found my dear wife in tears and lamentations', began Simonds D'Ewes after the death of his twin boys in 1633. 'And though I were struck with a sad apprehension of mine own extream losses...yet I comforted her [his wife, Anne] what I might, and concealed part of my grief and disconsolation from her', he stated.[161] Three years later, D'Ewes suffered the loss of another son, and wrote that 'I being desirous to minister comfort' to his wife, 'I suppressed the outward expression of mine own grief, and used the best arguments I had to mould and frame her to patience and moderation'.[162] Thus, although this man did not believe that his grief was less profound than his wife's, he tried to restrain his expressions of sadness. It would be all too easy to ignore this distinction between the expression and feeling of grief, interpreting evidence of men's emotional control as proof of less intense feelings. These extracts indicate that people thought it possible to temper the passions, confirming Linda Pollock's assertion that emotions could be 'elicited and regulated...provoked or silenced, moderated or enhanced'.[163] D'Ewes was not alone in his attempts to moderate his wife's grief: after the death of two children in 1687 Symon Patrick wrote that although it was 'the saddest day my wife and I ever saw', 'I upheld and comforted

---

[157] Ann Fanshawe, *Memoirs of Lady Fanshawe,* ed. Richard Fanshawe (1829), 303.

[158] John Evelyn, *John Evelyn's Diary: A Selection,* ed. Philip Francis (1963), 388.

[159] Robert Sidney, *Domestic Politics and Family Absence: The Correspondence (1588–1621) of Robert Sidney, First Earl of Leicester, and Barbara Gamage Sidney,* eds Margaret P. Hannay, Noel J. Kinnamon, and Michael G. Brennan (Aldershot: 2005), 227.

[160] *A handkercher for parents wet eyes, upon the death of children* (1630), 1–2, 7.

[161] D'Ewes, *The Autobiography,* vol. 2, 88–90.

[162] Ibid. vol. 2, 147.

[163] Pollock, 'Anger and the Negotiation', 589.

her' (his wife), who was 'overcome with grief'.[164] Perhaps fathers acted in this way because they believed women needed more help in controlling their passions than men. This was implied by John Owen in 1680:

> Men being always accounted the more hardy and invulnerable, are less liable to the impressions of sorrow then Women, whose very constitution does give a lift and advantage to their Passions; for being weaker Vessels they cannot well contain their resentments, and support their spirits in affliction, as those that are stronger.[165]

As was suggested earlier, fathers may have made these statements because they were trying to remind themselves of the need for rational control—a crucial attribute in males.[166] They were engaged in a process of gender construction.[167]

Nevertheless, this gender difference should not be overstated: some mothers believed that they were better at controlling their grief than their husbands. When her three-year-old daughter died of the plague in 1625, Grace Wallington admonished her husband for his 'grieeving for this childe so much', and warned him that 'you offend God'.[168] Similarly, when Mary Rich's son Charles died in 1662, she noted that she was 'enabled from above with some degree of patience, that I did endeavour to comfort my sad and afflicted husband, who, at the news of his death . . . cried out so terribly that his cry was heard a great way'.[169] At another time, after the death of their baby daughter Elizabeth, this mother admitted 'I was much afflicted; but my husband as passionately so ever I saw him; he being most exceedingly fond of her'.[170] These examples indicate that fathers grieved for both daughters and sons.

An examination of the circumstances that exacerbated parents' grief provides insights into the nature of family relationships. Firstly, the absence of one's spouse seemed to heighten parental distress. In 1685, Elizabeth Freke's seven-year-old son was 'like to dye' from the smallpox: she complained that 'to [add] to my great torture and distraction, Mr Frek [is] all the while in Ireland from me'.[171] After the deaths of children, couples craved one another's support, and its absence was sorely missed. Mary Verney told her husband that the 'affliction' of her children's deaths, 'joined with being absent from thee is . . . a heavier burthen then can be borne'.[172]

Grief was also worse when the sick or deceased child had been the only living child. The death of two-year-old Anne 'would have been the greater trouble unto us

---

[164] Symon Patrick, 'A Brief Account of My Life with a Thankful Remembrance of God's Mercies to Me', in J. H. Parker (ed.), *The Works of Symon Patrick in Nine Volumes* (Oxford, 1858), vol. 9, 407–569, at 507–8.

[165] Owen, *Immoderate mourning*, message to the reader.

[166] Foyster, *Manhood in Early Modern England*, 29–30.

[167] Gender construction in males is an increasingly popular subject—see, for example, Tim Hitchcock and Michele Cohen (eds), *English Masculinities 1660–1800* (1999), and Foyster, *Manhood in Early Modern England*, 28–54.

[168] Guildhall Library, London, MS 204, p. 409.

[169] Mary Rich, *Autobiography of Mary Countess of Warwick*, 30–1.

[170] Ibid. 17.

[171] Elizabeth Freke, *The Remembrances of Elizabeth Freke*, ed. Raymond Anselment, Camden Fifth Series, vol. 18 (Cambridge: 2001), 54–5.

[172] Verney (ed.), *The Verney Memoirs*, vol. 1, 382.

because she was at this time our only child', wrote Simonds D'Ewes in 1632.[173] Parents were especially loath to part from sole children because they had formed extremely close bonds with them. The deaths of only sons were also particularly 'sore trials' for parents: Nehemiah Wallington lamented that the death of his 'sweete sonne' in 1628 was 'A bitter portion indeed', because this child was 'an onely sonne'.[174] Contemporaries often assumed that the death of a son would be 'a very great affliction' for fathers in particular, as 'A Son . . . continues the [family] name, and supports the family'.[175] This seems to have been the case for William Thornton in 1660: his wife reported that he was 'soe afflicted' by the death of 'deare Willy', and added 'beeing an [only] son he takes it more heavily'.[176] However, only daughters were also subjects of special grief: in 1613 the London clergyman William Gouge bewailed, 'My sweetest child, mine only daughter, is gone', after the death of his little girl.[177] Thus, it seems that grief was exacerbated by the uniqueness of the child's status within the family, rather than its sex in general. This seems to challenge the view that 'husbands preferred boys to girls'.[178]

Occasionally, the deaths of older children elicited more distress than those of babies.[179] 'We both found the sorrow for the loss of this child', two-year-old Clopton, 'on whom we had bestowed so much care and affection . . . far . . . surpassed our grief for the disease of his three . . . brothers, who, dying almost as soon as they were born, were not so endeared to us as this was', confessed Simonds D'Ewes in 1636. The longer children live, the more 'deeply imprinted in our hearts' they become, he explained.[180] However, this heightened suffering at the decease of an older child does not mean that parental sorrow at the loss of infants was insubstantial—many parents expressed acute sadness at these times.[181] The idea that the intensity of grief was sometimes affected by the child's age or gender status may seem to contradict my earlier assertion that when the child was suffering pain, parental distress was the same for all their offspring. However, these conclusions are not incompatible: the circumstances provoking parental grief—pain and death—were different, and therefore it is reasonable that parents' emotional responses differed.

The occurrence of multiple illnesses and deaths within the family also augmented parents' grief. When fourteen-year-old Sarah Howley lay dying in 1670, her mother cried, 'how shall I bear parting with thee, when I have scarce dried my eyes for thy Brothers[?]'[182] Fathers as well as mothers were affected by these multiple

---

[173] D'Ewes, *The Autobiography*, vol. 2, 67.

[174] Guildhall Library, London, MS 204, p. 421.

[175] John Flavel, *A token for mourners* (1674), 3.

[176] Thornton, *The Autobiography*, 126.

[177] Cited by Fletcher in *Growing Up*, 87.

[178] Ingrid Tague, 'Aristocratic Women and Ideas of Family in the Early Eighteenth Century', in Helen Berry and Elizabeth Foyster (eds), *The Family in Early Modern England* (Cambridge and New York: 2007), 184–208, at 195.

[179] This has been suggested by Houlbrooke, *Death, Religion and the Family*, 234–6; Fletcher, *Growing Up*, 81–4, 86.

[180] D'Ewes, *The Autobiography*, vol. 2, 147.

[181] Anselment, *The Realms of Apollo*, 65.

[182] *An account of the admirable conversion of one Sarah Howley, a child of eight or nine years old* (Edinburgh: 1704), 7.

deaths. In 1658, George Purefoy complained that he had had 'dailye neewe causes of sorrowes' which 'succeed[ed] one another soe fast wee . . . [are in] soe sadd estate': in the course of only a week, his 'good sonne Hales' had died, his daughter Nell was 'dangerously sicke', and 'little George . . . is falne sicke'.[183] These 'sorrows upon sorrows' brought parents close to breaking point, threatening their health and their religious faith. After the death of two children 'in small space' in 1679, Isaac Archer admitted that his 'confidence was dashed, and God is unaccountable for what he doth'. He exclaimed that the 'double stroake' was so afflicting to his wife Anne that 'it might have killed her!'[184] Isaac's own father, a minister, had undergone a similar experience in 1648: he had lost his wife, daughter, and youngest son: the 'treble losse so grieved my father that he could take no rest at home, nor preach, but rode up and downe [on horseback] to find comfort'.[185]

How did poorer mothers and fathers respond to the deaths of their offspring? Until recently, historians have painted unfavourable pictures of poor parents, even suggesting that they may have welcomed the deaths of their children, as a way of escaping the costs of parenthood.[186] Such an interpretation probably derives from contemporary observations. M. Underwood, for instance, declared that the poor 'express great thankfulness, when any of their Children died'.[187] However, Patricia Crawford has argued that parents' feelings were 'far more complex and ambivalent', involving 'grief at their wasted efforts to sustain a child's fragile life, and relief that there was one less mouth to be fed'.[188] While 'we lack first-person statements from [the] poor . . . about their grief . . . we should not assume indifference', she warns. In particular, mothers 'may have been deeply disturbed by the deaths of children', even to the extent that they believed themselves insane.[189]

Popular ballads about child death contain powerful expressions of poor parents' grief. *A wonderful prophesie* (1684–86) describes the reaction of a humble Cornish couple to the death of their daughter Christian James:

> Her aged father did lament,
> her mother did shed many a tear,
> she wep't, she waild, she wrung her hands,
> for loss of this her Daughter dear:
> Alas, alas my child she said,
> how dearly I have tendered thee,
> and wilt thou now forsake the world,
> and leave me in this misery.
> I would my birth have been my death,
> then never had I seen this day,

---

[183] Hampshire Record Office, Winchester, 44M69/F5/2/2, this manuscript is unfoliated (Jervoise letters).

[184] Archer, *Two East Anglian Diaries*, 159–61.

[185] Ibid. 47.

[186] Stone, *Family, Sex and Marriage*, 65.

[187] M. Underwood, *A treatise of the disorders of children* (1797), vol. 3, 121, cited by Crawford, *Parents of Poor Children*, 129.

[188] Ibid. (Crawford), 129.

[189] Ibid. 187, 189.

this grievous moan the mother made.[190]

This mournful outpouring conveys succinctly the dolour of a grieving mother, and is strikingly similar in tone to the expressions of elite parents above. Of course, we cannot be sure that the ballad was based on a real event—as historians have cautioned, the 'boundary between fiction and fact...remains very vague' in these texts.[191] Nevertheless, it was probably necessary for authors to write about subjects in such a way as would have been deemed acceptable to consumers of all social levels, and therefore it seems likely that grief was seen as a plausible response among the poor, and one with which most people could empathize.[192] Ballads about child murder also provide clues into parents' attitudes to the deaths of their children. *The childrens cryes* (1696) is about a lowly gravedigger who killed his son. It describes the reaction of the boy's mother:

> Now for to see the Mother of this Lad,
> How destracted she's run since he is dead;
> Cruel hearts must shed tears
> To see her in dispair,
> Raving and pull her hair for her dead son.[193]

Admittedly, the story is about murder rather than illness, but it does offer insights into cultural ideas about grief: the woman in this ballad is experiencing 'distracted grief', the early stage of mourning examined earlier. Although it is maternal grief which features most prominently in the above examples, fathers were not depicted as immune to sorrow. In *A lamentable ballad* (1686–88), it is chiefly the father who mourns the death of his two murdered infants: he begs the killer to spare his children's lives, and even cuts off his own nose in an attempt to make a bargain with the murderer. Seeing the bodies of his murdered children 'made the Father wring his hands and grievously to weep'.[194] Newspaper advertisements for medicines also indicate that grief was experienced by both sexes. An advertisement from 1717 states that the alehouse keepers Charles and Mary Pearce 'thought and expected in Sorrow and Tears' their baby's death because he was 'so very ill'.[195] These parents seem to have been experiencing the 'pre-mourning' stage of grief, identified earlier.

What did parents miss about their deceased children? An examination of the qualities that were eulogized and pined over by parents and relatives sheds light on the nature of family relationships, and provides opportunities for a comparison between contemporary notions of ideal boyhood and girlhood.[196] Firstly, parents missed the physical presence of the child. In 1678, the mother of six-year-old Joseph Scholding 'took up his Fingers' and said, 'These Fingers will not be long

---

[190] *A wonderful prophesie* (1684–86).
[191] Walsham, *Providence*, 41.
[192] See Introduction, p. 27.
[193] *The childrens cryes* (1696).
[194] *A lamentable ballad of the tragical end of a gallant lord* (1686–88).
[195] OBP, reference: a17170117-1 (accessed 14 January 2011).
[196] For discussions of memorialization, see Woods, *Children Remembered*.

here'.[197] The idea that the child's body would become lifeless, and eventually decompose, was unbearable.[198] Linked to their physical presence, parents remembered the child's beauty. At the death of Sarah Disney in the 1640s, her family wrote, 'She was esteemed one of the beautifullest Children that ever was seen, her Hair being Milk white, and Complexion pure white and red'.[199] Somewhat surprisingly, the beauty of boys was mentioned almost as regularly as the attractiveness of girls. When young Richard Cholmley died, his father recorded, 'He was much fairer and more beautifull then other my brood for his haire was amber couller his eies gray and his complction as fayre white and red as ever I saw'.[200] The fact that similar features of beauty were identified in girls and boys indicates that notions of attractiveness in childhood were not necessarily gendered.

Parents longed for their child's company. 'Oh such a Child and Comrad as she hath been!', cried the mother of ten-year-old Christian Karr after her death in 1702.[201] Sometimes parents missed specific interactions with their children. The father of four-year-old Samuel Disney had taken 'much delight' in his son's 'pretty Talk', and remembered nostalgically 'walking Hours' in the garden chatting about all sorts of things.[202] In the case of older children, it was often their companionship that parents grieved over: when nine-year-old Ann Fanshawe died in 1654, her mother lamented the loss of 'the dear companion of my travels and sorrows', implying that her daughter had been her confidante.[203] The idea that parents regarded their children as friends suggests that parent–child relationships were not always as rigidly hierarchical as has been assumed by scholars. By contrast, younger children and infants were more likely to be missed for their affection and emotional dependence. Elizabeth Egerton recalled that two-year-old Kate had taken 'delight in nothing but me . . . never was there so fonde a child of a mother'.[204]

Another attribute eulogized by parents was the child's intellect. Young Samuel Disney was 'a Child of most pregnant Parts . . . extraordinarily Inquisitive, and would usually demand a Reason for every Thing'.[205] We might expect these qualities to have been celebrated more in sons than daughters, because intelligence was associated especially with masculinity, and was often denigrated in females.[206] However, this is not the case, for parents frequently remembered their daughter's

---

[197] Bidbanck, *A present for children*, 81.
[198] Houlbrooke, *Death, Religion and the Family*, 220.
[199] Gervase Disney, *Some remarkable passages in the holy life and death of Gervase Disney* (1692), 12–13.
[200] Hugh Cholmley, *The Memoirs and Memorials of Sir Hugh Cholmley of Whitby 1600–1657*, ed. Jack Binns, Yorkshire Archaeological Society, vol. 153 (Woodbridge: 2000), 91.
[201] Archibald Deans, *An account of the last words of Christian Karr, who dyed at Edinburgh . . . 1702, in the eleventh year of her age* (Edinburgh: 1702), 6.
[202] Disney, *Some remarkable passages*, 13–14.
[203] Fanshawe, *Memoirs of Lady Fanshawe*, 123.
[204] BL, Egerton MS 607, pp. 120–2 ('True coppies of scertaine loose Papers left by the Right honourable Elizabeth Countesse of Bridgewater, Collected and Transcribed together here since her Death Anno Dm 1663').
[205] Disney, *Some remarkable passages*, 13–14.
[206] Fletcher, *Growing Up*, 13, 33.

mental capacities. Ralph Josselin pronounced his eight-year-old daughter Mary 'a child of ten thousand, full of wisedome . . . [and] knowledge'.[207]

Perhaps more highly prized than intellect, was piety. The adolescent Elizabeth Walker, 'besides a blameless Conversation . . . she was very conscientious in the Duties of Religion [and] . . . would always speake the Truth'.[208] This attribute was celebrated in both genders. 'For his piety in God, never did I see the age of 14 so seasoned with piety & devotion', wrote a relative of Henry Curwen in 1636.[209] It is not surprising that parents were keen to recall their children's religiosity: such behaviour was evidence of their likely salvation after death. Parents sometimes alluded to this in their eulogies. Four-year-old Betty Egleton, for instance, had showed such 'Angel-like Carriage, and Heavenly Behaviour' that 'one would have thought she had lived a little while in Heaven before she got thither'.[210]

Finally, parents grieved over the loss of various other personal virtues, including kindness, meekness, obedience, and modesty. Six-year-old Mary Walker was 'a sweet tender hearted obedient Child', whilst her sister Elizabeth was 'meek of Spirit' and 'dutiful' in her 'loving Obedience to her Parents'.[211] Historians have shown that many of these attributes, and especially obedience and meekness, were regarded as essential components of femininity.[212] However, these qualities were also mentioned in reference to boys: young Henry Curwen was 'adorned . . . with humility, and modesty . . . obedient and Dutifull'.[213] Similarly, twelve-year-old Joseph Briggins was *'always ready to obey . . . very bashful . . . a very manly, meek and sober Child, not given to quarrel with any'*.[214] The juxtaposition of 'meek' and 'manly' may appear paradoxical, since gender prescriptions commanded boys to 'not be bashful'.[215] One could interpret the use of these terms as evidence of a greater blurring of gender ideologies than has been recognized by historians.[216] However, I would argue that the gendering of these qualities has been overstated in the historiography: all Christians, whether male or female, child or adult, were expected to display meekness and deference to God, and as such, these attributes were not regarded as incompatible with notions of manliness—they were Christian, rather than specifically feminine, virtues.[217] In the case of children, the

---

[207] Josselin, *The Diary of Ralph Josselin*, 203; Walker, *The vertuous wife*, 96–7, 107.

[208] Walker, *The vertuous wife*, 107.

[209] Charles Croke, *A sad memorial of Henry Curwen Esquire* (Oxford: 1638), 18.

[210] E. C., *Some part of the life and death of Mrs Elizabeth Egleton, who Died . . . 1705 in the fifth year of her age* (1705), 21.

[211] Walker, *The vertuous wife*, 96–7, 107, 110.

[212] Fletcher's chapter on 'girlhood' has outlined these characteristics, in *Growing Up*, 23–36.

[213] Croke, *A sad memorial of Henry Curwen*, 13, 16–17.

[214] *The living words of a dying child . . . Joseph Briggins* (1675), 'to the reader'.

[215] Fletcher, *Growing Up*, 16.

[216] Fletcher, for example, asserted that notions of ideal girlhood and boyhood were so different that 'it is difficult to talk about prescriptions for bringing up English children as opposed to those for English boys and English girls': ibid, 5.

[217] Jeremy Gregory has shown that Christian virtue in males was not regarded as being incompatible with 'manliness': in fact, religious literature implied that masculinity required piety: '"Homo Religiosus": Masculinity and Religion in the Long Eighteenth Century', in Hitchcock and Cohen (eds), *English Masculinities*, 85–110.

Commandment, 'Honour thy parents', undoubtedly played a large part in encouraging the ideals of obedience and meekness in both sexes.

Although the illnesses and deaths of children elicited extreme grief, parents also expressed resignation. 'Resignation' was defined as the acceptance of, or 'submission to' the will of God.[218] This response was regarded as virtuous, because it demonstrated a respect for the Lord, and a trust in His providences. In addition, resignation helped to moderate and ease extreme grief, which otherwise was in danger of becoming 'immeasurable, obstinate, [and] desperate'.[219] Whereas it was acceptable to show wild grief at the illness of the child, to 'indulge' in excessive grief after the death was considered 'both unreasonable and unchristian', because it implied resentment of God's will.[220] This attitude stemmed from the Biblical passage 2 Samuel 12, verses 15–23: when David's child lay sick and in pain, he 'fasted and wept', but as soon as he had died, the father 'washed his face and sat up and ate', on the grounds that there was nothing he could do to bring his child back. This did not mean that parents were expected to show no grief: to be 'void of *sorrow* [would be] *inhuman*'.[221] But it had to be restrained, and tempered with resignation.

As soon as the child became ill, parents and other relatives expressed their attempts at resignation. When Abigail Harley's niece was seized with 'violent fitts' in 1660, she prayed 'god fitt…us to submit to his will if another sad providence must pass upon us'.[222] Lucinda Becker has implied that women may have found it easier to submit to God's will than men, since they had been socialized into obedience.[223] However, resignation was expressed by fathers as well as mothers. 'Children all not well, especially John', wrote Philip Henry in 1665. 'Wee made a fresh Deed of gift resigning them up to the will of God', he declared.[224] This example of male submission supports my earlier comment that certain virtues, such as meekness and resignation, were encouraged in all Christians regardless of sex. After the deaths of children, parents renewed their commitments to resignation: James Clegg uttered the words, 'Father not as I will but as thou wilt and now the will of God is done and I do acquiesce in it and endeavour after a calm and composed spirit', after the death of his twelve-year-old daughter Margaret.[225] There is no evidence to show that parents' expressions of 'positive resignation' became less common after 1680.[226]

[218] OED Online.
[219] *A handkercher for parents,* 7.
[220] Owen, *Immoderate mourning for the dead,* 91.
[221] *A handkercher for parents,* 7.
[222] BL, Additional MS 70115, this manuscript is unfoliated (Harley papers).
[223] Becker, *Death and the Early Modern Englishwoman,* 103–26; Houlbrooke, *Death, Religion, and the Family,* 185.
[224] BL, Additional MS 42,849, fol. 30r (Henry family letters).
[225] Clegg, *The Diary of James Clegg,* 20.
[226] Woods, *Children Remembered,* 183, 211.

Parents were put under considerable pressure to resign themselves. Friends and relatives routinely sent letters of condolence to the bereaved family advising them to be resigned. The Cambridge Platonist Henry More beseeched the grieving Lady Anne Conway to 'pluck up a good courage and perfectly resigne yourself to God in all thinges, and trouble your minde with nothing but the composing yourself to that rule' when her baby son died in 1660.[227] Conduct literature and sermons also targeted parents with this counsel, warning that a failure to resign was 'sinful' and 'ungrateful'.[228] Poorer parents as well as those of high status were expected to heed this advice. When the child of a lowly wet nurse died in 1640 and 'mourned for it', eleven-year-old Cecily Puckering gave her 'grave counsel', saying, *'Seeing Gods will is done in taking away your childe, take heed of offending God by murmuring'.*[229] Elizabeth Clarke has implied that more pressure was put on mothers to resign themselves than fathers.[230] However, men were also subject to these admonishments. Sir Edmund Verney, for instance, instructed his son to 'not repine his [God's] decrees' during the illness of his four-year-old daughter Anna Maria in 1638.[231]

Owing to all these demands for resignation, parents' expressions of submission to God's will cannot be taken as irrefutable evidence of their feelings of resignation. Parents may have been making statements of resignation as a means of 'self-fashioning'—trying to attain the necessary composure through writing down what they should be feeling.[232] This was the case for Nehemiah Wallington at the death of his grandson John in 1654: he confessed, 'though I say Thy will be done in earth as it is in heaven[,] it coming not from my heart, [my] conscience tells me I lye'.[233] Parents may have been saying what they knew their relatives and friends wanted to hear, while in secret, not fully experiencing the sentiments they were describing. This is suggested in some letters sent between members of the Symth family in the 1630s: after the death of her baby daughter Betty, Florence Smyth wrote to her father assuring him that she had made 'pious resolutions' to resign herself. But a short while later, her father received news from her brother Jack that she was 'plunged into melancholy and fitted with passion which doth not agree to those good . . . resolutions' she had expressed.[234]

Parents regularly recorded their struggles at reaching a state of resignation.[235] After receiving advice from the aforementioned Henry More about the necessity

---

[227] Anne Conway, *The Conway Letters: the Correspondence of Anne, Viscountess Conway, Henry More, and their Friends, 1642–1684*, ed. Marjorie Hope Nicolson (Oxford: 1992, first publ. 1930), 168–9.

[228] Flavel, *A token for mourners*, 31.

[229] John Bryan, *The vertuous daughter* (1640), 13.

[230] Clarke, 'A Heart Terrifying Sorrow', 69.

[231] Verney, *The Verney Memoirs*, vol. 1, 219.

[232] This has been implied by Avra Kouffman in, 'Maternity and Child Loss in Stuart Women's Diaries', in Kathryn M. Moncrief and Kathryn R. McPherson (eds), *Performing Maternity in Early Modern England* (Aldershot and Burlington, VT: 2007), 171–82.

[233] Nehemiah Wallington, *The Notebooks of Nehemiah Wallington, 1618–1654, A Selection*, ed. David Booy (Aldershot: 2007), 301.

[234] Smyth, *The Earlier Smyths*, 114.

[235] Many historians agree that resignation was difficult to achieve: Thomas, 'Parent-Child Relationships and Childhood Experiences', 187; Linda Pollock, *A Lasting Relationship: Parents and*

of submitting to God's will, Lady Conway confessed, 'I find my proficiency' in resignation 'so smale, and my weaknesse so great, that though such considerations [of religion] may enable me to bear lesser crosses, yet I lie open to receive the assaults of greater'.[236] Sometimes parents felt that their resignation was incomplete, coexisting with other, less commendable emotions. Upon the death of her baby in 1688, Sarah Savage complained, that though her '*judgment* is quiet', she 'could not keep my passions in bounds', implying that her resignation was accompanied by more rebellious feelings of grief.[237] Parents often depicted the internal struggle between their passions and their resignation as a battle, during which they strove to 'take the Field' and 'gain a full, a glorious Victory' over their 'insulting Passions'.[238] The inability or difficulty of achieving the necessary resignation was, in turn, a source of guilt and anxiety: parents worried that they might be punished by further afflictions. During the illness of her son in the 1680s, Lady Russell acknowledged that 'a quiet submission is required', but confessed that 'unfit thoughts... haunt me', and that 'I do secretly repine'. This unsuccessful resignation caused her to fear that she 'shall provoke my God to repeat those threatenings... making yet more bitter that cup I have drank so deeply out of'.[239]

Although it is possible that parents sometimes expressed more resignation than they were actually feeling, to discount entirely the evidence of this response would be wrong. There were several convincing theological arguments that helped parents to cultivate a degree of resignation, even if this resignation was mixed with other, often contradictory, emotions. An examination of these arguments reveals that early modern passions were thought to be malleable: they could be moulded and framed to resignation.[240] Firstly, parents referred to the 'God as nurse' metaphor. At the death of his three-year-old son in 1628, Grace Wallington told her husband,

> Husband, say wee should put our childe forth too norsse [nurse]; and when wee see time fette [fit] wee sende for our childe, and if norsse should denie us our childe and should thinke much at us that wee feeah [fetch] it home againe wee should then be very angry with her[.] [E]ven standes the case with us for God gave us this childe to norse for him for a while: and now he requires it of us againe; therefore Let us give it to him willingly.[241]

By regarding themselves as wet nurses, parents were able to rationalize the loss of their children, and make resignation easier. Conduct literature for the bereaved routinely invoked this metaphor.[242]

Children Over Three Centuries (1987), 95; David Cressy, *Birth, Marriage, and Death: Ritual, Religion and the Life Cycle in Tudor and Stuart England* (Oxford: 1997), 393; Sara Heller Mendelson, 'Stuart Women's Diaries and Occasional Memoirs', in Mary Prior (ed.), *Women in English Society 1500–1800* (London and New York, 1985), 181–212, at 197–8.

[236] Conway, *The Conway letters*, 180–1.

[237] Sarah Savage, *Memoirs of the Life and Character of Mrs Sarah Savage*, ed. J. B. Williams (1821), 72–4.

[238] Chudleigh, 'On the Death of my Dear Daughter', 99.

[239] Russell, *Letters of Rachel, Lady Russell*, vol. 1, 140.

[240] See Pollock, 'Anger and the Negotiation of Relationships', 567–90.

[241] Guildhall Library, London, MS 204, pp. 421–2.

[242] For example, *A handkercher for parents*, 34–5, 43; Owen, *Immoderate mourning*, 99.

Secondly, parents tried to 'count their blessings', dwelling on the positive things in their lives. After the death of her young son in 1652, Mary Carey listed the mercies that she enjoyed:

> [God] hath given me all my senses, food and raiment...loving parent, & good husbands...lovely children...two yet with me...I have been kept in health in the plague time...I have lived forty-five years and never yet wanted anything that was absolutely necessary.[243]

Parents considered that the deaths of their children were not the worst things that could have befallen them: 'it is a great mercy we are not singled out for some uncommon and *extraordinary* judgment, but visited with the same that many are tried with', wrote Ann Hulton when her children were ill of smallpox in 1695.[244] Fathers as well as mothers voiced these positive thoughts. James Clegg noted that the death of his infant Ebenezer 'might have been much more wide and afflicting' if God had 'taken from me my Dear wife' as well: 'I have reason to be thankful it is no worse', he wrote.[245] Likewise, after the death of a baby son in 1675, Isaac Archer considered, 'God might have taken wife, or the other son, or all of them, etc., and hath taken the poore babe only'. This thought 'comforts mee somwhat', he added.[246] Condolence letters regularly reminded grieving parents of these considerations.[247]

Far more helpful than the above, was the belief that the dying child would go to heaven. When eight-year-old Mary Josselin was dying in 1650, her father declared, 'to the Lord I have resigned her...to receive her into his everlasting arms...she shall enjoy [life] in heaven not here'. He noted that this thought 'hath taken the feare of it [her death] from my heart, and helpes mee in bearing it'.[248] One of the most comforting features of heaven for parents, was that it was a place free from pain. 'The Lord was pleased to free her from all her paines by takeing her to His mercy, when she sweetly fell asleep', wrote Alice Thornton at the death of her baby daughter Joyce.[249] Naturally, it was during particularly painful illnesses that relatives mentioned this feature of heaven. 'Every day appears more melancholly when I see poor Jem in such piteous and languishing condition...the sooner God is pleased to take him the happier, for he has endured more than can be possibly imagin'd', lamented John Yorke during the illness of his nephew James in 1726.[250] Considering how distressing it was to witness a child suffer, it is unsurprising that parents resigned their offspring for this reason. It did not seem to occur to parents that death might bring even greater suffering to their children: heaven rather than

---

[243] Carey, *Meditations from the Note Book,* 44–50.
[244] Hulton, 'The Memoirs of Mrs Anne Hulton', 321.
[245] Clegg, *The Diary of James Clegg,* 12.
[246] Archer, *Two East Anglian Diaries,* 151.
[247] See, for example, a letter from the Bishop of Oxford to Lady Hatton, dated 3 July 1680: [Hatton], *Correspondence of the Family of Hatton being Chiefly Addressed to Christopher, First Viscount Hatton, 1601–1704,* ed. Edward Maunde Thompson, Camden Society (vols 22–3) (1878), vol. 1, 229–30.
[248] Ralph Josselin, *The Diary of Ralph Josselin 1616–1683,* ed. Alan Macfarlane (Oxford: 1991), 202–3.
[249] Thornton, *The Autobiography,* 150–1.
[250] Clavering, *The Correspondence,* 162.

hell was always the destination for dying children. This is intriguing because in theology, children were not excluded from hell: as James Janeway had warned, 'children . . . are not too little to dye, they are not too little to go to Hell'.[251] Parents actively encouraged their children to think about hell as well as heaven while ill, thus implying that either destination was a possibility, and children themselves sometimes expressed fears of damnation.[252] Nevertheless, when it came to the actual deaths of children, parents invariably assumed that they would go to heaven. It may have been too emotionally painful to consider the alternative.

Another aspect of heaven that generated comfort was the thought that it was a place of eternal happiness, where the child would enjoy the company of Christ. 'He . . . now partakes in bliss, the reward,that is prepared for such as liv'd like him', wrote Thomas Brockbank to his parents after learning of his adolescent brother's death. He reminded them, 'let these happy considerations of his happiness gently and by degrees put a period to your afflictions'.[253] Relatives often mentioned the affectionate physical contact between the child and Christ, perhaps enjoying vicariously the embraces that Jesus would be giving to their offspring. Ten-year-old Mary Warren's mother told her 'I trust thou art going to the embracings of the Lord Jesus'.[254] These words of comfort were occasionally spoken by the siblings of the deceased child. When baby Willy Thornton died in 1660, his four-year-old sister Nally asked their mother,

> [W]hy doe you morne and weepe soe much for my brother Willy?...would you or my father have my brother to live with you, when as God has taken him to Himselfe to heaven, wher he has noe sickness, but lives in happines? Would you have him out of heaven againe, where he is in joy and happiness? Deare mother, be patient . . . for my brother is in happiness with God in heaven.[255]

This advice made a deep impression on the mother. Nonetheless, the happiness of the child was not enough to eradicate parents' grief. Ralph Verney broke the news of his daughter's death with the words, 'Oh . . . my poor Peg is happy but I am . . . most afflicted and unfortunate'.[256]

To persuade themselves to accept their child's departure to heaven, parents and relatives compared death to a divine wedding. 'Consider it is your daughters weading day and will you grieve to see your daughter goe home to her Husband Jesus Christ, where she shall never want, but have the fullness of joy evermore?', asked Grace Wallington of her husband after the death of three-year-old Elizabeth.[257] Occasionally, dying children themselves mentioned this analogy: eight-year-old Tabitha Alder cried, 'I shall be with Jesus, I am married to him, he is my husband, I am his Bride, I have given my self to him, and he hath given himself to

---

[251] Janeway, *A token for children* (part 1), 'to the teachers of children'.
[252] See Ch. 6 for a discussion of children's fears of hell.
[253] Brockbank, *The Diary and Letter Book*, 4–5.
[254] H. P.,*A looking-glass for children* (1673), 10.
[255] Thornton, *The Autobiography*, 126.
[256] Verney, *The Verney Memoirs*, vol. 1, 381.
[257] Guildhall Library, London, MS 204, p. 409.

me, and I shall live with him for ever.'[258] Since marriage was one of the most momentous occasions in a female's life, this analogy may have been especially consoling to the parents of dying girls: they could consider that their daughter was not missing out on the joyous occasion of her wedding. The metaphor was not confined to daughters, however: John Vernon wrote that 'it pleased God to visit' his twelve-year-old son Caleb 'with sickness, to perfect his compleature for his Bridegroom'.[259] The use of this metaphor suggests that marriage was of crucial importance for males as well as females.[260]

Arguably the most consoling aspect of heaven was the possibility of family reunion.[261] When six-year-old John Henry was 'dangerously ill of the chincough' in 1666, his father expressed a hope that 'I shall meet him again with comfort, at the right hand of Jesus'.[262] Moments before the death of six-year-old Frances Archer, her father assured her she 'was going to heaven to her brothers and sisters, and that we should all meet againe'.[263] Husbands and wives frequently reminded one another of this prospect to temper their grief. After the death of two children, Ralph Verney told his wife,

> I shall endeavour to leave deploring their losse . . . wee should rather rejoyce at their happiness . . . Tis true they are taken from us . . . but we shall goe to them . . . is it not better both for us and them, that wee should rather assend to heaven to partake of theire perpetuall blisse, then they descend to Earth to share with us our misfortunes.[264]

By seeing death as only a temporary separation from their children, parents were able to compose their emotions to resignation. Poor parents may also have derived comfort from this thought. A pamphlet published in 1708 recounted the sad tale of 'The Cruel Mother', Elizabeth Cole, who had thrown her five-year-old daughter into the Thames. Upon returning home, she told her family she had 'sent my dear Child to Heaven, and am resolv'd to go after her'.[265] Although this is a case of murder rather than child illness, it does reveal something of the hopes of a mentally disturbed mother: she wanted to see her daughter again in paradise.

It must be pointed out, though, that not all sick children died. Judging from the fact that three quarters of children lived beyond the age of ten, it seems likely that recovery was a common experience.[266] Historians have often overlooked this positive

[258] James Janeway, *A token for children. The second part* (1673), 21.
[259] Vernon, *The compleat scholler,* 19. According to Elizabeth Maddock Dillon, this strange image—of a male marrying the male Christ—indicates that puritan religion could usurp gender barriers, and serve to 'feminize' the male body: Elizabeth Maddock Dillon, 'Nursing Fathers and Brides of Christ: the Feminized Body of the Puritan Convert', in Janet Moore Lindman and Michele Lise Tarter (eds), *A Centre of Wonders: the Body in Early America* (Ithaca, NY and London: 2001), 129–44.
[260] Ira Clark, *Comedy, Youth, Manhood in Early Modern England* (London and Newark, NJ: 2003), 15–16; Foyster, *Manhood in Early Modern England,* 65.
[261] See Thomas's book *The Ends of Life,* for a discussion of family reunion in heaven, 230–1.
[262] Henry, *The Diaries and Letters,* 205.
[263] Archer, *Two East Anglian Diaries,* 160–1.
[264] Verney, *The Verney Memoirs,* vol. 1, 385.
[265] *The cruel mother: being a strange . . . account of one Mrs Elizabeth Cole* (1708), 5.
[266] Edward Anthony Wrigley and Roger Schofield, *The Population History of England, 1541–1871: A Reconstruction* (Cambridge: 1981), 249.

outcome. When children got better, parents responded with joy and relief. In the 1650s, four-year-old Betty Newcome had suffered from rickets for many months: her parents decided to send her to 'Mr Wilson's of Poppythorne', hoping that he could cure her. When the girl's parents 'went one day to see her . . . she met us on her feet, which was a great rejoicing to us', and she was even able to 'dance to the virginals'.[267] The 'victorious' recovery of fourteen-year-old Mary Glover from diabolical possession in 1602 provides a moving insight into the experience of a child's recovery:

> [T]here was heard amongst us . . . abundance of most joyful tears . . . The father . . . took her by the hand as not being able to speak a word. And the Mother went, and taking away the handkerchief with which her daughter sat covering her blubbering face, with like watery cheeks kissed her . . . They also gave her to drink a kind of posset, which she took and drank with ease, to their marvel and rejoicing.[268]

Just as parents found it difficult to express grief without tears, they found it hard to articulate their joy. Poor parents as well as wealthier parents responded in this way. An advertisement for a medicine, printed in 1717, describes the response of the London alehouse keepers Charles and Mary Pearce to the successful workings of the medicine: 'We . . . hereby affirm' that 'the Child got up upon his Feet to play, to our great Amazement, and has ever since so visibly recover'd and thriv'd'.[269]

These happy passions could be so potent that they improved the parent's health. When five-year-old William Archer 'revived' from his worms and fever in 1675, his mother Anne 'upon his mending . . . began to be better'.[270] Thus, joyful passions could impact on the body in the same manner as negative feelings. Common phrases used by parents to describe their experience of recovery were 'heaviness endured for a night, but joy came in the morning', and 'God . . . pleases to turn our mourning into joy'.[271] These lines, which were taken from Psalm 30 verse 5 and 11, captured effectively the extraordinary transformation of parents' emotions, revealing that recovery could happen in a short space of time.[272]

CONCLUSION

Overwhelmed by grief, fear, and guilt, the sickness or death of a child was 'one of the most sad and dismal occasions' that ever befell parents.[273] It is difficult to tell which was more agonizing: watching children suffer pain, or realizing they were dying. These dolorous experiences, which may have cut across socio-economic

---

[267] Newcome, *The Diary of the Rev. Henry Newcome*, 93.

[268] Swan, 'A true and briefe Report', 318–21.

[269] OBP, reference: a17170117-1 (accessed 14 January 2011).

[270] Archer, *Two East Anglian Diaries*, 150.

[271] To give a few examples, Newcome, *The Autobiography of Henry Newcome*, 97; Guildhall Library, London, MS 204, p. 433 (A Record of the Mercies of God: or A Thankfull Remembrance' by Nehemiah Wallington); Russell, *Letters of Rachel, Lady Russell*, 249.

[272] These verses are 'weeping may endure for a night, but joy cometh in the morning' (Psalm 30:5); 'Thou hast turned for me my mourning into dancing' (Psalm 30:11).

[273] D'Ewes, *The Autobiography*, vol. 2, 143.

divides, underwent little alteration over the course of the early modern period.[274] Nevertheless, we have seen that parents' misery was sometimes tempered by attempts to reach a state of emotional and spiritual resignation, which was in turn facilitated by a consideration of the Christian doctrines of providence and salvation. God, the loving author of affliction, brought pain for the spiritual benefit of its sufferers, and therefore, parents could rest assured that something good would come out of their suffering. 'A bitter portion indeed . . . yet it was wholesome', mused Nehemiah Wallington at the death of his son in 1628.[275] Parents could also comfort themselves with the thought that their dying child would soon be enjoying bliss in heaven, where the whole family would eventually be reunited. These cathartic aspects of Protestant doctrines seem to have endured throughout the period. However, it is important not to overstate the positive side to providentialism: owing to the direct link between personal sin and affliction, child sickness also sparked painful feelings of guilt. Finally, it must be remembered that children did not always die: when they recovered, parents experienced a 'double joy': not only was their child better, but God had shown a sign of His love by answering their prayers. By drawing attention to parents' responses to their children's recoveries, as well as their deaths, this chapter opens up an area of history that has previously been neglected.

The experiences of mothers and fathers seem to have been virtually indistin-guishable: children's pains and deaths were sources of profound grief for both parties. Perhaps the only marked difference was the way that some fathers at-tempted to conceal 'part' of their grief so that they could turn their energies to helping their wives reach a state of resignation. This is not evidence that men were less emotionally attached to their children, or that their sadness was less extreme than mothers'. Rather, men's attempts at controlling their grief were probably motivated (possibly unknowingly) by a desire to assert and construct their mascu-line identities, since the display of rationality was necessary for the attainment of what Elizabeth Foyster has termed 'full manhood'.[276]

Little evidence has been found to show that parents grieved more deeply for sons than for daughters: rather, the pains and deaths of children of both sexes elicited acute distress. Children were missed for their individual qualities rather than their gender. On the rare occasions when parents did mention the child's gender as a reason for heightened sorrow, they referred to daughters as well as sons, and implied that it was the child's status as 'only son' or 'only daughter' rather than its gender, that occasioned this grief. Likewise, we have seen that the gendering of girlhood and boyhood ideologies was far less clear-cut than has been suggested in the historiography, for many attributes were celebrated in both sexes.

An underlying concern of this chapter has been the distinctive way in which early modern people conceptualized and depicted the emotions. In keeping with the findings of Gail Kern Paster and others, it has been demonstrated that the

---

[274] This continuity is confirmed in Amanda Vickery's brief examination of the experiences of eighteenth-century child illness: *The Gentleman's Daughter,* 117–20.
[275] Guildhall Library, London, MS 204, p. 421.
[276] Foyster, *Manhood in Early Modern England,* 30.

passions were imagined as powerful liquids, which literally (rather than figura-
tively) welled up within the human body, heart, and soul. The passions were thus
inexorably linked with the bodily humours: they were fluids that needed to be purged
or tempered. Although there is a 'clear recognizability' of the basic emotions represented in the primary sources, 'what is imagined to happen in a body gripped by
passion has radically changed over time'.[277]

[277] Kern Paster, *Humoring the Body*, 244–5.

PART III

THE CHILD'S EXPERIENCE

5

'Very Much Eased':
Being a Patient

Taking the elusive perspective of the child, this chapter asks what it was like being a patient during the early modern period: it explores the social, emotional, physical, and spiritual experiences of patienthood. The terms 'patienthood' and 'being a patient' usually denote the 'state or condition of receiving . . . medical treatment'.[1] However, in this chapter, the definition is extended to encompass all the other aspects of care that were provided during illness in addition to physic, such as prayer, nursing, sick-visiting, and the religious preparation for death.[2] Thus, children's experiences of all these components of care will be examined, and a number of key themes will be identified.

While historians have occasionally considered patients' attitudes to taking medicine, they have rarely investigated the experiences of other forms of patient care. They have also tended to paint deeply negative pictures of early modern patienthood, which centre on the backwardness of medicine at this time. Michael MacDonald, for example, declared that treatments were 'notoriously violent and dangerous', and that 'Laymen were . . . painfully aware of the perils and discomforts of seventeenth-century medicine'.[3] Other scholars have compared taking medicine to 'hitting yourself over the head with a hammer', or 'leaping out of the frying pan into the fire'.[4] In what follows, it is shown that the experiences of patients were actually far more complicated and mixed, involving some agreeable as well as disagreeable elements. For instance, sick children experienced power and powerlessness, hope and despair, relief and pain. Thus, this chapter promotes a more holistic, and less pessimistic, approach to the history of early modern medicine. It also asserts that the fundamental experiences of ill children did not alter drastically over the course of the 140 years covered by this study, despite the notable developments occurring in the wider contexts.

---

[1] OED Online.
[2] The aspects of care are described in Ch. 3.
[3] Michael MacDonald, *Mystical Bedlam: Madness, Anxiety and Healing in Seventeenth-Century England* (Cambridge: 1981), 191.
[4] Lucinda McCray Beier, *Sufferers and Healers: The Experience of Illness in Seventeenth-Century England* (1987), 107; Roy Porter and Dorothy Porter, *In Sickness and in Health: The British Experience, 1650–1850* (1988), 105; a similar statement is made by Guy Williams, *The Age of Agony: The Art of Healing, c. 1700–1800* (1975).

This chapter is not concerned with the experience of illness, such as physical pain and the anticipation of death. Rather, the focus here is the experience of the practical consequences of sickness: patienthood or care. The final chapter of this book is devoted to the experience of sickness. Of course, this distinction between patienthood and illness is artificial: a closer examination of the definitions of 'patient' reveals that as well as referring to the receipt of medicine, it means 'A person who suffers from an injury or disease; a sick person . . . A sufferer'.[5] This meaning stems from the Latin, 'patior', which means 'to suffer'.[6] Thus, 'patient' refers to both the bodily affliction and the care received. Nevertheless, it is necessary to draw a distinction in order to organise the content of these two chapters. The word 'patient' is often associated with passivity and subjection; the ensuing discussions suggest that such connotations do not adequately capture the complexity of patienthood in the early modern period. While patients did sometimes behave submissively, they also wielded considerable power, and took active roles in their care regimes.

SYMPATHY AND AFFECTION

Perhaps the most striking feature of patienthood was the great compassion and love shown by carers to sick children. 'I am sorry your eyes have bine soore', wrote Lady Brilliana Harley to her son Ned in 1639. She added, 'I can not but pitty you . . . for by experience, I know it is to be a great paine; for once I had sore eyes, and . . . feele how tender the eye is'.[7] In cases of serious illness, relatives often expressed their sympathy in tears. The 'very greevous' pain of thirteen-year-old Thomas Darling 'moved many' of his family members 'to shed tears' and 'weepe . . . to behold his miserie' in 1596.[8] It is possible that boys in particular derived consolation from this sympathy, because it was not likely to have been a common experience in their everyday lives: contemporary prescriptive literature warned against showing too much tenderness to sons on the grounds that it would foster the undesirable effeminate qualities of 'weakness, softness and delicacy'.[9] Nevertheless, there is evidence that some children regarded pity as a source of further distress. In the 1670s 'nothing grieved' eleven-year-old John Harvy more than observing 'the sorrow that he saw his Mother to be in'.[10] The boy's love for his mother, and his precocious ability to empathize with her feelings, are conveyed here.

Parents and relatives showed their sympathy and concern by asking ill children how they were feeling. Historians have acknowledged that this was a standard question directed at the sick.[11] When eleven-year-old Martha Hatfield from

---

[5] OED Online.   [6] Ibid.

[7] Brilliana Harley, *Letters of the Lady Brilliana Harley*, ed. Thomas Taylor Lewis (1853), 37.

[8] I. D., *The most wonderfull and true storie . . . as also a true report of the strange torments of Thomas Darling, a boy of thirteene yeres of age* (1597), 3, 6–7.

[9] Anthony Fletcher, *Growing up in England: The Experience of Childhood 1600–1914* (London and New Haven, CT: 2008), 15.

[10] James Janeway, *A token for children. The second part* (1673), 86.

[11] Ralph Houlbrooke, *Death, Religion and the Family in England, 1480–1750* (Oxford: 1998), 191–2.

Yorkshire became ill of 'spleen-wind' in 1652, her mother asked, 'Ah my dear Childe... how doest thou?'[12] Absent relatives made these enquiries by letter: the nun Winefrid Thimelby wrote to her niece Gertrude Aston, asking for information about 'all perticulers of y[ou]r indispositions, that I may better know how to direct my prayers'.[13] By giving children the opportunity to say how they were feeling, these questions probably made suffering more bearable, since it was believed at this time that 'the body finds relief in complaining'.[14] Sick children might have been engaging in what Stephen Pender has termed 'rhetorical therapy'.[15] Today, psychologists agree that 'proclaiming one's pain... has a direct effect on the reality of the experience', bringing 'relief by liberating... the feeling'.[16] Perhaps this was the case for ten-year-old Jane Throckmorton in the 1590s: during a diabolical fit, she answered her family's questions of 'how she did' with the statement that she 'was marvellously sick and full of pain'.[17] The practice of questioning children in this way indicates that it was considered acceptable for the sick to complain about pain: they were not expected to suffer in silence.[18]

It has often been assumed that early modern parents did not lavish their offspring with hugs and kisses, owing to their fears of 'cockering' their children.[19] The sources suggest that during serious illness this was not the case. In 1661, ten-year-old Mary Warren was permitted to 'Clasp... her Arms around her Mothers Neck' in an embrace.[20] A few decades later, eight-year-old Sarah Camm, who had the smallpox, exchanged kisses with her 'Father and Mother... Grandmother and others', and was held 'in her Fathers Arms'.[21] Boys were also shown this affection:

[12] James Fisher, *The wise virgin, or, a wonderfull narration of the hand of God... in afflicting a childe of eleven years of age* [Martha Hatfield] (1653), 147.
[13] Arthur Clifford (ed.), *Tixall Letters: or, The Correspondence of the Aston Family*, 2 vols (1815), vol. 2, 75–6.
[14] Stephen Pender, 'Seeing, Feeling, Judging: Pain in the Early Modern Imagination', in Jan Frans van Dijkhuizen and Karl A. E. Enenkel (eds), *The Sense of Suffering: Constructions of Physical Pain in Early Modern Culture*, Yearbook for Early Modern Studies, vol. 12 (Leiden and Boston: 2008), 469–95, at 484. Michael Schoenfeldt has made a similar statement in 'Aesthetic and Anesthetics: the Art of Pain Management in Early Modern England', 34 (in the same volume as Pender).
[15] Ibid. (Pender) 484.
[16] Roselyne Rey, *The History of Pain*, trans. Louise Elliot Wallace, J. A. Cadden and S. W. Cadden (London and Cambridge, Mass.: 1998, first publ. 1993), 4–5; Lisa Smith, '"An Account of an Unaccountable Distemper": the Experience of Pain in Early Eighteenth-Century England and France', *Eighteenth-Century Studies*, 41 (2008), 459–80, at 466, 472.
[17] 'The most strange and admirable discovery of the three Witches of Warboys... for betwitching of the five daughters of Robert Throckmorton' (1593) in Philip Almond (ed.), *Demonic Possession and Exorcism in Early Modern England: Contemporary Texts and their Cultural Contexts* (Cambridge: 2004), 75–149, at 121.
[18] For attitudes to pain expression, see Lucinda McCray Beier 'In Sickness and in Health: A Seventeenth Century Family's Experience', in Roy Porter (ed.), *Patients and Practitioners: Lay Perceptions of Medicine in Pre-Industrial Society* (Cambridge: 2002, first publ. 1985), 101–28, at 125; Esther Cohen, 'The Animated Pain of the Body', *American Historical Review*, 105 (2000), 36–68, at 58–9.
[19] This tendency has been highlighted by Fletcher, *Growing Up in England*, 55.
[20] H. P., *A looking-glass for children being a narrative of God's gracious dealings with some little children* (1673), 10.
[21] *The admirable and glorious appearance of the eternal God... through a child of the age of betwixt eight and nine years, upon her dying bed* (1684), 6.

in the early 1700s, one Mrs Heath was 'always embracing and Caressing' her two sons, seven-year-old Joseph and three-year-old Benjamin, whilst they were ill of the smallpox.[22] The fact that parents and children of both sexes were subject to physical affection suggests that the emotional attachment between these family members was equally intense, and that it was considered acceptable for affection to be expressed across genders. Clearly, early modern fathers were not the aloof figures commonly depicted in the historiography.[23] Siblings also offered kisses to sick children: Martha Hatfield's four-year-old sister, 'being . . . very fond of her', would 'lie by her . . . oftentimes kissing . . . her'.[24] Half a century later, the Countess of Nottingham observed that her little girl 'gott into' her son's room, 'and kissed himm' when he had the smallpox.[25] These instances of brotherly and sisterly affection demonstrate the loving relationships between siblings, thus shedding light on an area of history that has often been overlooked.[26] Occasionally, however parents prevented their ill children from touching their healthy offspring because they did not want the disease to be passed on. This was the case for plague-stricken Susanna Bicks in 1664: when she tried to kiss her baby sister, her father took the 'poor little Child away . . . from the hazard of that fiery distemper', and told Susanna that 'he already [had] too much to bear'.[27] Examples of this kind provide insights into laypeople's understandings of contagion. Nevertheless, parents them-selves rarely forbore these intimate gestures, choosing instead to take the risk of catching the disease. Susanna Bicks was kissed by her parents despite the fact that they would not allow their other children to do the same.[28] Such acts testify to the deep love of parents for their children.

Other forms of affectionate physical contact bestowed by carers included cra-dling sick children on their laps, and sitting with their arms around them. The clergyman Isaac Archer noted in 1679 that his six-year-old daughter Frances 'slept with my arme under her more then halfe an houre'.[29] Roughly forty years later, the Countess of Hertford, Frances Seymour, mentioned that her seven-year-old daughter Betty, who 'has a sad cold . . . is half asleep upon my lap'.[30] Children of all ages, genders, and economic backgrounds might be held in this way. In 1663, a

---

[22] BL, Sloane MS 4034, fol. 21r–21v.

[23] Joanne Bailey agrees that fathers 'provided hugs' to their children, though in reference to a later period: ' "A Very Sensible Man": Imagining Fatherhood in England, c.1750–1830', *History*, 95 (2010), 267–92.

[24] Fisher, *The wise virgin*, 145 (dated *c.* 1652).

[25] [Hatton], *Correspondence of the Family of Hatton being Chiefly Addressed to Christopher, First viscount Hatton, 1601–1704*, ed. Edward Maunde Thompson, Camden Society (1878), vol. 2, 212.

[26] Peter Stearns has mentioned this deficiency, in 'Challenges in the History of Childhood', *Journal of the History of Childhood and Youth*, 1 (2008), 35–42, at 36. Some work has begun on this subject, though, including Naomi J. Miller and Naomi Yavneh, *Sibling Relations and Gender in the Early Modern World: Sisters, Brothers and Others* (Aldershot and Burlington: 2006).

[27] Janeway, *A token for children* (part 2) 49–50.

[28] Ibid. 49.

[29] Isaac Archer, *Two East Anglian Diaries 1641–1729*, ed. Matthew J. Storey, Suffolk Record Society, vol. 36 (Woodbridge: 1994), 160–1.

[30] Frances Seymour, *The Gentle Hertford: Her Life and Letters*, ed. Helen Hughes (New York: 1940), 78.

twelve-year-old servant called Thomas Sawdie, who was 'exceeding sore', was 'fed on a Womans knees'.[31] An Assize deposition from 1656 states that the illegitimate infant of a beggar woman from West Riding 'died in her arms' as she sat awaiting relief from her neighbours.[32] It is likely that physical affection comforted children, and ameliorated their sufferings. This was implied by Dr John Symcotts in his medical casebook: when little 'Mistress Elms' fell sick of a 'strange disease' in 1642, the only thing that soothed her was being 'carried in one's arms into the yard, or roundly about [the] house, or in a coach'.[33]

As well as giving physical affection, families and friends indulged sick children with verbal affection and praise. This might seem surprising given the fact that puritan parents have often been stereotyped as harsh and critical, acutely aware of their children's innate depravity.[34] Clearly this was not always so: in 1665, twelve-year-old Caleb Vernon, who was suffering from consumption, was 'very much eased' and 'pleased' upon hearing his father's 'expressions of affection' for him.[35] Daughters were also recipients of praise. In 1664, Susanna Bicks' father assured her that she had brought him much 'satisfaction and joy' through her exemplary godliness 'in reading the Word, in Prayer and gracious Discourse'.[36] The most poignant expressions of love were uttered when the child was dying. Fourteen-year-old Sarah Howley's mother asked, 'how shall I bear parting with thee[?]'[37] It is conceivable that for some children such instances of praise and affection were rare, reserved for the emotionally intense deathbed; perhaps this element of patienthood was therefore cherished. Although it is more difficult to ascertain if children lower down the social scale received praise in this context, Patricia Crawford has suggested tentatively that 'praise and approval may have mattered more' among the poor, since these parents were unable to afford 'tangible gifts'.[38]

ATTENTION

Today, historians usually concur that although parent–child relations were often loving in the early modern period, society was still 'far removed from the cult of the

---

[31] *A return of prayer: or a faithful relation of some remarkable passages of providence concerning Thomas Sawdie* (1664), 12.

[32] Cited in Patricia Crawford and Laura Gowing (eds), *Women's Worlds in Seventeenth-Century England: A Sourcebook* (2000), 118–19.

[33] John Symcotts, *A Seventeenth Century Doctor and his Patients: John Symcotts, 1592?-1662*, eds F. N. L. Poynter and W. J. Bishop, Bedfordshire Historical Record Society, vol. 31 (Streatley: 1951), 76.

[34] One exception is Angela Margaret Thomas, 'Parent-Child Relationships and Childhood Experiences: the Emotional and Physical Aspects of Care for Children in Early Modern Britain, 1640–1800' (unpubl. PhD thesis, University of Reading, 2000), ch. 3.

[35] John Vernon, *The compleat scholler; or, a relation of the life . . . of Caleb Vernon*(1666), 72.

[36] Janeway, *A token for children* (part 2), 26–7, 48.

[37] *An account of the admirable conversion of one Sarah Howley, a child of eight or nine years old* (Edinburgh: 1704), 7.

[38] Patricia Crawford, *Parents of Poor Children in England, 1580–1800* (Oxford: 2010), 145.

child'—children were not the centre of attention during everyday life.[39] This situation was transformed by serious illness, for patienthood brought extraordinary attention.[40] Perhaps the most obvious form of attention was nursing. In 1635, the antiquary and baronet, Simonds D'Ewes, was 'near' his sick two-year-old son Clopton 'all the time', 'bestowing my heavy tears, deep sighs, and humble prayer, upon him' while carrying out the task of watching.[41] Five years later, Brilliana Harley noted approvingly that her son Tom's nurse, Blechly, 'takes a great deale of paines with him, watches every ... night with him, rises every night to him'.[42] Barbara Hanawalt has asserted that in medieval England, nurses probably sat up longer with sick boys because 'they had a higher social value' than girls.[43] However, there is little evidence to suggest that this was the case during the early modern period: parents regularly recorded their attentive nursing of daughters as well as sons. Isaac Archer 'sate by' his little daughter 'all night ... I was almost always by her'.[44] Perhaps it could even be postulated that parents may have found it ideologically easier to nurse their daughters, since the traditional qualities of femininity, such as weakness and dependence, matched the connotations of patienthood.[45] Children often appreciated this attentive nursing: Elizabeth Walker recorded that her adolescent daughter 'would express her loving Affections and Thankfulness for my Care of her' during her illness in 1674.[46] Likewise, twelve-year-old Caleb Vernon thanked his parents for their 'tenderness to him' and told his mother, '*I love your company dearly*'.[47] Nevertheless, since politeness was a crucial trait in children, it is difficult to determine the extent to which children's expressions of gratitude reflect 'genuine' feeling, or were in fact examples of good manners.[48]

Other significant forms of attention bestowed upon ill children were sick-visiting and communal prayer days. Scholars of witchcraft and possession have shown that the demoniac 'would become the centre of a dramatic ritual of prayer and healing in which he was treated with affectionate concern'.[49] Many examples can be found to support this claim: in 1594, the bewitched girl Jane Ashton 'layd on a couch in the

---

[39] Gerald F. Moran and Maris A. Vinovskis, 'The Great Care of Godly Parents: Early Childhood in Puritan New England', *Monographs of the Society for Research in Child Development*, 50 (1985), 24–37, at 28.

[40] Isabelle Robin-Romero agrees that during illness children were lavished with attention: 'L'Enfant Malade dans les Écrits Privés du XVIIIe', *Histoire Économie et Société*, 22 (2003), 469–86, at 478–9.

[41] Simonds D'Ewes, *The Autobiography and Correspondence of Sir Simonds D'Ewes, Bart.*, ed. J. O. Halliwell, 2 vols (1845), vol. 2, 144.

[42] Harley, *Letters of the Lady Brilliana Harley*, 120.

[43] Barbara Hanawalt, *Growing Up in Medieval London: the Experience of Childhood in History* (Oxford and New York: 1993), 58–9.

[44] Archer, *Two East Anglian Diaries*, 160–1.

[45] Gianna Pomata has highlighted these connotations of patienthood: *Contracting a Cure: Patients, Healers, and the Law in Early Modern Bologna* (London and Baltimore, MD: 1998), 24.

[46] Elizabeth Walker, *The vertuous wife: or, the holy life of Mrs Elizabeth Walker*, ed. Anthony Walker (1694), 111.

[47] Vernon, *The compleat scholler*, 55, 62–3.

[48] Anthony Fletcher, 'Courses in Politeness: The Upbringing and Experiences of Five Teenage Diarists, 1671–1860', *Transactions of the Royal Historical Society*, 12 (2002), 417–30, at 417.

[49] Keith Thomas, *Religion and the Decline of Magic* (1991, first publ. 1971), 574.

midst' of fifty visitors, who prayed for her throughout the day.[50] A decade later, the possessed fourteen-year-old, Mary Glover, sat 'in the middle of the chamber in a low wicker chair', while twenty-four visitors, including six preachers, surrounded her and prayed continuously for her recovery.[51] James Sharpe has implied that possessed females in particular would have enjoyed this attention because it was not something they were accustomed to on a daily basis.[52]

The diabolically ill were not the only recipients of these forms of attention: prayer and sick-visiting were standard procedures during any type of serious distemper, natural or unnatural.[53] When ten-year-old Mary Warren became ill of a stomach disease in 1661, her family and friends, including '*John Simpson,* and Mr *Palmer* ... Mr *Jessey* ... Mr *Greensmith* and his Wife; also that grave Matron Mrs. *Adkins,* a Ministers Widow; with divers other Christian friends' attended a day dedicated to prayers for her recovery.[54] A few years later, Martha Hatfield received so many visitors that one person complained 'the room was not able to bear so many'.[55] Children sometimes took comfort in this attentive care. 'Her delight was very great in these days of Prayer', recalled the relatives of four-year-old Mary Stubbs in the 1680s. 'Her Love was so great to those that prayed with her, and for her, that she would weep and mourn when they took their Leave of her, she was unwilling to lose their Company', they recalled.[56]

Perhaps the greatest source of attention for patients derived from the religious preparation for death, for this was a matter of eternal significance. As was established in an earlier chapter, this process, which involved various acts of piety, was essential for convincing the sick and their families that they were destined for heaven. The patient's religious behaviour was proof of faith, which in turn was evidence of God's grace, and his or her likely salvation.[57] Consequently, it was only natural that parents and friends keenly 'watched for signs' and 'tangible evidence' of their child's faith during serious illness, taking note of every scrap of religious behaviour in the hope it would assure them of their child's heavenly future.[58] Of course, according to the doctrine of predestination, no amount of piety on the deathbed could influence the salvation of the Christian, since such matters had

---

[50] John Darrel, *A true narration of the strange and grevous vexation by the Devil, of 7. persons in Lanchashire* (1600), 13, 19.

[51] John Swan, '"A True and Briefe Report, of Mary Glovers Vexation" (1603)', in Almond (ed.), *Demonic Possession,* 291–330, at 299, 304.

[52] James Sharpe, *The Bewitching of Anne Gunter: A Horrible and True Story of Football, Witchcraft, Murder, and the King of England* (1999), 156.

[53] Lucinda McCray Beier, 'The Good Death in Seventeenth-Century England' in Ralph Houlbrooke (ed.), *Death, Ritual and Bereavement* (London and New York: 1989), 43–61, at 44.

[54] H. P., *A looking-glass for children,* 10–11.

[55] Fisher, *The wise virgin,* 138.

[56] William Bidbanck, *A present for children. Being a brief, but faithful account of many remarkable and excellent things utter'd by three young children* (1685), 53–4.

[57] Andrew Wear, 'Puritan Perceptions of Illness in Seventeenth Century England', in Roy Porter (ed.), *Patients and Practitioners: Lay Perceptions of Medicine in Pre-Industrial Society* (Cambridge: 2002, first publ. 1985), 55–99, at 64.

[58] David Cressy, *Birth, Marriage, and Death: Ritual, Religion and the Life Cycle in Tudor and Stuart England* (Oxford: 1997), 390.

been predetermined by the Almighty. But, in practice, patients and their families retained the hope that they might exert some leverage.[59] An example of this attention is provided in the possession case of Mary Glover: when she 'began to gasp and strive to speak' words of prayer in 1602, her family and friends were seen 'laying their ears to her head' to catch what she was saying.[60] This image—of numerous adults straining to hear the words of a sick child—encapsulates the experience of patienthood, wherein attention was paramount. Attention to the religious preparation for death endured into the eighteenth century. In 1720, Sarah Savage recorded in her spiritual diary that the parents of five-year-old Jacky Gardner earnestly observed him 'repeat his prayers' and 'lift up his little hands in Devotion' during his illness from the smallpox, hoping that this was evidence of his impending salvation.[61]

Particular attention was paid to the religious activity that had been initiated by the children themselves, for this behaviour was regarded as especially indicative of spiritual grace and election. John Evelyn noted that his five-year-old son Richard 'would of himselfe select the most pathetical Psalmes, & Chapters out of Jobe, to reade' during his illness in 1658.[62] When children succeeded in carrying out these religious actions in exemplary fashion, the attention was often mixed with expressions of praise and admiration. After hearing how 'solidly, profitably and spiritually' five-year-old Anne Lane spoke in 1640, her family expressed 'joy and delight'.[63] It is possible that children's piety was sometimes motivated by a craving for this praise. This is implied in the biography of an anonymous five-year-old boy, in which it is noted that 'When no body hath been speaking for a while he ... would burst out into tears ... [saying] that the very thoughts of Christ[']s love to sinners in suffering for them, made him ... cry'.[64] This child may have hoped that his dramatic religious statement would attract notice from his relations.

Besides seeking evidence of their child's salvation, parents' attention to the preparation for death was spurred by the belief that their child was acting as a mouthpiece for the Holy Spirit. The dying were thought to be especially close to God, and so by witnessing the child's religiosity, parents were literally observing the works of their deity. When Mary Stubbs prayed in an unusually holy manner during her illness in the 1680s, her family believed the cause was the 'Spirit' of God, which was 'flowing' out of the girl 'like a ... Stream'.[65] Upon observing the piety of eleven-year-old Christian Shaw a few decades later, her relatives mused, 'althou[gh] she was a Girle of a pregnant Spirit ... yet we doubt not but ... the Lord did by His good Spirit graciously afford her more than ordinary measure of Assistance'.[66]

[59] Houlbrooke, *Death, Religion, and the Family*, 154.
[60] Swan, 'A True and Briefe Report', 306.
[61] Bodleian Library, Oxford, MS Eng. Misc. e. 331, p. 253 (Diary of Sarah Savage, 1714–23).
[62] John Evelyn, *John Evelyn's Diary: A Selection*, ed. Philip Francis (1963), 385–8.
[63] Janeway, *A token for children* (part 2), 16–18.
[64] James Janeway, *A token for children being an exact account of the conversion, holy and exemplary lives and joyful deaths of several young children* (1671), 53.
[65] Bidbanck, *A present for children*, 51–2.
[66] Francis Grant Cullen, *A true narrative of the sufferings and relief of a yong girle [called Christian Shaw]* (Edinburgh: 1698), p. xiv.

Frequently quoted by parents during these moments of 'heavenly behaviour' were Jesus' words in Matthew 21 verse 16: *'Out of the mouths of Babes and Sucklings thou hast perfected thy Praise'.*[67] This verse was used as evidence that God spoke through children; it succinctly captures the amazement of parents, as they realized that such unassuming beings as little children, were capable of 'flashes of startling divine insight'.[68] Since it was God who inspired children's religiosity, parents and relatives sometimes directed their commendation at Him, rather than at their offspring: children had little personal responsibility for their own spiritual behaviour. This situation may have been frustrating to those children who desired praise from their families.

Attention was not just attracted by great acts of piety: sick children also commanded notice through their more mundane behaviour. At eight o'clock one October evening in 1625 when Grace Wallington was washing the dishes, her three-year-old daughter Elizabeth asked her, 'What doe you heere?' Later that night when she was in bed, she said to her father, 'Father I goe abroode tomorrow and bye [buy] you a plomee pie'.[69] The reason these everyday sentences were remembered by Elizabeth's parents was that 'These were the last words that I did heere my sweete child speeke', for the next day, she died. Some forty years later, John Vernon recalled the words of his dying son, twelve-year-old Caleb: he had spoken of his pet bird, saying *'I will give it to my Sister Betty, who hath none, for Nancy* [another sister] *hath one already'.*[70] Thus, parents' awareness of the likelihood of death endowed children's words and actions with special importance. Mothers and fathers paid great attention to the thoughts and behaviour of their sick children, painfully conscious that these might soon be treasured as final memories. These moving insights into the ordinary preoccupations of sick children demonstrate that parents took seriously the words of their offspring however trivial they might appear in hindsight.

Thus far, the underlying assumption has been that attention was comforting to child patients. However, this was not always the case: 'Sometimes sick persons can ill bear noise', warned the conduct book writer John Kettlewell in 1695, 'or would be troubled, not relieved, by the presence of others'.[71] At times, children probably felt so unwell that they simply wished for peace and quiet, and found the attention of nurses, doctors, family and visitors, exhausting. This is apparent in the biography of Caleb Vernon: he complained to his mother that the 'noise being made among the little ones', his younger sisters, *'hurt[s] me'.*[72] Especially tiring was making polite conversation with visitors: when thirteen-year-old Thomas Darling was questioned on 'poeticall and other schoole points' in 1597, he grew 'wearie' of his visitor's 'companie and conference . . . as indeede he had great reason, being unfitt for such

[67] Bidbanck, *A present for children*, 52.
[68] Alexandra Walsham, '"Out of the Mouths of Babes and Sucklings": Prophecy, Puritanism, and Childhood in Elizabethan Suffolk', in Diana Wood (ed.), *The Church and Childhood*, Studies in Church History, vol. 31 (Oxford: 1994), 285–300, at 295–6.
[69] Guildhall Library, London, MS 204, pp. 407–9.
[70] Vernon, *The compleat scholler*, 53–4.
[71] John Kettlewell, *Death made comfortable* (1695), 56–7.
[72] Vernon, *The compleat scholler*, 59.

an occasion . . . and desired to be carried into another chamber'.[73] Listening to the prayers of relatives and friends could be similarly exhausting. After tolerating hours of prayer, the adolescent Hannah Crump 'at last . . . rose and . . . in a very great rage', cried out that she wanted them to '*let her alone . . . and be quiet*'.[74] Although the child's family interpreted this outburst as the voice of Satan, it does nevertheless reveal something of the feelings of this child at the time.

The attention directed towards the preparation for death could also be burdensome.[75] In 1674, sixteen-year-old Elizabeth Walker confessed to her physician that 'health was the fittest time to prepare for death, for in sickness she could do little more than to consult her ease', implying that she found the process most arduous.[76] In the same decade, Isaac Archer recorded in his diary that when he had tried to persuade his six-year-old daughter Frances to say her catechism, she had found 'speaking was painfull', and therefore she 'look't earnestly on mee, but said nothing'.[77] Families were often sensitive to their children's difficulties, noticing when they were struggling, and leaving them in peace. When Mary Glover attempted to participate in the religious devotion organized on her behalf, her parents perceived her to be 'wax pale-coloured, weeping, and answering faintly', and in response, took a 'little pause', so that she 'might . . . refresh' herself.[78]

Another context in which children sometimes did not relish the attention of patienthood, was when they were being looked after away from their parents or their homes. These children occasionally felt so homesick that they remained inconsolable however diligent the care. When the schoolboy James Clavering fell ill of a languishing disease in the 1720s, he was tended by his uncle, John Yorke. Yorke wrote to James' father, telling him that the boy's 'impatience to see you, and return home, makes him fret and very uneasie, as he was this morning, which provoked a violent fit of coughing'.[79] As well as confirming that there was thought to be a causal link between emotional and physical distress, this extract implies that it was considered quite acceptable for an adolescent boy to desire the presence of his parents during illness, even though the ideology of masculinity demanded independence in boys.[80] Daughters as well as sons missed their parents. In 1709, Lady Elizabeth Hervey told her husband that their ill daughter Angellica, 'comes down and looks in your place every morning, and calls [for] you, and then holds up her hands and says all is gone'. A few years later, their other sick daughter, Pegg, told her mother

---

[73] I. D., *The most wonderfull and true storie*, 16.

[74] 'A true relation of the wonderful deliverance of Hannah Crump', in John Barrow, *The Lord's arm stretched out in an answer of prayer* (1664), 17–20, at 19.

[75] Lucinda Becker, *Death and the Early Modern Englishwoman* (Aldershot and Burlington, VT: 2003), 17.

[76] Walker, *The vertuous wife*, 109.

[77] Archer, *Two East Anglian Diaries*, 160–1.

[78] Swan, 'A True and Briefe Report', 301–3.

[79] Sir James Clavering, *The Correspondence of Sir James Clavering*, ed. Harry Thomas Dickinson, Surtees Society, vol. 178 (Gateshead: 1967), 159–60.

[80] Fletcher, *Growing Up in England*, 15.

'she shall not recover till [her father] come[s]'.[81] These intimate insights into the feelings of two sisters testify the deep love of daughters for their fathers.[82]

Sick children were not always the centre of attention: sometimes they were left without proper care. Following a bout of smallpox in December 1657, seventeen-year-old Isaac Archer bewailed, 'I knew not what course to take, for my tutour was out of the colledge, [and] I had none to look after mee but my bed-maker, who was none of the skilfullest'.[83] This situation, which was caused by the chance absence of the boy's tutor, was an unnerving experience for Isaac, eliciting feelings of helplessness and indignation. Inattentive care could also be the consequence of disorganization or misunderstanding. In 1709, Anne Clavering confessed that her twelve-year-old half-sister Betty, who was suffering from an ague, was 'in distress of a nurse' because the 'laxfull woman' who had agreed to nurse her 'went quite away' in the night, having 'gott intelligence that we had' another nurse 'in reserve'. When the girl awoke,

[S]he call'd, and having no answer fell asleep, wakes again and calls. Nobody answers so then the child riss out of bed, walkd round the room, opens the chamber door, and calls and [it] was some time before she make the house hear. I bless myself she was not kill'd by it. Thank God itt only renew'd her cough.[84]

Evidently, Anne was angry with the nurse, and anxious for Betty, believing that the child's distress had exacerbated her illness. The above examples reveal something of the expectations of patients and their families: they anticipated patienthood to be a time of attention and care, and felt deprived if it was denied.

Another situation where sick children were not the centre of attention was when family members sickened simultaneously or consecutively, as was usual in outbreaks of infectious disease. The consequence was the stretching of the available resources between the patients. In 1689, Dr van Diemerbroeck recorded in his casebook that a 'Lad of Fourteen Years of Age', the son of Isaac Schorer, 'was taken in *September* with a Fever and Small Pox', but by the fourteenth day of his illness, 'his Brother . . . was taken in the same manner'; several days later, his sister Mary, about 'Ten Years of Age', fell sick of the same Distemper', before finally the youngest daughter, Maud 'had the Small Pox come very thick upon her'. It seems inevitable that the attention—in terms of nursing, visitors, sympathy and so forth—would have been limited in this context. Nevertheless, van Diemerbroeck emphasized that the medical care he provided was not deficient, stating that because they 'were all of one Family', he had the opportunity to 'see them [all] every hour' during their distempers.[85] However, the situation

---

[81] John Hervey, *Letter-Books of John Hervey, First Earl of Bristol*, ed. S. H. A. Hervey, 3 vols (Wells: 1894), vol. 1, 247, and vol. 2, 161.

[82] Ralph Houlbrooke agrees that fathers and daughters could develop affectionate relationships, *The English Family 1450–1700* (1984), 185.

[83] Archer, *Two East Anglian Diaries*, 54–5.

[84] Clavering, *The Correspondence of Sir James Clavering*, 60–1.

[85] Ysbrand van Diemerbroeck, *The anatomy of human bodies . . . to which is added a particular treatise of the small pox* (1689), 31.

was probably far worse during epidemics of plague: historians have shown that whole communities probably died without any care at all.[86]

During these occasions of multiple illnesses, parents occasionally favoured one child with more attention than the others. Lady Fanshawe admitted that when both her 'eldest daughters had the smallpox at the same time ... I neglected them, and day and night attended my dear son'.[87] Her preference may have stemmed from a bias towards sons. However, it should not be inferred that girls were always likely to suffer in these contexts, for there is evidence to suggest that daughters were sometimes preferred to sons. In 1711, Lady Elizabeth Hervey confessed to her husband that she was most 'particular' for her daughter, whom she had affection- ately nicknamed 'Sweet-Face'.[88] Nevertheless, parental favouritism did not always result in the neglect of the less favoured children. 'I ever concealed what passion I had for her', confided Ralph Verney to his wife in 1647 shortly after the death of his favourite child Pegg. He admitted that he had 'rather appeared to neglect her ... least ... over fondnesse should spoyle her, or make the others jellous'.[89] A popular ballad from the 1670s suggests that favouritism was a familiar concept, though it was frowned upon: 'let all Parents that this Ditty hear, Have equal kindness for your Children dear; Those that you think scarce worthy of your love Do sometimes the greatest Blessings prove'.[90]

Although the link between levels of medical attention and socio-economic status is far from clear-cut, it does seem likely that poverty would have acted as a limiting factor to the amount of care that could be provided to a sick child. Poor parents may have found it more difficult to afford the services of nurses and medical practitioners, and they may have been unable to carry out the care duties themselves owing to the pressures of paid employment. A rather extreme example is provided in the Proceedings of the Old Bailey: in 1714, a one-year-old boy, who had the smallpox, was found abandoned with nothing but 'a piece of green Rug pinn'd about' him.[91] There is no indication as to why he had been left, but one could speculate that it might have been because the parents could not afford to care for him in his ailing state. Around the same time, in France, the son of a labourer called Valentin Jamerey-Duval, contracted the smallpox; the only care he received was being put in the middle of the sheepfold and wrapped in 'straw and manure' for warmth.[92] Ralph Houlbrooke has suggested that poorer patients, 'Without servants ... [or] a kinship network which could be activated by the hope of reciprocal services', would probably have been more likely to spend their illness 'alone or in the company of one or two other people'.[93] Nevertheless, Patricia Crawford has asserted

[86] Paul Slack, *The Impact of Plague in Tudor and Stuart England* (Oxford: 1990), 41.
[87] Ann Fanshawe, *Memoirs of Lady Fanshawe*, ed. Richard Fanshawe (1829), 133–4.
[88] Hervey, *Letter-Books of John Hervey*, vol. 1, 302.
[89] Frances Verney (ed), *The Verney Memoirs, 1600–1659*, 2 vols (1925, first publ. 1892), vol. 1, 395.
[90] *The downfall of pride* (1675–96).
[91] OBP, reference: OA17140716 (accessed 14 January 2011).
[92] Colin Heywood, *Growing Up in France from the Ancien Régime to the Third Republic* (Cambridge: 2007), 180.
[93] Houlbrooke, *Death, Religion, and the Family*, 192.

that many parents from the lowest social levels provided 'devoted' care to their ill children.[94] Cheaper forms of care could be accessed, such as home-made medicines composed of herbs grown in local meadows. Those in desperate straits could also apply for help from the parish, and obtain the services of parish nurses.[95] Towards the end of the seventeenth century, young patients were more likely to be cared for within an institutional setting, such as workhouses or hospitals.[96] The shortage of qualitative evidence about poorer children makes it very difficult to uncover their emotional experiences of patienthood.

EXEMPTION FROM ROUTINES

In 1975, the sociologist Talcott Parsons claimed that an essential feature of patienthood or 'the sick role' was 'exemption from ordinary daily obligations and expectations' such school or work.[97] This seems to have been true for early modern children. In the 1650s, Winefrid Thimelby informed her brother-in-law Herbert Aston that his daughter Kate's 'ill health was so continuall' that she 'could not have [been] sett . . . seriously to any thing', and consequently, 'learnt . . . little'.[98] About ten years later, the same concern was voiced by Ralph Verney in relation to a young boy he was looking after: 'I thought him a greate stranger . . . to learning', wrote Ralph to the boy's father, 'for by reason of . . . his . . . Ague' he had only attended about 'five days' of school during the period of 'five moneths'. He added, 'your sonn must not be pressed too hard till [he] is absolutely freed [from] this troublesome ague', and assured the father that, 'my owne Boy, by reason of his sisters & his owne sicknesse hath had greate hindrances too'.[99] Children may have relished their exemption from school. Edward Gibbon, in the mid-eighteenth century, 'secretly rejoiced in those infirmities which delivered me from the exercises of school and the society of my equals'.[100] Indeed, it is possible that children sometimes feigned or induced their illnesses on purpose, in the hope that it would release them from school. This was so for twelve-year-old James Fraser in 1651: having been 'grievously awed' at school, and 'ordinarily whipt whether I deserved it or not', he decided to 'procure a Sickness' in order to 'rid' himself of this 'grievous bondage'. His method was to pick 'green Fruits' and 'eat nothing but that, and . . . go naked all Night'.[101] However, not all children enjoyed being excused from their education

---

[94] Crawford, *Parents of Poor Children*, 128.

[95] Jeremy Boulton, 'Welfare Systems and the Parish Nurse in Early Modern London, 1650–1725', *Family and Community History*, 10 (2007), 127–51. A similar service was provided in France: Susan Broomhall, *Women's Medical Work in Early Modern France* (Manchester: 2004), 162, 179.

[96] Crawford, *Parents of Poor Children*, 182, 189.

[97] Talcott Parsons, 'The Sick Role and the Role of the Physician Reconsidered', *The Milbank Memorial Fund Quarterly. Health and Society*, 53 (1975), 257–78, at 262.

[98] BL, Additional MS 36452, fol. 76r (Private letters of the Aston family, 1613–1703).

[99] BL, M.636/8, this manuscript is unfoliated (Verney papers on microfilm, 1646–50; a letter dated 22/12 December 1647).

[100] Cited in Porters, *In Sickness and in Health*, 190.

[101] James Fraser, *Memoirs of the Life of . . . Mr James Fraser* (Edinburgh: 1738), 19.

in this way: in 1660, seven-year-old John Harvy was afflicted with 'sore eyes' which 'kept him from School' and prevented him from reading 'any Book whatsover at home'. The child was 'grieved', for he loved school 'as well as many boys do their play'.[102]

For children lower down the social scale, illness may have been one of the few occasions when work was suspended.[103] In 1659, eleven-year-old James Yonge was apprenticed to a 'morose, ill-natured' surgeon, who had kept him 'perpetually working'. Yonge was so unhappy that he 'often wished ... [himself] dead'. Only when he was ill of a 'malign fever', was he permitted to rest.[104] Historians have shown that poor children as young as seven were subjected to extremely arduous employment: as parish apprentices, they were engaged in work similar to servants, but under harsher conditions.[105] By the end of the seventeenth century, it was becoming increasingly common for local authorities to send poor children to workhouses, where they were expected to engage in intense labour discipline.[106] The 'College of Infants' in Middlesex required girls to knit and sew, while the boys living in a Cambridgeshire workhouse spent their days ploughing fields.[107] Some children found the work so exhausting that they were prepared to feign illness. This is implied in a rulebook for a workhouse in Buckinghamshire, published in 1725: it states that 'if any Person will not work, pretending Sickness, which may be discover'd by their Stomachs or otherwise, they shall be severely punish'd'.[108]

As well as missing school or work, sick children may have escaped discipline. Since 'Discipline and restraint were central elements' of children's lives, this feature of patienthood may have been especially appreciated by children.[109] In 1661, the adolescent Hannah Crump, who had been suffering from demonic fits, rose from bed 'in a very great rage' and 'struck her father and sisters' violently. Rather than punish his daughter for her behaviour, her father saw his child as 'an object of Pity' because her actions were induced by the 'bonds of Satan'.[110] In orthodox theology, it was wrong to blame the Devil in this way, since humans had been 'endowed with the capacity to resist the temptations of Lucifer'.[111] But, in practice parents probably found it emotionally easier to regard their children as blameless in these situations. Children suffering from natural illnesses were also excused from

---

[102] Janeway, *A token for children* (part 2), 72–3.
[103] For a description of children's work, see Ilana Krausman Ben-Amos, *Adolescene and Youth in Early Modern England* (1994), 40–5.
[104] James Yonge, *The Journal of James Yonge (1647–1721), Plymouth Surgeon*, ed. F. N. L. Poynter (1963), 32, 39.
[105] Crawford, *Parents of Poor Children*, 157. See also, Steven Hindle, '"Waste" Children? Pauper Apprenticeship under the Elizabethan Poor Laws, c.1598–1697', in Penelope Lane, Neil Raven, and K. Snell (eds), *Women, Work and Wages in England 1600–1850* (Woodbridge: 2004), 28–9.
[106] Crawford, *Parents of Poor Children*, 212.
[107] Ibid. 212.
[108] *An account of several work-houses for employing and maintaining the poor* (1725), 76.
[109] Houlbrooke, *The English Family*, 141.
[110] 'A true relation', 19–20.
[111] Alexandra Walsham, *Providence in Early Modern England* (Oxford: 2003, first publ. 1999), 14, 331.

discipline in some instances. When first taken ill of a fever in 1589, ten-year-old Jane Throckmorton turned to one of her elderly visitors, and shouted, 'look where the old witch sits . . . Did you ever see . . . one more like a witch than she? . . . I cannot abide to look on her'. Her mother, though 'very angry with her child', imputed this rude outburst to 'some lightness in the child's brain by reason of her great sneezing and want of sleep', and therefore 'laid her down upon a bed' and did not punish her.[112] Thus, as patients, children's responsibility for their behaviour was lifted, because contemporaries believed that disease affected the mind as well as the body. Parents may have also thought that illness itself was a punishment, and therefore the infliction of further correction was unnecessary. This was the case in the Isham household during the 1620s: Elizabeth Isham recalled in her autobiography that her mother was always 'much pitt[y]ing & sparing' her sister from punishment on the grounds that the child 'was [already] corrected by thy hand O Lord' in the form of illness 'from her berth'.[113]

There were occasions, however, when young patients were not excused from their daily routines. During trivial illness, schooling and apprenticeships were often continued. While suffering from an eye condition in 1538, eleven-year-old James Lisle informed his mother that, 'Each day I go to lectures with my fellows . . . After . . . I return to my chamber, where . . . my tutor, repeateth with me my lessons'.[114] Roughly a century and a half later, when young Tom Browne had diarrhoea for a week, his grandmother wrote cheerfully that it 'did pull him not to kepe from scoole but 2 days'.[115] Occasionally, discipline may have also been maintained, although this usually occurred when children were suspected of counterfeiting illness. Thirteen-year-old James Barrow was 'stript and whipt' when he first showed signs of possession in 1661, because his father thought that 'the Boy dissembled'.[116] Poor servants and apprentices were especially vulnerable to harsh discipline during sickness, as is revealed in various court proceedings. In 1595, a nine-year-old servant called Thomas Lincolne, who was already weak from illness, was whipped so harshly by his mistress that he died from his wounds.[117] Over a century later, James Durant, a wigribbon-weaver, was tried for beating to death 'a very little Boy', his thirteen-year-old apprentice, for idleness: the child had been suffering from diarrhoea and cough.[118]

---

[112] 'The most strange and admirable discovery', 77–8.

[113] Elizabeth Isham, '*My Booke of Rememenberance*': [sic] *The Autobiography of Elizabeth Isham*, ed. Isaac Stephens; PDF file on the internet, website address: http://history.ucr.edu/people/grad_students/stephens/TheAutobiography.pdf, 6 (accessed June 2009).

[114] St Clare Byrne (ed.), *The Lisle Letters*, vol. 4, 502.

[115] Sir Thomas Browne, *The Works of Sir Thomas Browne*, ed. Geoffrey Keynes (1931), 196.

[116] John Barrow, *The Lord's arm stretched out in an answer of prayer, or, a true relation of the wonderful deliverance of James Barrow, the son of John Barrow* (1664), 12–13.

[117] Cited by Terence Murphy, '"Woeful Childe of Parents' Rage": Suicide of Children and Adolescents in Early Modern England, 1507–1710', *Sixteenth-Century Journal*, 17 (1986), 259–70, at 267.

[118] Cited by Crawford, *Parents of Poor Children*, 159.

HOPE AND RELIEF

Historians of medicine have often implied that being a patient in the early modern period was an utterly miserable experience, owing to the backwardness of medicine. Guy Williams, in his aptly named book, *The Age of Agony*, declared that the 'horrors' that the sick endured 'scarcely bear repeating'.[119] Such an approach privileges modern scientific ideas about past medicine over contemporary perceptions and experiences. Perhaps a more appropriate approach is to examine what patients themselves thought about taking physic, while resisting the temptation to assess retrospectively whether such medicine could have 'really worked'. There is evidence that children sometimes did believe their treatments were effective. Following several months of wearing a brace to cure his rickets in the 1650s, fifteen-year-old Edmund Verney wrote to his father, declaring triumphantly, 'I may truly say the cure is almost perfected'; he added with glee that 'I am almost as tall, if not taller than my cousin Spenser'.[120] He was clearly delighted to be able to send such good news to his father. Younger children also shared this therapeutic experience: when the infant Willey Morris was given 'a clyster & some Medicines for the Wind' in the early eighteenth century, his father noted that the child felt 'much the better'.[121] Although we cannot be sure how far this little boy agreed with his father's interpretation, these examples do seem to contradict the notion that 'seventeenth-century . . . people did not expect . . . medicines to cure them'.[122] The question of whether the positive responses stemmed from the efficacy of the medicine or from a 'placebo' seems irrelevant.

As well as appearing to cure illnesses, children often believed that their pains were soothed by taking physic. When an 'ointment of Roses' was applied to the swelled legs of one of the Verney boys in 1647, the child felt 'much ease[d]', and noted that the sore was 'suppled'.[123] Over twenty years later, ten-year-old Hannah Martindale reported she felt 'somewhat better' from the rickets after taking a bath in 'cow-bellies new killed'.[124] Although this last treatment might sound repulsive, the use of animal carcasses was common in the early modern period, so it probably elicited a different reaction.[125] Children sometimes actively requested particular treatments because they anticipated the analgesic effects. In 1681, the schoolboy Tom Browne 'begged to bleed a little and to go into a *balneum dulce*' in the hope that it would

---

[119] Williams, *The Age of Agony*, 51, 66.

[120] BL, M.636/12 (Verney papers on microfilm, 1646–50; a letter dated 22 July 1653). My thanks to Leona Archer, a Cambridge PhD student, for translating this letter from French into English.

[121] Claver Morris, *The Diary of a West Country Physician, 1648–1726*, ed. Edmund Hobhouse (1935), 58.

[122] McCray Beier, 'The Good Death', 44.

[123] BL, M.636/8, this manuscript is unfoliated (Verney papers on microfilm, 1646–50; a letter dated 24 November 1647).

[124] Adam Martindale, *The Life of Adam Martindale*, ed. Richard Parkinson, Chetham Society, vol. 4 (Manchester: 1845), 214–15.

[125] See Lisa Silverman, *Tortured Subjects: Pain, Truth, and the Body in Early Modern France* (2001), 144.

make him feel better.[126] It is perhaps not surprising that pain relief was a common experience for children in this period: as we saw in an earlier chapter, the mitigation of suffering was a key priority in children's physic. Doctors frequently insisted that it was necessary to '*First abate pain*' when treating children, by adding small quantities of opium and various other ingredients to the medicines.[127]

Sick children sometimes liked the taste of their medicines. Edmund Verney was given a 'diet drink' to cure him of various ailments, which his father declared he 'likes...very well'.[128] This same father gave a similar drink to the young son of his friend Mr Busby: 'I...boyle Hartshorne...in all the water he drinks', 'which is very cordiall' to him.[129] The authors of domestic recipe books often reminded their readers to add sugar to children's medicines to improve the taste, and to avoid 'ungrateful' ingredients. Anne Glyd suggested that her medicine for 'chin cough' should be put into 'hony' or 'what ever the child likes best'.[130] Medical texts and casebooks replicated this advice. John Pechey, for example, suggested that medicines for killing worms should contain 'things that are more pleasant', while 'bitter things...as Wormwood, Scordium, and the like' must be avoided because 'Children will not easily take them'.[131]

While some medicines probably did bring relief from suffering, others appear to have been less effective. In 1667, fourteen-year-old Samuel Jeake complained that the 'Vesicatory', which had been applied to his neck to cure his headache, 'took not away the pain'.[132] When young James Hervey was sick of an ague fifty years later, his mother lamented, 'I don't find that either the bleeding, blistering, or purging gives him any relief'.[133] Her words convey a strong sense of frustration. Doctors also reported cases of ineffective medicines. In 1650, Dr Thomas Willis complained that the physic he had prescribed to the four-year-old son of Mrs Dapwell was 'without any profit. In fact everything grew worse'.[134] A few decades later, the surgeon Richard Wiseman acknowledged that the 'cephalick Emplaster' that he had applied to the head of his six-month-old patient had 'made such an itching and soarness' to the skin that it had had to be quickly removed.[135] Although the above examples do not reveal the children's emotional responses to these medicines, it seems likely that they would have shared the frustration of the doctors and parents.

As well as being ineffective, medicines themselves could 'inadvertently or directly increase the pain of the patient'.[136] This aspect of physic is revealed in a letter

[126] Browne, *The Works of Sir Thomas Browne*, 222–3.
[127] See Ch. 2 for further details.
[128] BL, M.636/8, this manuscript is unfoliated (Verney papers on microfilm, 1646–50; a letter dated 9 February 1648).
[129] Ibid. (a letter dated 5 January/26 December, 1647/8).
[130] BL, Additional MS 45196, fol. 51r (Brockman Papers, 'Ann Glyd Her Book 1656').
[131] John Pechey, *A general treatise of the diseases of infants and children* (1697), 123–4.
[132] Samuel Jeake, *An Astrological Diary of the Seventeenth Century: Samuel Jeake of Rye*, ed. Michael Hunter (Oxford: 1988), 92. A 'Vesicatory' was a sharp substance that provoked a blister.
[133] Hervey, *Letter-Books of John Hervey*, 371.
[134] Thomas Willis, *Willis's Oxford Casebook (1650–52)*, ed. Kenneth Dewhurst (Oxford: 1981), 105.
[135] Richard Wiseman, *Several chirurgical treatises* (1686, first publ. 1676), 133.
[136] Schoenfeldt, 'Aesthetic and Anesthetics', 21.

written by fifteen-year-old Edmund Verney to his father in 1653 about the brace he wore to correct his rickets:

> [A]fter first wearing the brace I found that I was in great pain . . . each time they tightened it, it seemed worse than I could bear because I felt as if I was being pressed, and such extreme pain that I believe my senses lapsed and I had to be taken home . . . the leather covering my brace on the inside . . . .when all nine screws are in place [cause] the continual heat of my body [which] is trapped in me always, with the effect that the heat gives off such a strong smell that it's quite intolerable, and each day ruins the white shirts I'm wearing.[137]

The discomfort caused by the tightness of the brace and its heating effects, was almost insupportable for Edmund. Evacuative treatments, such as vomits, purges, and blisters, were notoriously 'unpleasing, ful of pain and molestation to Children', according to the medical writer Francis Glisson.[138] After taking several purges, one patient of four years old 'cried at the very sight' of her doctor.[139] Dr William Brownrigg recorded that his eleven-year-old patient, Jonathan Kelsick, became 'very anxious and miserable' upon the contemplation of blistering 'vesicatories' (ointments) being 'applied to his feet'.[140] Treatments which elicited the greatest distress were surgical procedures. In the early 1600s, the young sister of the North-ampton autobiographer Elizabeth Isham had been so afraid of having her thigh bone reset after a break that 'her teeth would chatter in her head for very feare'.[141] Considering that there was no effective anaesthetic in this period, it is hardly surprising that surgery provoked this response.[142] As soon as the child spied the 'Knife', felt the 'smart', and saw the 'bloud trickel down', crying and terror would inevitably result, according to the surgeon Richard Wiseman.[143] Another surgeon, Daniel Turner, complained that after carrying out an operation on a boy of fourteen in 1714, the boy 'cry'd out in Passion' that 'he would die before' he would allow him to 'cut' him for a second time.[144] Children from all socio-economic levels seem to have feared operations. The Proceedings of the Old Bailey report that a poor girl of nine years old, Phillis Holmes, who had been raped, was to 'make her tell' the identity of the rapist through the threat that the local surgeon would 'have her cut to pieces' unless she confessed.[145] Nevertheless, it must be

---

[137] BL, M.636/12, this manuscript is unfoliated (Verney papers on microfilm, 1646–50; a letter dated 24 March 1653; translated by Leona Archer into English from French).
[138] Francis Glisson, George Bate, and Assuerus Regemorter, *A treatise of the rickets being a diseas common to children*, trans. Philip Armin (1651), 317.
[139] Wiseman, *Several chirurgical treatises*, 288.
[140] William Brownrigg, *The Medical Casebook of William Brownrigg, MD, FRS (1712–1800) of the Town of Whitehaven in Cumberland*, eds Jean E. Ward and Joan Yell, Medical History Supplement, vol. 13 (1993), 55.
[141] Isham, '*My Booke of Rememenberance*' [sic], 10.
[142] See Peter Stanley, *For Fear of Pain: British Surgery, 1790–1850* (Amsterdam and New York: 2003) and Silverman, *Tortured Subjects*, 133–51.
[143] Wiseman, *Several chirurgical treatises*, 278.
[144] Daniel Turner, *De morbis cutaneis, a treatise of diseases incident to the skin* (1714), 213.
[145] Cited by Crawford, *Parents of Poor Children*, 147.

noted that practitioners did endeavour to mitigate the painfulness of treatment where possible, and frequently abstained from surgical procedures.[146]

While painful medicines were unpleasant, they may not have been entirely devoid of therapeutic effect. There was a long held belief that in order for a medicine to work, it had to be 'as bitter as the disease', and therefore the suffering induced by treatment may have actually served to elicit hope of recovery.[147] Perhaps this was the case for the aforementioned Edmund Verney, who told his father he was 'very hopeful that I will become perfectly right soon, because after first wearing the brace I found that I was in great pain, but within three days . . . I began gaining strength'.[148] Possibly, the association between pain and therapy stemmed from the religious notion that divine punishment was necessary for the good of the soul.[149] Children may have been especially aware of this association, due to their familiarity with corporal punishment, and the idea that it was 'for their good'. As Sarah Toulalan has suggested, when pain is regarded as benevolent, the whole experience of suffering is 'transformed', and becomes more bearable, and even occasionally desirable.[150] From today's perspective this positive attitude to suffering is challenging, but in the early modern period, it was an entrenched element of the religious culture. It is also possible that the painfulness of medical treatment served as a useful 'distraction from another pain', the pain of illness: 'violent purges . . . may have been in the production of a kind of distress that distracted one from the primary pain'.[151]

Another advantage of painful physic was that it provided an occasion for 'virtuous and praiseworthy exhibition of stoic forbearance', eliciting commendation from parents and friends.[152] Five-year-old Richard Cholmley was applauded by his father for his 'courridge and resolution', and lack of 'whimpering' during an unpleasant surgical procedure in the mid-seventeenth century.[153] In 1709, Daniel Turner was so impressed by the bravery of his young patient, a boy of six, that he called him a 'little Champion' and a 'little *Hero*', and congratulated him for his 'Manly Courage' during a painful operation to his head.[154] Such praise may have been especially rewarding for boys, for it gave them the opportunity to demonstrate courage, an attribute of particular importance in males.[155] Nevertheless, girls were also praised for their bravery, which suggests that they too may have derived satisfaction from this aspect of patienthood. When Elizabeth Isham's sister allowed her doctor to reset her broken thigh bone, a relative remarked

---

[146] See Ch. 2 for detail about pain mitigation.

[147] Ariel Glucklich, *Sacred Pain: Hurting the Body for the Sake of the Soul* (Oxford and New York: 2001), 22.

[148] BL, M.636/12, this manuscript is unfoliated (Verney papers on microfilm, 1646–50; a letter dated 24 March 1653; translated by Leona Archer from French into English).

[149] See Glucklich, *Sacred Pain*.

[150] Sarah Toulalan, *Imagining Sex: Pornography and Bodies in Seventeenth-Century England* (Oxford and New York: 2007), 124.

[151] Schoenfeldt, 'The Art of Pain Management', 32.

[152] Ibid. 26.

[153] Hugh Cholmley, *The Memoirs and Memorials of Sir Hugh Cholmley of Whitby 1600–1657*, ed. Jack Binns, Yorkshire Archaeological Society, vol. 153 (Woodbridge: 2000), 91.

[154] Daniel Turner *A remarkable case in surgery . . . in a child about six years old* (1709), 11, 25, 39.

[155] Elizabeth Foyster, *Manhood in Early Modern England: Honour, Sex, and Marriage* (1999), 31.

that she had shown the bravery of 'a Marter', to their 'great comfort and Joy'.[156] Another girl, Mary Anne Schimmelpenninck, stoically endured the drawing of four teeth without any pain relief: her medical practitioner was impressed, telling her mother that 'Thy little girl is too much of a philosopher'.[157] These examples indicate that although the endurance of pain was applauded in both sexes, the ideological underpinnings may have differed slightly for males and females: boys' stoicism was associated with the ideology of masculinity, whereas girls' bravery carried connotations of saintliness and martyrdom.

Prayer as well as medicine could be a source of hope and comfort to young patients. 'We know the prayers of the faithful are very powerful with the Lord', proclaimed eleven-year-old Margaret Muschamp during her illness in 1646. 'God had laid it on her, and God would take it off her', she declared.[158] A few decades later, Caleb Vernon cried, '*Why, I know God will help me, and I will trust in him*', while sick of consumption.[159] Children's positive attitude to prayer is demonstrated by their tendency to actively request it themselves. In 1596, thirteen-year-old Thomas Darling cried out, 'O pray, pray, never more need to pray'.[160] The apparent spontaneity of this boy's demand suggests that he genuinely believed that prayer would bring him relief. Even very young children were able to derive hope from this practice. William Bidbanck, the author of several children's biographies, recorded that an infant of two and a half years, when lifted from her cradle, would ask to 'see such a Minister', and demand that he '*Pray for Miss,* (as she always call'd her self, from hearing others so call her)'.[161] After hearing the prayers, the child showed her appreciation by kissing the minister 'many times'.[162] Of course, it must be borne in mind that these positive responses may have been exaggerated, since the authors wanted to emphasize the children's piety. This was especially likely in the biographies of pious children, since these documents were intended to act as models for ideal conduct. Nevertheless, the fact that other types of sources also contain evidence of this response does suggest that it is credible. A ballad entitled *The happy damsel* (1693), tells the story of a 'poor lame Creature' from Westminster, thirteen-year-old Maria Anna Mollier, who was convinced she would be 'heal'd her by a Mighty Hand'. She prayed, 'I do believe thou able art to cure me still'.[163] The author claimed that the story was true, but even if it was not, it demonstrates that contemporaries thought it quite believable that children of all socio-economic levels could derive hope from prayer.

Prayer did not always elicit hope of recovery, however: children sometimes despaired of God's mercy. This was the case for the possessed adolescent Mary

---

[156] Isham, '*My Booke of Rememenberance*' [sic], 11.
[157] Cited in Porter, *In Sickness and in Health*, 100–1.
[158] Mary Moore, '"Wonderful News from the North. Or, a True Relation of the Sad and Grievous Torments, Inflicted on the Bodies of Three Children of Mr George Muschamp, Late of the County of Northumberland, by Witch-Craft" (1650)', in Almond (ed.), *Demonic Possession*, 363–90 at 365.
[159] Vernon, *The compleat scholler*, 25–6.
[160] I. D., *The most wonderfull and true storie*, 28.
[161] Bidbanck, *A present for children*, 34–5.
[162] Ibid. 35.
[163] *The happy damsel* (1693).

Glover: when her family and friends engaged in passionate prayer, she was observed 'sitting, weeping bitterly . . . casting out words of fear that God would not hear us in calling on him' for her recovery.[164] Some children found prayer upsetting because it was accompanied by tears and desperate pleadings. When twelve-year-old Caleb Vernon saw his father's 'gushed out . . . tears' during his illness in the 1660s, he 'said earnestly . . . weeping, *Pray Father do not weep*'.[165] Prayer could also be a source of boredom. Joseph Lister reminisced in his autobiography that as a boy of ten or eleven, he was 'often weary' of 'those weeping, praying, and wrestling sermons' that had been kept with such 'strictness and severity'; he had 'longed to see those nights and days over'.[166] Similarly affected was the possessed boy James Barrow in 1661: on the third morning of communal prayer, he cried out, '*What three dayes! two dayes was enough . . . What, nothing but pray! what, all pray! all mad! will you kill your selves with praying? Three dayes is too much . . .*'[167]

POWER

In the early modern household, children occupied the bottom rung of the domestic hierarchy, possessing limited control over their daily routines.[168] This situation was upheld by religion, law, and the doctrine of patriarchy. Parents provided protection and provision to their offspring, and in return, children were expected to honour and obey their fathers and mothers.[169] However, as Roy and Dorothy Porter have stated, 'Sickness . . . was an anarch, replacing order with a certain confusion . . . parents waited upon the children they normally commanded'.[170] There were several ways by which children exerted power during illness. Firstly, they demanded things from their carers. In 1626, the two-year-old son of Nehemiah Wallington called to his maid, 'Jane, [']some beare[']', and it was promptly given to him.[171] Girls as well as boys exercised this authority: in 1705, four-year-old Betty Egleton 'called her Aunt . . . to read the *Bible*', and then, seeing her uncle 'Eating some Milk', she 'desired to eat some with him'; later, she decided that she would like to be 'carried . . . Two or Three times about the Room', before finally requesting 'to be laid down to go to Sleep'.[172] Females may have derived special satisfaction from this newfound power, because in their everyday lives they were probably subject to greater

[164] Swan, 'A True and Briefe Report', 303.

[165] Vernon, *The compleat scholler*, 73.

[166] Joseph Lister, *The Autobiography of Joseph Lister of Bradford, 1627–1709*, ed. A. Holroyd (Bradford: 1860), 7.

[167] Barrow, *The Lord's arm stretched out*, 17.

[168] Houlbrooke, *The English Family*, 144–5.

[169] Colin Heywood, *A History of Childhood: Children and Childhood in the West from Medieval to Modern Times* (Cambridge: 2001), 102; James Sharpe, 'Disruption in the Well-Ordered Household: Age, Authority and Possessed Young People', in Paul Griffiths, Adam Fox, and Steve Hindle (eds), *The Experience of Authority in Early Modern England* (Basingstoke: 1996), 187–212, at 191, 197–9, 205.

[170] Porter and Porter, *In Sickness and in Health*, 192.

[171] Guildhall Library, London, MS 204, p. 421.

[172] E. C., *Some part of the life and death of Mrs Elizabeth Egleton, who Died . . . 1705 in the fifth year of her age* (1705), 23–4.

authority than boys.[173] Sometimes children's requests were quite extreme: twelve-year-old Caleb Vernon asked his parents for '*a young Lamb, Pigeon, Rabbit or any thing*' to be brought to his bed, in order to 'divert' him from his pains, and provide '*pretty company for me*'. Remarkably, his parents granted his request, deciding that a pet squirrel would be best, because 'it might easily be procured'.[174] What is striking about children's demands, is the assertiveness with which they were delivered: they often lacked the usual deference and politeness required of the young. 'O! Mother, pray, pray for me', cried fourteen-year-old Sarah Howley, without saying please or thank you.[175] Nonetheless, some children did maintain their manners: Isaac Archer remarked approvingly that his six-year-old daughter Frances, when requesting her father to come to her, added 'if you please', thus 'shewing her selfe dutifull, as all her life long so, to the last'.[176] The above examples demonstrate that patients were not passive, as is implied in modern discussions of the meaning of the word 'patient', but in fact were active agents, directly involved in their own care.

Another way that sick children exerted power was by admonishing those around them on religious issues. This was part of the process of preparation for death, necessary for demonstrating one's faith and God's grace.[177] These admonitions were often thought to be inspired by the Almighty, or even flowing from a divine presence within the sick themselves.[178] Consequently, ill children could assume a higher status than ever before, advising and reprimanding their elders unreservedly, in the knowledge that whatever they said, however apparently impertinent, would be respected as God's 'works of wonder'.[179] After ten days of delirium in 1581, eleven-year-old William Withers 'sharpely taunted' one of his visitors, '*Smith*', the friend of Master Ashly, a 'Gentleman of greate credite and worship', telling him that 'it were better for him to put on sackcloth & mourn for his sinnes, then in such abhominable pride to pranke up himselfe like the divels darling, the very father of pride and lying . . . in monstrous ruffes'. This harsh reproof was accepted humbly by the man, who proceeded to 'rent' off his 'great . . . ruffes', the subject of the boy's lecture, and vow that he would 'never . . . weare the like again'.[180] Thus, owing to his proximity to death, and to God, this child could usurp the traditional hierarchy, behaving in a way that would not normally have been tolerated. Alexandra Walsham has suggested that this boy may have enjoyed the rare opportunity.[181]

Girls as well as boys could offer spiritual admonitions during illness. In 1602, Mary Glover interrupted a sermon with her religious meditations: 'the maid's words were now waxing loud', recalled a witness, so that the onlookers found it 'confusing'

---

[173] Houlbrooke, *The English Family*, 186.
[174] Vernon, *The compleat scholler*, 65.
[175] *An account of the admirable conversion*, 4–5.
[176] Archer, *Two East Anglian Diaries*, 160–1.
[177] Houlbrooke, *Death, Religion, and the Family*, 158, 160–2.
[178] Ibid. 186.
[179] A very similar notion has been offered by Sharpe, but in relation to possessed children: 'Disruption in the Well-Ordered Household', 200.
[180] J. Philip, *The wonderfull worke of God shewed upon a chylde whose name is William Withers . . . eleven yeeres of age* (1581), document image 10.
[181] Walsham, 'Out of the Mouths of Babes', 299.

listening to both the girl and the preacher simultaneously; eventually, the preacher was obliged to 'cease . . . and gave us leave to hearken to her'. Mary's words were received with 'joyful attendance and silence' because they were thought to be imbued with God's spirit.[182] This extraordinary situation—where a young girl was permitted to interrupt an esteemed minister with her own religious advice—could only have been legitimized by her state of serious illness and her perceived closeness to the Lord.[183] Girls also admonished their male relatives. 'Father,' cried fourteen-year-old Sarah Howley in 1670, 'O take use of time to get Christ for your Creator before you come to a sick bed, put not this great work [off] til then, for then you will find it a hard work indeed'.[184] Older brothers were targeted too: four-year-old Mary Stubbs, while seriously ill, would speak to her brother 'for near a quarter of an hour' at a time, telling him to 'get alone into some private place, and pray to God, instead of playing'.[185] Considering that daughters were usually obliged to behave submissively around male family members, they may have relished this unusual situation. Mary Stubbs certainly did, for she admitted that she had had a 'great desire' to 'get an Opportunity to speak her Mind to her Brother largely'.[186] Historians agree that the preparation for death provided 'exceptional opportunities' for females: where previously they were forbidden to speak in church, 'they might now utter prayers, exhortations, and statements of faith which were heard with a special respect'.[187]

A briefer, less formal way in which young patients exerted power during the preparation for death was by 'answering back' to parents' advice. As before, this behaviour was tolerated because the sick were thought to possess a divine authority. When Caleb Vernon was speaking about religious issues in 1665, his family tried to 'restrain him from talking more', concerned that he needed rest: the boy answered, '*to speak of the things of God was not wearisome but refreshing*'.[188] Five years later, Sarah Howley's grandmother told her 'she [was] spend[ing] her self too much' in prayer; Sarah replied, 'I care not', and continued her prayers.[189] In both cases, the families did not reproach their children for their insolent responses, but interpreted them as evidence of their offspring's holiness.

A form of power that was probably exercised more widely was the child's refusal to take medicines or submit to surgical procedures. 'Children . . . cannot be gotten to take any inward Medicine at all', complained one anonymous medical author.[190]

[182] Swan, 'A True and Briefe Report', 306–7.
[183] This point has been made by Ralph Houlbrooke, but in relation to adult females, *Death, Religion, and the Family*, 186.
[184] *An account of the admirable conversion*, 9–10.
[185] Bidbanck, *A present for children*, 49.
[186] Ibid.
[187] Houlbrooke, *Death, Religion, and the Family*, 185; Becker, *Death and the Early Modern Englishwoman*, 7. For a critique of this interpretation, see Sarah Apetrei, *Women, Feminism and Religion in Early Enlightenment England* (Cambridge: 2010): this scholar objects to the way that religion is often regarded as an 'inadvertent platform' for female power, and argues that instead, the theology itself was 'potentially seminal to the whole intellectual . . . process of conceiving a feminist critique': 29.
[188] Vernon, *The compleat scholler*, 28.
[189] *An account of the admirable conversion*, 11.
[190] *An account of the causes of some particular rebellious distempers* (1670), 74.

This complaint was echoed by physicians and surgeons across the period, and was an everyday clinical experience.[191] Dr van Diemerbroeck, for instance, stated that his six-year-old patient 'loath'd Physic', and refused all internal medicine.[192] Laypeople also recorded this behaviour: John Yorke bemoaned that his nephew James 'is . . . so refractory [about] taking what is proper for him', that '[it is] a hard taske to govern him'. Yorke had to 'use all my perwasion' to get the child 'to take what the Dr order'd'; in particular, he 'wou[l]d by no means submit to a glister to cool his body'. Eventually, through bribing James with a copy of *Robinson Crusoe*, the uncle managed to coax his nephew into taking the medicine, but even then, 'he grew very outrageous and wou[l]d not keep the glister [in for] two minutes so it cou[l]d not have the full desired effect'.[193] So, although the child did submit eventually, he was still allowed to decide when the treatment was over. Children of all ages and genders could exert this power: John Verney lamented that his infants Molly and Ralph 'will not . . . take anything but small Beare, nor that if anything be mingled with it, that we have trouble enough'.[194] Occasionally, children used spiritual arguments to justify their rebellions. 'I may not have any more Physick given to me', insisted ten-year-old Mary Warren to her mother in 1661: the reason she gave was, 'doctors . . . look more at the Physick, than at the Power of God'. She added the ominous warning, 'if you suffer them to give me any more things the Lord will be angry with you, and will bring greater affliction upon you in some of my other Sisters'.[195] This argument was highly effective, for it transformed what could have been regarded as childish disobedience into precocious holiness, and consequently, parents had no alternative but to acquiesce. Since obedience was one of the primary obligations of children, it is possible that they took some consolation from this rare outlet provided by sickness and patienthood.[196]

Finally, children could exercise power by refusing to prepare spiritually for death, or by disrupting the prayers of their relatives and friends. This behaviour was especially likely during cases of possession, since one of the key symptoms of unnatural disease was abhorrence of anything religious.[197] 'Nothing in the World would so discompose her as Religious Exercises', wrote an eye-witness of the possessed eleven-year-old, Christian Shaw, in 1696. '[I]f there were any discourses of God or Christ', or any attempts to persuade her to 'repeat any of the Psalms' or listen to prayer, 'she would suddenly be struck Dumb and lay as one stiff Dead', and then utter 'reproachful Talk' to whoever was praying, 'calling him Dog', and 'Laughing . . . Singing' and 'pulling her head Cloaths down over her Face'.[198] Sometimes the disruptive activities became violent. When the possessed adolescent Anne Baldwin was asked to read the Bible in 1704, she said, '*I can't endure it, I will tear it*', and then she sprang 'out of the Chair she sat in, and leap[t] . . . about the

[191] For example, Paul Barbette, *Thesaurus chirurgiae: the chirurgical and anatomical works of Paul Barbette* (1687, first publ. 1676), 359. See Ch. 2 for more examples.
[192] Van Diemerbroeck, *The anatomy of human bodies*, 138.
[193] Clavering, *The Correspondence of Sir James Clavering*, 158–60.
[194] Verney, *The Verney Memoirs*, vol. 2, 376.   [195] H. P., *A looking-glass for children*, 14.
[196] Houlbrooke, *The English Family*, 140–5.   [197] Almond (ed.), *Demonic Possession*, 5.
[198] Cullen, *A true narrative of the sufferings*, pp. xx, xviii.

Room' lashing out and screaming '*I'll kill ye, I'll kill ye*' to her carers.[199] It is possible that these girls derived satisfaction from this behaviour, since it was the antithesis to the usual ideals of feminine conduct, such as obedience and modesty. Although the majority of the children in the possession cases were girls, there are occasional examples of possessed boys who levied this power. The adolescent John Starkie, for instance, when instructed to read the Bible and pray, called the sacred book 'bible bable bible bable', and then took to 'nicknaming every word in the Lord's prayer' and other 'horrible blasphemy'.[200] Thus, during possession, children of both sexes could behave in ways that would not have usually been tolerated, mocking and rejecting the spiritual elements of their care without punishment, since the Devil was accountable. It is impossible to ascertain the extent to which children's rebellions resulted from their conscious desires to escape their strict religious upbringings, or in fact, were motivated by a genuine belief that Satan was coercing them to act in this way. Perhaps this does not matter, for the essential point applies in both cases: possessed children possessed power.[201]

It was not just victims of possession who enjoyed authority: those children who were afflicted with natural disease could also be very disruptive during the spiritual elements of care. When Mary Stubbs became ill of a languishing disease in the 1680s, she was 'very unwilling to hear any things spoken to her of Death', and 'would be very angry' if anyone tried to prepare her for this event.[202] Like possessed children, the rebellious behaviour of naturally ill patients was attributed to the temptations of the Devil, because even when he did not directly possess his victim, he was still thought to be an active presence during grave illness.[203] This was the case for eight-year-old Tabitha Alder in 1644: when she expressed reluctance to prepare spiritually for death, her family believed that 'it was Satan that did put it into' her mind.[204]

Thus far, it has been argued that patienthood was an empowering experience. However, it could also be quite the opposite: children sometimes remained submissive during sickness, yielding to rigorous care regimes. At the most basic level, young patients were usually made to stay in bed during their illnesses. In 1711, Elizabeth Freke noted that her grandson's smallpox had 'confined him to his bed . . . for a full month before hee rose'.[205] Mary Ann Lund agrees that 'the action

[199] Thomas Aldridge, *The prevalency of prayer . . . of the deplorable case of the children of John Baldwin of Sarret* (1717), 7–8.
[200] This has been cited by Sharpe in 'Disruption in the Well-Ordered Household', 201.
[201] For discussions of the power brought by possession, see Michael MacDonald, *Mystical Bedlam: Madness, Anxiety and Healing in Seventeenth-Century England* (Cambridge: 1981), 202; Sharpe, *The bewitching of Anne Gunter*; Sharpe, 'Disruption in the Well-Ordered Household', 191, 197–9, 205.
[202] Bidbanck, *A present for children*, 43.
[203] Walsham, 'Out of the Mouths of Babes'.
[204] Janeway, *A token for children* (part 2), 19–22.
[205] Elizabeth Freke, *The Remembrances of Elizabeth Freke*, ed. Raymond Anselment, Camden Fifth Series, vol. 18 (Cambridge: 2001), 196.

of taking to . . . bed' and feeling 'the sheets pressing down like iron doors' created an unpleasant sensation of 'confinement and imprisonment' in patients.[206]

Children also submitted to the taking of physic. In 1704, four-year-old Betty Egleton 'was extreamly Obedient in every Thing her Aunt would have her do; and though her Medicines were very nauseous, she would force her self to take them'.[207] One might expect girls to have submitted more readily than boys, on the grounds that they had been taught to 'live under obedience', but this was not the case.[208] In 1665, young Caleb Vernon assured his father '*I will never be disobedient to you, nor my dear Mother*', and therefore took a medicine, despite the fact he was 'averse to taking any thing'.[209] This boy's compliance seems to have been motivated by his fear of the sin of disobedience. Parents sometimes persuaded their children to accept physic by appealing to their sense of duty. The father of six-year-old Joseph Scholding told his son, 'If you love me, take it', to which, the boy responded, 'to satisfy you, I will take it'.[210] Relatives employed the 'carrot and stick' to ensure cooperation: the governess of little Tom Browne, 'Madame Cobbe' was said to have 'use[d] play things, Cakes . . . and the like' to keep him 'in awe', and through the combination of 'smart words & partly by rewards . . . upon her authority wee can get him to take physick or what hee hath noe liking of'.[211] Occasionally, medical practitioners may have resorted to force: the medical author Theophile Bonet suggested that, because 'Children are averse to all sorts of Medicines', they must be 'forced' through use of 'a Spoon' which was put between the teeth, and a 'large Pipe', which was 'thrust . . . into the Mouth to the Jaws', so that the medicines could be 'poured in'.[212] However, this is one of very few examples of forced medication, which suggests that it was rare. Probably a more common method was to apply psychological pressure to the patient. This was the tactic used by the surgeon Richard Wiseman: he admitted that he had succeeded in persuading his thirteen-year-old patient to drink '2 quarts of *Barnet*-water to purge her' by 'plying' her ''till she had drank it all'.[213]

Even when children submitted willingly to the treatments, the administration of these remedies sometimes demanded an extraordinary degree of cooperation on the part of patients: medicines often had to be taken several times a day over a long period. For instance, the Trumbell family's recipe book contains the following course of medicines for children suffering from the smallpox:

> [G]ive a Glyster of milk & sugar, and that evening or next morning . . . vomit with Ipecacuanna . . . The morning after the vomit . . . let blood be taken . . . At the

---

[206] Mary Ann Lund, 'Experiencing Pain in John Donne's "Devotions Upon Emergent Occasions" (1624)', in Jan Frans van Dijkhuizen and Karl A. E. Enenkel (eds), *The Sense of Suffering: Constructions of Physical Pain in Early Modern Culture*, Yearbook for Early Modern Studies, vol. 12 (Leiden and Boston: 2008), 323–45, at 332.

[207] E. C., *Some part of the life and death*, 8.

[208] Linda Pollock, '"Teach Her to Live Under Obedience": the Making of Women in the Upper Ranks of Early Modern England', *Continuity and Change*, 4 (1989), 231–58.

[209] Vernon, *The compleat scholler*, 68.

[210] Bidbanck, *A present for children*, 70.

[211] Browne, *The Works of Sir Thomas Browne*, 225.

[212] Theophile Bonet, *A guide to the practical physician* (1684), 324.

[213] Wiseman, *Several chirurgical treatises*, 266–7.

appearance of the specks [the pustules] let the Patient take a dose of Gascoin's powder
in a spoonfull of the Julep ev'ry eight hours . . . When the patient is restless, quieting
Medecines must be given . . . twice or thrice a day . . . on the eight day . . . anoint the
face, night & morning with the oyntment, for two or three days . . . On the 21 day let
blood, & purge next day or the day after, which purging must be repeated 3 or 4
times intermitting 3 or 4 Days.[214]

Although children were usually expected to take their medicines less frequently
than adults, the regimes could still be considerably gruelling. In short, children
often submitted to the taking of medicines, and therefore, patienthood could be
experienced as a time of subjection rather than power.

Children eventually succumbed to other elements of patient care, such as the
spiritual preparation for death. In 1596, thirteen-year-old Thomas Darling, who
had previously been 'cast into a fit' whenever he had been 'caused . . . to read upon
the bible', later became 'desirous to have the Booke, that he might read himself'.[215]
This example supports James Sharpe's assertion that 'The challenges to authority
offered' by possession 'like many such challenges in the early modern period, [were]
short-lived and doomed to failure'.[216] Children suffering from natural illness also
complied with these spiritual aspects of care. Upon finding that their little daughter
Mary Stubbs was reluctant to answer questions about her readiness to die in the
early 1680s, her parents decided to 'not forbear' this questioning procedure, and
continued asking her 'Whither she should go if she died?' until she eventually replied,
'she knew not'. Unsatisfied with this response, they 'asked the same Question' several
more times, despite the fact that she showed 'much dislike'. Eventually, to the relief of
her family, this child, 'beyond all Expectation . . . did appear . . . very sensible of her
Condition', and answered with confidence that she would 'go to Heaven'.[217] Thus,
through unremitting pressure, children were sometimes persuaded to relinquish their
powers. This case of Mary Stubbs might seem, from today's perspective, to be verging
on abuse. However, Mary's parents had their daughter's best interests at heart: they
insisted that they acted in this way for 'the good of her Soul'.[218] Furthermore, as will
be shown in the next chapter, through this process many children eventually came to
a sense of peace and resignation, and overcame their fears of dying.

SENSELESSNESS

The premise in the discussions so far has been that children were conscious of their
experiences of care and patienthood. It must be acknowledged that this was not
always the case: children were sometimes delirious during sickness, or to use the
words of contemporaries, 'senseless' or 'insensible'. This was especially likely in
cases of convulsions or high fevers, or when death was approaching. In 1661, Philip

---

[214] BL, Additional MS 72619, fol. 123v–124v ('Book of recipes for the Trumbell's household').
[215] I. D., *The most wonderfull and true storie*, 12, 19.
[216] Sharpe, 'Disruption in the Well-Ordered Household', 208–9.
[217] Bidbanck, *A present for children*, 43–4.   [218] Ibid.

Henry lamented that Margaret, the young daughter of his friend, 'hardly understood' his prayers 'through extremity'; he concluded mournfully, 'I know not how to deal with persons in sickness, lord help mee'.[219] This child was probably unable to derive hope or comfort from her visitor's prayers. Children may have also been oblivious to the visits of family and friends when they were very ill. Simonds D'Ewes complained that his ten-year-old sister 'was dying as soon as we heard she was sick' in 1620, and therefore by the time he and his two elders sisters had 'hastened on foot to the place where she lay', she was 'past all sense'.[220] Around the same time, Samuel Rogers lamented that when he rode home to see his adolescent sister Mary, she was 'scarse knowing mee, but roving [raving] and erring'.[221] These circumstances caused great distress in parents and visitors because they worried about the child's ability to prepare spiritually for death.[222]

CONCLUSION

Being a patient was a fundamentally mixed experience for early modern children: it was often a time of sympathy, love, attention, and power, but it could also be distressing, tedious, painful, and disempowering. This argument challenges the historiographical view that patienthood was a wholly negative experience, as well as the notion that finding out 'what it was like to be ill' as a child is beyond the scope of historical study.[223] Children's experiences seem to have undergone very little change between the late sixteenth and early eighteenth centuries: the themes identified in this chapter were important throughout. This continuity stemmed from the fact that the basic elements of care provided to the sick remained the same, as did the emotional character of family relationships: most parents loved their children, and wished to provide attentive care during illness. In fact, affection and kindness seem to have permeated every element of the care provided to young patients. What might appear through modern eyes to be cruel treatments, such as painful medicines and the spiritual preparation for death, had benevolent intentions.

The meanings of the words 'patient' and 'patienthood' have been explored in this chapter: these terms referred not just to the receipt of medical treatment, but in fact encompassed a great range of components, including prayer, nursing, sick-visiting, and the spiritual preparation for death. The usual connotations of patienthood, such as passivity and subjection, have also been disputed, since they fail to convey the full ambivalence of the patient's position: whilst the sick did at times behave submissively, they were also active agents in their care regimes, exercising considerable power over those around them. The next and final chapter will further

---

[219] Philip Henry, *The Diaries and Letters of Philip Henry of Broad Oak, Flintshire, A.D. 1631–1696*, ed. M. H. Lee (1882), 94.

[220] D'Ewes, *The Autobiography and Correspondence*, vol. 1, 156–8.

[221] Samuel Rogers, *The Diary of Samuel Rogers, 1634–1638*, ed. Tom Webster and Kenneth Shipps, Church of England Record Society, vol. 11 (Woodbridge: 2004), 152–4.

[222] Houlbrooke, *Death, Religion and the Family*, 198.

[223] Heywood, *A History of Childhood*, 146.

investigate the meaning of 'patient', by showing that its most important association was probably the patient acceptance to God's afflictions—an idea which links clearly with the connotations of submissiveness mentioned above.

Historians have asserted that every aspect of children's lives was gendered. It has been shown here that the basic features or themes of patienthood—such as power, attention, and love—seem to have applied to children of both sexes. This finding indicates that in the context of sickness at least, there was a greater dichotomy between gender prescriptions, and gender practices, than has been often assumed. Nevertheless, this line of argument does not preclude the possibility that the girls and boys might have experienced these various features of patienthood slightly differently. In fact, it has been tentatively suggested that certain aspects of patient-hood, such as power, may have been relished with greater enthusiasm by girls, since in everyday life daughters probably held less authority than their brothers. Likewise, boys may have derived more comfort from other aspects of patient care, such as the tender sympathy they were shown.

6

'Ill in My Body, but Well in God':
Suffering Sickness

'The Sick Child' (1660), by the Dutch artist Gabriel Metsu (1629–1667), inspired the subject of this chapter.[1] The ailing child gazes listlessly out of the painting, her fragile, pale form contrasting against the solid, bright presence of her nurse or mother.[2] Her expression is serene and peaceful, despite the weakness of her body. What is this child thinking? Is she in pain, and if so, what emotions has this suffering provoked? Is the child aware that she might die, and what does she think will become of her after death?

This chapter seeks to reconstruct the experience of illness through the eyes of the child: it explores the physical, emotional, and spiritual dimensions of sickness, pain, and death. The central argument is that children's experiences were characterized by profound ambivalence: whilst sickness was often painful, frightening, and a source of spiritual guilt and grief, it could also be a time of emotional and spiritual fulfilment, and even occasionally, joy.[3] The more positive side stemmed from the deeply entrenched Christian beliefs about the spiritual value of pain and illness, and the doctrines of providence and salvation. Sickness, as a benevolent gift from the Lord, cleansed the soul of its impurities and helped to convince the Christian of his or her heavenly future: bodily disease could improve the health of the soul. However, these religious beliefs had paradoxical psychological effects, for as well as having a cathartic impact, they could provoke unpleasant emotions such as guilt and fear, and probably also make the physical pain of illness harder to bear. This interpretation challenges the historiographical assumption that sickness was a purely negative event in the early modern period.[4] It also enriches our understanding of the psychological culture of Protestantism, and contradicts the views of John Stachniewski and others, who have claimed that Protestant doctrines were wholly pernicious.[5] It is difficult to determine how far children's experiences of illness differed from those of adults: few studies have been published about the experiences of patients of any age. Nevertheless, it will be

---

[1] This painting is shown on the front-cover of the book; my thanks to the Rijsmuseum for granting permission for the use of this image.

[2] The art historian Catrionia Murray confirms that this child is female.

[3] Jenny Mayhew has also argued that physical pain could be experienced positively, in: 'Godly Beds of Pain: Pain in English Protestant Manuals (ca. 1550–1650)', in Jan Frans van Dijkhuizen and Karl A. E. Enenkel (eds), *The Sense of Suffering: Constructions Pain in Early Modern Culture,* Yearbook for Early Modern Studies, vol. 12 (Leiden and Boston: 2008), 299–322.

[4] See Ch, 5, footnotes 3–4.   [5] See Introduction, footnote 21.

possible to make some tentative suggestions about how sickness might have been distinctive for children. An underlying theme throughout this chapter is the depth of love between parents and their offspring, and in particular, children's emotional attachment to their parents. While historians have provided convincing evidence of parental love, fewer remarks have been made about children's feelings for their parents.

The historiography of patients has tended to focus on patients' actions during their illnesses, rather than their feelings or experiences. Lucinda McCray Beier's book, *Sufferers and Healers* (1987), for example, asks 'what did people of that time do when they became ill'.[6] Nevertheless, certain historians have explored selected aspects of the experience of illness. Mary Ann Lund has used the autobiographical work of John Donne to illuminate the physical sensation of pain.[7] Likewise, Lisa Smith has analysed collections of patients' correspondence to unearth the bodily and emotional experiences of disease in eighteenth-century England and France.[8] Other scholars have examined the spiritual side of illness, asking how puritans interpreted illness and pain.[9] Finally, some research has been conducted on patients' emotional responses to death.[10] While these works have greatly enhanced our understanding of what it was like to be ill in the early modern period, they do not provide a comprehensive picture, since they tend to focus on one or two particular facets of sickness.[11] This chapter takes a more holistic approach, by exploring the physical, emotional, *and* spiritual dimensions of illness. Three key aspects of this experience have been identified, around which the discussions are structured: physical pain, the notion that sickness was providential, and the anticipation of death.

PAIN AND SUFFERING

To gain an insight into children's experiences of pain, it is necessary to analyse the types of metaphors that were used to describe their sufferings.[12] This analysis will

---

[6] Lucinda McCray Beier, *Sufferers and Healers: The Experience of Illness in Seventeenth-Century England* (1987), 4. Michael Stolberg's new monograph on patients, *Experiencing Illness and the Sick Body in Early Modern Europe* (November, 2011) was published when *The Sick Child* was already under publication, and therefore, unfortunately, it has not been possible to evaluate its contribution to the historiography of patients.

[7] Mary Ann Lund, 'Experiencing Pain in John Donne's "Devotions Upon Emergent Occasions" (1624)', in Jan Frans van Dijkhuizen and Karl A. E. Enenkel (eds), *The Sense of Suffering: Constructions of Physical Pain in Early Modern Culture*, Yearbook for Early Modern Studies, vol. 12 (Leiden and Boston: 2008), 323–45.

[8] Lisa Smith, '"An Account of an Unaccountable Distemper": the Experience of Pain in Early Eighteenth-Century England and France', *Eighteenth-Century Studies*, 41 (2008), 459–80.

[9] See Introduction, footnote 24.

[10] For example, Lucinda M. Becker, *Death and the Early Modern Englishwoman* (Aldershot and Burlington, VT: 2003), and Ralph Houlbrooke, *Death, Religion and the Family in England, 1480–1750* (Oxford: 1998).

[11] The exceptions include Roy and Dorothy Porter, *In Sickness and in Health: The British Experience, 1650–1850* (1988), which contains several chapters about pain and the spiritual side to illness. Likewise, a number of the chapters in the edited volume *The Sense of Suffering* explore the physical, emotional, and spiritual experience of pain.

[12] A similar method has been used by Lund in 'Experiencing Pain', 323–34.

also shed light on the cultural meanings of pain, since the language used in the accounts carries distinctive connotations.[13] The underlying supposition to the discussions is that 'cognition and sensation are so tightly interrelated that the manipulation of thoughts can affect what a person physically feels'.[14] In other words, the types of words that were used to describe pain, and the meanings they held, may have affected the physical sensation of suffering. As such, by examining this language, we come closer to glimpsing the experience of pain. Some scholars might question this methodology, on the grounds that physical pain is an 'interior and unsharable' experience, which can never be adequately verbalized or accessed. Elaine Scarry, for example, has asserted that pain is so difficult to describe that it 'actively destroys language'.[15] However, I take a more optimistic stance, agreeing with Joanna Bourke that 'the experience of pain can actually generate language': the English language is 'swollen' with 'metaphor, metonynmy, and analogy' which can enable sufferers to communicate pain with eloquence.[16] In some ways, the experience of early modern pain may be especially accessible to historians: unlike today's clinical vocabularies, early modern descriptions of physical sensations lend themselves to the expression of bodily feeling. As Michael Schoenfeldt has stated, once one 'gets over the initial unfamiliarity of a particular description of a bodily process, one is struck by the fact that this is indeed how bodies feel as if they are behaving'.[17]

There remain several large obstacles to accessing children's experiences of pain, however. One, already discussed elsewhere, is that the majority of the sources were written by adults rather than by the young patients themselves, and as a result, our view into the child's experience is indirect.[18] Another problem is the tendency of the sources to rarely give much detail on the subject of children's pain.[19] Diarists and letter writers usually stated that their child was 'sore' or 'in pain', offering no further information. This paucity may reflect parents' reluctance to dwell on their children's suffering, since it was undoubtedly a source of emotional distress. Contemporaries may have assumed that pain was self-evident, requiring no description, or perhaps they found it too difficult to describe suffering, owing to its elusive, intangible nature.[20] Alternatively, by omitting details of pain, parents may have hoped to emphasize their offspring's stoicism and patience, responses that were

---

[13] Barbara Duden, *The Woman Beneath the Skin: A Doctor's Patients in Eighteenth-Century Germany*, trans. Thomas Dunlap (Cambridge, Mass.: 1991), 89.

[14] Mayhew, 'Godly Beds of Pain', 299.

[15] Elaine Scarry, *The Body in Pain: The Making and Unmaking of the World* (New York and Oxford: 1985), 16.

[16] Joanna Bourke, in *Pain and the Politics of Sympathy, Historical Reflections, 1760s to 1960s: Inaguaral Address* (Utrecht, 2011), 6. Ariel Glucklich makes a similar comment in, *Sacred Pain: Hurting the Body for the Sake of the Soul* (Oxford and New York: 2001), 44.

[17] Michael Schoenfeldt, *Bodies and Selves in Early Modern England: Physiology and Inwardness in Spenser, Shakespeare, Herbert, and Milton* (Cambridge: 1999), 3, 6.

[18] See the 'Sources' section of the Introduction.

[19] This problem has been recognized by Isabelle Robin-Romero, in: 'L'Enfant Malade dans les Écrits Privés du XVIIIe', *Histoire Économie et Société*, 22 (2003), 469–86, at 479.

[20] On the difficulties of expressing pain, see Scarry, *The Body in Pain*, 3–5; Esther Cohen, 'Towards a History of European Physical Sensibility: Pain in the Later Middle Ages', *Science in Context*, 8 (1995), 47–74, at 48.

considered highly desirable in Christian thinking. Doctors were also frustratingly laconic in their accounts of children's pain, usually offering no more detail than stating which bodily region was hurting. However, these shortcomings do not preclude an exploration of children's experiences, since even the briefest descriptions provide some sort of insight. Besides, certain genres of source do tend to give more detail, especially the possession cases and the biographies of children.

Metaphor is by far the most common linguistic technique in the descriptions of children's sufferings. Elaine Scarry explains why this is the case: 'Because the existing vocabulary contains only a small handful of adjectives, one passes through direct descriptions very quickly and . . . almost immediately encounters an "as if" structure' in accounts of pain.[21] Metaphors are needed because 'It is difficult for us to communicate, perhaps even imagine, the nature of pain . . . without resorting to metaphors of agency or instrumentality.'[22] These linguistic devices 'work' by transferring the unintelligible idea of pain into a more concrete, and familiar setting.[23]

Several types of metaphor appear consistently in the descriptions of children's pain: firstly, those associated with torture or torment.[24] In 1653, the biographer of eleven-year-old Martha Hatfield bemoaned that her convulsion fits held her 'on the rack for many weeks, nay moneths, in which she endured grievous torturings'.[25] Half a century later, Charles Trelawny lamented that his child 'is at this minute upon the Rack with convulsion fitts, which makes the mother almost mad'.[26] The violent contraction of the body's muscles in convulsions probably seemed to resemble the physical effects of the rack. This is suggested explicitly in the possession case of the Throckmorton children: five sisters, aged nine to fifteen, suffered from strange convulsions in 1589. As they 'fell into their fits', they uttered 'terrible screeches', and were 'wonderfully tormented, as though they would have been torn to pieces'.[27] However, it was not just the pains of convulsions that were described using this metaphor: any acute suffering might be represented in this way. In 1647, Pegg Verney's 'great deflustion in her cheeke' (mouth ulcer) 'tortured her both night & day', according to her father.[28] Although there is no way of telling whether the children themselves used these terms, the language does provide clues into the sensation of suffering.

It is not surprising that torture features so regularly in the accounts of pain: it was a deeply ingrained element of early modern culture, depicted in a wide variety of media, including poetry, drama, and prose. For puritans, the most important

---

[21] Scarry, *The Body in Pain*, 15.   [22] Glucklich, *Sacred Pain*, 44.   [23] Bourke, *Pain*, 10.

[24] Smith agrees, in 'An Account of an Unaccountable Distemper', 467.

[25] James Fisher, *The wise virgin, or, a wonderfull narration of the hand of God . . . in afflicting a childe of eleven years of age* [Martha Hatfield] (1653), 135.

[26] BL, Additional MS 28052, fol. 100r (Domestic correspondence of the Godolphin family, 1663–1782).

[27] ' "The most strange and admirable discovery of the three Witches of Warboys . . . for betwitching of the five daughters of Robert Throckmorton" (1593)', printed in Philip Almond, *Demonic Possession and Exorcism in Early Modern England: Contemporary Texts and their Cultural Contexts* (Cambridge: 2004), 75–149, at 85.

[28] BL, M.636/8, this manuscript is unfoliated (Verney papers on microfilm, 1646–50).

source of information on this subject was the literature of Christian martyrdom, including John Foxe's famous tome, *Acts and Monuments,* which went through nine editions between 1563 and 1684.[29] This text describes graphically, in words and images, the gruesome tortures inflicted upon Christian martyrs from Biblical times onwards.[30] Children as well as adults would have been familiar with this book, since it often formed the basis of their religious education, along with the Bible.[31] It is highly likely therefore, that the linguistic choices of pious parents and their offspring would have been influenced by this literature when describing pain.

The use of the torture metaphor may have had a positive impact on children's experiences of pain: its implicit connection with the ordeals of martyrs could potentially ennoble their sufferings, making sickness more bearable.[32] This was possibly the case for twelve-year-old Charles Bridgeman in 1632: when considering his pains, he 'called to mind that Martyr *Thomas Bilney*', who had burned his own finger in a candle to give himself a taste of what it would be like to burn at the stake. Charles had read of this martyr in the aforementioned *Acts and Monuments,* and clearly identified with him, declaring, 'O . . . had I lived then, I would have run through the fire to have gone to Christ'.[33] Girls as well as boys mentioned martyrs in this way. Fourteen-year-old Mary Glover compared herself to her grandfather, who died a martyr, by repeating his dying words, 'The comforter is come. O Lord, you have delivered me.' Upon hearing his daughter speak, her father declared, with the 'triumph of a conquering army', that her words were those of 'her Grandfather going to be burned' at the stake.[34] This father's obvious pride may have been a source of satisfaction for his daughter. The reason martyrdom carried such positive connotations was that the sufferings of the dying martyr represented the pains of Christ on the cross, which in turn was the key to the redemption of the whole of mankind from eternal death.[35] However, the cathartic effects of the metaphor should not be overstated, for it is probable that many children were unaware that it was being used to describe their pains. Moreover, the language of torture also

---

[29] Sharon Howard, 'Imagining the Pain and Peril of Seventeenth-century Childbirth: Travail and Deliverance in the Making of an Early Modern World', *Social History of Medicine,* 16 (2003), 367–82, at 374.

[30] Thomas Freeman and Thomas Meyer, *Martyrs and Martyrdom in England, c.1400–1700* (Woodbridge: 2007), 1–2.

[31] Gillian Avery, 'Intimations of Mortality: the Puritan and Evangelical Message to Children', in Gillian Avery and Kimberley Reynolds (eds), *Representations of Childhood Death* (Basingstoke: 2000), 87–110, at 95.

[32] Esther Cohen, 'Towards a History of European Physical Sensibility', 69.

[33] James Janeway, *A token for children being an exact account of the conversion, holy and exemplary lives and joyful deaths of several young children* (1671), 46–7. The story of Thomas Bilney is given in John Foxe, *Foxe's Book of Martyrs* [*1576*] Variorum Edition Online (version 1.1—Summer 2006), website address: http://www.hrionline.ac.uk/johnfoxe/, book eight, 985.

[34] John Swan, ' "A True and Briefe Report, of Mary Glovers Vexation" (1603)', in Almond (ed.), *Demonic Possession,* 291–330, at 318.

[35] Esther Cohen, 'The Animated Pain of the Body', *American Historical Review,* 105 (2000), 36–68, at 45–7; Lisa Silverman, *Tortured Subjects: Pain, Truth, and the Body in Early Modern France* (Chicago and London: 2001), 8–9; Thomas S. Freeman, ' "Imitatio Christi with a Vengeance": The Politicisation of Martyrdom in Early-Modern England', in Freeman and Mayer (eds), *Martyrs and Martyrdom,* 35–69, at 41.

carried a set of far more negative connotations: those of the pains suffered by the damned in hell, which will be discussed below.

Another metaphor that appears in the accounts of children's pains refers to the sensation of temperature. In the 1620s, thirteen-year-old Elizabeth Isham complained of stomach pain that felt like 'faintnes or coldness'; the sensation was 'so cold' that she thought she 'should never leave the eating of somwhat to warme' herself.[36] About forty years later, a boy of the same age, James Barrow, was taken ill of 'a violent burning, so great' that his parents feared 'that . . . it would cost him his life'.[37] Lisa Smith has suggested that the origin of these metaphors lies in the Galenic tradition of the four humours, each of which was characterized by its temperature.[38] Pain was caused by the imbalance of the humours, and the resulting overheating or cooling of the body. Doctors and laypeople regularly mentioned the humours when describing the sensation of pain, which suggests that the humoral origin of this metaphor is plausible. In 1641, Dr John Symcotts recorded in his casebook that 'Mr Woodman's daughter' fell into 'a great distemper . . . with great burning' and 'a sharp red, fiery humour' which was 'exceedingly painful'.[39] Owing to this association with the humours, it is possible that references to temperature were intended to be literal rather than metaphorical: it was believed that the humours could actually rise or drop in temperature, and boil, burn, and freeze, within the human body.[40]

An equally convincing derivation of the temperature metaphor, however, was the Christian notion of hell, and its horrible punishments of burning and freezing. Contemporary sermons and religious treatises taught that hell was a real, physical place, wherein the damned were tortured with fire. *Tormenting tophet; or a terrible description of hell* (1650), by Henry Greenwood, states that hell is 'a treasure of . . . fire kept under the Earth to punish'.[41] Cold as well as heat was associated with hell, for the damned were tortured with 'cold intolerable' as well as 'fire unquenchable'.[42] The vocabulary used in the descriptions of children's pain is remarkably similar to the language used in accounts of hell. Thomas Darling cried out, 'Flames of fire, flames of fire' during his illness in 1596, while four-year-old Mary Stubbs was said to have endured 'very sore nights & days' in 'the Furnace'.[43] All these terms—flame, fire, and furnace—abound in the eschatological literature and sermons. By using the language of hell in this way, it is possible that children and their families were subconsciously, or consciously, linking their pains to the sufferings of the damned.

---

[36] Elizabeth Isham, *'My Booke of Rememenberance'*: [sic] *The Autobiography of Elizabeth Isham*, ed. Isaac Stephens; PDF file on the internet, website address: http://history.ucr.edu/people/grad_students/stephens/TheAutobiography.pdf, 37.

[37] John Barrow, *The Lord's arm stretched out in an answer of prayer, or, a true relation of the wonderful deliverance of James Barrow* (1664), 5–7.

[38] Smith, 'An Account of An Unaccountable Distemper', 462, 465.

[39] John Symcotts, *A Seventeenth Century Doctor and his Patients: John Symcotts, 1592?-1662*, eds F. N. L. Poynter and W. J. Bishop, Bedfordshire Historical Record Society, vol. 31 (Streatley: 1951), 72.

[40] Gail Kern Paster, *Humoring the Body: Emotions and the Shakespearean Stage* (Chicago: 2004), 20–6.

[41] Henry Greenwood, *Tormenting tophet; or a terrible description of hell* (1650, first publ. 1618), 241.

[42] Ibid, 240.

[43] I D., *The most wonderfull and true storie . . . as also a true report of the strange torments of Thomas Darling, a boy of thirteene yeres of age* (1597), 7; William Bidbanck, *A present for children. Being a brief, but faithful account of many remarkable and excellent things utter'd by three young children* (1685), 52.

Since puritan children were 'weaned' on a diet of 'prophetic preaching' and 'sermon repetition exercises', it is understandable that they employed the same language as their religious teachers when describing their pains.[44]

The use of these hellish metaphors may have exacerbated children's sufferings, since damnation probably evoked feelings of guilt and fear.[45] Unlike the tortures of martyrs, the pains of the reprobate were 'deserving [of] condemnation rather than sympathy'.[46] However, it is likely that the metaphors also had a therapeutic effect: the idea of hell may have helped some children to put their own sufferings into perspective. This was because earthly pains, however excruciating, were considered but 'flea-bitings' to the everlasting sufferings of the damned.[47] As explained by the theologian Christopher Love,

> Upon earth, you have diseases haply; but though some parts are afflicted, other parts are free... there is no disease that puts the whole body in pain at once: but in hell it is not so, in hell all the parts of your bodies, and powers of your souls shall be tormented.[48]

Sick children were sometimes able to draw consolation from this notion, viewing their own pains as comparatively mild. In 1661, ten-year-old Mary Warren considered that, 'My pains are nothing to the pains of Hell, where they will never be an end'.[49] About a decade later the adolescent Elizabeth Walker 'would bless God that what she suffered was not Hell, where the Damned had not a drop of water to cool their Tongue'.[50]

Besides mentioning torture and temperature, the metaphors involved attacks from animals or weapons. In 1596, the adolescent Thomas Darling suffered 'many sore fits' which felt like 'the pricking with daggers or stinging of Bees'. He cried out, 'A beare, a beare... he teareth me, he teareth me' and 'Daggers, Daggers'.[51] A century later, a similar combination of metaphors was used by eleven-year-old Christian Shaw: as she fell into her diabolical fits, she made 'hideous Outcryes, telling those about her that Cats, Ravens, Owles and Horses were destroying and pressing her down in the Bed', and 'uttered horrid Schreeks' that she had been 'pierced thorow with Swords'.[52] Sensations of sharpness and compression are

---

[44] Alexandra Walsham, '"Out of the Mouths of Babes and Sucklings": Prophecy, Puritanism, and Childhood in Elizabethan Suffolk', in Diana Wood (ed.), *The Church and Childhood*, Studies in Church History, vol. 31 (Oxford: 1994), 285–300, at 291–2.

[45] Cohen, 'The Animated Pain of the Body', 54–5, 68.

[46] Ibid. 55.

[47] See Philip C. Almond, *Heaven and Hell in Enlightenment England* (Cambridge and New York: 1994), 89. The quotation ('flea-bitings') is taken from Christopher Love, *Hells terror: or, a treatise of the torments of the damned* (1653), 44.

[48] Ibid. (Love) 43.

[49] H. P., *A looking-glass for children* (1673), 16.

[50] Elizabeth Walker, *The vertuous wife: or, the holy life of Mrs Elizabeth Walker*, ed. Anthony Walker (1694), 110.

[51] I. D., *The most wonderfull and true storie, of a certain witch... as also a true report of the strange torments of Thomas Darling, a boy of thirteene yeres of age* (1597), 6, 8, 21.

[52] Francis Grant Cullen, *A true narrative of the sufferings and relief of a yong girle* [*Christian Shaw*]; (Edinburgh: 1698), pp. xxx, xix.

evoked by the use of these metaphors: these feelings may have been associated with the ordeals of certain martyrs, who were crushed to death for refusing to plea.[53] In both the above cases, it was clearly the children rather than the adult witnesses who described their pains using this language. However, it is less obvious as to whether the children were aware that their descriptions were allegorical: their pains may have matched the sensations associated with the metaphorical agencies so perfectly that they were unable to differentiate between the two. It is also possible that these children were hallucinating.

One explanation for the use of the animal metaphor, especially in the context of possession, is the belief in 'familiar spirits'. Familiar spirits were animal-shaped evil spirits used by witches to harm or possess their victims. According to Keith Thomas, children were especially likely to have known about these creatures, owing to the traditions of storytelling.[54] The association between pain and evil animals could be terrifying to sick children. Thomas Darling, who linked his 'sore fits' with a certain 'blacke Cat', was said to have 'shriked pitifully and fearfully, desiring them to take away' the animal.[55] The imagery associated with weaponry, by contrast, may transcend historical and cultural barriers, for it seems to be used almost universally to describe pain.[56] Nonetheless, the seventeenth century was a time of extensive warfare, so it is possible that children were particularly familiar with these objects, as well as the injuries caused by daggers and other weapons.

The descriptions of physical suffering often incorporate the language of emotion. In the 1650s, Oliver Heywood wrote in his diary that his seven-year-old son Eliezer was 'grievously pained and moaned sadly several days' during his fever.[57] Roughly half a century later, James Clegg recorded that his twelve-year-old daughter Margaret suffered 'grievous pain' in her 'stomach and Bowells', accompanied by 'frequent and painful vomiting'.[58] As well as mentioning grief, the accounts of pain refer to sadness or anguish: Margaret Muschamp, aged eleven, was afflicted with 'sad and grievous torments' in the 1640s.[59] The language of emotions was used in this way because contemporaries believed that there was a very 'close relationship between physical and emotional suffering', with physical pain tending to lead to emotional pain.[60] Indeed, Michael Schoenfeldt has asserted that early modern culture made 'no hard and fast distinction between physical and emotional pain', and therefore what we might consider to be the language of emotions was regarded

---

[53] Andrea Mckenzie, '"This Death Some Strong and Stout Hearted Man Doth Choose": The Practice of Peine Forte et Dure in Seventeenth- and Eighteenth-Century England', *Law and History Review*, 23 (2005), 25–6.

[54] Keith Thomas, *Religion and the Decline of Magic* (1991, first publ. 1971), 566.

[55] I. D., *The most wonderfull and true storie*, 8.

[56] Scarry, *The Body in Pain*, 16–17.

[57] Oliver Heywood, *The Rev. Oliver Heywood, B.A: His Autobiography, Diaries, Anecdote and Event Books*, ed. Horsfall Turner, 4 vols (1883), vol. 1, 203.

[58] James Clegg, *The Diary of James Clegg of Chapel-en-Frith 1708–1755*, vol. 1 (1708–36), ed. Vanessa S. Doe, Derbyshire Record Society, vol. 5 (Matlock: 1978), 20.

[59] Moore, 'Wonderful News', 363.

[60] Smith, 'An Account of an Unaccountable Distemper', 464–5.

in the early modern period as equally applicable to physical sensations.[61] As such, it may be anachronistic to class adjectives like 'grievous' as words denoting emotion, because contemporaries probably intended this language to refer literally to all pains, physical and emotional.

In short, physical pain was often experienced as intense and severe, resembling the violent stabbing of a knife, or the torture of the rack. Rather than pushing 'the nature of pain . . . into deeper obscurity', this metaphorical language has actually facilitated empathy.[62] To use the words of Mary Ann Lund, metaphors 'draw . . . the reader into the experience [they] depict, into the sickbed, almost', and enable us to imagine what it may have been like to suffer pain.[63] It has also been shown that pain carried mixed connotations in the early modern period: it was associated both with the positive sufferings of Christian martyrs, and with the ghastly torments of the damned in hell.

How did children respond emotionally to pain? This is an important question not only because the emotional side of sickness was a major part of the illness experience, but because this question sheds light on early modern ideas about the relationship between the body and the soul, and more specifically, the impact of physical pain on the passions. While many historians have explored beliefs about the effects of the mind on the body, very few have considered the perceived influence of the body on the mind and emotions.[64] The problems presented by the task of uncovering the emotions of people from the past have already been discussed in Chapter 4, and therefore will not be repeated here. But it should be added that the challenges are multiplied in the context of children's emotions, because the young rarely speak directly in the primary sources.

Children's emotional responses to pain depended upon its duration and intensity. During prolonged or severe pain, young patients often expressed melancholy or sadness.[65] In 1647, Ralph Verney informed Robert Busby that his son was 'sad and melancholy' by reason of his 'troublesome ague', which 'hath been his constant companion for 9 or 10 weekes togeather'.[66] The words 'melancholy' and 'sad' were often used interchangeably, which suggests that they were regarded as almost synonymous. Dr van Diemerbroeck, for instance, noted that one of his child patients, a boy of six, grew 'Melancholy' at the time of his illness, while another child, a boy of eight, 'became sad' during his illness from epilepsy.[67] Other words that were used to

---

[61] Michael Schoenfeldt, 'Aesthetic and Anesthetics: the Art of Pain Management in Early Modern England', in Jan Frans van Dijkhuizen and Karl A. E. Enenkel (eds), *The Sense of Suffering: Constructions of Physical Pain in Early Modern Culture*, Yearbook for Early Modern Studies, vol. 12 (Leiden and Boston: 2008), 19–38, at 29.

[62] Scarry, *The Body in Pain*, 18

[63] Lund, 'Experiencing Pain in John Donne's "Devotions"', 343.

[64] See Introduction, footnote 26, for a summary of this historiography.

[65] For discussions of melancholy, see Stanley Jackson, *Melancholia and Depression from Hippocratic Times to Modern Times* (1986); Angus Gowland, 'The Problem of Early Modern Melancholy', *Past and Present*, 191 (2006), 77–120.

[66] BL, M.636/8, this manuscript is unfoliated (Verney papers on microfilm, 1646–50; a letter dated 22/12 December 1647).

[67] Ysbrand van Diemerbroeck, *The anatomy of human bodies . . . to which is added a particular treatise of the small pox* (1689), 137–8, 190.

describe children's unhappy feelings were 'joyless', 'mournful', 'doleful', and 'heavy'. In 1602 Joan Thynne informed her husband John that their daughter Doll, who was sick of the smallpox, 'takes it very heavily and mourns very much by reason of the soreness and store of them'.[68] Half a century later, Ralph Josselin lamented that his 'very ill' eight-year-old daughter Mary 'is heavy, and joylesse'.[69] These words could refer to physical as well as emotional states: 'doleful' for example, as well as meaning 'full of . . . dole or grief', denoted the condition of being 'full of pain'.[70] This duality of meaning is indicative of the inseparability of mind and body in early modern understanding, and confirms Lisa Smith's assertion that suffering had a 'flexible vocabulary, concurrently describing physical and emotional pains'.[71] Children themselves sometimes recognized when their pains were making them unhappy. In 1665, twelve-year-old Caleb Vernon was sick for over nine months of 'consumption'. His father recorded that he was in so much pain that 'he [was] not being able to endure so much as a . . . Gown upon him, his bones were so bare'. In response to this suffering, Caleb told his parents 'I find my self inclining to melancholy'.[72]

The reason pain elicited these sorrowful passions, according to early modern philosophers, related to the intimate connection between the soul and body. Jean-François Senault (1601–1672) explained in 1649, 'The Soul is unhappy in the miseries of her body' owing to 'the love which she beareth to her Body, [which] obligeth her to resent with sorrow the pains which it endureth'.[73] The religious writer John Norden (c.1547–1625) offered a similar explanation: '[I]f the body be overmuch tormented with the grievousnesse of sicknesse, the soule cannot but feele, (through a mutuall love, which is between the soule and the body) a kinde of griefe and sorrow'.[74] Thus, the body and the soul (or mind), were personified as close friends, who sympathized with one another's sufferings. The relationship was also depicted in contractual terms, or as one between master and servant: 'the pains of the Mistress become the diseases of the Slave; the Chains that bind them together, are so straight, that all their good and bad estate is shared between them . . . Since the Soul hath contracted so straight a society with the Body, she must suffer with it'.[75] Given this entwining of body and soul, the unhappy responses of sick children were probably regarded as natural and inevitable.

[68] [Thynne] *Two Elizabethan Women: Correspondence of Joan and Maria Thynne 1575–1611*, ed. Alison D. Wall, Wiltshire Record Society, vol. 38 (Devizes: 1983), 22–3.

[69] Ralph Josselin, *The Diary of Ralph Josselin 1616–1683*, ed. Alan Macfarlane (Oxford: 1991), 200.

[70] OED Online.

[71] Smith, 'An Account of an Unaccountable Distemper', 463.

[72] John Vernon, *The compleat scholler; or, a relation of the life, and latter-end especially, of Caleb Vernon*(1666), 65.

[73] Jean-François Senault, *The use of passions*, trans. Henry Earl of Monmouth (1671, first publ. 1649), 480–2.

[74] John Norden, *A pathway to patience* (1626), 78.

[75] Senault, *The use of passions*, 478, 480.

Other common responses to pain were helplessness, anxiety, and panic.[76] When six-year-old Frances Archer contracted an ague in 1679, she 'could not forbeare shrieking most of the night', saying 'she had the crampe, and alas a day I know not what to doe'.[77] Boys as well as girls exhibited these emotions. Twelve-year-old Caleb Vernon cried, '*What shall I do?*', in the midst of his sufferings.[78] These anxious emotions were sometimes accompanied by feelings of self-pity. While ill from worms in 1650, young Mary Josselin called out, 'poore I poore I'.[79] Early modern philosophers wrote sympathetically about these responses to sickness, regarding self-pity in particular as natural: '[who] shall blame the Soul, if she have compassion on her own body? Wherefore shall we accuse her of Abjectness, if she share in the sorrows that assail it, in that thing which, of all the world she loves best'.[80]

Pain also sparked irritation and anger. In 1656, Ralph Josselin recorded that his two-year-old daughter Ann had been 'very froward' during her 'sad trouble'.[81] A few years later, Alice Thornton's infant son William grew 'very angery and froward' by reason of the pain of the smallpox.[82] The term 'froward' denoted an irritable or cross disposition or mood.[83] Once again, contemporaries believed that pain sparked these emotions due to the link between the mind and the body. Senault, for instance, stated that 'when the body is assaulted... by the rage of Sickness, she [the soul] is constrained to sigh with it; the Cords which fasten them together, make their miseries common'.[84] The 'rage' of the body thus provoked the rage or irritation of the emotions. But in addition, pain may have acted indirectly, disrupting children's sleep, and causing them to become irritable through tiredness. This was the case for one-year-old Jack Hervey in 1697: his mother complained that he cried 'night and day' because of his sore teeth 'and sleeps very little'.[85] The detrimental effects of sleep deprivation were associated especially with children, for it was understood that this age group required more rest than adults. As explained by the midwifery writer W. S. in 1704, 'Children for some time after they come into the World sleep not moderately, as having had a long Repose in the Womb, and therefore is naturally in its Infancy desirous of Rest'.[86] Children remembered sleeping the womb, and therefore needed much sleep to remain healthy and happy.

---

[76] See Andrew Wear, 'Fear, Anxiety and the Plague in Early Modern England: Religious and Medical Responses', in John Hinnells and Roy Porter (eds), *Religion, Health and Suffering* (1999), 339–63, and David Gentilcore, 'The Fear of Disease and the Disease of Fear', in William Naphy and Penny Roberts (eds), *Fear in Early Modern Society* (Manchester and New York: 1997), 184–208.

[77] Isaac Archer, *Two East Anglian Diaries 1641–1729*, ed. Matthew J. Storey, Suffolk Record Society, vol. 36 (Woodbridge: 1994), 160–1.

[78] John Vernon, *The compleat scholler; or, a relation of the life... of Caleb Vernon*(1666), 25–6.

[79] Josselin, *The Diary of Ralph Josselin*, 201.

[80] Senault, *The use of passions*, 480.

[81] Josselin, *The Diary of Ralph Josselin*, 369.

[82] Alice Thornton, *The Autobiography of Mrs Alice Thornton*, ed. Charles Jackson, Surtees Society, vol. 62 (1875), 124–5.

[83] OED Online.

[84] Senault, *The use of passions*, 478.

[85] John Hervey, *Letter-Books of John Hervey, First Earl of Bristol*, , ed. S. H .A., 3 vols (Wells: 1894), vol. 1, 117.

[86] W. S., *A family jewel, or the womans councellor* (1704), 50. See Chs 1 and 2 for further discussions of children's need for sleep.

While children's 'frowardness' was often mentioned in the sources, references to extreme anger are rare. Some authors explicitly noted the absence of this emotion. In 1638, eleven-year-old Cecily Puckering was 'never seene to open her mouth in discontent, nor to be angry or pettish with any that were about her', even though her illness was exceedingly painful.[87] The reason anger appears so infrequently in these documents is probably that it was an emotion of dubious moral repute, associated with the sin of wrath.[88] In the context of illness, it may have attracted particular censure, because it could be regarded as a sign of the patient's rebellion against the will of God. Consequently, pious parents may have omitted mention of this emotion in order to emphasize their child's godliness during illness, and likely salvation in the event of death.

Finally, children occasionally responded to pain with a degree of resignation and patience. In the late 1600s, thirteen-year-old John Clap 'endured the Hand of God' with 'great Patience', expressing 'a profound Submission to the Will of God' during his illness.[89] Likewise, six-year-old Frances Archer was 'naturally patient' while sick in 1679, assuring her father that 'I would beare it if I could'.[90] The word 'patience' referred to 'the calm . . . endurance of affliction, pain, [or] inconvenience', while 'resignation' was defined as the acceptance of, or 'submission to' the will of God.[91] Whether or not these responses were seen as emotions is unclear, but what is more evident, is that they were regarded as highly desirable reactions to affliction among the godly. Thomas Becon beseeched Christians to 'behave them selves paciently and thankefully in the tyme of sycknesse', and avoid 'murmur and grudge against God'.[92] Patience was appropriate because it demonstrated a person's trust in God, and showed a respect for His providences. The origin of this attitude was Biblical: the Lord's Prayer states '*Thy Will be done on Earth, as it is in Heaven*', and the character Job was a 'Pattern of true *Patience*' during all his afflictions.[93] So important were patience and resignation, they were often taken as general measures of a person's religiosity and likely salvation. As a result, children's expressions of these sentiments were greeted with much praise and relief from parents. In 1665, twelve-year-old John Sudlow was commended for his 'admirable patience under the hand of God' during his sickness from the plague.[94] Patience may have been especially praiseworthy in children because contemporaries assumed it was particularly difficult for the young to achieve this state: children were associated with

---

[87] John Bryan, *The vertuous daughter* (1640), 17.

[88] For attitudes to anger, see Peter Stearns, *Anger: The Struggle for Emotional Control in America's History* (London and Chicago: 1986), Linda Pollock; 'Anger and the Negotiation of Relationships in Early Modern England', *The Historical Journal*, 47 (2004), 567–90; Gwynne Kennedy, *Just Anger: Representing Women's Anger in Early Modern England* (Carbondale: 2000).

[89] Cotton Mather, *A token, for the children of New-England* (Boston, 1700), 7–9.

[90] Archer, *Two East Anglian Diaries*, 160–1.

[91] OED Online.

[92] Thomas Becon, *The sycke mans salve wherin the faihfull Christians may learne . . . how to behave them selves paciently and thankefully* (1561).

[93] Richard Allestree, *The art of patience* (1694, first publ. 1684), 2–4.

[94] Janeway, *A token for children* (part 1), 12.

impatience.[95] Given this emphasis on patience, it can be conjectured that the very word used to denote the sick person ('patient') was linked with the Christian insistence on patience during affliction: patients were those who suffered patiently. In a similar way, 'sufferer' referred both to the sick person, and to his or her resignation to God's providential punishments: 'suffer' meant 'to submit'.[96]

When children's pains lessened, any negative feelings were quickly usurped by more cheerful emotions. In 1681, Lady Dorothy Browne recorded that 'Poor Tommy,' her grandson, 'has bin very hott and his Coffe very troblesom', but fortunately, 'his stomach is now better and less hott and the coffe Batter' so that 'he is now cherfall, I bless God'.[97] Doctors' casebooks provide similar evidence. Dr Symcotts noted that in 1636 his fourteen-year-old patient, Elizabeth Burgoyne 'vomited no more, nor complained of the pain of her stomach as before', so that by the following morning she was 'very cheerful, without all pains' and 'grew better and better still'.[98] The tendency for physical relief to lead to emotional relief was once again attributed to the sympathy between the body and the soul. This was implied by the minister Edward Lawrence when discussing recovery from illness in 1672: he stated, 'consider how lately the *multitude of thy bones* were tortured *with strong pains*... yet now God hath given thee health, he hath caused *thy bones to rejoyce,* and *filled thy heart with... gladness*'.[99] The idea that the bones themselves could rejoice epitomizes the notion that relief from physical pain brought emotional cheer.

In short, children's emotional responses to pain seem to have varied according to its severity and longevity: fear, sadness, and irritability were more likely during extremely painful bouts of illness, while happier emotions, such as cheerfulness were more evident when the symptoms of disease began to ease. Thus, a strong link existed between the body and mind in early modern culture. However, as will become apparent below, this connection was sometimes disrupted by certain religious beliefs, which helped children to feel more positive emotions even whilst suffering the most grievous pain. In these situations, the relationship between the mind and body seems to have been reversed, with the happy emotions taking control over the body, and serving to lessen the perception of pain.

THE PROVIDENTIAL ORIGIN OF SICKNESS

It is essential to ask how children responded emotionally to the idea that their pains were sent from God, because the majority of the children in the primary sources were from puritan families, who believed strongly in providence. The discussions below will show that this doctrine held intrinsically ambivalent implications for the

---

[95] Isaac Watts, *Preservative from the sins and follies of childhood and youth* (1734), 9.
[96] OED Online.
[97] Thomas Browne, *The Works of Sir Thomas Browne*, ed. Geoffrey Keynes (1931), 222–3.
[98] Symcotts, *A Seventeenth Century Doctor*, 61.
[99] Edward Lawrence, *Christ's power over bodily diseases* (1672), 261–2.

sick, making pain and illness both more and less bearable.[100] The belief in providence persisted beyond the end of the seventeenth century.

A common response to the providential origin of sickness was guilt. 'Oh my sin is the cause of it', cried eleven-year-old Martha Hatfield in 1652 following the onset of her distemper of the spleen. 'Lord reveale unto me what is the cause of this affliction, what sin it is that lies unrepented of', she prayed.[101] The reason for these guilty feelings was simple: God had brought illness as a punishment for sin, and therefore the sick had only themselves to blame for their afflictions.[102] It was necessary to dwell on these sins during sickness as part of the curative process, since God would only consider removing the illness once the patient had repented.[103] When young Caleb Vernon fell sick in 1665, he told his parents that 'one sin of his' that 'had often lain heavy upon his heart' was 'his disobedience to his Mother once, [in] not going to bed when she had commanded it'.[104] Other sins commonly listed were lying, gluttony, oversleeping, playing on the Sabbath, and original sin. It was not just the subjects of the pious biographies who felt guilty for their illnesses: children in various genres of primary source, such as letters, expressed this emotion. In 1726, the uncle of schoolboy James Clavering informed the boy's father that his son attributed his languishing disease to his 'irregular life' at school, and 'many of the pranks he committed there', thereby suggesting that the child himself felt remorse for his improper behaviour.[105]

Occasionally, children's guilty feelings became so intense that they were almost unbearable. Sixteen-year-old Elizabeth Walker would often 'sit and Weep most bitterly' during the smallpox in 1674 because she was 'much troubled with a wicked thing'. She confided to her mother, 'my dear Mother, you cannot conceive what passes through my poor head, nor what your poor child endures'.[106] These emotions sometimes kept children up at night with worry, or caused nightmares. When six-year-old Joseph Scholding's mother asked him 'Why dost thou not lie still' in the night, he replied that 'he dreamed such desperate things as did affright him', including the fear that he might commit the sin of swearing.[107] For these children it is likely that the emotional distress occasioned by the doctrine of providence outweighed the physical pain of illness, serving to exacerbate the overall misery of sickness. This was the case for a nine-year-old poor boy from the parish of Newington-Butts: he declared that 'though his pains were great, and the distemper

---

[100] See Ch. 4, pp. 130–1 for a summary of the debate about providence.

[101] Fisher, *The wise virgin*, 11.

[102] Andrew Wear, 'Puritan Perceptions of Illness in Seventeenth Century England' in Roy Porter (ed.), *Patients and Practitioners: Lay Perceptions of Medicine in Pre-industrial Society* (Cambridge: 2002, first publ. 1985), 55–99, at 71.

[103] David Harley, 'Spiritual Physic, Providence and English Medicine, 1560–1640', in Ole Peter Grell and Andrew Cunningham (eds), *Medicine and the Reformation* (1993), 101–17, at 106.

[104] Vernon, *The compleat scholler*, 27.

[105] Sir James Clavering, *The Correspondence of Sir James Clavering*, ed. Harry Thomas Dickinson, Surtees Society, vol. 178 (Gateshead: 1967), 157–8.

[106] Walker, *The vertuous wife*, 108–10.

[107] Bidbanck, *A present for children*, 77.

very tedious, yet the sense of his sin, and the thoughts of the miserable condition that he feared his soul was still in, made his trouble ten times greater'.[108]

Guilt was not always such an unpleasant experience, however. Some children may have derived a degree of satisfaction from observing the reactions of onlookers to their expressions of repentance. When the aforementioned nine-year-old from Newington-Butts declared himself 'the vilest creature he knew', his family and friends were 'filled ... with astonishment and joy', praising him for his 'knowledge, experiences, patience, humility, and self-abhorrency'.[109] This positive reaction to the confession of guilt sprang from the belief that an awareness of sin was a crucial component of ideal Christian sick behaviour, necessary for eliciting God's forgiveness, and for proving that one was not complacent about salvation. Such a preoccupation with sin and guilt may have also served as a useful distraction from the actual illness itself, 'a form of conversion hysteria in reverse'.[110]

Children did not always feel guilty during illness. Often, their distempers were attributed to the sins of their parents rather than to their own transgressions. When Frances Archer fell sick in 1678, her father mused, 'Upon this occasion I considered that children are not capable of emproving [provoking] afflictions; that they were chastnings sent by God for the good of parents'.[111] Children who overheard their parents talking in this way may have felt absolved from responsibility. This was the case for fifteen-year-old Susanna Whitrow from London: having overheard her mother repeatedly warn her father that *'The Lord would visit him with sore and grievous Judgment if he did not Repent'*, when she became sick in 1677, she instantly deduced that 'the Lord is broke in upon us' to punish her father, and duly beseeched the Lord to 'Remember not his Offences'.[112] It is possible that the practice of parents acting as scapegoats was one way in which children's experiences of sickness were distinguished from those of adults: there were fewer opportunities for ill adults to shift the blame for their providential afflictions. This was because childhood was 'the most innocent Part of our Lives' in which time parents shouldered the chief responsibility for the child's spiritual well-being.[113] The notion that God used the illnesses of children to punish parents was rooted in the Biblical passage 2 Samuel 12, verses 8–23: the Lord 'struck' David's child so that 'it was very sick' to punish him for committing adultery with a woman called Bathsheba and then having her husband killed.

The providential origin of sickness, though capable of inspiring feelings of guilt, was also a source of tremendous emotional and spiritual comfort to sick children. This was because it was believed that God's providences, however unpleasant, were always benevolent, and therefore the sick could patiently accept their illnesses in the knowledge that something good would emerge from their sufferings.[114] This notion

---

[108] Janeway, *A token for children* (part 1), 61.   [109] Ibid. 63–6.
[110] Wear, 'Puritan Perceptions of Illness', 75.   [111] Archer, *Two East Anglian Diaries*, 156.
[112] Rebecca Travers, *The work of God in a dying maid ... Susanna Whitrow* (1677), 16–17.
[113] John Bunyan, *Meditations on the several ages of man's life* (1700), 14.
[114] For the spiritual benefits of pain, see Wear, 'Puritan Perceptions of Illness'; and Jan Frans van Dijkhuizen, 'Partakers of Pain: Religious Meanings of Pain in Early Modern England', in Jan Frans Van Dijkhuizen and Karl A. E. Enenkel (eds), *The Sense of Suffering: Constructions of Physical Pain in*

may have actually affected the physical sensation of pain, making it more bearable.[115] To give a few examples of this more positive side to providentialism, one morning in 1669, six-year-old Mary Walker confessed to her maid that 'she was very sick; but God would doe her good by that sickness, and she would love him the better for it'.[116] Around the same time, eleven-year-old John Heywood, when 'very sick' of the smallpox, told his father that 'tho[ugh] he be in pain, yet . . . his heavenly father takes care of him'.[117] To make sense of this seemingly paradoxical idea, children and their families often invoked certain metaphors. In 1652, while in 'great extremity of pain', eleven-year-old Martha Hatfield was heard to say,

> As the Father calleth his childe when he hath done amiss, and . . . gives him correction: so God he gives his children correction, but it is for their good . . . God . . . whippeth his children, but he will not give them one whip, nor one lash more then is for their good . . . the Patient must taste of the bitter potion before his stomack be cleared.[118]

Here, disease is likened to the corporal punishment inflicted by a loving father to correct his children's transgressions, and also to a medicinal purge, which though noxious to the taste, is curative to the body.[119] Thus, like purges and correction, sickness was both unpleasant and therapeutic: it hurt the body, but benefited the soul.[120] According to Jenny Mayhew, the constant reiteration of these metaphors may have induced a 'psychotropic transformation', making physical pain seem more bearable, or even 'delightful': being told 'again and again' that sickness was a spiritual purge or correction would lead the patient 'imaginatively and emotively' to believe that 'suffering is good'.[121] This seems to have been the case for eleven-year-old Margaret Muschamp in the late 1640s: upon the consideration that her illness was a 'Godly chastisement', she declared, 'My pains [are] always joy, never sorrowful'.[122] This metaphor may have been particularly helpful to children, because it involved a situation with which they were especially familiar—punishment was common in childhood. The idea of positive correction was rooted in the Bible: 'My Son, despise not the Chastening of the Lord: neither be weary of his Correction. For whom the Lord loveth he correcteth, even as a Father the Son, in whom he delighteth'.[123]

But what exactly were the spiritual benefits of illness and pain, and how was God 'taking care' of these children by sending disease? Often, the sick did not articulate the precise advantages of illness, but instead wrote rather vaguely that affliction

---

Early Modern Culture, Yearbook for Early Modern Studies, vol. 12 (Leiden and Boston: 2008), 189–220.

[115] Mayhew, 'Godly Beds of Pain'.

[116] Walker, *The vertuous wife*, 96–100.

[117] Heywood, *The Rev. Oliver Heywood*, 235–6.

[118] Fisher, *The wise virgin*, 33–4, 69, 133.

[119] Ariel Glucklich has discussed the use of the medicine metaphor in, *Sacred Pain*, 21, 23. See also David Harley, 'Medical Metaphors in English Moral Theology, 1560–1660', *Journal of the History of Medicine*, 48 (1993), 396–435.

[120] An example of a theological treatise which mentions the medicine/punishment metaphors, is Richard Younge, *A Christian library* (1660, first publ. 1655), 9.

[121] Mayhew, 'Godly Beds of Pain', 312–14.

[122] Moore, 'Wonderful News', 382, 384.   [123] Proverbs 3: 11–12 (KJV).

would 'purify', 'cleanse', or 'perfect' the soul. Occasionally, however, more specific benefits were alluded to. Firstly, affliction was thought to awaken Christians to their sins, and draw them closer to God. As the theologian Richard Younge declared in 1660, '*repentance* seldom meets a man in *jollity,* but in *affliction* the heart is made *pliable* and ready for all *good impressions*... And indeed seldome is any man *thoroughly awakened* from the sleep of sin, but by *affliction*'.[124] It is obvious why repentance followed sickness: sin was the cause of man's afflictions, and therefore the cure lay in its renunciation. It seems that ailing children appreciated this purpose of illness, for they usually started repenting as soon as they fell unwell. When four-year-old Mary Stubbs sickened in the 1680s, she 'began to be very sensible of her Condition, and to cry and mourn' for her sins; after thoroughly repenting, her soul grew 'vigorous and lively' and she became happier about her spiritual health.[125]

Another function of sickness was to remind Christians to empathize with the suffering of Christ on the cross. In 1661, ten-year-old Mary Warren described the various tortures endured by Christ: 'he suffered a great deal more for me... he was bruised, buffeted, and spit on; and they platted a Crown of Thorns and put upon his Head, and gave him Vinegar to drink... And they came out against Christ with Swords and Staves'.[126] Over thirty years later, the adolescent Daniel Williams, 'being full of Pain', said, 'Jesus Christ bore more than this, and He Dyed for me'.[127] By empathizing with Christ, children were able to raise their own spiritual standings, and put their pains into perspective. Michael Schoenfeldt has suggested that an actual 'analgesic effect' can result when a sick person meditates on the pains of others.[128] The reason empathy was so essential from a religious perspective was that it was the means through which the Christian could attain a true appreciation of Christ's sacrifice. Although Protestant theologians did not believe it was possible to share fully the burdens of Jesus, the identification with His passion did enable the Christian to forge a 'fellowship with Christ'.[129] This empathy was especially important for puritans because they often believed that 'Christ's redemptive work was for the elect only': hence, to meditate upon 'the depths of the suffering... that Christ had plumbed' on their behalf was 'especially comforting'.[130]

Providential pain also served to make 'visible the intrinsically invisible pleasures of health'.[131] Brilliana Harley reminded her ill son Ned of this in the early 1640s: 'My deare Ned', she wrote, 'as some sharpenes gives a better relish to sweet meats, soe some sence of sickenes makes us tast the benefit of health'.[132] Roughly eighty years later, the Norfolk architect John Buxton told his thirteen-year-old son Robert

[124] Younge, *A Christian library*, 9–11.   [125] Bidbanck, *A present for children*, 43–68.
[126] H. P., *A looking-glass for children*, 16.
[127] Mather, *A token, for the children of New-England*, 23.
[128] Schoenfeldt, 'The Art of Pain Management', 34.
[129] Van Dijkhuizen, 'Partakers of Pain', 231.
[130] Dewey D. Wallace, *Puritans and Predestination: Grace in English Protestant Theology, 1525–1695* (North Carolina: 1982), 48–9.
[131] Schoenfeldt, 'The Art of Pain Management', 26.
[132] Brilliana Harley, *Letters of the Lady Brilliana Harley*, ed. Thomas Taylor Lewis (1853), 48.

that 'what you have gon thro[ugh]' during illness 'has been well worth the enduring', for it would enable him to 'put a true estimate upon health', a lesson that 'abundance of young men are strangers to'.[133] Periods of bodily discomfort would help children to fully appreciate the absence of pain, while also inspiring gratitude to God for His mercies. Children themselves frequently referred to this function: thirteen-year-old Margaret Andrews, having suffered from great pains, told those around her that '*God is very gracious in giving us pain, otherwise we should not know how to be thankful for ease*'.[134] It is possible that these thoughts helped rationalize suffering for children, making it easier to bear.

Finally, it was often implied that sickness had a direct impact on the individual's salvation. When the Cornish adolescent Anne Gwin became ill in the 1690s, she beseeched God to 'chastise for my Sins in this Life, and punish not me in that which is to come, that there I may live with thee in Glory Eternal, for ever and ever, *Amen*'.[135] This girl was hoping that her present suffering would forestall future, eternal punishment. Boys also expressed this wish: Caleb Vernon was heard 'blessing the Lord again for bringing this Sickness upon him, saying, *for these light afflictions which are but for a moment, work for me far more exceeding and eternal weight*', thereby implying that somehow his earthly pains would have a positive effect on his salvation.[136] A Biblical verse regularly quoted by children, which seemed to justify these hopes, was Hebrews 12 verse 11: 'no chastisement seemeth for the present joyous, but grievous, but after wards it yieldeth the peaceable fruit of righteousness to them which are exercised thereby'.[137] Hence, sickness, although unpleasant at the time, was recompensed by the bliss of heaven, the 'fruit of righteousness'.

The idea that sickness could influence the child's salvation was not endorsed by orthodox Protestant theology, however. According to John Calvin, the eternal destinies of souls were predestined—no amount of pain or sickness could affect the individual's eternal life.[138] John Stachniewski confirms that 'Nothing could coerce, alter, aid, or hinder God's purposes' in the eyes of orthodox Protestants.[139] The very idea that pain could affect a person's salvation could be deemed an 'intolerable impingement' on Christ's role as Saviour, since 'it is only God who works through pain, not humans themselves...pain is not productive in itself, does not have any *inherent* efficacy, but serves as an opportunity to cultivate *mental* attitudes of temperance and acceptance'.[140] In spite of this belief, however, the sick continued to make a link between earthly affliction and eternal bliss. They may have tried to

---

[133] John Buxton, *John Buxton, Norfolk Gentleman and Architect: Letters to his Son, 1719–1729*, ed. Alan Mackley, Norfolk Record Society, vol. 69 (Norwich: 2005), 45.

[134] *The life and death of Mrs Margaret Andrews...who died...1680, in the 14th year of her age* (1680), 59.

[135] Thomas Gwin, *A memorial of our dear daughter Anne Gwin*(1715), 29.

[136] Vernon, *The compleat scholler*, 26.

[137] James Janeway, *A token for children. The second part* (1673), 25.

[138] For an extended discussion of the doctrine of predestination, see Wallace, *Puritans and Predestination*.

[139] Stachniewski, *The Persecutory Imagination*, 19.

[140] Van Dijkhuizen, 'Partakers of Pain', 212–15.

reconcile the theological quandary by considering that God had preordained their illnesses for their spiritual benefit. Alexandra Walsham has commented on this tendency for laypeople to 'subtly edit, alter, and ignore' the elaborate tenets propounded by their preachers to meet their emotional needs.[141]

Thus, throughout the early modern period, the belief in providence had a mixed impact on children's experiences of illness. As well as provoking unpleasant feelings of guilt, the doctrine was a source of comfort to young patients, helping them to resign themselves patiently to their suffering in the knowledge that although it was detrimental to the health of their bodies, it was cathartic to the health of their souls. Thus, once again, patients were required to be patient; they were supposed to 'suffer' (submit to) their sufferings.

THE ANTICIPATION OF DEATH

In his book *The Hour of our Death* (1981), Philippe Ariès argued that during the Middle Ages, death was regarded as a 'familiar friend', eliciting no great sense of fear from the sick and dying, but that by the end of the early modern period, it had come to be viewed as the 'king of terrors'.[142] The cause of this shift, he asserted, was the emergence of 'individualism' (the awareness of 'self'), which made people increasingly concerned for their own fates. David Stannard offered a similar interpretation, but suggested that the heightened fear stemmed from the Reformation, and the resulting abolition of the doctrines of purgatory and intercessory prayer, and increased emphasis on the helplessness of man to influence his own salvation.[143] Since the 1990s, historians have questioned these interpretations. Ralph Houlbrooke argued that there is 'little firm evidence' to show that the decline of purgatory induced a 'serious or widespread psychic crisis': rather, most people 'reassured themselves with the simple reflection that God was too loving . . . to send them to hell'.[144] He implied that death may actually have been becoming *less* frightening towards the end of the period, owing to growing scepticism among some individuals about the reality of hell.[145] The following paragraphs offer a fresh perspective on these issues: I argue that children's emotional responses to

---

[141] Alexandra Walsham, *Providence in Early Modern England* (Oxford: 2003, first publ. 1999), 331.

[142] Philippe Ariès, *The Hour of Our Death*, trans. Helen Weaver (London and New York: 1981), and his article, 'The Reversal of Death: Changes in Attitudes Toward Death in Western Societies', *American Quarterly*, 26 (1974), 536–60.

[143] David Stannard, 'Death and the Puritan Child', *American Quarterly*, 26 (1974), 456–75, and his, *The Puritan Way of Death: a Study in Religion, Culture, and Social Change* (Oxford: 1977). Claire Gittings believes that the rise of individualism combined with the Protestant Reformation created 'more anxiety-provoking attitude towards death' during the early modern period: *Death, Burial and the Individual in Early Modern England* (1984), 50.

[144] Houlbrooke, *Death, Religion and the Family*, 54. Likewise, Peter Marshall has stated that 'there appears to have been a broad cultural presumption in later Reformation England that salvation was widely accessible': *Beliefs and the Dead in Reformation England* (Oxford: 2002), 201.

[145] Ibid. (Houlbrooke), 55–6. This view was probably informed by Daniel Pickering Walker's thesis about the 'decline of hell': *The Decline of Hell: Seventeenth-Century Discussions of Eternal Torment* (1964).

death seem to have undergone little alteration in the early modern period. Throughout, dying children reacted in various ways, sometimes expressing fear, and at other times, experiencing emotions that verged on ecstasy.[146] The cause of this ambivalent response was the ingrained doctrine of salvation, and its hauntingly divergent fates of eternal happiness and eternal torment. While hell may have been doubted in some quarters, it remained a powerful presence in the imaginations of children into the eighteenth century.

Sick children were made aware of the likelihood of death. 'My Dear, Are you so ill that you think you shall die?', enquired the mother of thirteen-year-old Margaret Andrews three hours before her death in 1680.[147] As was established in an earlier chapter, a key facet of patient care was helping the sick person to prepare spiritually for death. This process of preparation, which involved various acts of piety, was supposed to enable the dying to reach a state of confidence about their eternal future. Thus, parents and relatives were obliged to inform their children of the possibility of death. In 1642, eight-year-old Elizabeth Angier was asked by her father 'whether she was willing to die'.[148] While this practice of questioning children about such a foreboding a subject might seem cruel today, in this period it was considered quite the opposite, because it was essential for the child's eternal happiness. Children also learned of their potential mortality from witnessing the deaths of family members or neighbours. In the 1650s, four-year-old John Sudlow's baby brother died: seeing the little body 'without breath, and not able to speak or stir, and then carried out of doors, and put into a pit-hole', made this boy 'greatly concerned', and caused him to ask his parents 'whether he must die too', to which they replied in the affirmative.[149] Over half a century later, Sarah Savage recorded that her 'young ones' saw her neighbour, 'Mr Starky' die: they were 'much affected' at 'seeing him at the very Entrance of a boundless inconceivable Eternity', and witnessing his 'ghastly looks & gasping after a fleeting breath'.[150] Occasionally, children did not need to be told that they would die: they seemed to already know, almost instinctively, that their time was soon up. In 1636 Dr John Symcotts recorded in his casebook that his fourteen-year-old patient, Elizabeth Burgoyne, confided 'to her friends that she must die', for she had undergone 'the greatest agony' from a 'worm of 3 quarters of a foot long'.[151] It may have been the intensity of their pain that fuelled these children's premonitions. Of course, not all children were aware of their impending deaths—many were probably too ill, or else

---

[146] Gillian Avery agrees that the dying experienced a 'paradoxical' array of emotions, in her chapter, 'Intimations of Mortality', 103. Ralph Houlbrooke also shows that emotional responses to death could be diverse, ranging from ecstasy to fear: 'Death in Childhood: the Practice of the Good Death in James Janeway's "A Token for Children"', in Anthony Fletcher and Stephen Hussey (eds), *Childhood in Question: Children, Parents and the State* (Manchester: 1999), 37–56, at 41–2, and his book, *Death, Religion and the Family*, 147, 195–6, 200–2, 207.

[147] *The life and death of Mrs Margaret Andrews*, 60.

[148] John Angier, *Oliver Heywood's Life of John Angier of Denton together with Angier's Diary*, ed. Ernest Axon, Chetham Society, vol. 97 (Aberdeen: 1937), 126.

[149] Janeway, *A token for children* (part 2), 2–3.

[150] Bodleian Library, Oxford, MS Eng. Misc. e. 331, p. 35 (Diary of Sarah Savage, 1714–23).

[151] Symcotts, *A Seventeenth Century Doctor*, 61.

deteriorated so rapidly that they had no time to think about such things. As Ralph Houlbrooke has cautioned, 'scores' of people probably 'passed out of the world suddenly, confused, prostrated by fever, or slipped into oblivion without full awareness of their approaching end'.[152]

Children sometimes responded to the anticipation of death with great fear and anxiety. When seven-year-old Tabatha Alder became ill in 1644, she confessed that 'she was greatly afraid that she should go to hell' because 'she did not love God'. When asked why she did not love God, she said she 'found it a hard thing to love one she did not see'.[153] About forty years later, four-year-old Mary Stubbs underwent a similar experience: her mother, trying to make her daughter aware of the necessity of repentance during illness, had warned her that 'all that died, did not go' to heaven. Subsequently, the girl had begun to 'cry and mourn, fearing that she should go to Hell'.[154] Thus, children's fears centred on the idea of hell, and could be sparked by their parents' words. Such fear could be so intense that it kept children awake at night, or caused nightmares. In 1670, Sir Edward Harley told his wife that their son Robin 'waked in the night' with worries about sin, crying 'with tears' that 'he was afraid if he died he should go to hell'.[155] These emotions sometimes seemed to dwarf the pain of illness by comparison: when the nine-year-old boy from Newington-Butts contracted the plague, he complained that 'Now the plague upon his body seemed nothing to that which was in his soul', because he feared he 'should go to hell'.[156] Even those children who were not convinced of their own damnation seem to have been preoccupied with hell. When six-year-old Joseph Scholding's mother went to the oven to attend to dinner one evening in 1678, the boy 'seeing a great Fire flaming out of the Oven' said, 'a great and grievous Fire: little do wicked Men think what God is; he hath a worse Fire to burn wicked Men in'.[157] This concern about damnation indicates that it was such an entrenched part of the religious culture that no one was entirely free from fear.

The fear of hell was not confined to the children of the socio-economic elites. The Proceedings of the Old Bailey show that damnation evoked anxiety across a wide spectrum of society. In 1678 the nine-year-old daughter of a lowly craftsman, Elizabeth Hopkins, who had contracted venereal disease from being raped, only confessed to the incident when her family warned her that she would be 'in danger of hanging in Hell' unless she spoke out.[158] Clearly the child had sufficient knowledge of the afterlife to be convinced by this threat. Patricia Crawford has confirmed that poor parents 'threatened children with fears of hell... to

[152] Houlbrooke, *Death, Religion, and the Family*, 383.
[153] Janeway, *A token for children* (part 2), 19–20.
[154] Bidbanck, *A present for children*, 44–5.
[155] Cited by Arthur W. M. Bryant (ed.), *Postman's Horn: an Anthology of the Family Letters of Later Seventeenth Century England* (1946), 5.
[156] Janeway, *A token for children* (part 1), 62.
[157] Bidbanck, *A present for children*, 76 (dated *c.* 1678).
[158] POB, reference: t16781211e-2 (accessed 14 January 2011).

terrify them into behaving'.[159] The above evidence seems to challenge the view that the fears of dying children are elusive to historical study.[160]

One has only to cast a glance at the contemporary eschatological literature to discover why hell elicited such extraordinary fear.[161] Henry Greenwood's treatise, first published in 1618, describes hell as, a 'most lamentable and wofull place of torment . . . where there shall be scretching and screaming, weeping, wayling, and gnashing of teeth for eternity . . . easelesse, endlesse, remedylesse'.[162] Religious writers emphasised the intensity of the pain suffered by the reprobate, comparing it to the comparatively mild suffering experienced on earth:

> You may fancy the most terrible things can be dreaded; of Fire and Brimstone, Wracks and Tempests, boiling Pitch, scalding Lead . . . But all we can hereby reach to conceive, of the Pains of Hell, falls as much short of the Torments of the Damned . . . 'Tis impossible for the most awakened Conscience to conceive the Horrour of it.[163]

Thus, humans were incapable of fully understanding the true horror of hell—it was beyond anything they might experience on earth. The two extracts above were separated by almost a century, and yet they convey very similar ideas about hell.

One might question whether these terrible descriptions would have been shared with children. However, conduct literature written specifically for children did depict the hellish horrors.[164] One writer warned children, 'Consider that you may perish as young as you are; there are small Chips, as well as great Logs in the Fire of Hell . . . The Child that will tell a Lye, must one Day roar in Hell, for a Drop of Water to cool his Tongue!'[165] Robert Russel's *A Little book for children* went into still greater detail:

> [If] thou wilt continue to be a naughty wicked Child . . . Then thou with all thy wicked Companions shall be tumbled into the Lake that burns with Fire and Brimstone; there thou shalt endure such unspeakable Pain . . . which cannot be conceived . . . there thou shalt always be crying and roaring under those great intollerable Flames . . . O my dear Child, Hell is a dreadful place, worse Ten thousand times than thy Parents beating thee.[166]

Authors tailored their descriptions of hell to their young audiences, making them especially relevant to children by mentioning corporal punishment, schoolfellows, and angry parents. Children's literature also contains vivid pictures of the damned in hell, such as **Figure 7**, which depicts a woman in the jaws of hell, surrounded by flames.

---

[159] Patricia Crawford, *Parents of Poor Children in England, 1580–1800* (Oxford: 2010), 147.

[160] Gittings, *Death, Burial and the Individual*, 12.

[161] For extended discussions of early modern ideas about hell see Almond, *Heaven and Hell*, Houlbrooke, *Death, Religion, and the Family*, 30, 33, 35, 39–40, and Marshall, *Beliefs and the Dead*, 9–10, 191–2, 195.

[162] Greenwood, *Tormenting tophet*, 239–40.

[163] John Shower, *Heaven and hell; or the unchangeable state of happiness or misery for all mankind in another world* (1700), 17–8.

[164] Gillian Avery states that hell was a regular theme of children's literature this period: 'Intimations of Mortality', 87–110.

[165] *A voice from heaven, the youth of Great Britain* (1690), image 7 (this treatise is unpaginated).

[166] Robert Russel, *A little book for children, and youth* (1693–96; this treatise is unpaginated).

Fig. 7. Woodcut of hell from *A voice from heaven, the youth of Great Britain* (1720); Copyright © The British Library Board.

Unsurprisingly, children who viewed these treatises often responded with trepidation. When fifteen-year-old Joseph Taylor read 'a little Book', which gave 'a Pathetical Description of Hell', he was 'put into sore Amazement and very great Terrour'. He sat 'groaning in the dark', crying *'O! How shall I do to bear this heavy Sentence! How shall I bear the tormenting Flames of Hell for ever and ever!'*[167] Even those children who did not have access to these books, such as the offspring of the poor, would have gained some knowledge of hellfire, because damnation was discussed routinely in sermons, ballads, and chapbooks—media that reached down to the lowest levels.[168] For instance, the ballad *St Bernard's vision* (1685) gives a 'brief discourse' between the soul and body of a damned man, and describes the 'frying flames' into which he was about to be plunged.[169] Although we do not know how poor children would have responded to these texts—whether they 'Reade and Tremble[d]', or 'cheerfully laugh[ed]'[170]—the fact remains that hell was part of everyone's cultural repertoire of early modern England.

Despite the widespread awareness of hell, it seems likely that some adults would have preferred to conceal the more gruesome details from their little ones, perhaps

---

[167] Joseph Taylor, *Grace, grace: or, the exceeding riches of grace* (1702), 7–8.
[168] Tessa Watt, *Cheap Print and Popular Piety 1550–1640* (Cambridge and New York: 1991), 110–12, 171, 283–9.
[169] *St Bernard's vision* (1685).   [170] Walsham, *Providence*, 39.

because they did not want to upset them. This can be inferred from the preface of Janeway's treatise, wherein he felt it necessary to coax and cajole parents into teaching their children about the realities of hell, thereby implying that there were significant numbers of parents who were reluctant to do so. He warned parents, 'Are you willing that they should be Brands of Hell? Are you indifferent whether they be Damned or Saved? ... [T]hey are not too little to dye, they are not too little to go to Hell'.[171] Thus, it seems probable that some parents preferred to skim over the more terrifying aspects of hell, confining their children's knowledge of this place to a tamed version.[172] This milder attitude does not seem to have followed a chronological pattern: no evidence has been found to indicate that over the course of the early modern period parents were increasingly reluctant to teach their children about hell.

It was not just the thought of hell that provoked fears in sick children: death was frightening for many other reasons besides. Some children worried about the practical problems of death and salvation. Young Joseph Scholding, 'one Morning as he lay in his Bed very ill', said to his mother, 'Mother ... I am thinking how my Soul shall get to Heaven when I die; my Legs cannot carry it, the Worms shall eat them.'[173] Another concern provoked by the thought of death was the separation from family and friends that it would bring.[174] While suffering from 'vapours' in 1720, seven-year-old Betty Seymour 'laid her head' in her mother's lap and 'fell into a passion of crying', saying that if she died she 'should not have so good a Mama, and that she would keep this Mama'.[175] This fear was not restricted to females: in the 1670s, six-year-old Jason Whitrow took his mother 'by the hand, and said, *Mother, I shall dye, oh that you might dye with me, that we might both go to the Lord together*'.[176] These extracts, as well as elucidating the preoccupations and anxieties of dying children, reveal the deep affection felt for mothers by both sons and daughters. Historians have usually concentrated on parents' feelings about their children, rather than the other way round.

While the prospect of dying was undoubtedly frightening, the idea of heaven helped mitigate these unpleasant feelings, enabling children to respond to death with a degree of resignation. In 1632, twelve-year-old Charles Bridgeman told his parents, 'I desire to dye, that I may go to my Saviour ... Now I am well, my pain is almost gone, my joy is at hand'.[177] About sixty years later, the adolescent Anne Gwin expressed a similar sentiment, telling her family that '*She had no Cause to be afraid to die*' because '*She knew she was going to a God gracious and merciful,*

---

[171] Janeway, *A token for children* (part 1), preface.

[172] Mary Clare Hewlett Martin believes that 'most parents did not frighten their children with threats of death and hell' in the eighteenth and nineteenth centuries, in her thesis 'Children and Religion in Walthamstow and Leyton, 1740–1870' (unpubl. PhD thesis, University of London, 2000), 196.

[173] Bidbanck, *A present for children*, 76.

[174] Stannard, *The Puritan Way of Death*, 63.

[175] Frances Seymour Countess of Hertford, *The Gentle Hertford: Her Life and Letters*, ed. Helen Hughes (New York: 1940), 77.

[176] Travers, *The work of God in a dying maid*, 47–8.

[177] Janeway, *A token for children* (part 1), 46–9.

whose Face she hoped to see with Comfort.[178] Parents and friends played a large part in helping children to reach this state of soteriological confidence. For several days during her illness in 1644, eight-year-old Tabitha Alder had been in a 'desponding condition', fearing that she might be damned; but after a 'dear friend' of the family spent a day talking to the girl, and praying with her, she gradually became convinced that 'she loved the Lord Jesus dearly' and therefore would be saved.[179]

Sometimes these feelings of resignation blurred into outright happiness and joy, as children positively looked forward to their heavenly future.[180] When eleven-year-old Martha Hatfield lay ill in 1652, she 'was enabled with great alacrity to express the joy of Heaven', declaring that 'I am now going to Heaven', and seeming to be 'exceedingly rapt up with joy . . . laughing, and spreading her arms', and crying out 'I have found my Christ, O, I have found my Christ, how sweet he is to me!'[181] Boys as well as girls experienced these emotions: when at last the poor boy from Newington-Butts managed to overcome his fears of hell, and attain a confidence in his salvation, he felt so happy that 'he hath been ready almost to leap out of his bed for joy'.[182] These blissful feelings often served to distract children from their physical pains, making the suffering more bearable. In 1661, ten-year-old Mary Warrren mused that although 'I am very sore, from the crown of my head to the sole of my foot, I am so full of Comfort and joy that I do feel but little of my pain'.[183] Over half a century later, young Betty Keay, who was suffering from smallpox, said:

> When I have formerly read of that martyr in flames, who said he felt no more pain than if on a bed of roses, I knew not then what he meant – but I bless God now I know, and am so swallowed up of joy as not to regard my outward pains.[184]

The martyr to whom Betty was referring was probably James Baynam, whose death at the stake in 1532 was described in John Foxe's *Acts and Monuments*: while 'in the middest of the flaming fire', Baynam had declared, 'in this fire I feele no more paine, then if I were in a bed of Downe: but it is to me as sweete as a bed of roses', because he was thinking of his future in paradise.[185] By identifying with this martyr, Betty not only assuaged her pains, but also temporarily raised her own social and religious status.[186] Godly parents frequently reminded their children of heaven with the intention of easing their pains. When thirteen-year-old Caleb Vernon cried out that

---

[178] Gwin, *A memorial of our dear daughter*, 9–10.

[179] Janeway, *A token for children* (part 2), 20–1.

[180] Ralph Houlbrooke agrees, in *Death, Religion and the Family*, 195–6, 200.

[181] Fisher, *The wise virgin*, 6.

[182] Janeway, *A token for children* (part 1), 67.

[183] H.P., *A looking-glass for children*, 12–13.

[184] Sarah Savage, *Memoirs of the Life and Character of Mrs Sarah Savage*, ed. J. B. Williams (1821), 203–6.

[185] Foxe, *Foxe's Book of Martyrs*, book eight, 1002.

[186] This theme has also been discussed at length by Susan Hardman Moore: '"Such Perfecting of Praise out of the Mouth of a Babe": Sarah Wight as Child Prophet', in Diana Wood (ed.), *The Church and Childhood*, Studies in Church History, vol. 31 (Oxford: 1994), 313–24, and by Walsham, 'Out of the Mouths of Babes', 285–99.

'*His Bones were sore*' in 1665, his father replied, 'but your soul is not', reminding him of his healthy spiritual state and heavenly future. Hearing this, the boy 'presently forgot his pains, and was refreshed'.[187] Occasionally, children found the thought of heaven so cathartic that they demanded their relatives to 'speak of Heaven, nothing but Heaven' at times of great physical dolour.[188] The reason thoughts of heaven mitigated the patient's sensation of pain, according to early modern philosophers, related to the relationship between the soul and the body: just as the body could influence the passions, the passions could influence the body, and therefore happy emotions could bring physical comfort, reducing the body's sense of pain. This notion was lucidly articulated by F. N. Coeffeteau in 1621: he stated that the 'contemplation' of heaven or other good things 'is so sweete and delightfull of it self, as it expels and disperseth all' a person's physical 'cares and *Griefe* . . . . In regard whereof some Martyres have give a thousand testimonies of joy in the midst of their torments'.[189]

These feelings of resignation and joy may seem implausible. It is possible that they may have been exaggerated, or worse still, completely invented by the authors, who wanted to convey a prescriptive message about ideal Christian responses to death, or wished to convince themselves of their child's salvation.[190] Patience and joy on the deathbed demonstrated the person's submission to God's will, and were often taken as signs of his or her faith and likely salvation: consequently, there was a need to emphasize this behaviour.[191] Parents may have also unintentionally put pressure on their children to voice more confidence than they were actually feeling, because they desperately wanted to believe that their offspring would go to heaven.[192] This was probably the case for eleven-year-old John Harvy in the 1660s: his mother told him, 'if thou hadst but an assurance of Gods love I should not be so much troubled', to which he replied, 'I am assured, dear Mother, that my sins are forgiven, and that I shall go to Heaven'. The boy admitted that 'nothing . . . grieved him' more than 'the sorrow that he saw his Mother to be in for his death', from which it can be deduced that he may have been trying to comfort his mother with his expressions of confidence.[193] His words also show his love and concern for his mother.

While a degree of scepticism is healthy, to disregard entirely the evidence of children's joyful deaths would be wrong. A closer examination of the words of the dying children reveals that they had particularly vivid imaginations of heaven, which may explain why they looked forward to going there. When ten-year-old Christian Karr was seriously ill in 1702, she told her family, 'O I think I see Heaven, I think I see Heaven, That is a glorious sight indeed . . . the Walls and the

---

[187] Vernon, *The compleat scholler*, 66.
[188] The quotation relates to four-year-old Mary Stubbs: Bidbanck, *A present for children*, 59–60.
[189] F. N. Coeffeteau, *A table of humane passions* (1621), 352–3.
[190] Houlbrooke, *Death, Religion and the Family*, 62.
[191] See Richard Wunderli and Gerald Broce, 'The Final Moment before Death', *Sixteenth Century Journal*, 20 (1989), 259–75.
[192] This has been suggested by Lucinda McCray Beier in her essay, 'The Good Death in Seventeenth-Century England', in Ralph Houlbrooke (ed.), *Death, Ritual and Bereavement* (London and New York: 1989), 43–61, at 46.
[193] Janeway, *A token for children* (part 2), 84–5.

streets of that City are like burning God. And I think I see all the Saints, arrayed in Whyte there'.[194] Ralph Houlbrooke has implied that children may have believed more literally in the afterlife than adults, perhaps because they had a tendency to accept what they are taught unquestioningly.[195]

There were several convincing reasons why death could be seen as desirable. Firstly, it would bring a termination to physical suffering, replacing it with permanent comfort and happiness. Mary Warren's mother, 'going softly to the Chamber-door', overheard her daughter uttering the words, *'Come Lord Jesus, come quickly, & receive they [sic] poor Creature out of all my pains'*. This girl later assured her mother, *'I know it, that when I go from hence, I shall go into health and happiness'*.[196] Naturally, it was at moments of particularly devastating pain that this aspect of heaven seemed most alluring. Having wasted away over the course of several months in 1665, twelve-year-old Caleb Vernon's bones had become 'so sharp as if they would pierce his skin, having no flesh to interpose in any part'. Overcome with 'weariness and impatience', he cried that *'It is better for me now to dye than to live'*, because he knew that in heaven his agony would be at an end.[197] Theological literature confirms that paradise was envisaged as a place free from pain, where people are forever happy.[198] When one considers that there were few effective painkillers in this period, it seems understandable that children may have wished to die to escape their suffering.[199]

Children sometimes looked forward to death because they wished to meet Christ. In 1644, eight-year-old Tabitha Alder had 'a longing to be with' God, declaring 'in a kind of extasie of joy' that she 'shall be with Jesus . . . and I shall live with him for ever'.[200] It is entirely reasonable that devout children longed to be in Christ's company, because they had been taught so much about Him. Particularly enticing was the prospect of being embraced by Jesus, and seeing His face for the first time. In his final hours, John Harvy said to his mother, 'O Mother, I shall presently have my head in my Fathers bosome'.[201] Parents sometimes reminded their dying children of Christ's affection, perhaps hoping that this would familiarize and demystify the potentially daunting occasion of meeting the Lord, while also reassuring children that life after death would not be devoid of the kind of love that they were accustomed to on earth. When ten-year-old Mary Warren clasped her arms around her mother's neck, her mother said, 'Thou embracest me, but I trust thou art going to the embracings of the Lord Jesus'.[202] This idea of Christ's affection to children sprang from the Biblical passage, 'Suffer little children to come unto me, for of such is the kingdom of heaven, and he took them into his

---

[194] Archibald Deans, *An account of the last words of Christian Karr, who dyed . . . in the eleventh year of her age* (Edinburgh: 1702), 7.

[195] Houlbrooke, 'Death in Childhood', 49.

[196] H. P., *A looking-glass for children*, 9.

[197] Vernon, *The compleat scholler*, 66. Caleb probably took these words from Jonah, ch. 4, verse 3.

[198] William Gearing, *A prospect of heaven* (1673), 114–15.

[199] See Ch. 2 for a discussion of pain relief in children's medicine.

[200] Janeway, *A token for children* (part 2), 21–2.

[201] Ibid. 84–5.

[202] H. P., *A looking-glass for children*, 9.

arms, and laid his hands on them and blessed them'.[203] Religious writers supported the notion of Christ's affectionate welcome: William Gearing stated that, 'God will most affectionately receive all his Children to himself; with much love and tenderness of affection at the last day, they shall be received into the arms of his embraces'.[204] The image of Christ invoked in the above extracts—as a loving, affectionate father—seems far removed from the stern, angry God commonly associated with Puritanism in this period.[205]

Arguably the most comforting aspect of heaven was the possibility for family reunion after death. In 1620, ten-year-old Cecilia D'Ewes contracted the smallpox; her mother had died a short time previously, and therefore, the girl appeared not to mind dying, but instead 'would speak of her religious mother', crying with relief, 'I will go to my mother, I will see her; I shall shortly be with her'.[206] It was common for children to lose one or both of their parents in the early modern period: in Elizabethan Rye, for instance, nearly 60 per cent of the fathers who died left children under the age of fourteen.[207] Peter Laslett has calculated that 29 per cent of children would have lost their fathers by the age of fifteen.[208] It is therefore not surprising that dying children looked forward to heaven—they missed their parents. They also wished to be reunited with siblings who had died: in 1664, thirteen-year-old Susanna Bicks told her parents 'I go to my brother *Jacob* .... And to my little sister, who was but three years old when she died'.[209] The death of siblings was even more widespread than the deaths of parents: a quarter to a third of children died before the age of fifteen.[210] While the occasional churchman questioned the notion that souls in heaven would be able to recognize one another, the majority agreed with William Gearing that 'Parents, Children, Relations . . . shall meet all together', enjoying a 'sweet familiarity with one another' in paradise.[211] Ultimately, dying children hoped to eventually meet all their family members, living and dead. When young John Brockbank observed his mother's grief, he took her, 'about the neck with his pocky arm; and kist her with his scabbed lips', and told her, 'I pray God send us merry meeting in the kingdom of Heaven where we shall be for Ever More'.[212] Even very young children were able to derive comfort from

---

[203] This verse was quoted by thirteen-year-old Susanna Bicks in 1664: Janeway, *A token for children* (part 2), 42.

[204] Gearing, *A prospect of heaven*, 166–7.

[205] Ivy Pinchbeck and Margaret Hewitt, for example, stated that early modern children had a 'cruelly distorted image of God' owing to all the emphasis on death and its perils: *Children in English Society. Vol. 1, from Tudor Times to the Eighteenth Century* (1969), 265.

[206] Simonds D'Ewes, *The Autobiography and Correspondence of Sir Simonds D'Ewes, Bart.*, ed. J. O. Halliwell, 2 vols (1845) , 157.

[207] Crawford, *Parents of Poor Children*, 115.

[208] Peter Laslett, 'Parental Deprivation in the Past', in his *Family Life and Illicit Love in Earlier Generations* (Cambridge: 1977), 162–3.

[209] Janeway, *A token for children* (part 2), 54.

[210] See Introduction, footnote 4.

[211] Gearing, *A prospect of heaven*, 239. For a discussion of the social relations in heaven, see Peter Marshall, 'The Company of Heaven: Identity and Sociability in the English Protestant Afterlife, c. 1560–1630', *Historical Reflections*, 26 (2000), 311–33.

[212] Thomas Brockbank, *The Diary and Letter Book of the Rev. Thomas Brockbank 1671–1709*, ed. Richard Trappes-Lomax, Chetham Society New Series, vol. 89 (Manchester: 1930), 5–7.

this prospect: four-year-old Mary Stubbs, for example, 'was very desirous that her Father and Mother, Brother and Sister' should 'mind Heaven', so that 'they might live together in Heaven'.[213] Parents often reminded their dying children of this reunion, so as to comfort them during their last moments. A few hours before her death in 1679, Isaac Archer told his six-year-old daughter Frances 'she was going to heaven to her brothers and sisters, and that we should all meet againe'.[214] The idyllic image of the reunited family evoked in the above extracts demonstrates the deeply loving nature of many family relationships.

Of course, children did not always die: two thirds to three-quarters of children lived past the age of fifteen, and therefore it is likely that recovery was a common experience. Martha Hatfield's biography provides a touching insight into the experience of recovery:

> Soon . . . she knew her Mother, and rejoiced to see her with laughing and stroaking her face, and clasping her armes about her neck; and then her Father came, and asked her, if she knew him, and . . . she did the like to him . . . all the afternoon she played with some odde little toyes, and Spice, which Neighbours had brought her . . . her Mother being set upon the bed by her, she laughed, and rejoiced, and said, Mother, ah Mother, how do you? Ah my deare Childe, (said her Mother) how doest thou? She answered, Me is pretty well, I praise my God . . . she felt the strength come into her Legs . . . It trickled down, and came into her thighs, knees, and ankles, like warm water.[215]

Evidently, this child felt great joy and relief upon recovering. She particularly enjoyed the sensation of regaining strength, and being able to once more recognize her family.

CONCLUSION

The experience of one child, twelve-year-old Caleb Vernon, encapsulates the argument of this chapter. Upon falling sick of 'Feaver and Plurisie' in 1665, he began to feel guilty for his sins, worrying in particular about 'his disobedience to his Mother once' in 'not going to bed when she had commanded it'. These feelings, which sprang from his assumption that his illness was a providential punishment, served to exacerbate his misery, making his physical pains harder to bear. However, after being assured by his mother that 'God had pardoned it and all other his sins in Christ', he gradually attained 'hope and some joy (yet mixed at first with more fears and doubtings)' about his eternal state, which eventually transformed into a firm belief that 'I shall go to Heaven'. The boy confided to his parents that he could almost 'forget pain', as '*God hath as it were taken me into his Arms this night, and assured me of his Love.*' He was '*very ill . . . in my Body, but well in God*'.[216]

Sickness could be a time of emotional and spiritual turmoil for children, as they veered through an array of feelings, from fear and guilt, to resignation, patience,

[213] Bidbanck, *A present for children*, 63.   [214] Archer, *Two East Anglian Diaries*, 160–1.
[215] Fisher, *The wise virgin*, 145–59.   [216] Vernon, *The compleat scholler*.

and ecstasy. The fundamental causes of this ambivalent experience were the Christian beliefs in providence, the soul, and salvation. Sickness, as a divine rod of correction, was good for the soul, serving to purge it of iniquity, and ultimately helping to convince the individual of his or her eternal happiness. Thus, while illness harmed the body, it perfected the soul, and consequently, even excruciating pain could be experienced positively. The belief in heaven transformed death from 'the King of Terrours into the King of Desires'.[217] Essentially, human health seems to have been experienced on two levels—those of soul and body—and since the soul was immortal, its well-being assumed the greater importance. It was this duality of existence which enabled the sick to feel contented during illness: they might be ill in their bodies, but their souls could be well. However, the flip side of this belief system was that the soul was also vulnerable to ill health: when sickness of the body combined with sickness of the soul, the distress of the patient was 'ten times greater'.[218] Ironically, it was during bodily illness that spiritual illness was most likely, since the doctrine of providence directly linked personal sin with affliction—sickness was a punishment. The sense of guilt sparked by this notion could lead the sick to become obsessed with their own wickedness, and occasionally, to fear '*the worst thing of all*': damnation.[219]

The above interpretation challenges the widespread assumption in the historiography that patienthood in the early modern period was a wholly miserable experience.[220] It also undermines the ingrained view that Calvinist doctrines had a purely negative impact on the emotions of Protestants.[221] It is difficult to determine the extent to which children's experiences were distinctive: more work needs to be conducted on the perspectives of patients of different ages before any definite comparisons can be made. But it does seem that certain aspects of the experience may have been unique, including the tendency of parents to blame their children's diseases on their own sins rather than their children's, together with the child's especially vivid imaginations of heaven and hell, which may have made death seem more desirable or terrifying depending on which eternal place they anticipated.

Children's experiences of illness do not seem to have undergone much change over the course of the early modern period: similar language was used to describe pain across the period, and suffering seems to have elicited comparable emotional responses. This continuity demonstrates that the changes in medical provision in the early modern period, such as the expansion of the trade in drugs, had little impact on the actual experience of sickness, at least at a spiritual and emotional level. This may have been because the two doctrines that held most sway during sickness, providence and salvation, endured across the period. While there may have been a rise in scepticism about the existence of hell among some early

---

[217] This quotation was taken from the pious biography of ten-year-old Christian Karr: Deans *An account of the last words of Christian Karr,* 8.

[218] Janeway, *A token for children* (part 1), 61.

[219] This quotation of damnation as the '*worst thing of all*' was uttered by eleven-year-old Priscilla Thornton, from New England: Mather, *A token, for the children of New-England,* 14.

[220] See Ch. 5, footnotes 3–4 for examples.

[221] See the Introduction, footnote 21.

eighteenth-century individuals, it seems that pious children continued to believe wholeheartedly in this place.[222]

This chapter has shown that the age of the child did not have a significant impact on the experience of illness. Contrary to the claims of certain scholars, younger children were not always shielded from ideas about hell, nor were they considered any less capable of religious faith than older children.[223] Rather, children of a variety of ages expressed similar sentiments in response to death, including fears of hell and excitement about heaven. This was because puritan culture nurtured and encouraged precocious spirituality even in the smallest infants. As Janeway had asserted, children were not 'too little to dye' or 'go to Hell, they are not too little to serve their great Master, to[o] little to go to Heaven'.[224]

A number of themes have emerged in this chapter: firstly, the notion that the sick should be patient during their afflictions. Such a response was facilitated by the belief in the benevolence of God's providences, and the possibility of eternal bliss after death. In this context, it seems likely that the very word 'patient', used to denote the ill person, was associated with the idea that it was necessary to *be* patient during sickness. Similarly, the term 'suffer' referred both to pain, and to the Christian duty of submission to God's providences.[225] Another theme is the perceived influence of the body on the passions in early modern England. It has been shown that just as the emotions could influence the body, bodily sensations could impact on the emotions. This relationship between the mind and body was two-way, for when a person contemplated 'the sweete Idea...of the glory of heaven', their happy emotions could render physical pains more bearable.[226] A third theme concerns the close emotional bond between parents and children. Children's fears of separation from their families in death, together with their hopes for eventual reunion in heaven, indicate that parental love was reciprocated. By exploring children's feelings for their parents, this chapter has sought to balance our knowledge of parent–child relationships, since hitherto, historians have usually concentrated on parents' attitudes to their children.

[222] See the Introduction, footnote 32.
[223] Houlbrooke, 'Death in Childhood', 39, 45–6, 48.
[224] Janeway, *A token for children* (part 1), preface.
[225] OED Online.   [226] Coeffeteau, *A table of humane passions*, 353.

Conclusion

The Sick Child has sought to bridge the gap between the history of childhood and the history of medicine by unearthing a concept of 'children's physic' in early modern England. Children's physic constituted a collection of medical beliefs and practices which centred around the physiological distinctiveness of the young, and their need to be 'cur'd in a different manner in them then they are in other Ages'.[1] Children's uniqueness resided in their humours—their bodies and minds were moist and warm, soft and weak, abounding in the humour blood. These characteristics crept into every aspect of children's physic, from notions about diagnosis and prognosis, to ideas about the causation and treatment of their diseases. Medical practitioners and laypeople adapted children's remedies in various ways to make them as safe and pleasant as possible, conscious that young patients 'by reason of the weakness of their bodies, cannot undergo severe methods or strong Medicines'.[2] These findings, which challenge the notion that early modern doctors did not differentiate between child and adult patients, bring the history of medicine in line with the current consensus among historians of childhood about the existence of a concept of 'childhood' in the past. The book has also sought to draw attention to the importance of age more generally as a category in early modern medicine: age mattered when it came to perceiving and treating the sick. Children were distinguished not just from adults, but from the other 'ages of man', youths and the elderly.

While children were regarded as distinctive, they were not entirely unique, however. Their bodies and minds, maladies and remedies, were understood in terms of their humours, substances contained within all living creatures. Nor were children a homogeneous group: within the age of childhood, distinctions were drawn between individual children in relation to their age, size, strength, and occasionally, gender. The most important of these variables was age: as children grew older, their humoral constitutions gradually altered—they became physically and mentally stronger in response to the rise in temperature and the decline in moisture. The least significant variable, by contrast, was gender: doctors and laypeople rarely distinguished between girls and boys when describing children's constitutions, disease causation, and treatment. This was because the defining characteristics of children in medical opinion were their moisture and weakness, qualities shared by both sexes. These findings have implications for the historiography of childhood and gender, since hitherto it has been assumed that from the age of seven, every aspect of children's lives was differentiated according to sex. Further work on the perceived relationship between age and gender is required, in order to reach a deeper

---

[1] J.S., *Paidon nosemata; or childrens diseases both outward and inward* (1664), 5.
[2] John Pechey, *A general treatise of the diseases of infants and children* (1697), 15.

understanding of these issues. In particular, it would be fruitful to examine medical perceptions of youths and the elderly, and the ways in which gender and age intersected in medical theories and treatments. If gender was relatively unimportant in childhood, at what point did it begin to assume greater significance? Was gender mentioned in the context of the diseases and treatments of the elderly?

This book has shown that parents' experiences of child sickness and death were characterized by emotional, spiritual, and physical exhaustion. Mothers, fathers, and other relatives devoted 'great care and pains' to their ill offspring, busying themselves with nursing, medicine-making, prayer, and the spiritual preparation for death.[3] The spectacle of a child in pain was perhaps one of the most unbearable aspects of parenting in this period: parents felt as though their minds were 'on the rack', tortured by the horrible passions of grief and fear. The death of the child was similarly excruciating, and grief often persisted for many years. Mary Verney's agony at the discovery of her little daughter's death in 1647 encapsulates the experience of early modern parents: 'I am nott able to say one word more but that at this time there is nott a sadder creature in the world'.[4] The conviction that parental sin lay behind the pains and illnesses of children added guilt to the other dolorous emotions borne by parents. Nonetheless, the picture is not entirely negative: the Christian doctrines of providence and salvation provided a measure of comfort, by reassuring parents that some good would emerge from their sufferings, and that a joyful reunion after death was possible.

By seeing illness through the child's eyes, this book has sought to enrich our knowledge of early modern childhood, and demonstrate that it *is* possible to capture the experiences of the young, even though the evidence is incomplete. It has been argued that children's experiences of sickness were profoundly ambivalent: on the one hand, illness was often painful, frightening, exhausting, and a source of spiritual guilt and grief. But on the other hand, it could be a time of compassion, attention, affection, and power, and occasionally, spiritual and emotional ecstasy. When eleven-year-old Martha Hatfield lay very sick in 1652, she became impressed with a deep sense of her own unworthiness, crying 'What a naughty, naughty Lass was I'. But a short time later, she was 'exceedingly rapt up with joy', because she believed she was 'now going to Heaven'.[5] This emotional ambivalence stemmed from the religious beliefs in the soul, salvation, and the value of suffering, as well as the more practical and social consequences of patienthood, such as love, attention, and power. This interpretation helps to nuance our picture of early modern illness, showing that it was not as negative as has often been suggested in the historiography. Such a positive attitude to pain might seem strange from a modern-day perspective, but it is ubiquitous in the primary sources: children regularly saw suffering as an avenue to spiritual improvement, hoping that the end result would be their salvation. In a

---

[3] Simonds D'Ewes, *The Autobiography and Correspondence of Sir Simonds D'Ewes, Bart.*, ed. J. O. Halliwell, 2 vols (1845), vol. 1, 24.

[4] Frances Verney, *The Verney Memoirs, 1600–1659*, vol. 1 (1925, first publ. 1892), 384.

[5] James Fisher, *The wise virgin, or, a wonderfull narration of the hand of God . . . in afflicting a childe of eleven years of age* [Martha Hatfield] (1653), 6, 9.

sense, life in this period seems to have been experienced on two planes: those of the body and the soul. It was this duality of existence which enabled the sick to exhibit joy on their sickbed—their bodies might be deteriorating, but their souls could be healthy and vigorous. When twelve-year-old Caleb Vernon was asked how he was feeling in 1665, he replied, '*Very ill . . . in my body, but well in God*'.[6]

The extent to which children's experiences of illness differed from those of adults, is hard to tell. Further work needs to be conducted on the emotional and physical experiences of other ages before definite comparisons can be drawn. Nevertheless, it seems likely that the empowering aspects of patienthood may have been especially rewarding to children, whose usual status within the household was comparatively lowly. It is also possible that there may have been more opportunities for children to displace their feelings of providential guilt than adults, since children's illnesses could be seen as punishments for parental sin. The anticipation of death may have been slightly different for children as well, since their imaginations of the afterlife seem to have been particularly vivid.

As has been implied above, an underlying theme in this book is that sickness was as much a religious experience as a physical one, since God sent illness for the spiritual improvement of believers. The sick and their families were required to consider what sins had provoked God's wrath, and promptly repent and pray, in the hope that He would lift His afflicting hand. Young patients were encouraged to prepare spiritually for death by performing various acts of piety, such as declaring their willingness to die, and reading the Bible. Death and the afterlife were major preoccupations during illness, because the sick were acutely aware of their own mortality. By drawing attention to the importance of religion in this context, I hope to encourage a greater degree of constructive communication between historians of medicine and religion.

Patricia Crawford has argued that the experiences of childhood and parenthood among the poor were entirely different to those of the elites: the priority of these parents was economic survival, and many of the ideologies harboured by the wealthy were probably 'irrelevant' to the lower groups.[7] My book has suggested that child sickness may have been one aspect of life that cut across social levels. The basic feelings of pain, grief, exhaustion, and guilt, which sprang from witnessing and experiencing the illness and death of a child, were probably common to rich and poor. Contributing to the overlapping of experiences was the fact that the religious culture of early modern England was shared by everyone: sermons, church attendance, and popular print communicated the key principles of Christianity to a wide audience. Consequently, the spiritual side of illness, including its providential origin, and the anticipation of heaven and hell, may have been universal experiences. Of course, there were some aspects of sickness that *were* different for the poor. For instance, the destitute poor may have been unable to nurse their ill

[6] John Vernon, *The compleat scholler; or, a relation of the life, and latter-end especially, of Caleb Vernon*(1666, 72.
[7] Patricia Crawford, *Parents of Poor Children in England, 1580–1800* (Oxford: 2010), 9. Also see my review of this book, in *Women's History Review* (2011), DOI: 10.1080/09612025.2011.632941.

offspring owing to employment pressures and family stratification, and medical treatment was probably more rudimentary. Nevertheless, these conclusions are tentative: further research is required in order to fully capture the experiences of poorer children.

One of the most controversial arguments of this book concerns gender. It has been asserted that, during serious illness, the gender roles of mothers and fathers were flexible. Both parents shared the tasks of nursing and domestic medicine, even though mothers may have carried out the more intensive physical care, and both experienced extreme anguish upon the diseases and deaths of their offspring. The instances when men emphasized their wives' grief and downplayed their own distress should not be taken as evidence of a lack of sadness on the part of fathers, but should instead be interpreted as signs of gender construction: people tried to create ideal masculine and feminine identities through performance. Children's experiences seem to have been similarly devoid of gender distinctions: girls and boys usually received care of a similar standard and nature, and responded to physical suffering, providence, and death in like ways. The limited gendering of children's experiences was probably due to the fact that the Christian beliefs in salvation and providence, doctrines of huge significance during illness, applied equally to both genders, since all Christians were children of God. This argument does not contradict the notion that other areas of children's lives were affected by gender: historians have provided convincing evidence to indicate that boys and girls' upbringings were often different.[8] Rather, this book demonstrates that illness was a context in which these gender distinctions receded.

Medical ideas about children seem to have changed very little over the course of the early modern period. The essential foundation to children's physic, the notion that children were humid and tender, endured throughout, and was embraced by Galenists and chemists alike. Similarly, the types of treatments administered to children, and the various ways in which the medicines were adapted, do not appear to have undergone any significant alteration. The experience of patienthood was also characterized by continuity: when children fell ill, they were usually prayed over, nursed, and plied with physic. There is no clear evidence to show that parents increasingly turned to physicians as time progressed: rather, they obtained the services of a multifarious array of lay and learned healers across the period. A striking absence of change has also been observed in relation to the experiences of sickness: the pain of disease, together with the emotional and spiritual responses of children and parents, were described using comparable language across the period. This may have been because the aforementioned doctrines that had the most direct impact on the sick and their loved ones—providence and salvation—continued to loom large in the minds of the godly throughout the centuries. The continuity may also be a reflection of the biases inherent in the sources, many of which were products of the providential traditions.

---

[8] Anthony Fletcher, *Growing up in England: The Experience of Childhood 1600–1914* (London and New Haven, CT: 2008).

This book has explored the reciprocal relationship between the mind and the body in early modern thought and experience, showing that these two realms were depicted as close friends that shared one another's sorrows and joys. The pain of the body produced sad emotions, while the sorrowful passions caused bodily deterioration. As Jean-François Senault declared in 1671, the 'Soul and the Body... cannot be separated in their suffering... the torment of the one, must of necessity be the others punishment'.[9] The relationship could also be positive, however: when the passions were happy, as was the case when a sick child contemplated heaven, the body was distracted from its pain, and felt eased. Historians have often explored ideas about the impact of negative emotions on the body, but they have rarely considered the bodily effects of joyful passions, nor the influence of the body's sensations on the emotions.

Finally, what has emerged most strikingly in this book is the depth of love between parents and children in early modern England. The sheer effort, time, and emotion devoted to sick and dying children testifies the extraordinary affection that both mothers and fathers felt for their offspring. This deduction is supported by evidence of direct statements of love, affectionate physical contact, and expressions of distress at the separation brought by death. '[H]ow shall I bear parting with thee[?]', cried the mother of fourteen-year-old Sarah Howley in 1670.[10] Historians have tended to focus on parents' relationships with their children, seeing children's feelings for their parents as beyond the scope of historical enquiry. *The Sick Child* has tried to challenge this view by exploring children's emotional relationships with their parents. Children's appreciation of their parents' tender care, together with their fears of separation from their families in death, and hopes of eventual reunion in heaven, indicate that parental love was passionately reciprocated. Ending, as we began, with the words of an early modern child, young Elizabeth Walker told her mother, moments before her death in 1674, 'my dear Mother, you will remember what I now sa[y] to you[:]... I could be content to be a little Child again, that I might lie at your Breast and Bosom'.[11]

---

[9] Jean-François Senault, *The use of passions,* trans. Henry Earl of Monmouth (1671, first publ. 1649), 481–2.

[10] *An account of the admirable conversion of one Sarah Howley, a child of eight or nine years old* (Edinburgh: 1704), 7.

[11] Elizabeth Walker, *The vertuous wife: or, the holy life of Mrs Elizabeth Walker,* ed. Anthony Walker (1694), 111.

Bibliography

MANUSCRIPT SOURCES

London

British Library

Additional MS 5858 (Religious diary of a female cousin of Oliver Cromwell, 1687/90–1702)

Additional MS 19253 (Letterbook of Philip Stanhope, Earl of Chesterfield)

Additional MS 21935 ('Historical notes and meditations, 1588–1646' by Nehemiah Wallington)

Additional MS 27466 ('Recipe-Book of Mary Doggett', 1682)

Additional MS 28050 (Domestic correspondence of the Osborne family, 1637–1761)

Additional MS 28052 (Domestic correspondence of the Godolphin family, 1663–1782)

Additional MS 34722 (Lady Anne Loules and others, medical and culinary recipes, 1650)

Additional MS 36452 (Private letters of the Aston family, 1613–1703)

Additional MS 38089 (Collection of medical recipes, seventeenth and eighteenth centuries)

Additional MS 42,849 (Letters of the Henry family)

Additional MS 45196 (Brockman Papers, 'Ann Glyd Her Book 1656')

Additional MS 56248 (Recipe Book of Lady Mary Dacres, 1666–96)

Additional MS 70115 (Harley papers)

Additional MS 72516 (Trumbell papers, the letters of Anne Dormer)

Additional MS 72619 ('Book of recipes for the Trumbell's household', late seventeenth century)

Additional MS 75355 (Althorp papers and the correspondence of the Spencer family, 1664–82)

Additional MS 78337 (Evelyn papers, medical and culinary recipes, 1651–1700s)

Egerton MS 607 ('True coppies of scertaine loose Papers left by the Right honourable Elizabeth Countesse of Bridgewater, Collected and Transcribed together here since her Death Anno Dm 1663')

Egerton MS 2,214 ('Thomas Davies' medical recipes arranged in alphabetical order of common complaints', 1680)

Egerton MS 2415 (Recipe book of Mary Birkhead, 1681)

MS 636/7-10 (Verney papers on microfilm, 1646–50)

Sloane MS 153 (Casebook of Joseph Binns, 1633–63)

Sloane MS 1367 ('Lady Ranelagh's Medical Receipts')

Sloane MS 4034 (Correspondence of Sir Hans Sloane 1720–30)

Sloane MS 4454 (Diary of Katherine Austen)

Guildhall Library

MS 204 ('A Record of the Mercies of God: or A Thankfull Remembrance' by Nehemiah Wallington)

Wellcome Library

MS 1 (Grace Acton, collection of cookery and medicinal receipts, 1621)

MS 108 (Jane Baber, 'A Booke of Receipts', *c.* 1625)

MS 160 (Anne Brumwich and others, 'Booke of Receipts or medicines', *c.* 1625–1700)

MS 169 (Elizabeth Bulkeley, 'A boke of hearbes and receipts', 1627)

MS 184a (Lady Frances Catchmay, 'A booke of medicens' *c.* 1625)

MS 212 (Arthur Corbett, collection of medical receipts, mid-seventeenth century)

MS 213 (Mrs Corylon, 'A Booke of divers medecines', 1606)

MS 311 (Joan Gibson, 'A booke of medicines', 1632–[1717])

MS 363 (Sarah Hughes, 'Mrs Hughes her receipts', 1637)

MS 373 (Jane Jackson, 'A very shore and compendious Methode of Phisicke and Chirurgery', 1642)

MS 1026 (Lady Ayscough, 'Receits of phisick and chirurgery', 1692)

MS 1071 (Barrett family, 'Select receipts', *c.* 1700)

MS 1340 (Katherine Jones, Lady Ranelagh, collection of medical receipts, *c.* 1675 1710)

MS 1511 (Mrs Carr, collection of cookery and medical receipts, 1682)

MS 1548 (Mary Chantrell and others, 'Book of receipts', 1690)

MS 1662 (Mary Clarke, collection of cookery, medical and other receipts, *c.* 1700)

MS 2840 (Mrs Elizabeth Hirst and others, collection of medical and cookery receipts, 1684–*c.* 1725)

MS 2844 (Martha Hodges and others, collection of cookery receipts, including a few medical receipts, *c.* 1675–1725)

MS 2954 (Sarah Hudson, 'Her book', 1678)

MS 2990 ('Madam Bridget Hyde her receipt book', 1676–90)

MS 3107 (Katherine Kidder, collection of cookery and medical receipts, 1699)

MS 4338 ('Johanna St John Her Booke' 1680)

MS 7113 (Lady Ann Fanshawe, recipe book 1651–78)

Oxford
Bodleian Library

MS Rawlinson D. 1262–3 (Autobiographical memoirs and spiritual diary of Anne Bathurst, 1679)

MS Eng. Misc. e. 331 (Diary of Sarah Savage, 1714–23)

Winchester
Hampshire Record Office

44M69/F5/2/2 (Jervoise letters, 1658)

44M69/F6/1/2 (Jervoise letters, 1683–86)

44M69/F6/1/3 (Jervoise letters, 1692–95)

63M84/347 (Letters of Mary Yonge, 1720–21)

PRINTED SOURCES

The place of publication is London, unless otherwise stated.

An account of the admirable conversion of one Sarah Howley, a child of eight or nine years old (Edinburgh: 1704)

An account of the causes of some particular rebellious distempers (1670)

An account of the general nursery, or colledg of infants (1686)

An account of several work-houses for employing and maintaining the poor (1725)

Acton, George, *A letter in answer to certain quaeries and objections against . . . chymical physick* (1670)

Aldridge, Thomas, *The prevalency of prayer . . . of the deplorable case of the children of John Baldwin* (1717)

Allestree, Richard, *The art of patience* (1694, first publ. 1684)

Almond, Philip (ed.), '"The most strange and admirable discovery of the three Witches of Warboys . . . for betwitching of the five daughters of Robert Throckmorton" (1593)', in *Demonic Possession and Exorcism in Early Modern England: Contemporary Texts and their Cultural Contexts* (Cambridge: 2004), 75–149

Angier, John, *Oliver Heywood's Life of John Angier of Denton together with Angier's Diary*, ed. Ernest Axon, Chetham Society, vol. 97 (Aberdeen: 1937)

Archer, Isaac, *Two East Anglian Diaries 1641–1729*, ed. Matthew J. Storey, Suffolk Record Society, vol. 36 (Woodbridge: 1994)

Bacon, Francis, *Historie naturall and experimentall, of life and death* (1638)

Bantock, Anton (ed.), *The Earlier Smyths of Ashton Court From their Letters, 1545–1741* (Bristol: 1982)

Barbette, Paul, *Thesaurus chirurgiae: the chirurgical and anatomical works of Paul Barbette* (1687, first publ. 1676)

Barrow, John, *The Lord's arm stretched out in an answer of prayer, or, a true relation of the wonderful deliverance of James Barrow* (1664)

Basse, William, *A helpe to discourse. Or, a miscelany of merriment* (1619)

Baxter, Richard, *The saints everlasting rest, or, a treatise of the blessed state of the saints* (1650)

Becon, Thomas, *The sycke mans salve wherin the faihfull Christians may learne . . . how to behave them selves paciently and thankefully* (1561)

St Bernard's vision (1685)

Bidbanck, William, *A present for children. Being a brief, but faithful account of many remarkable and excellent things utter'd by three young children* (1685)

Blundell, William, *Cavalier: Letters of William Blundell to his Friends, 1620–1698*, ed. Margaret Blundell (1933)

Bonet, Theophile, *A guide to the practical physician* (1684)

Boursier, Louise Bourgeois, *The compleat midwife's practice enlarged* (1663)

Brockbank, Thomas, *The Diary and Letter Book of the Rev. Thomas Brockbank 1671–1709*, ed. Richard Trappes-Lomax, Chetham Society New Series, vol. 89 (Manchester: 1930)

Brown, John, *A compleat discourse of wounds* (1678)

Browne, Thomas, *The Works of Sir Thomas Browne*, ed. Geoffrey Keynes (1931)

Brownrigg, William, *The Medical Casebook of William Brownrigg, MD, FRS (1712–1800) of the Town of Whitehaven in Cumberland*, eds Jean E. Ward and Joan Yell, Medical History Supplement, vol. 13 (1993)

Bruele, Gualtherus, *Praxis medicinae, or, the physicians practice* (1632)

Bryan, John, *The vertuous daughter* (1640)

Bryant, Arthur Wynne Morgan (ed.), *Postman's Horn: an Anthology of the Family Letters of Later Seventeenth Century England* (1946)

Bullein, William, *The government of health* (1595, first publ. 1558)

Bunyan, John, *Meditations on the several ages of man's life* (1700)

Burton, Robert, *The anatomy of melancholy* (1621)

Buxton, John, *John Buxton, Norfolk Gentleman and Architect: Letters to his Son, 1719–1729*, ed. Alan Mackley, Norfolk Record Society, vol. 69 (Norwich: 2005)

C., E., *Some part of the life and death of Mrs. Elizabeth Egleton, who Died . . . 1705 in the fifth year of her age* (1705)

Calvin, John, *The institutes of Christian religion* (1559; first publ. 1536)

Camm, Thomas, *The admirable and glorious appearance of the eternal God... through a child... upon her dying bed* (1684)

Carey, Mary, *Meditations from the Note Book of Mary Carey, 1649–1657*, ed. Sir Francis Meynell (1918)

Cartwright, Thomas, *An Hospitall for the diseased* (1597)

Case, Thomas, *Correction instruction, or a treatise of afflictions* (1653, first publ. 1652)

Chamberlayne, Thomas, *The compleat midwife's practice* (1659)

Chamberlen, N., *A few queries relating to the practice of physick* (1694)

The childrens cryes (1696)

The children's example (1700)

Cholmley, Hugh, *The Memoirs and Memorials of Sir Hugh Cholmley of Whitby 1600–1657*, ed. Jack Binns, Yorkshire Archaeological Society, vol. 153 (Woodbridge: 2000)

Chudleigh, M., 'On the Death of my Dear Daughter Eliza Maria Chudleigh' in M. Chudleigh, *Poems on several occasions* (1713), 95

Clavering, Sir James, *The Correspondence of Sir James Clavering*, ed. Harry Thomas Dickinson, Surtees Society, vol. 178 (Gateshead: 1967)

Clegg, James, *The Diary of James Clegg of Chapel-en-Frith 1708–1755*, vol. 1 (1708–36), ed. Vanessa S. Doe, Derbyshire Record Society, vol. 5 (Matlock: 1978)

Clifford, Anne, *The Diaries of Lady Anne Clifford*, ed. D. D. H. Clifford (Stroud: 1990)

Clifford, Arthur (ed.), *Tixall Letters: or, The Correspondence of the Aston Family*, 2 vols (1815)

Coeffeteau, F.M., *A table of humane passions* (1621)

Collins, Thomas, *Choice and rare experiments in physick and chirurgery* (1658)

Comber, Thomas, *The Autobiographies and Letters of Thomas Comber, Sometime Precentor of York and Dean of Durham*, ed. C. E. Whiting, 2 vols, Surtees Society, vols 156–57 (Durham: 1941–42)

The compleat midwifes practice (1656)

Conway, Anne, *The Conway Letters: the Correspondence of Anne, Viscountess Conway, Henry More, and their Friends, 1642–1684*, ed. Marjorie Hope Nicolson (Oxford: 1992, first publ. 1930)

[Cornwallis], *The Private Correspondence of Jane Lady Cornwallis, 1613–1644*, ed. Lord Braybrooke (1842)

Cotta, John, *A short discoverie of severall sorts of ignorant and unconsiderate practisers of physicke* (1619)

Croke, Charles, *A sad memorial of Henry Curwen Esquire* (Oxford: 1638)

Crooke, Helkiah, *Mikrokosmographia a description of the body of man* (1615)

The cruel mother: being a strange... account of one Mrs. Elizabeth Cole (1708)

Cuffe, Henry, *The differences of the ages of mans life* (1607)

Cullen, Francis Grant, *A true narrative of the sufferings and relief of a yong girle* [*Christian Shaw*] (Edinburgh: 1698)

Culpeper, Nicholas, *Culpeper's Complete Herbal* (Ware: 1995)

——*Culpeper's directory for midwives: or, a guide for women... the diseases and symptoms in children* (1662)

D., I., *The most wonderfull and true storie... as also a true report of the strange torments of Thomas Darling, a boy of thirteene yeres of age* (1597)

D'Ewes, Simonds, *The Autobiography and Correspondence of Sir Simonds D'Ewes, Bart.*, ed. J. O. Halliwell, 2 vols (1845)

Darrel, John, *A true narration of the strange and grevous vexation by the Devil, of 7. persons in Lanchashire* (1600)

Deans, Archibald, *An account of the last words of Christian Karr, who dyed . . . in the eleventh year of her age* (Edinburgh: 1702)

Diemerbroeck, Ysbrand van, *The anatomy of human bodies . . . to which is added a particular treatise of the small pox* (1689)

Disney, Gervase, *Some remarkable passages in the holy life and death of Gervase Disney* (1692)

Dolaus, Johann, *Systema medicinale. A compleat system of physick* (1686)

The downfall of pride (1675–96)

Edwards, *A treatise concerning the plague and the pox* (1652)

Evelyn, John, *John Evelyn's Diary: A Selection*, ed. Philip Francis (1963)

The evil spirit cast-out (1691)

Fanshawe, Ann, *Memoirs of Lady Fanshawe*, ed. Richard Fanshawe (1829)

Ferrand, Jacques, *Erotomania or a treatise discoursing . . . love, or erotique melancholy* (1640)

Fisher, James, *The wise virgin, or, a wonderfull narration of the hand of God . . . in afflicting a childe of eleven years of age* [Martha Hatfield] (1653)

Flavel, John, *A token for mourners* (1674)

[Fleming], *The Flemings in Oxford*, ed. John Richard Magrath, Oxford Historical Society, vol. 44 (Oxford: 1904)

Foxe, John, *Foxe's Book of Martyrs [1576] Variorum Edition Online (version 1.1—Summer 2006)*, website address: http://www.hrionline.ac.uk/johnfoxe/

Fraser, James, *Memoirs of the life of . . . Mr. James Fraser* (Edinburgh: 1738)

Freke, Elizabeth, *The Remembrances of Elizabeth Freke*, ed. Raymond Anselment, Camden Fifth Series, vol. 18 (Cambridge: 2001)

Fulwood, William, *The enemie of idlenesse* (1568)

Galen, Claudius, *Galens art of physick* (1652)

Gearing, William, *A prospect of heaven* (1673)

Glisson, Francis, Bate, George, and Regemorter, Assuerus, *A treatise of the rickets being a diseas common to children*, trans. Philip Armin (1651)

Gouge, William, *Of domesticall duties eight treatises* (1622)

Greenwood, Henry, *Tormenting tophet; or a terrible description of hell* (1650, first publ. 1618)

Guillemeau, Jacques, *Child-birth, or the happy delivery of women . . . To which is added, a treatise of the diseases of infants* (1635, first publ. 1612)

Gwin, Thomas, *A memorial of our dear daughter Anne Gwin* (1715)

Halkett, Anne, *The Autobiography of Anne Lady Halkett*, ed. John Gough Nichols, Camden Society New Series, vol. 13 (1875–76)

Hall, John, *Select observations on English bodies* (1679)

A handkercher for parents wet eyes, upon the death of children (1630)

The happy damsel (1693)

Harley, Brilliana, *Letters of the Lady Brilliana Harley*, ed. Thomas Taylor Lewis (1853)

Harris, Walter, *An exact enquiry into, and cure of the acute diseases of infants*, trans. William Cockburn (1693)

Harrold, Edmund, *The Diary of Edmund Harrold, Wigmaker of Manchester 1712–15*, ed. Craig Horner (Aldershot: 2009)

Harward, Simon, *Harwards phlebotomy: or a treatise of letting of bloud* (1601)

[Hatton], *Correspondence of the Family of Hatton being Chiefly Addressed to Christopher, First Viscount Hatton, 1601–1704*, ed. Edward Maunde Thompson, Camden Society (1878), vol. 2, 212.

van Helmont, Joan Baptista, *Van Helmont's works, containing his most excellent philosophy, physick, chirurgery, anatomy* (1664)

Henry, Philip, *The Diaries and Letters of Philip Henry of Broad Oak, Flintshire, A. D. 1631–1696*, ed. M.H. Lee (1882)

Herbert, Edward, *The Life of Edward, First Lord Herbert of Cherbury written by himself*, ed. J. M. Shuttleworth (1976)

Hervey, John, *Letter-Books of John Hervey, First Earl of Bristol*, ed. S. H. A. Hervey, 3 vols (Wells: 1894)

Heywood, Oliver, *The Rev. Oliver Heywood, B. A: His Autobiography, Diaries, Anecdote and Event Books*, ed. Horsfall Turner, 4 vols (1883)

Hippocrates, *The eight sections of Hippocrates aphorismes* (1665)

Hoby, Margaret, 'Diary of Lady Margaret Hoby', in Charlotte Otten (ed.), *English Women's Voices 1450–1700* (Florida: 1992)

Hulton, Anne, 'The Memoirs of Mrs Anne Hulton, Youngest Daughter of the Rev. Henry Hulton', ed. [and narrated] Matthew Henry in Sarah Savage, *Memoirs of the Life and Character of Mrs Sarah Savage* (1821)

Hyperius, Andreas, *The practice of preaching* (1577)

Isham, Elizabeth, *'My Booke of Rememenberance': The Autobiography of Elizabeth Isham*, ed. Isaac Stephens; PDF file on the internet, website address: http://history.ucr.edu/people/grad_students/stephens/TheAutobiography.pdf

Janeway, James, *A token for children being an exact account of the conversion, holy and exemplary lives and joyful deaths of several young children* (1671)

——*A token for children. The second part* (1673)

Jeake, Samuel, *An Astrological Diary of the Seventeenth Century: Samuel Jeake of Rye*, ed. Michael Hunter (Oxford: 1988)

Johnson, G., *A thousand more notable things . . . to prevent diseases in children . . . rules for bloodletting . . . to order children rightly, and to prevent diseases incident to them* (1706)

Johnson, Robert, *Praxis medicinae reformata: or, the practice of physick* (1700)

Johnson, Samuel, *An Account of the Life of Dr. Samuel Johnson, from his Birth to his Eleventh Year, Written By Himself* (1805)

Josselin, Ralph, *The Diary of Ralph Josselin 1616–1683*, ed. Alan Macfarlane (Oxford: 1991)

Kettlewell, John, *Death made comfortable* (1695)

Kidder, Richard, *The Life of Richard Kidder D. D. Bishop of Bath and Wells Written by Himself*, ed. Amy Edith Robinson, Somerset Record Society, vol. 37 (1924)

Lake, Edward, *Diary of Dr. Edward Lake, Chaplain and Tutor to the Princesses Mary and Anne, 1677–1678*, ed. Henry Ellis, Camden Miscellanies, vol. 1 (1847), 5–31

A lamentable ballad of the tragical end of a gallant lord (1686–88).

Lane, Joan, *John Hall and his Patients: The Medical Practice of Shakespeare's Son-in-Law* (Stratford-upon-Avon: 1996)

Lawrence, Edward, *Christ's power over bodily diseases* (1672)

Lemnius, Levinus, *The secret miracles of nature* (1658, first publ. 1559)

——*The touchstone of complexions*, trans. Thomas Newton (1576)

The life and death of Mrs. Margaret Andrews . . . who died . . . 1680, in the 14th year of her age (1680)

Lister, Joseph, *The Autobiography of Joseph Lister of Bradford, 1627–1709*, ed. A. Holroyd (Bradford: 1860)

The living words of a dying child . . . Joseph Briggins (1675)

Locke, John, *The Correspondence of John Locke*, 8 vols, ed. E. S. De Beer (Oxford: 1976–89)

——*John Locke (1632–1704): Physician and Philosopher: A Medical Biography, with an Edition of the Medical Notes in his Journals*, ed. Kenneth Dewhurst (1963)

Love, Christopher, *Hells terror: or, a treatise of the torments of the damned* (1653)

MacMath, James, *The expert midwife...[and the] various maladies of new born babes* (Edinburgh: 1694)

Martindale, Adam, *The Life of Adam Martindale*, ed. Richard Parkinson, Chetham Society, vol. 4 (Manchester: 1845)

Mather, Cotton, *A token, for the children of New-England* (Boston: 1700)

Mauriceau, François, *The diseases of women with child... With fit remedies for the several indispositions of new-born babes* (1710)

Maynwaringe, Everard, *The method and means of enjoying health* (1683)

Medicus, Alius, *Animadversions on the medicinal observations of... Frederick Loss* (1674)

Mildmay, Lady Grace, 'Medical Papers' in Linda Pollock, *With Faith and Physic: the Life of a Tudor Gentlewoman, Lady Grace Mildmay, 1552–1620* (1993)

Moore, Mary, ' "Wonderful News from the North. Or, a True Relation of the Sad and Grievous Torments, Inflicted on the Bodies of three Children of Mr George Muschamp, Late of the County of Northumberland, by Witch-Craft" (1650)', in Philip Almond (ed.), *Demonic Possession and Exorcism in Early Modern England: Contemporary Texts and their Cultural Contexts* (Cambridge: 2004), 363–90

Mordaunt, Elizabeth, *The Private Diarie of Elizabeth Viscountess Mordaunt* (Duncairn: 1856)

Morris, Claver, *The Diary of a West Country Physician, 1648–1726*, ed. Edmund Hobhouse (1935)

Mulcaster, Richard, *The training up of children* (1581)

Newcome, Henry, *The Autobiography of Henry Newcome*, ed. Richard Parkinson, Chetham Society, vol. 26 (Manchester: 1852)

Newton, Evelyn Caroline Legh, *Lyme Letters, 1660–1760* (1925)

Norden, John, *A pathway to patience* (1626)

The nurse's guide (1729)

Owen, John, *Immoderate mourning for the dead, prov'd unreasonable* (1680)

P., H., *A looking-glass for children* (1673)

Paston, Lady Katherine, *The Correspondence of Lady Katherine Paston, 1603–1627*, ed. Ruth Hughey, Norfolk Record Society, vol. 14 (1941)

Patrick, Symon, 'A Brief Account of My Life with a Thankful Remembrance of God's Mercies to Me', in J. H. Parker (ed.), *The Works of Symon Patrick*, 9 vols (Oxford: 1858), vol. 9, 407–569

Pechey, John, *The complete midwife's practice enlarged* (1698)

——*A general treatise of the diseases of infants and children* (1697)

Pemell, Robert, *De morbis puerorum, or a treatise of the diseases of children* (1653)

Perkins, William, *A salve for the sicke man. or a treatise containing... the right manner of dying well* (1611, first publ. 1597)

Phaer, Thomas, ' "The Booke of Children: The Regiment of Life by Edward Allde" (1596, first publ. 1544)', in John Ruhrah (ed.), *Pediatrics of the Past* (New York: 1925), 157–95

Philip, J., *The wonderfull worke of God shewed upon a chylde whose name is William Withers* (1581)

Primrose, James, *Popular errours, or the errours of the people in physick*, trans. Robert Wittie (1651)

R., E., Esquire, *Bracteola aurea, or, filings of gold drawn from the life and death of that lovely child, Mrs. Joanna Reynell* (1663)

Raymond, John, *Folly in print, or a book of rymes* (1667)

A return of prayer: or a faithful relation of some remarkable passages of providence concerning Thomas Sawdie (1664)

Reynolds, Edward, *A treatise of the passions and faculties of the soule of man* (1640)

Rich, Mary, Countess of Warwick, *Autobiography of Mary Countess of Warwick*, ed. Croker Crofton (1848)

Roesslin, Eucharius, *The byrth of mankynde, otherwise named the womans book*, trans. Richard Jonas (1613, first publ. 1540)

Rogers, Samuel, *The Diary of Samuel Rogers, 1634–1638*, ed. Tom Webster and Kenneth Shipps, Church of England Record Society, vol. 11 (Woodbridge: 2004)

Rueff, Jacob, *The expert midwife* (1637)

Ruscelli, Girolamo, *The thyrde and last parte of the secretes of the reverende Maister Alexis of Piemount* (1562)

Russel, Robert, *A little book for children, and youth* (1693–96)

Russell, Lady Rachael Wriothesley, *Letters of Rachel, Lady Russell*, 2 vols (1853, first publ. 1773)

S., J., *Paidon nosemata; or childrens diseases both outward and inward* (1664)

S., W., *A family jewel, or the womans councellor* (1704)

Salmon, William, *Medicina practica, or, practical physick* (1692)

Savage, Sarah, *Memoirs of the Life and Character of Mrs Sarah Savage*, ed. J. B. Williams (1821)

Schimmelpenninck, Mary Anne, *The Life of Mary Anne Schimmelpenninck*, ed. C. C. Hankin, 2 vols (1858)

Searle, A. (ed.), *Barrington Family Letters, 1628–1632* (1983)

Senault, Jean-François, *The use of passions*, trans. Henry Earl of Monmouth (1671, first publ. 1649)

Sennert, Daniel, *Practical physick the fourth book in 3 parts: section 2: of diseases and symptoms in children* (1664)

Seymour, Frances, *The Gentle Hertford: Her Life and Letters*, ed. Helen Hughes (New York: 1940)

Sharpe, Jane, *The midwives book* (1671)

Shower, John, *Heaven and hell; or the unchangeable state of happiness or misery for all mankind in another world* (1700)

Sidney, Robert, *Domestic Politics and Family Absence: The Correspondence (1588–1621) of Robert Sidney, First Earl of Leicester, and Barbara Gamage Sidney*, eds Margaret P. Hannay, Noel J. Kinnamon, and Michael Brennan (Aldershot: 2005)

Skinner, *Some observations made upon the Russia seed . . . curing the rickets in children* (1694)

St Clare Byrne, Muriel (ed.), *The Lisle Letters*, 6 vols (Chicago: 1981)

Swan, John, ' "A True and Briefe Report, of Mary Glovers Vexation" (1603)', in Philip Almond (ed.), *Demonic Possession and Exorcism in Early Modern England: Contemporary Texts and their Cultural Contexts* (Cambridge: 2004), 291–330

Sydenham, Thomas, *The compleat method of curing almost all diseases* (1694)

Sylvius, Franciscus, *New idea of the practice of physic* (1675)

——*Dr. Franciscus de le Boe Sylvius of childrens diseases* (1682)

Symcotts, John, *A Seventeenth Century Doctor and his Patients: John Symcotts, 1592?–1662*, eds F. N. L. Poynter and W. J. Bishop, Bedfordshire Historical Record Society, vol. 31 (Streatley: 1951)

Tauvry, Daniel, *A treatise of medicines containing an account of their chymical principles* (1700)

Taylor, Joseph, *Grace, grace: or, the exceeding riches of grace* (1702)

Thornton, Alice, *The Autobiography of Mrs Alice Thornton*, ed. Charles Jackson, Surtees Society, vol. 62 (1875)

[Thynne], *Two Elizabethan Women: Correspondence of Joan and Maria Thynne 1575–1611*, ed. Alison D. Wall, Wiltshire Record Society, vol. 38 (Devizes: 1983)

Travers, Rebecca, *The work of God in a dying maid . . . Susanna Whitrow* (1677)

'A true relation of the wonderful deliverance of Hannah Crump', in John Barrow, *The Lord's arm stretched out in an answer of prayer* (1664), 17–20

A true sence of sorrow (1671–1702)

Turner, Daniel, *De morbis cutaneis, a treatise of diseases incident to the skin* (1714)

——*A remarkable case in surgery . . . in a child about six years old* (1709)

Verney, Frances (ed.), *The Verney Memoirs, 1600–1659*, vol. 1 (1925, first publ. 1892)

Vernon, John, *The compleat scholler; or, a relation of the life . . . of Caleb Vernon* (1666)

A voice from heaven, the youth of Great Britain (1690)

A voice from heaven, the youth of Great Britain (1720)

Walker, Elizabeth, *The vertuous wife: or, the holy life of Mrs. Elizabeth Walker*, ed. Anthony Walker (1694)

Wallington, Nehemiah, *The Notebooks of Nehemiah Wallington, 1618–1654, A Selection*, ed. David Booy (Aldershot: 2007)

A warning to all lewd livers (1684–86)

Watts, Isaac, *Preservative from the sins and follies of childhood and youth* (1734)

Willis, Thomas, *Dr Willis's practice of physick* (1684, first publ. 1681)

——*Willis's Oxford Casebook (1650–52)*, ed. Kenneth Dewhurst (Oxford: 1981)

Wiseman, Richard, *Several chirurgical treatises* (1686, first publ. 1676)

A wonderful prophesie (1684–86)

Wright, Thomas, *The passions of the minde* (1630, first publ. 1601)

Wurtz, Felix, '"An Experimental Treatise of Surgerie in Four Parts . . . Whereunto is Added . . . the Childrens Book", trans. Lenertzon Fox (1656)', in John Ruhrah (ed.), *Pediatrics of the Past* (New York: 1925), 198–220

Yonge, James, *The Journal of James Yonge (1647–1721), Plymouth Surgeon*, ed. F. N. L. Poynter (1963)

——*Wounds of the brain proved curable . . . the remarkable history of a child four years* (1682)

Younge, Richard, *A christian library* (1660, first publ. 1655)

ELECTRONIC SOURCES

Early English Books Online

Eighteenth Century Collections Online

Proceedings of the Old Bailey

    Reference: t16800526-6

    Reference: a17140630-1

    Reference: a17170117-1

    Reference: a17170117-1

    Reference: OA17140716

    Reference: t16781211e-2

Index

NOTE: specific diseases are listed under 'diseases', and particular emotions, under 'emotions'. Bodily organs, fluids, and processes can be found under 'bodies'. Children's names are listed by surname, and are followed by 'child'. All other persons mentioned in the main text are ordered by surname.